# APPLYING MUSIC IN EXERCISE AND SPORT

Costas I. Karageorghis
PhD, CPsychol, CSci, FBASES, AFBPsS
Brunel University London, UK

HUMAN
KINETICS

**Library of Congress Cataloging-in-Publication Data**

Names: Karageorghis, Costas I., 1969- author.
Title: Applying music in exercise and sport / Costas I. Karageorghis.
Description: Champaign, IL ; London, UK : Human Kinetics, [2017] | Includes bibliographical references and index.
Identifiers: LCCN 2016010699 (print) | LCCN 2016013475 (ebook) | ISBN
    9781492513810 (print) | ISBN 9781492530695 (ebook)
Subjects: LCSH: Music and sports. | Music--Psychological aspects. |
    Exercise--Psychological aspects. | Sports--Psychological aspects. |
    Exercise music--Discography.
Classification: LCC ML3830 .K36 2017 (print) | LCC ML3830 (ebook) | DDC
    781.5/94--dc23
LC record available at http://lccn.loc.gov/2016010699

ISBN: 978-1-4925-1381-0 (print)

The web addresses cited in this text were current as of May 2016, unless otherwise noted.

**Acquisitions Editor:** Chris Wright; **Developmental Editor:** Kevin Matz; **Senior Managing Editor:** Carly S. O'Connor; **Copyeditor:** Patsy Fortney; **Permissions Manager:** Martha Gullo; **Graphic Designer:** Dawn Sills; **Cover Designer:** Jonathan Kay; **Photograph (cover):** iStock/wundervisuals; **Photographs (interior):** © Human Kinetics, unless otherwise noted; **Photo Asset Manager:** Laura Fitch; **Photo Production Manager:** Jason Allen; **Senior Art Manager:** Kelly Hendren; **Associate Art Manager:** Alan L. Wilborn; **Illustrations:** © Human Kinetics, unless otherwise noted; **Printer:** United Graphics

Printed in the United States of America    10  9  8  7  6  5  4  3  2  1

The paper in this book is certified under a sustainable forestry program.

**Human Kinetics**
Website: www.HumanKinetics.com

*United States:* Human Kinetics
P.O. Box 5076
Champaign, IL 61825-5076
800-747-4457
e-mail: info@hkusa.com

*Canada:* Human Kinetics
475 Devonshire Road Unit 100
Windsor, ON N8Y 2L5
800-465-7301 (in Canada only)
e-mail: info@hkcanada.com

*Europe:* Human Kinetics
107 Bradford Road
Stanningley
Leeds LS28 6AT, United Kingdom
+44 (0) 113 255 5665
e-mail: hk@hkeurope.com

*Australia:* Human Kinetics
57A Price Avenue
Lower Mitcham, South Australia 5062
08 8372 0999
e-mail: info@hkaustralia.com

*New Zealand:* Human Kinetics
P.O. Box 80
Mitcham Shopping Centre, South Australia 5062
0800 222 062
e-mail: info@hknewzealand.com

E6225

This book is dedicated to some inspirational teachers I have met along life's path:

Professor Peter C. Terry, Professor N.C. Craig Sharp,
John J. Myhill, Junior G. Field, and Richard A. Glover (1949-2013).

And to inspirational teachers everywhere.

# CONTENTS

# FOREWORD

## PART I: THE ATHLETE'S PERSPECTIVE

Dina Asher-Smith is a Great Britain Olympic track athlete and member of Blackheath and Bromley Harriers Athletics Club in southeast London. She is the first British woman to have broken the 11-second barrier over 100 meters. Asher-Smith has achieved numerous honors that include winning gold medals at the 2013 European Junior Championships (200 meters), 2014 World Junior Championships (100 meters), and 2016 World Junior Championships (100 meters). In 2015, Asher-Smith took a silver medal at the European Indoor Championships (60 meters) and equalled the British record of 7.08 seconds. In the same year, she placed fifth at the World Athletics Championships in Beijing where she broke Kathy Cook's long-standing British record over 200 meters with a time of 22.07 seconds. She capped 2015 with the Sunday Times/Sky Sports Young Sportswoman of the Year award. Alongside her daily commitments on the track, Asher-Smith is reading for a degree in history at King's College London. She is the British 60-meter, 100-meter, and 200-meter record holder and fastest British woman in history.

When I was growing up in South London, I listened to a lot of the music that my mum and dad liked—what I would often refer to as their '80s mega-mix. Since then I have developed my own music taste, which has a strong hip-hop and R&B flavor. The kind of music that I listen to in my everyday life often has a bearing on the music that I choose to listen to in preparation for competition. The songs with which I am most familiar tend to make me feel most comfortable in the often inhospitable domain of international track and field.

For many athletes, music listening has become a staple for competition because it's a great way to block out the pressure and control feelings. In particular, I find that music is an ideal way to achieve my desired mood state. Given how much of my sport depends on psychological readiness, this can make a telling difference. If I feel extremely nervous, I will listen to something calming like Ed Sheeran's *Thinking Out Loud* that will put me on an even keel emotionally. Contrastingly, if I've had a long flight the night before or feel tired, I use music to get fired up about an hour before I am due to compete. In these instances, I select a powerful, up-tempo track such as "Not Letting Go" by Tinie Tempah or "Run The World (Girls)" by Beyoncé.

The nature and personality of the artist performing a song can be an important factor for me. Beyoncé, for example, is an incredible role model for women the world over. She is such a strong person, so tenacious and hardworking, plus she likes to rule the roost—they don't call her Queen B for nothing! These are all qualities that I like to bring to the sprint events, so when I play one of Beyoncé's songs during the crucial pre-competition phase, my association with her approach to performing on stage helps me get zoned in. The importance of the personal connection with an artist *and* the artist's music is something that comes across strongly in this book. Accordingly, I would encourage up-and-coming athletes to think carefully about musical role models as well as sporting ones.

Life can be lonely on the circuit, and I don't always have my coach John alongside me. It seems that my music can serve many purposes: at times as a companion, often as a means by which to wind down and relax, and at other times as a rhythmic cue to get my legs turning over just that little bit faster. I feel incredibly lucky and blessed to have gotten as far as I have in my sport, and, looking toward the future, I take comfort in knowing that my music will continue to be with me every step of the way.

Dina Asher-Smith

# PART II: THE COACH'S PERSPECTIVE

I have to declare from the outset that, like most athletics coaches, I am not particularly musical! Nonetheless, I am realizing more and more the important role that music plays in the preparation of my athletes and elite sprinter Dina Asher-Smith in particular. There is hardly a circuit or strength and conditioning session that we do without musical accompaniment. It brightens up the atmosphere and dulls the pain. Having read a draft of this excellent book, I am not sure that I will ever again allow the strength and conditioning coach to monopolize the music selection!

It is perhaps in the competitive arena that my athletes truly experience the power of music. Many of them use it to psych up before a race, but Dina tends to use it mostly to switch off and unwind. A big race such as a world championship final makes Dina super-excited, and sometimes it is hard to put a lid on that excitement, particularly in between the rounds. A playlist of soothing music selections really seems to do the trick in terms of her mental state. Dina is able to blank the opposition, ignore the burden of public expectation, and just lock herself into a listening bubble. Because she has been so successful, the younger athletes in my squad tend to copy everything that she does—her routine getting into the blocks, the way she carries her arms, and even listening to some of the same music. From the content of this book, coaches can get a good handle on how specific qualities of music, such as the rhythmic structure or bass frequencies, can influence the mind-sets of their athletes.

Mark Shearman

John Blackie has been a track and field coach for over 15 years and is one of the directors of the 365 Athletics Academy, which attracts more than 400 children to attend coaching sessions each week. Blackie has been recognized through several honors for his coaching achievements, including England Athletics National Development Coach of the Year and UK Athletics Development Coach of the Year (both in 2011). He coaches a 25-strong athletics squad in southeast London and has facilitated the progression of his athletes toward numerous county, regional, and national titles. Among his current crop of athletes is the fastest woman in British history, Dina Asher-Smith as well as Shannon Hylton (UK top-ranked under 20 over 200 meters), Cheriece Hylton (UK third-ranked under 20 over 200 meters), Helen Godsell (multiple European sprint champion in the veterans' ranks), and Isabella Hilditch (UK second-ranked under 17 over 60-meter hurdles).

When I am coaching sprint hurdles, I find music to be particularly helpful. Hurdles are a very rhythmic event and so, in preparation, the athletes need something with a beat to get them into the rhythmic mode. One of our drills entails skipping over the side of a row of hurdles with either straight or bent legs; however, some athletes lack the all-important rhythm that the drill requires. In an attempt to counter this timing issue, I sometimes hum the chirpy tune of the can-can out loud, which immediately reminds the athletes that they need to keep the beat as they kick up to clear the edge of each hurdle.

Outside of track and field, I am a big fan of dressage. One of my favorite exponents of this sport is the British 2012 Olympic champion Charlotte Dujardin. It is simply amazing how she gets her horse Valegro to move in perfect time with the music. I only wish that I could get my athletes to exhibit a similar degree of rhythmic skill!

John Blackie

# PREFACE

*Music produces a kind of pleasure which human nature cannot do without.*

—Confucius

This Confucian quote aptly illustrates the long-running love affair that humankind has with music. In many guises, music touches almost every aspect of our lives, providing an auditory backdrop for the most formal public occasions as well as our most intimate moments. In recent decades, music has become a central part of people's experiences in exercise and sport—as participants and as spectators. This book will appeal to anyone who might use music in a physical activity context, be that for a jog in the park, to accompany a fitness class, or to prepare a professional sport team for a big game. Although the book will hold particular appeal for professionals in the realm of exercise and sport, I have striven to make the content equally relevant to exercisers and athletes who want to use music to enrich their experiences or enhance their performances. This book is also relevant to students and practitioners with an interest in sport psychology, music psychology, or both.

With the advent of new digital technologies, we now have the freedom to formulate our own playlists at the touch of a button. This was wholly unimaginable during my teenage years when vinyl was still very much de rigueur. Thousands of tracks can be stored in a device weighing just 3 ounces (85 g), and virtually everyone in Western society below the age of 50 owns a personal music player. The popularity of such audio tools coupled with online streaming and platforms such as YouTube provides the opportunity to listen to precisely what we want, whenever we want. This unlimited choice often leads me to consider how to optimize the use of music and maximize the benefits we derive from it.

My expertise lies in the scientific application of music in the domain of exercise and sport. I have a background in sport and music, both as a performer and as a researcher and practitioner.

People often ask what I do or even view it with skepticism. Certainly, no one is born a psycho-musicologist specializing in exercise and sport; therefore, I'd like to share a little of my background to illustrate how I came to forge a career in this field. This might help you to understand why I consider music such a potentially powerful tool for exercise and sport participants. My early life experiences had a profound influence on the direction my career would take—although I didn't know what exactly I would do, and my immediate environment was not awash with opportunity.

I grew up in the center of Brixton, a poor but culturally vibrant enclave of South London. Following a period of mass immigration to the United Kingdom from the British Commonwealth in the 1950s and 1960s, Brixton became one of the most multicultural and multi-ethnic parts of London. I was born in the final throes of the swinging sixties, and most of the people I knew while growing up were first-generation immigrants to the UK. These people brought musical traditions from their motherlands that I found both fascinating and enticing.

During my childhood years, the flat I shared with my parents and extended family was in the very heart of Brixton, above a store that sold second-hand vinyl records and audio equipment. Each morning, rather than waking to the sweet sound of birdsong as the sun broke gently through the net curtains, I was jolted out of bed by the boom of a gigantic subwoofer. My father often rushed down to complain to the store's proprietor, but the reggae beat of Bob Marley and Desmond Decker would drown out his protestations, and the music continued unabated. As I opened my sleepy eyes and looked out of my bedroom window at the busy street below, I noticed how the music influenced the facial expressions and movement patterns of passersby; pedestrians certainly appeared happier and more animated as they came within earshot of the music.

Although the shuddering floorboards were undeniably a perpetual nuisance, the music played by the lovable rogue downstairs became firmly lodged in my subconscious; it would linger in my mind like an unwanted voice that could not be silenced. Sometimes I would find myself singing short phrases even though I didn't really understand the meaning of the patois (Jamaican Creole dialect) used in the lyrics: "Hey, fatty bum bum, a sweet sugar dumpling. Hey, fatty bum bum, let me tell you something." It was unsurprising, then, that I grew up musically able as well as deeply interested in how music influenced and was influenced by the human condition.

In the first decade of the 21st century, technological advances in personal listening devices sparked an explosion in the use of music by individual exercisers and athletes. Consequently, the effect of music on the human psyche is an area of interest to many people. Although myriad books have been written about the application of music in everyday living situations and therapeutic environments (see the Further Reading section), none has sought to address specifically the domain of exercise and sport. I have spent almost every day of my academic career investigating and writing about the influence of music on exercisers and athletes. I have also had the privilege of working with many Olympic and world championship athletes from a wide range of sports and countries as a consultant psychologist. Such work has afforded me an opportunity to put my ideas and experimental findings into practice in the highest echelons of sport.

Moreover, I have worked as a consultant for major national and international organizations such as Nike, Red Bull, England RFU, IMG, Spotify, and Universal Music on sport- and exercise-related music projects; these engagements have enabled me to monitor the impact of music on various sections of the population. For example, most recently I have been examining the influence of music on enjoyment and physical exertion levels among participants in O2 Touch, a new form of physical activity that combines touch rugby with high-energy music. Such experiences have also taught me about the intricacies related to harnessing the power of music to improve people's mental states, increase their work output, sharpen their mental focus, and even enhance their lives.

In this book I share my findings and applied experiences as well as the insights of many scientist-practitioners who work in this emerging field. I have aimed to write in an accessible, nonscientific style to ensure that the material is fully relevant to practitioners and students with an interest in application and psychological interventions. I have also tried to keep the use of in-text citations to a minimum to avoid breaking up the flow of the narrative.

The citations reappear as full references at the end of the book. For those who wish to delve deeper into the scientific premises of the text, a section titled Further Reading includes a broader range of sources split into two sections: secondary sources under the heading Books and Book Chapters and primary sources under the heading Journal Articles. For those with an academic interest in this field, the further reading provides details of scholarly works that I have harvested over 25 years. This section does not include any of the sources presented in the references.

My purpose in writing this book is to share contemporary research and applied knowledge so that exercisers and athletes derive the greatest benefit from music and that they and those who guide them can select music based on scientific principles. It details the circumstances under which exercise participants and athletes are likely to derive the largest gains from music, as well as those in which music use is best avoided. It also provides the skills necessary for devising playlists for both groups and individuals, implementing a wide variety of music-related interventions, and comprehensively assessing the effects of music in the field.

I have drawn on the work of scholars in psychomusicology, psychobiology, psychoacoustics, and neuroscience to supplement research and applied material from the field of sport and exercise sciences. My guiding principle is to adopt a balanced approach to help people reach reasoned and well-informed decisions about the use of music in the domain of exercise and sport. Wise choices lead to greater enjoyment and, ultimately, better outcomes for exercisers and athletes and those who train and coach them. There are many examples of music tracks in the book and each of these can be located on YouTube—simply type in the name of an artist and the track title.

The book is organized in three parts, each with a distinct theme. Part I addresses the when, how, and why of music use in exercise and sport to provide a thorough grounding in the subject. Chapter 1 is a general introduction to the topic that includes explanations of key concepts and several examples to illustrate how music can influence people's behavior and feelings. A short section at the end of chapter 1 covers legal considerations for the use of music in exercise and sport environments. Chapter 2 delves into the scientific premise of the applications that follow in chapters 4 through 9 to enable practitioners to engage in evidence-based practice and fully understand the theoretical premise of music-related interventions. Chapter 3 provides a broad range of assessment methods that exercise and sport professionals can use to inform their selections of music. These methods are useful for measuring how effective music interventions are both with individuals and groups or teams.

Part II focuses on music applications in the exercise domain, although many of the principles will resonate with sport professionals who use musical accompaniment in their training programs. Chapter 4 addresses music use in individual exercise and workout sessions with reference to a range of training modalities that include strength, flexibility, and cardiorespiratory.

Chapter 5 takes a similar approach for group-based exercise and workouts and covers internationally popular classes such as spinning, dance aerobics, and circuit training. Chapter 6 provides case studies for individual and group-based exercise along with sample playlists to illustrate the principles outlined in chapters 4 and 5. The vivid examples are meant to inspire trainers and exercise leaders to consider how to incorporate music into the exercise routines of those in their charge. Exercisers can just as easily apply the principles to their own training programs.

Part III covers the use of music to enhance the training and performance of competitive athletes and teams. This part may also be of interest to exercise professionals who work with highly committed and performance-oriented exercisers whose regimens approximate those of elite athletes. Chapter 7 contains specific training and performance-related music applications for those participating in individual sports such as track and field, tennis, golf, cycling, and martial arts. Chapter 8 takes a parallel approach for team sports such as soccer, netball, basketball, rugby, and American football. Finally, chapter 9 provides two case studies—one for an individual and one for a team—as well as carefully crafted playlists that bring the principles of chapters 7 and 8 to life.

**eBook**
available at
HumanKinetics.com

# ACKNOWLEDGMENTS

I would like to thank Dr. David-Lee Priest for the research assistance he has provided since the inception of this project in the spring of 2011. David is a former doctoral student of mine (1998-2004), who has long since become a close friend and confidant. He often comes across to others as a rather modest and unassuming individual, although this outward persona belies a broad array of talents: David is a polymath, a polyglot, a multi-instrumentalist, a superb raconteur, and as he himself would testify, an aspiring racketeer! His meticulous fact finding, encyclopedic knowledge of musical subcultures, and critical commentary on numerous drafts of this opus have assisted me greatly in its production. David is an inspiration to all who know him.

I would also like to thank Dr. Leighton Jones for the research assistance he provided during the spring and summer of 2014. Another former doctoral student of mine (2010-2014), Leighton has been publishing with me for over a decade, throughout the course of his bachelor's and master's degrees. During his doctoral studies, Leighton blossomed into an independent researcher with notable recent successes that have included papers in the *Journal of Sport & Exercise Psychology* and *Annals of Behavioral Medicine*. I am particularly proud of the fact that Leighton was awarded a Vice-Chancellor's Prize for Doctoral Research at his graduation in July 2014.

Numerous work placement students from a range of UK institutions provided me with research assistance during the course of the project. Foremost among these were John Bird (BSc psychology, University of Bath), Nicole Cara (BSc psychology, Brunel University London), Jasmine During (BSc psychology, Brunel University London), and Daniel Payne (BSc sport and exercise science, Leeds Beckett University). While addressing the comments of peer reviewers during 2015, I was ably assisted by my current postgraduate students, Jonathan Bird (PhD exercise psychology) and Joel Shopland (MSc sport, health, and exercise sciences). I thank all of the aforementioned students for their unflinching commitment, enthusiasm, perspicacity, and superior (to mine!) IT skills.

I am grateful to my employer, Brunel University London, who granted a six-month period of research leave that afforded me the time to fully immerse myself in this project during the spring and summer of 2014. Our long-serving former head of school, Professor Susan Capel, is deserving of a special mention for the constant support and encouragement she gave throughout the formative years of my academic career.

Ted Miller (vice president of special acquisitions, USA) and Chris Wright (acquisitions editor, Europe) at Human Kinetics have been closely involved with this project since I pitched the idea to Ted during his visit to the London 2012 Olympic Games. Both have provided me with a clear sense of direction from the outset, copious feedback on drafts of each chapter, and colorful examples from the world of sport that duly found their way into part III of the book. It has been a distinct privilege and a pleasure to work with Ted and Chris over the last five years.

Finally, I would like to thank my caring wife, Tina, and our two teenage daughters, Anastasia and Lucia, who each appear to have grown taller by several inches during the course of this project—I have only *just* noticed. My family's enduring tolerance of the obsessive and unsociable behaviors that life in the academic realm demands can only be described as truly remarkable.

# What Do You Know About Music in Exercise and Sport?

Before you delve into the heart of this book, tackle the following 15 multiple-choice and 10 short-answer questions. This will help you gauge how much you presently know about the application of music in exercise and sport environments. Once you've answered all 25, go to the Answers to Quizzes section and give yourself one point for each correct answer.

Add the points of your correct answers and multiply this number by 4 to turn it into a percentage (e.g., if you get 10 correct answers, 10 × 4 = 40, which makes your score 40 percent). Answering these questions will reveal your strengths in the subject matter, and also where you have blind spots. Quiz 2 at the end of the book provides an additional 25 questions—at the same difficulty level as the ones presented here—that can help you gauge the degree to which your knowledge of the subject matter has improved.

## MULTIPLE-CHOICE QUESTIONS

1. Three important constituents of music that exercise and sport practitioners should always take into consideration when constructing a playlist are
   a. the lyrical content, gender of the artist, and quality of the sound system
   b. whether the track is instrumental or has a vocal element, whether the track slows down or speeds up, and whether the track made it into the top 10 of the billboard charts
   c. the lyrical content, tempo, and rhythmic qualities
   d. the beat, the familiarity of the artist(s), and any subliminal messages contained in the lyrics

2. What role does music play before, during, and after physical activity?
   a. Enables participants to experience positive imagery before they start; lock into the rhythm of the music during their activity; and feel better about themselves after the activity.
   b. Mentally prepares participants pre-task; provides a rhythmic stimulus in-task; and distracts attention from aching muscles post-task.
   c. Encourages participants to forget about the pain they are going to encounter before they start; distracts attention from fatigue-related sensations and raises mood during the activity; and helps prevent muscle soreness post-activity.
   d. Assists participants in the pre-task phase by priming them for the task at hand; provides an in-task stimulus that lifts mood, distracts attention from fatigue-related sensations, and facilitates moving to the beat; and enhances post-task recovery.

3. Exercising or training at a high intensity while listening to very loud music poses a particular health risk because
   a. the person is more likely to fall off the treadmill and get injured as a result of the distraction
   b. the blood flows away from the inner ear (the cochlea) toward the working muscles, making the inner ear far more susceptible to damage from the sound vibrations
   c. the hair cells in the inner ear are forced to vibrate at a high frequency, and the combination of this with the

exercise or training activity can induce migraines over time

    d. the inner ear is made to vibrate by the activity, and the additional vibration caused by the music causes the auditory system to swell, which leaves it susceptible to permanent damage

4. As a broad generalization, Madonna's music is superior to that of Rihanna for middle-aged white women in exercise classes because

    a. women in this demographic don't tend to listen to chart music and so would not be very familiar with the music of Rihanna

    b. it generally has a better beat for women in this demographic

    c. Rihanna's music has a Barbadian dance hall sound that they find difficult to relate to

    d. these women are likely to have grown up listening to Madonna's music, and thus, it holds a particularly special meaning for them

5. To prime a male athlete with an outgoing personality for a highly explosive task such as weightlifting or shot putting, the optimal music is likely to be

    a. of a relatively high tempo, of loud intensity, and rather evocative

    b. of a moderate tempo, with crashing guitars, and a thumping bass line

    c. evocative, loud, and nonlyrical

    d. either gangsta rap or heavy rock with an aggressive lyric

6. Male adult exercisers and athletes tend to prefer music with stronger bass frequencies than their female counterparts do because

    a. they associate this with high bass frequencies resonating from their cars, which implies social status

    b. males generally have larger frames than females and so are better able to absorb low-frequency sound

    c. at school, boys are more drawn to playing instruments that produce low-frequency sounds (e.g., tenor saxophone, bass guitar, timpani), whereas the converse holds for girls (e.g., violin, treble recorder, oboe); this creates differences in how people respond to high and low frequencies during adulthood

    d. the male voice is generally an octave lower than the female voice, and this difference may account for gender differences in how sound frequencies are processed by the brain

7. Music has been shown to enhance the flow state during exercise- and sport-related tasks. This state can be described as

    a. complete immersion in an activity to the point at which nothing else seems to matter

    b. a state in which movements flow to such a degree that they feel technically superior to the movements of others nearby

    c. being absorbed in a task to the point of becoming wholly unaware of other people nearby

    d. a mental and physical state similar to a Zen-like state of awareness that borders on meditation

8. Which three key attributes should a piece of music have to be used as part of a pre-match routine for a sport team?

    a. It should rouse the crowd, put the coach in a positive mood, and calm the players.

    b. It should be quite aggressive, have a high tempo, and build up to a crescendo or climax.

    c. It should lift the mood of the players, create a sense of team identity, and use predominantly major (happy) harmonies.

    d. It should conjure the type of imagery desired by the team for the task at hand, instill a sense of unity and cohesion, and include strong lyrical affirmations.

9. How does music enhance the efficiency of repetitive movements such as running and cycling?

a. People believe that they're working less hard with music.

b. Music reduces inefficiencies in the movement chain when applied synchronously.

c. Synchronous music is akin to exercising with a metronome; a tick-tock pulsation is constantly in the mind as a significant distraction.

d. Because humans have a natural predisposition to respond to the rhythmic qualities of music, it makes the activity seem easier.

10. Music can reduce ratings of perceived exertion during exercise or training of moderate-to-low intensity by approximately what percentage?

a. 4 to 8 percent

b. 6 to 10 percent

c. 8 to 12 percent

d. 10 to 14 percent

11. Young adult males find rap music particularly beneficial when they run because

a. the relatively slow tempo is almost perfect for taking a stride cycle to each beat

b. most harbor an inner desire to appear in rap videos and be surrounded by attractive females

c. they get drawn into the rapid-fire lyrics and thus completely forget about the pain associated with the run

d. it creates brain wave patterns that are perfectly suited to running

12. The combination of music and video in an exercise environment can be more beneficial than music alone because

a. people are less likely to fixate on the appearance of others in the gym and negatively compare them with themselves

b. the visual distraction greatly increases the effects of auditory distraction, making all workouts considerably easier

c. the combination of sound and vision is what people are most accustomed to in their own homes, so they tend to perform better when MTV is showing in the gym

d. using auditory and visual stimuli in combination facilitates greater distraction than using either auditory or visual stimuli alone

13. It is long established that the use of music during exercise and training activities promotes dissociation, which means that

a. attention is focused on things unrelated to the task, such as problem solving, daydreaming, or music

b. the mind drifts, heightening the influence of sensory information from the body (e.g., a pounding heart or acidosis in the muscles)

c. external stimuli such as music or video block messages from the musculature to the central nervous system and cause a kind of out-of-body experience

d. people daydream and are able to tolerate the full gamut of exercise intensities with relatively little pain and self-reported perceived exertion

14. A good way to enhance the intrinsic motivation of people in an exercise class is by

a. playing music that the class prefers only if they achieve agreed-on performance targets

b. getting members of the class to compare the suitability of their personal music collections with each other and then integrating the collections of one or two members into the class

c. using really unusual tunes that few people have heard to pique their interest during the class

d. canvassing class members and highlighting when a track suggested by a particular person is used

15. Music can enhance task-specific imagery in exercise and sport because

a. people associate music with exercise and sport so strongly that virtually any well-known piece of music promotes imagery

b. it conjures images that have become associated with the music through prior life experiences, TV, film, radio, or the Internet (e.g., striving for Olympic glory and Vangelis' *Chariots of Fire* theme from the movie of the same name)

c. the rhythmic qualities of music directly stimulate the occipital lobe, a part of the brain near the back of the head that is responsible for imagery

d. the lyrical content of the music activates visual images as people process its meaning

## SHORT-ANSWER QUESTIONS

16. Which unit is commonly used to measure music tempo?

17. Briefly describe what musical meter is.

18. What are three documented ways well-selected music can enhance a person's psychological state during an exercise or training session?

19. What are the main influences on people's music preferences in an exercise or training context?

20. Briefly describe the relationship between exercise or training heart rate and preference for music tempo (i.e., how should music tempo be selected in response to expected changes in heart rate?).

21. What is the optimal range for music volume during exercise or training?

22. What are three advantages of exercisers or athletes using their own music devices when working out?

23. Why are music-related interventions particularly effective when working with young people in exercise and sport contexts?

24. Briefly describe the application of synchronous music.

25. When should music use be avoided during exercise and sport instruction?

Answers on page 215.

# PART I

# How Music Can Help Exercisers and Athletes

In part I, the first three chapters of this book set the scene for what's to come in part II and part III, and also provide a thorough grounding in the subject matter. Chapter 1 begins with a brief overview of the historical and cultural significance of music, touching on its ubiquity and its antiquity, a notion popularized by the Canadian scientist Daniel Levitin. It goes on to examine the music and exercise revolution of the 1980s, for which Hollywood actress Jane Fonda stood at the helm. The close relationship between music and the Olympic movement is touched on, and the components of a musical composition (e.g., melody, harmony, rhythm) are then explained and placed into context. The application of music in exercise and sport is introduced, and the main effects associated with music use for exercisers and athletes are highlighted. Chapter 1 ends with the important but patchily understood issue of how

to use music legally in the domain of exercise and sport.

Chapter 2 provides an overview of the scientific study of music in exercise and sport. It considers some of the key questions addressed by researchers, delves into how the brain responds to music, embraces the findings of landmark studies, and presents a new theoretical model to guide practitioners and researchers. Chapter 2 also addresses the matter of when music is used relative to performance—that is, pre-task, in-task, and post-task.

Chapter 3 deals with the sometimes thorny issue of selecting music and how to do so in a systematic manner for both individuals and groups or teams. It also presents a series of psychometric instruments, accompanied by detailed instructions, which enable practitioners to measure people's responses to music (e.g., the Music Mood-Regulation Scale, Feeling Scale, and Felt Arousal Scale).

# 1

# Music in Exercise and Sport

*Music expresses feeling and thought, without language; it was below and before speech, and it is above and beyond all words.*
—Robert G. Ingersoll (1833-1899), politician, orator, and lecturer

In one form or another, music has formed part of every human society since the dawn of civilization. It is almost as though music is part of humanity's genetic blueprint—a constant through the millennia that people of all ages and cultures engage in spontaneously. Music permeates many aspects of our lives and plays a variety of roles throughout the life span. Infants are sent to sleep by their mothers' gentle lullabies, and senior citizens appear spritely and rejuvenated during weekly sing-alongs in nursing homes. Adolescents define themselves in terms of the musical subculture they embrace, and their parents are all too willing to release their inhibitions and take to the dance floor when a familiar old song is played at a family wedding. It is quite a challenge to think of family occasions that do not revolve around the use of music in some form, be it a congratulatory chant at an anniversary party or a somber and reflective piece at a funeral.

The well-respected neuropsychologist Daniel Levitin maintains that music is unusual among all human activities for both its ubiquity and its antiquity (Levitin, 2007). In its earliest forms, music was produced using drums created by stretching animal skins over hollowed sections of tree trunks. Such drums were used

for communication, ceremonial purposes, and entertainment; similar activity is evident today among remote tribes in Africa and Australasia. For instance, the Yamatji aboriginal people from the Murchison, Gascoyne, and Pilbara regions of Western Australia use distinctive mud drums for religious rites. Anthropologists have speculated that the music made by primitive people on the sub-Saharan plains represented an attempt to imitate the heartbeat.

Available evidence indicates that the human species likely engaged in music making long before speaking. Archeological digs in Slovenia have revealed bone flutes made from the femur (thigh bone) of a now-extinct European bear. This prehistoric instrument is believed to be some 50,000 years old. One wonders whether the bear was driven to extinction as a consequence of our primitive ancestors' desire to make music!

The history of human conflict tells us much about the seminal role of music in rallying soldiers before entering the fray. Going back to ancient Greece, the only type of music known by the Spartans, the most feared fighting force of the ancient world, was war songs. An integral part of their military strategy was to march into battle to the sound of flute players accompanied by lyrists and harpists. This enabled the troops to advance evenly, step in time, and not break their order (a common failing of large armies at the moment of engagement).

In the American Civil War (1861-1865) between the southern Confederate states and northern Union states, music played a big part on both sides. On occasion, the opposing forces would engage in a type of battle of the bands on the night before the real battle ensued. At the Battle of Williamsburg in May 1862, it was famously said that the music was the equivalent of a thousand men. More recently, U.S. military personnel have had heavy metal music piped into their tanks as they enter battle to raise their testosterone levels and possibly numb their senses.

One of the key roles of music in a military context has been to accompany and pace the advance of marching soldiers. Marching troops have different levels of motivation, tolerance, fitness, and mental endurance. The military's use of marching bands such as the Royal Artillery Band and the Band of Her Majesty's Royal Marines in Great Britain created a common framework for all the men in time and space. Thus, it served to instill discipline, enhance esprit de corps, and even numb the pain of the march. All such benefits can be translated to the realm of physical exercise. Although the context is much different, many of the motivational challenges and deeply held inhibitions are remarkably similar.

## MUSIC AND EXERCISE REVOLUTION

Many people who are not habitual exercisers experience difficulties beyond their initial attempts to engage in an exercise routine. In addition to a general lack of motivation, well-documented barriers to regular participation include work and family commitments taking precedence; gym memberships perceived to be prohibitively expensive (despite the recent budget gym revolution); a lack of safe outdoor spaces in large towns and cities; boredom and lack of enjoyment; the absence of companionship and social support; and the fact that exercising makes people feel sweaty, breathless, and phys-

ically uncomfortable (Biddle, Mutrie, & Gorely, 2015).

Exercise professionals such as Hollywood actress-turned-fitness guru Jane Fonda realized in the late 1970s that if exercise for the masses could be coordinated with music, people would be far more likely to enjoy it and thus maintain a daily routine. During the 1980s and early 1990s, Fonda released some 22 exercise videos that sold in excess of 17 million copies worldwide. She was clearly onto something. The baby boomers, who were seeing the first signs of middle-age spread at that point, idolized Fonda and everything she stood for. An exponential rise in the number of exercise-to-music classes occurred during the 1980s, and the decades since have seen many permutations of the original dance-based classes: aqua aerobics, step aerobics, spinning, Boxercise, Zumba, BodyPump, and so on (see chapter 5).

Modern technologies have done much to promote the use of music in both exercise and sport settings. For example, the popularity of Fonda's exercise videos compelled many people to buy VHS video players in the 1980s. In terms of activities at the individual level, the Sony Walkman made walking and jogging to music a popular form of physical recreation during the same decade. Stadium staff have taken advantage of music editing technologies such as Audacity and Cubase to create soundtracks for sporting events to inspire the athletes and engage the fans. From an individual perspective, the essential personal music accessory of the 21st century—the iPod—has enabled exercise participants and athletes to create their own listening bubble. One consequence of this is that music listening and appreciation has become more of a lone pursuit than the social pursuit it was for previous generations. The relative merits of lone and group listening are explored in later chapters.

## MUSIC AND THE OLYMPIC GAMES

Music's place at the pinnacle of human culture is shown to stunning effect every two years in the celebration of the winter and summer olympiads. This illustrious link was originally forged in the ancient Olympic Games in Greece, where rhythmic clapping and drumming accompanied several events, including running races. The modern Olympic Games have continued to strengthen the association between music and sporting endeavors.

Music is integral to Olympic events such as figure skating and the floor exercise component of artistic gymnastics; it is also a prominent feature of the opening and closing ceremonies. One of the most spectacular examples of this came during the closing ceremony of the London 2012 Olympic Games—billed as *A Symphony of British Music*—where the late Freddie Mercury was projected onto large screens to perform a stirring call-and-response routine with the 80,000-strong crowd and athletes on the infield. Kim Gavin's orchestration cleverly fused Freddie's vintage 1986 Wembley performance with a modern-day celebration of sport. The screen ghost of the rock idol gave me the chills before the remaining members of Queen took center stage with songstress Jessie J to continue the homage to stadium rock. It was a truly mesmerizing way to close the Games and has remained etched in the memories of many who attended and the estimated 750 million TV viewers worldwide.

> *To watch the rousing performance by Queen and Jessie J at the closing ceremony of the London 2012 Olympics, search "Jessie J and Queen London 2012 Performance" on YouTube.*

This chapter addresses the nature of music as well as its key constituents. This will facilitate the selection processes that flow throughout parts I and II. Any terms that appear frequently throughout the book are explained in detail and accompanied by examples (you can also refer to the glossary). I examine the historical context of music in exercise and sport and present some of the more robust scientific findings reported by contemporary researchers. I draw on music-related anecdotes from sport and other spheres of popular culture to set the scene for what is to follow. The essential purpose of this introductory chapter is to provide a plate to put your dinner on.

# WHAT IS MUSIC?

The fundamental question "what is music?" needs to be addressed for the content of this book to be fully appreciated and the impact of music applications to be maximized. In many societies, the cultural pursuit of music has been elevated to an almost mystical level. Its best-known performers are perceived as enigmatic characters who are both revered and celebrated by the masses. We have all encountered artists and composers who appear to speak to us or can represent the human condition through their music in a form that we relate to.

In a physical activity context, whether jogging in a park or warming up for a judo contest, music can seem like a relatively simple stimulus that is effortlessly absorbed and appreciated. A piece of music, however, requires the careful organization of a number of elements: melody, harmony, rhythm, tempo, meter, timbre, and dynamics. In the case of a song or a piece of vocal music, lyrics can be added to this list. Let's explore these elements one by one and then consider how they function in unison to create the musical whole that might inspire optimal performance. A basic understanding of these musical building blocks, even if you have very little knowledge of music theory, will enable you to fully absorb and implement the music applications that feature in parts II and III of this book.

## Melody

Melody is often the highest-pitched part, or tune, of a piece of music. Most likely, you have caught yourself singing, humming, or whistling along to the melody. The melody line is distinctive and memorable; people can often name a piece of music after hearing just the first three or four notes of the melody. For example, if I were to play you the first three notes of the main motif of one of my favorite sporting compositions—"Gonna Fly Now (Theme From Rocky)" by Bill Conti—you may be able to hum the remainder of the uplifting tune without even thinking. Melodies are constructed using a scale or combination of scales. A scale is an arrangement of notes in a specific order of whole and half steps. A large part of the emotional tone of the music can be transmitted by the melody. The *Rocky* theme, for example, signifies a sense of optimism in the battle against adversity, as well as striving toward personal achievement.

## Harmony

Harmony is created when notes or melodies sound simultaneously, such as the rich sonic blend produced when members of a barbershop quartet sing in unison. This meshing of notes acts, in part, to shape the mood of the music to make people feel happy, sad, surprised, anxious, or calm. Harmony is what gives music its distinctive flavor, from the simplicity of bubblegum pop to the sophisticated blend of sonic ingredients in a Beethoven symphony. Complex harmony can challenge a listener emotionally and entails waves of aural tension and pleasantness—an array of dissonance and consonance. A good example from rock music is Queen's "Bohemian Rhapsody," which has a particularly complex harmonic structure for a pop song. A concept that is closely related to harmony is the key of a piece of music. This represents the tonal center of a piece that can be shifted up or down to create color and challenge the listener's expectations. In simple terms, the tonal center is a related series of pitches that serve as a fixed reference point to the ear—a kind of aural home base, to use a sporting analogy.

*To watch a video of Queen's "Bohemian Rhapsody," search "Queen Bohemian Rhapsody" on YouTube.*

Composers of film scores are particularly adept at manipulating the feelings of moviegoers during each scene through their masterful use of harmony and key changes; they may move a piece out of its initial tonal center—the home base—and sometimes return to it to give the listener a sense of resolution or satisfaction. A much-loved sport film such as the classic *Hoosiers* is rendered every bit as gripping and evocative by its well-crafted soundtrack as it is by the imagery and storyline of a small-town Indiana high school team that overcomes considerable odds to win the state basketball championship. As well as evoking primary emotions such as sadness and happiness, composers create subtler shades of feeling such as suspense, anticipation, joy, and tranquility just by changing the way they blend notes. Of course, those who make commercials are just as clever in their use of harmony. The next time you watch TV, compare the music used to sell an everyday product such as baked beans with that used to sell luxury items such as sports cars.

## Rhythm

Rhythm concerns the way notes are distributed over time and accented. Putting it more simply, rhythm concerns how the energy of the music is transmitted. When completing any sort of physical task in time with music, rhythm is a primary consideration. When I go swimming, for example, I often play famous waltzes in my mind because the three beats in a bar, with the emphasis on the first, coincide with a strong kick to every arm stroke, which is followed by two softer kicks (*one* two three, *one* two three). Similarly, when I perform my conditioning circuit early most mornings, I like to play energetic disco classics, which have a strong four-beats-to-the-bar rhythm. Not only does the music lift me out of my slumber, but its rhythmic regularity directs my push-ups and abdominal crunches in a way that makes the workout seem a little more bearable for my aging body. So, Johann Strauss' *Blue Danube Waltz* for the front crawl and "Disco Inferno" by The Trammps for circuits!

## Syncopation

Another aspect of musical rhythm that is relevant to the exercise sphere (see chapter 4) is known as syncopation. This occurs when rhythmic emphasis is placed off the main beat to create an unexpected rhythmic feel that many people equate with the notion of groove (e.g., That track has an infectious groove—it really makes me want to move!). In the case of common time, which has four quarter-note beats to the bar, the strongest beat is the first in the bar, and the second strongest is the third in the bar. Popular styles of music such as swing and reggae that place strong emphasis on the second and fourth beats of the bar (what musicians call the backbeat) are based on the principle of syncopation.

Most forms of popular music use syncopation to great effect, particularly when the music is used for dancing (e.g., funk, hip-hop, dubstep). Some forms of music are based on a highly syncopated rhythmic feel; Latin music is particularly well known for its use of syncopation (e.g., samba and salsa styles). This means that keeping in time with the rhythms used in classes such as Zumba may require greater information processing and coordination than those used in classes such as step or aqua aerobics. Of course, if you have grown up in Havana, Cuba, syncopated salsa rhythms will be the norm for you and will not necessarily require greater mental effort for you to translate the music into movement!

Although virtually all forms of popular music employ syncopation to a degree, as an illustration of the concept, and to assist you in your own selection processes, table 1.1 provides some classic examples of highly syncopated tracks that might be used in the exercise and sport domain (column 2) along with examples of tracks that have straighter rhythms or are relatively unsyncopated (column 1).

A musical technique that is closely related to syncopation is that of the breakbeat. This is when the music cuts out for a syncopated percussive break (typically a drum solo), or even a series of breaks. These breakbeats often introduce a new rhythm into the piece that is busier and more complex than the elementary rhythmic structure. The technique was popularized in early hip-hop music, which used samples from funk recordings of the late 1960s and early 1970s. To complicate matters, this sampled beat (examples of which appear in table 1.2) is sometimes referred to as a breakbeat in its own right, regardless of how it is

**Table 1.1**  Tracks Predicated on Relatively Unsyncopated (Straight) Rhythms (Column 1) and Highly Syncopated Rhythms (Column 2)

| Tracks with relatively unsyncopated rhythms | | | Tracks with highly syncopated rhythms | | |
|---|---|---|---|---|---|
| Title | Artist | Year | Title | Artist | Year |
| Keep On Running | Spencer Davis Group | 1966 | Mas Que Nada | Jorge Ben | 1963 |
| When Will I See You Again | Three Degrees | 1974 | Get On The Good Foot | James Brown | 1972 |
| Mamma Mia | ABBA | 1975 | Superstition | Stevie Wonder | 1972 |
| Do Ya Think I'm Sexy? | Rod Stewart | 1978 | Jive Talkin' | Bee Gees | 1975 |
| Scarface (Push It To The Limit) | Paul Engemman | 1983 | Don't Stop 'Til You Get Enough | Michael Jackson | 1979 |
| Teddy Picker | Arctic Monkeys | 2007 | Summer Of '69 | Bryan Adams | 1985 |
| I Kissed A Girl | Katy Perry | 2008 | Bamboléo | Gypsy Kings | 1987 |
| You've Got The Love | Florence and the Machine | 2009 | Smooth | Santana feat. Rob Thomas | 1999 |
| Firework | Katy Perry | 2010 | Livin' La Vida Loca | Ricky Martin | 1999 |
| Sweat | Snoop Dogg vs. David Guetta | 2011 | They Don't Want Music | Black Eyed Peas feat. James Brown | 2005 |
| For The First Time | The Script | 2010 | Grace Kelly | Mika | 2007 |
| Give Me Everything | Pitbull feat. NeYo, Afrojack, and Nayer | 2011 | Gangnam Style | PSY | 2012 |
| Of The Night | Bastille | 2013 | Feel This Moment | Pitbull feat. Christina Aguilera | 2013 |
| Come And Get It | John Newman | 2015 | Dibby Dibby Sound | DJ Fresh vs. Jay Fay feat. Ms Dynamite | 2014 |
| Adventure Of A Lifetime | Coldplay | 2015 | Hold Up | Beyoncé | 2016 |

*Note:* All of these tracks can be located on YouTube.

**Table 1.2** Classic Examples of Breakbeats in Popular Music

| Track title | Artist | Year | Timepoint |
|---|---|---|---|
| Amen Brother | The Winstons | 1969 | 1:26 min |
| Funky Drummer | James Brown | 1970 | 5:35 min |
| The Power | Snap! | 1990 | 12 sec |
| On A Ragga Tip | SL2 | 1996 | 1:52 min |
| Firestarter | The Prodigy | 1996 | 20 sec |
| Apache | Incredible Bongo Band | 2006 | 2:20 min |
| Warrior Dance | The Prodigy | 2009 | 41 sec |
| Calling All Hearts | DJ Cassidy feat. Robin Thicke and Jessie J | 2014 | 3:45 min |

*Note:* All of these tracks can be located on YouTube.

used in a piece of music. Particularly in the 1980s and 1990s, it was not uncommon for hip-hop tracks to be backed by the Amen break (see table 1.2) for the entire duration of the piece! When they appear in their guise as drum solos, breakbeats imbue a track with energy and add an unexpected twist that dancers and other performing artists often capitalize on in their movement patterns.

## Tempo

Tempo concerns the speed, or rate, at which music is played and is most commonly expressed in beats per minute (bpm). Generally speaking, pieces of music with fast tempi tend to be regarded as happy and stimulating, whereas pieces with slow tempi sound sad and can be sedative. This generalization holds up fairly well across the music of various cultures and ethnic groups. It is also the case that a given rhythm (e.g., a march) can be played at a fast or slow tempo, although the terms *rhythm* and *tempo* are often interchangeably. Chapter 2 touches on the relationship between exercise heart rate and the preference for music tempo. It was previously thought that this was a straightforward linear relationship—that is, as heart rate goes up, people prefer music of correspondingly higher tempi. However, as detailed in chapter 2, this relationship is more complex.

On occasion, tempo can be relatively slow while the melody is fast and invigorating—as is the case with "Something Inside So Strong" by Labi Siffre (80 bpm). One can imagine getting ready to perform a 3-repetition maximum lift on the bench press while hearing this piece; the tempo approximates the slow, deliberate movement required, while the lyric carries affirmations of strength and personal pride (more on this later).

It is worth noting that the tempo relates to the underlying pace of a piece of music and that lyrical content or a melody can flow at a slow, medium, or fast pace over a slow underlying tempo. In experimental research conducted with colleagues in the UK, United States, and Australia, I have found that many subjects interpret rap music as being of a fast tempo, when in actuality it has a relatively slow tempo (usually 75 to 95 bpm). These people are interpreting the machine-gun lyrical content and complex rhythmic structures using bass and percussion as contributing to the tempo. They are perhaps mistaking tempo with the closely related concept of meter.

*To watch a performance of "Something Inside So Strong," search "Labi Siffre Something Inside So Strong" on YouTube.*

## Meter

Meter concerns how fast a piece of music feels regardless of its tempo. It entails how tones are grouped over time; thus, meter depends on the listener's perception of what the pulse is and when it is expected to occur. To put it another way, meter relates to when you tap your foot hard versus light, and how this series of taps comes together to create larger units. For example, many musicians count in the Monkees' hit "I'm A Believer" at 80 bpm, whereas most listeners feel the song at 160 bpm (i.e., at twice the speed at which musicians count it). This is because the combination of the busy guitar riff and the tambourine playing on every offbeat gives it an up-tempo feel. The song can, of course, just as easily be counted at 160 bpm, in which case the tambourine is perceived as playing a standard backbeat on the second and fourth beats of each bar, rather than on each offbeat (see figure 1.1). The point here is that for an exercise or sport professional, the meter (perceived pulse), and not the tempo, is the critical consideration when marrying music with activities of varying intensities.

> *To watch a performance of "I'm A Believer" by the Monkees, search "The Monkees I'm A Believer" on YouTube. Look at figure 1.1 to match the notated rhythm with the sound of the track.*

## Lyrics

Lyrics are the words of a song, which we normally hear in the form of verses and choruses. The meaning of song lyrics can either be explicit or implicit; this means that they can make direct statements that are easy to comprehend (explicit) or suggested statements that are not directly expressed (implicit). Often bearing a close relationship to poetry, song lyrics can express meaning implicitly through the use of literary devices such as similes and metaphors.

A simile compares one thing with another thing of a different kind. It is used to make a description more emphatic or vivid, such as in the well-known lyric "Like a rock, I was strong as I could be" ("Like A Rock" by Bob Seger). A metaphor is a word or phrase applied to an object or action to which it is not literally applicable, as illustrated in this lyric that makes reference to New York: "If this town is just an apple, Then let me take a bite" ("Human Nature" by Michael Jackson). Sometimes lyrics conjure imagery that exercisers and athletes find highly inspiring; for example, R. Kelly's "I Believe I Can Fly" uses evocative lyrics to instill the notion that if you have sufficient self-belief, the sky is the limit in terms of what you might achieve. Lyrics can touch us emotionally or provide a source of affirmation because we can process our own language easily, they are attached to a melodic and rhythmic structure that often makes them far more accessible than spoken words, they are often repeated within a song (e.g., in the chorus), and they express the inner feelings of the artist by the way they are sung.

## Timbre

Timbre, which rhymes with *camber*, is the quality of the sound made by different instruments; it allows us to distinguish, for example, between a French horn and a vibraphone playing the same note. Timbre is an essential consideration in a sporting context and often determines the combination of instruments that are used in major events. For example, in team sporting events such as American football and soccer, the marching bands use instruments such as trumpets, bugles, tubas, flutes, and drums. The sound produced by these instruments cuts through the murmur

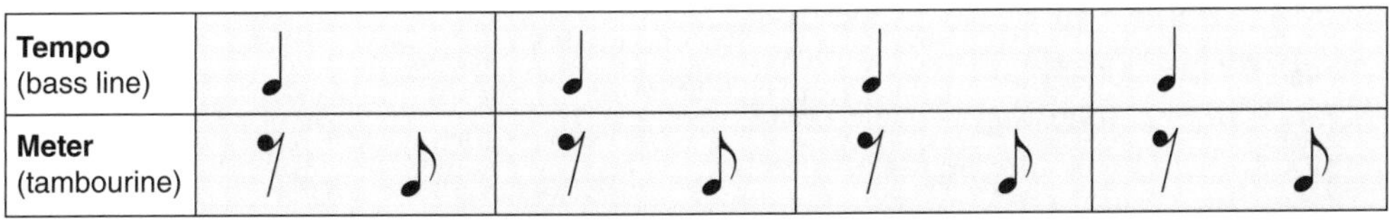

**Figure 1.1**   An illustration of the difference between tempo and meter and how this relates to the underlying rhythm of "I'm A Believer" by the Monkees. Each box in the tempo row represents one beat at the tempo of 80 bpm.

of the crowd and creates a suitable ambiance; when done well, the music of a marching band is stirring and uplifting. A string quartet or a jazz trio providing the pre-game and half-time entertainment, however, would simply not cut through sufficiently to have any significant impact on the players and spectators. Such musical collectives would be more suited to a champagne reception, where the music provides a warm backdrop to people's chatter.

## Dynamics

Dynamics concerns the energy transmitted by musicians through their touch or breath to affect the loudness of their instruments. For example, a drummer can stroke the snare drum with brushes in a typical jazz waltz, or hit the drum vigorously with sticks in a bright rock 'n' roll number. When a trumpet player forces the air out of his lungs and blows into the mouthpiece with all his might, the resultant sound is much louder than when he just tongues a note very gently. Along similar lines, a saxophone player can play quietly between the lyrics of a song or screech a high-decibel solo during an instrumental break.

In the music literature, a variety of terms denote loudness. In fact, loudness is the psychological manifestation of the physical strength, or amplitude, of a sound wave. The terms used to denote loudness or related characteristics of sound include *dynamics, volume, sound intensity,* and *sound pressure level.* We do not need to go into the distinctions between these, although full definitions are provided in the glossary. I generally use the term *volume,* which is widely understood, and when I refer to musicians making their instruments louder or softer, I use the term *dynamics.* Musicians are often instructed within a musical score to apply a crescendo (i.e., gradually get louder) or a diminuendo (i.e., gradually get softer). These principles can also be applied to the segueing of musical works for an exercise class or to hyping up a stadium crowd, as addressed in later chapters. In terms of a safe volume of music for exercise and training, the range 65 to 75 dBA is recommended (dBA represents the intensity of sound, as measured in decibels, at ear level).

## Musical Form

All of the aforementioned elements of music require an overarching structure for a piece to be readily absorbed and recognized by the listener. Composers and musicians refer to this structure as the form. A typical pop song might have the following form: intro, verse 1, verse 2, bridge 1, chorus 1, verse 3, bridge 2, chorus 2, chorus 3, chorus to fade. What makes popular music particularly accessible to exercise instructors is that it is normally broken into sections of four or eight bars, each containing four quarter beats. This makes it easy to coordinate blocks of movement with temporal blocks of the music (e.g., eight musical bars or measures). Figure 1.2 illustrates the anatomy of a regular pop song and how musical bars relate to each part of the form (e.g., verses and choruses).

Rhythm, tempo, and meter are the elements of music that are most likely to prompt a physical reaction in the listener. Indeed, London-based researchers Emily Wilson and Nick Davey noted that, even when people sit motionless, "it is often very difficult to suppress the natural urge to tap the feet or strum the fingers along with the beat of the music" (Wilson & Davey, 2002, p. 177). It appears that this propensity to react to the rhythmic aspects of music is hardwired; ostensibly, humans are musical beings (Levitin, 2007). This predisposition to respond to music, and in particular to the rhythmic qualities of music, is something that all exercise and sport professionals can capitalize on.

# MUSIC USE IN EXERCISE AND SPORT

The cultural phenomena of music and sport are combined seamlessly at modern-day events to the point that they appear to go almost hand in hand. Coaches blast music in the locker room to imbue players with a sense of shared purpose. Professional DJs are hired to make selections that engage supporters and rouse the players as they enter the fray. Also, many teams have adopted their own anthems or signature tunes that enhance their sense of identity and esprit de corps. For example, St Mary's Stadium at Southampton FC swings to the Dixieland favorite "When The Saints Go Marching In," whereas Anfield Stadium at Liverpool FC reverberates to the anthemic "You'll Never Walk Alone," a showtune popularized by the Liverpudlian group Gerry and the Pacemakers in the early 1960s.

| Song section | Timepoint | | Lyrics | Musical analysis |
|---|---|---|---|---|
| | Mins/Secs | Bars | | |
| **Intro** | 00:00 | 1–8 | (Because you know I'm) all about that bass, 'Bout that bass, 'bout that bass, no treble I'm all 'bout that bass, 'bout that bass, no treble I'm all 'bout that bass, 'bout that bass, no treble I'm all 'bout that bass, 'bout that bass | The singing is unaccompanied other than for a repeating two-beat rhythm (syncopated clapping ♫ ⅞ ♪). Final bar is a "rest," which gives greater impact to the start of the verse. |
| **Verse 1** | 00:16 | 9–16 | Yeah it's pretty clear, I ain't no size two But I can shake it, shake it like I'm supposed to do 'Cause I got that boom boom that all the boys chase All the right junk in all the right places | Uses a rest in bars 15 and 16 alongside a sung harmony section. |
| **Verse 2** | 00:31 | 17–24 | I see the magazines working that Photoshop We know that **** ain't real Come on now, make it stop If you got beauty beauty just raise 'em up 'Cause every inch of you is perfect From the bottom to the top | The lyrical affirmations counter distorted perceptions of female beauty that appear in the media. They also empower listeners to accept and celebrate their own body shape. |
| **Bridge 1** | 00:45 | 25–40 | Yeah, my momma she told me don't worry about your size She says, boys they like a little more booty to hold at night. You know I won't be no stick-figure, silicone Barbie doll, So, if that's what's you're into Then go ahead and move along | This has a Latin-influenced rhythmic feel and the meter seems to slow. |
| **Chorus 1** | 01:14 | 41–48 | Because you know I'm all about that bass, 'Bout that bass, 'bout that bass, no treble I'm all 'bout that bass, 'bout that bass, no treble I'm all 'bout that bass, 'bout that bass, no treble I'm all 'bout that bass, 'bout that bass | The chorus features an insistent rhythmic phrase that is repeated four times for emphasis; a hook that defines the song in listeners' memories. The rapid succession of sixteenth notes (♬♬) ushers in a faster meter, which lends the chorus greater energy than the verses. |
| **Verse 3** | 01:27 | 42–56 | I'm bringing booty back Go ahead and tell them skinny ******* that No, I'm just playing I know you think you're fat, But I'm here to tell you that, Every inch of you is perfect from the bottom to the top | A rhythmic trick is employed here: an unexpected rhythm break in the first bar in which there sits a harmony singing section with an upward 'slide' in pitch on the notes sung. |
| **Bridge 2** | 01:42 | 57–72 | Yeah, my momma she told me don't worry about your size She says, boys they like a little more booty to hold at night. You know I won't be no stick-figure, silicone Barbie doll, So, if that's what's you're into Then go ahead and move along | Another stylistic element is introduced here in the form of 'doo-wop' harmony fill-ins from the backing singers. An interesting facet of the song is the cheery melodic and harmonic elements alongside the infantile and pastel images in the video, which belie a sexual edge in the lyrics—this creates a rather intriguing tension. |
| **Chorus 5–8** | 02:11 | 73–104 | Because you know I'm all about that bass, 'Bout that bass, 'bout that bass, no treble I'm all 'bout that bass, 'bout that bass, no treble I'm all 'bout that bass, 'bout that bass, no treble I'm all 'bout that bass, 'bout that bass | Chorus is three-peated and then fades out |

**Figure 1.2**  The relationship of form to musical bars in a typical pop song ("All About That Bass" by Meghan Trainor).

In the United States, all collegiate teams have a series of supporting long cheers. One of the best known was used by Yale University during most of the 20th century and was taken in part from an Aristophanes play written circa 405 BC called *The Frogs*:

*Brekekekex, ko-ax, ko-ax, Brekekekex, ko-ax, ko-ax,*
*O-op, O-op, parabalou,*
*Yale, Yale, Yale,*
*Rah, rah, rah, rah, rah, rah, rah, rah, rah,*
*Yale! Yale! Yale!*

*To watch a performance of the Yale long cheer by a former Yale cheerleader, search "The Yale Long Cheer" on YouTube.*

As highlighted at the beginning of this chapter, the modern Olympic Games have played a pivotal role in formalizing the association between music and sporting feats. Composers such as Debussy, John Williams, and Vangelis were inspired by the Olympic ideals. Also, music was integral to many Olympic events such as rhythmic gymnastics and figure skating, and the best-known artists of the day performed at the opening and closing ceremonies. For example, the doyennes of British pop music, the Spice Girls, reformed to play at the closing ceremony of the London Olympic Games, each flanked by a jewel-encrusted London taxicab.

Songs associated with the Games often become smash hits. One of the most memorable examples of this relationship was Whitney Houston's "One Moment In Time," a track recorded especially for the 1988 Seoul Olympics, which many athletes have since used for its motivational qualities. More recently, the track "One Dream" by Canadian singer-songwriter Sarah McLachlan was used as the theme track of the 2010 Winter Olympics in Vancouver. The piece is characterized by plain rock-ballad instrumentation, a gradual buildup of energy, and lyrics that carry an inspirational message regarding self-actualization.

The national anthem of the gold medalist(s) is played at the medal ceremony, often reducing tough-as-nails athletes to tears in the emotional intensity of the moment. A good example of this is the British Olympian Rebecca Romero, who won a silver medal in rowing at the Athens 2004 Games, then had to take time out from rowing to rehabilitate a back injury. She found that cycling was particularly helpful to her rehabilitation program, and she also really enjoyed it. In fact, she was such a talented cyclist that she decided to (almost literally) jump ship and was subsequently selected to represent the Great Britain team at the 2008 Beijing Games. She went on to win a gold medal in the 3000-meter individual pursuit—a blue riband event. At the medal ceremony, Romero could not hold back her emotion; when "God Save The Queen" was played in the velodrome and the

British flag was hoisted, she had to wipe away the tears streaming down her face. It was suggested afterward that part of the reason for such a display of emotion at the medal ceremony was that her former rowing crew had won silver again in Beijing, and thus were not able to hear "God Save The Queen" played in their honor. Romero's tears flowed partly out of relief and partly out of joy.

A little-known fact is that in the period 1912 to 1948, artistic events were part of the Olympic festival, and medals were awarded for musical composition just as they were for athletic endeavors. The combination of art and music in a global festival was the desire of the founder of the modern Olympics, Baron Pierre de Coubertin. Artistic competitions were organized in five areas (architecture, literature, music, painting, and sculpture), with the premise that each work should be inspired by sport. The number of submissions by artists steadily grew, although there was a decline in Berlin (1936) and in the post-war Games hosted by London (1948). History books reveal that the juries often struggled to judge the pieces, which were submitted as scores only. Consequently, on two occasions, no award was given out at all! At the Berlin Olympics, also known as Hitler's Games, the winning pieces were played before an audience comprising dignitaries and members of the general public.

The judges at the Berlin Games (predominantly German) were shamelessly generous toward entries from their compatriots. In the orchestral work category, "Olympische Festmusik," composed by Werner Egk, took gold, and host nationals boasted a clean sweep in the choral category. According to my friend and colleague, the sports historian Anthony Bateman, many Germans believed that this proved the musical superiority of the master race, which was a natural extension of the Nazis' desire to demonstrate their physical superiority.

A modern-day irony, particularly in light of my own body of published research, is that many governing bodies of sport have either banned the use of music or are presently considering banning it in competition. For example, the International Association of Athletics Federations (IAAF) has banned music since 2006 owing, in part, to its potential work-enhancing effects but also to the fact that music can be so intoxicating that it places athletes in mass participation events, such as marathons, in danger. They might bump into each other, miss important instructions, or even get hit by a car. Moreover, in stadium events, the IAAF is concerned that coaches might transmit instructions to their athletes via music devices.

*The following examples shall be considered assistance and therefore not allowed: . . . (b) Possession or use of video recorders, radios, CD, radio transmitters, mobile phone or similar devices in the competition area.*

Rule 144.3 (b) of the International Association of Athletics Federations (Competition Rules 2016-2017, p. 153)

Not wanting to offend the governing organization USA Track and Field, the organizers of the New York City Marathon banned the use of personal music players at the 2007 event, which prompted vociferous objections from competitors and an interesting media debate. The banning of iPods and other MP3 devices in mass participation events is almost impossible to enforce without a dedicated music police; therefore, their use is likely to continue. Some race organizers have reacted to the ban on personal music players by organizing events accompanied by music from live bands or DJs. Music selections are made to match the physiological demands of the event and the demographic profile of participants (e.g., www .runtothebeat.co.uk; more on this in chapter 7).

Although there has been some recent curbing of the use of music in certain sports, the views of the organizers of Winter Olympic sports seem to be almost diametrically opposed to those of the the organizers of Summer Olympic sports. At the 2014 Sochi Games, bagpipers spurred on the athletes in curling, organ music interleaved segments of ice hockey games, lively selections accompanied half-pipe snowboarding, and skeleton sliders were immersed in their iPods while preparing mentally to throw themselves down a mountainside at 90 mph (145 km/h). Likewise, its use as an accompaniment for training or exercise has rapidly grown in popularity. Health and fitness chains take their selection of music very seriously, and although I believe they still have some way to go to optimize what they play and how they play it, they have made significant headway over the last two decades. Most chains have commissioned customer surveys and subsequently hired music consultants to improve the entertainment services offered to their customers.

My research group was commissioned to formulate a music policy for the David Lloyd Leisure chain in the UK. I worked on this project with my former doctoral student David-Lee Priest in the early 2000s (Priest, Karageorghis, & Sharp, 2004). We uncovered some interesting findings while surveying its members and staff. For example, females rated the importance of music higher than males did, different music selections were required for cardiorespiratory exercise than for resistance training, and music selections often favored younger gym members over their older counterparts. This held even in morning sessions, during which seniors were the predominant users. In the morning sessions, users generally preferred slower music selections when compared to the evening sessions. This could be due either to the lower level of stimulation required in the morning or to the need for more stimulation when mentally fatigued after a day's work. Either way, this finding needs to be explored further using a diverse range of samples.

In many instances the music played in health and fitness facilities is based on the preferences of duty managers; however, their musical predilections rarely coincide with those of their clientele. I recently received a letter from a man in Gloucester (UK) who was absolutely furious over the insistence of staff at his local gym to continually play gangsta rap rather than his preferred middle-of-the-road rock (e.g., "Why I'm Here" by Oleander). He wanted me to provide him with hard scientific evidence that rock was superior to rap when it came to working out! This illustrates how the imposition of one person's preferences or those of a subculture can stir deep feelings in those with entirely different preferences.

Throughout this book I provide numerous music recommendations for a variety of exercise modalities and intensities (e.g., moderate aerobic activity or high-intensity resistance training). These suggestions are for exercise instructors and managers of facilities as well as exercise participants who use personal listening devices or devise their own playlists. The recommendations are to use as a starting point and intended

## DORIAN, THE HEAVY METAL HERCULES

In the quasi-sport of bodybuilding, we find perhaps one of the most striking incidences of music empowering physical performance. Six-time Mr. Olympia winner Dorian Yates dominated the iron game for the best part of the 1990s. A colossus both physically and metaphorically, Yates' frame was sculpted and grown cell by cell over a career that saw him lift something in the order of 40,000 tons at the rate of between 11 tons (chest and arms) and 41 tons (legs) per workout. The argument is often advanced that leading bodybuilders have herculean physiques simply because they found themselves at the front of the queue when God was handing out pecs. Yates' progression stands in stark contravention of such thinking; when he began competing, he weighed in at a paltry 180 pounds (82 kg)—a mere mortal! A few years later, in an out-of-competition phase and properly hydrated, he was heavier by some 100 pounds (45 kg). The added muscle weight was compounded by extra bone, tendon, blood, heart muscle, guts, and skin.

How was this superhumanity achieved? To some extent, the heavy metal on his Walkman was just as important as the iron on his barbells. On back day, he strained to the strains of Aerosmith, whereas pounding tracks like Pearl Jam's "Spin The Black Circle" and "Go" were the soundtrack for chest, shoulders, abs, and arms development. Finally, Guns N' Roses was the catalyst for the insanity of leg day, for which he warmed up with a casual two sets of 12 reps at 1,047 pounds (475 kg) on the leg press followed by his Bulgarian split squats performed to the rousing lyric of "Welcome To The Jungle." His place in the iron-pumpers pantheon assured, Yates now runs a thriving gym business in the city of his birth, Birmingham (UK), which, like its most massive son, has swelled in proportions in recent decades.

to fire the imagination in formulating playlists. I am acutely aware of how fluid and indeed fickle musical preferences can be and how musical tastes morph over time. Nonetheless, I would argue that the principles underlying music selection in the exercise and sport domain remain relatively stable.

## MAIN EFFECTS OF MUSIC

Researchers have primarily explored three types of musical effects in the field of exercise and sport: psychological, psychophysical, and ergogenic. Psychological effects concern how music influences mood, emotion, affect (feelings of pleasure or displeasure), cognition (thought processes), and behavior. For example, one of the main foci of my good friend and colleague Andrew Lane (University of Wolverhampton, UK) has been how musical stimuli can be used to regulate the mood of athletes and exercise participants. His group has also developed an instrument that rates the degree to which a piece of music can regulate

mood: the Music Mood-Regulation Scale (MMRS; Hewston, Lane, & Karageorghis, 2008; see chapter 3). Whereas emotions are responses to specific stimuli, moods are more subtle, more enduring, and less intense.

Similarly, my group has addressed the influence types of music have on affect during exercise (Karageorghis et al., 2009, 2010, 2013; Karageorghis & Jones, 2014). It is possible to make an exercise or training session feel far more pleasurable with careful attention to music selection, even at relatively high workloads. Nonetheless, this message has taken a long time to permeate the academic sphere. For example, not until the summer of 2011 did the American College of Sports Medicine mention in a position statement that "Exercise environments with engaging distractions (e.g., music, an instructor, television, scenery) may also ameliorate affective experiences (and adherence), but additional confirmation is needed." (ACSM, 2011, p. 1347). I would argue that by 2016, an abundance of empirical evidence in the public domain supported the positive influence of well-selected music on affective experiences (see Clark, Baker, & Taylor, 2016; Karageorghis, 2016). The other forms of distraction or motivation mentioned by the ACSM do indeed require further investigation.

The psychophysical effects of music are studied by psychophysicists, who are interested in how the brain interacts with the physical world. These scientists usually employ stimuli that can be objectively measured, such as pure tones varying in loudness or lights varying in luminance. They then study how each of the senses (vision, hearing, taste, touch, smell) responds to these stimuli. Psychophysical effects of music are measured during exercise, but also sometimes during sport training, and the most common effect is the perception of physical exertion (Karageorghis & Priest, 2012a, 2012b; Karageorghis, 2016). This perception is often assessed using a Rating of Perceived Exertion (RPE) Scale. The RPE Scale, in its various guises, was devised by the well-known Swedish exercise psychophysicist Gunnar Borg, an emeritus professor at the University of Stockholm (Borg, 1982, 1998). The version of the scale that we use most often in our work—the 11-point scale—is presented in chapter 3. This scale is easy to apply and is administered while people are exercising to gauge how they feel. It is one of a range of popular in-task measures presented in this book.

Music has an ergogenic effect when it improves athletic or exercise performance by either delaying fatigue or increasing work capacity. Typically, this results in levels of endurance, power, productivity, or strength that exceed expectations. Accordingly, music can be used as a type of legal drug that enhances work output. In my daily work with Brunel's track and field athletes, I often use music to regulate their indoor conditioning sessions. The result is an increase in motivation, particularly if I allow the athletes to contribute to the music selection. They also find the sessions far more enjoyable. We explore the importance of democratizing music selection in chapters 5 and 8.

## HOW MUSIC IS USED

Music is used in three main ways within sport and exercise: synchronous, asynchronous, and pre-task. The synchronous application of music is typified by the use of the rhythmic, or tempo-ral, aspects of music as a type of metronome that regulates movement patterns. For example, in synchronized swimming, the athletes strive to keep their aquatic dance routines in perfect time with the accompanying music. As discussed in chapter 6, this approach can yield a particularly strong ergogenic effect when used to regulate endurance-type activities such as walking and cycling, thereby increasing their efficiency. As the term implies, the asynchronous use of music entails the absence of conscious synchronization. Music can also be used pre-task to arouse, relax, or regulate the mood of an individual or a team or exercise group prior to a competition or activity. Generally, fast, loud music has a stimulative effect, so it can be used as part of a psych-up routine; soft, slow music has a sedative effect, which means that it can be used as a sedative or relaxant. Most coaches believe that the role of music is always to arouse the athlete; however, given how extremely activated athletes can feel before competition, the ability of a well-selected piece to calm and deactivate the athlete is often discounted.

A good example of an athlete using music to psych down involves my former student, Audley Harrison, MBE. In 1998 he brazenly told fellow students that he was going to become the Olympic super-heavyweight boxing champion at the upcoming Sydney Games. However, when he got to the qualifying rounds and began to progress, nervousness set in. Years later he told me:

*Nothing had prepared me for the pressure cooker that was the Olympic Games—not even winning the Commonwealth title two years earlier in Kuala Lumpur. I really felt the weight of public expectation back home as well as the expectation of my family and support team. I needed something to calm me down and put me in the right frame of mind to give the performance of my life.*

To soothe his anxiety, he listened to Japanese classical music, which, like many Asian music forms, uses a pentatonic scale (e.g., the sound made by the five black keys on a piano). Such music can induce alpha brain wave activity, which is associated with mental calmness and enhanced concentration. Although many would argue that, given the energetic and aggressive nature of boxing, Japanese classical music was a somewhat counterintuitive choice, it did the trick for Audley, who was duly crowned Olympic champion. He went on to sign a lucrative contract with BBC Sport and enjoyed a decade-long professional career, of which the high points included WBF (2004) and European (2010) heavyweight titles. Reflecting on his Olympic triumph, Audley told me:

*Winning the Olympic title was a real turning point in my career and opened up all sorts of opportunities for me. I had been an urban music aficionado since my teens, but the Olympic experience created a kind of special relationship for me with pre-fight music. I would consider very carefully what I used in the lead-in to a big fight and in particular my walk-on music. That would set the tone for me and my fans. It would tell people that I had arrived and was ready for action.*

It is possible to use music in all three ways; for example, the West Indies cricket team listens to booming reggae music in the locker room while they mentally prepare. When they walk onto the pitch, they are accompanied by a throng of per-cussionists among their supporters (all pre-task). During the match, drums sound relentlessly in the background and thus exemplify the asynchronous use of music. However, while fielding, the team appears on occasion to lock into the calypso rhythms, which dictate the pace of play in a synchronous manner. The wall of sound has the added advantage of being a considerable distraction to their opponents; this may go some way toward explaining why teams around the world are often reticent to face the Windies—particularly when they are playing at their principal home ground, the Kensington Oval in Bridgetown, Barbados.

Legend has it that when the Windies play at their alternative home ground, the Kingston Oval in Jamaica, spectators can hear prisoners singing. Of course, this may have something to do with the fact that Kingston Prison is just beyond the fence! The supporters of each major cricket nation have their own way of using music either to inspire their heroes or to throw the concentration of rival teams. For example, Pakistani cricket supporters are well known for blowing horns. During a

Music punctuates many aspects of the West Indies cricket team's preparation and play.

JEWEL SAMAD/AFP/Getty Images

one-day international match against England at Edgbaston, they blew so loudly and so incessantly that Sky TV viewers phoned in to complain about the noise.

# MUSIC USE AND THE LAW

It is imperative that all exercise and sport professionals use music legally and under an appropriate license. Because the differences in laws across nations are subtle, my intention here is not to provide an exhaustive description for each jurisdiction. Rather, I hope to sensitize you to the fact that certain restrictions apply and that these are enshrined in law. Many exercise and sport leaders with whom I have discussed this matter describe the music licensing laws as a minefield, but nowadays, the Internet provides a wealth of information that is clear and easy to follow.

Music artists, producers, and record companies work hard to provide great tracks to use in fitness classes, at major championship events, and even as soundtracks to people's lives. Their reward comes in the form of royalties that are gathered on their behalf by performance rights organizations that exist in each of the developed nations around the world. Organizations such as BMI (Broadcast Music, Inc.) in the United States and PPL (formerly Phonographic Performance Limited) in the UK are diligent in ensuring that fitness and sport clubs and individuals who use music in public spaces pay the relevant annual license fees.

In the UK, PPL's tariff for the use of recorded music in exercise classes changed in 2013; exercise and fitness center operators are now responsible for holding a valid PPL license for using recorded music in their centers. Notably, exercise instructors are required to hold a valid PPL license for any class that takes place outside of exercise and fitness centers (e.g., hired halls, community buildings, and offices). Also, the legal requirement for a PPL license remains the same regardless of whether the use of recorded music is systematic/structured (e.g., in a dance aerobics class) or ad hoc/unstructured (e.g., as a backdrop for soccer players' warm-up in a stadium). The annual fee, however, differs according to the type of usage of recorded music, and PPL operates a range of tariffs. Performance rights organizations in other developed nations function in a similar manner.

Individual exercisers or athletes using music for personal use are not required to hold such a license. However, it is important that the music has been purchased over the counter or legally downloaded. Again, with the proliferation of illegal download sites on the Internet as well as bootleg CDs, some care is needed to stay within the bounds of the law. If the music is purchased on an original CD, downloaded from a recognized music provider such as iTunes, or provided on subscription by a music-streaming service such as Spotify, there is generally no problem: the record companies get their dues. Any individual or organization that broadcasts music or uses it for a group of exercisers, athletes, or sport fans needs to hold a valid license. For further details, visit the website of the performance rights society in your country (see table 1.3 for examples).

In addition to national jurisdictions, exercise and fitness instructors who segue music tracks to create bespoke playlists need to be aware of restrictions that apply when delivering exercise class formats under license. For example, the exercise programs BodyPump and BodyCombat, which are delivered under license by Les Mills, must use the associated playlists; there is no flexibility in how tracks are segued (see chapter 5). Some licensed exercise formats such as the Zumba range permit instructors to segue tracks from their catalogs, which can also be combined with non-Zumba tracks. Instructors wanting to use music that is produced under the Zumba banner must join the Zumba Instructor Network (ZIN) and pay a monthly subscription. I urge you to follow licensing laws—both national and exercise format related—that apply to you.

# SUMMARY

Music has played a role in early human civilizations as a form of communication and punctuates almost all rites of passage throughout the life span. Military strategists have embedded music into the theater of war since ancient times. Actress Jane Fonda sparked an exercise revolution by making exercising to music accessible to the masses. In the sport context, the Olympic movement played a seminal role in formalizing the link between sport and music. This relationship stemmed from the ancient Olympic Games and was given a new

**Table 1.3** Examples of Performance Rights Societies Around the World

| Country | Society's full name | Commonly used acronym | Website |
|---|---|---|---|
| Australia | Australasian Performing Right Association, Australasian Mechanical Copyright Owners Society | APRA AMCOS | www.apraamcos.com.au |
| Argentina | Argentine Society of Authors and Composers of Music | SADAIC | www.sadaic.org.ar |
| Belgium | Belgian Society of Authors, Composers and Publishers | SABAM | www.sabam.be |
| Brazil | Central Bureau for Collection and Distribution | ECAD | www.ecad.org.br |
| Bulgaria | Bulgarian Society of Authors and Composers for Performing and Mechanical Rights | MUSICAUTOR | www.musicautor.org |
| Canada | Re:Sound | N/A | www.resound.ca |
| China | Music Copyright Society of China | MCSC | www.mcsc.com.cn |
| Denmark | Koda | N/A | www.koda.dk |
| Finland | Teosto | N/A | www.teosto.fi |
| France | Society of Authors, Composers and Music Publishers | SACEM | www.sacem.fr |
| Germany | Society for Musical Performing and Mechanical Reproduction Rights | GEMA | www.gema.de |
| Greece | The Hellenic Society for the Protection of Intellectual Property | AEPI | www.aepi.gr |
| India | Indian Performing Right Society Ltd. | IPRS | www.iprs.org/cms/ |
| Italy | Italian Society of Authors and Publishers | SIAE | www.siae.it |
| Jamaica | Jamaica Association of Composers, Authors, and Publishers Ltd. | JACAP | www.jacapjamaica.com |
| Japan | Japanese Society for Rights of Authors, Composers and Publishers | JASRAC | www.jasrac.or.jp |
| Kenya | Music Copyright Society of Kenya | MCSK | www.mcsk.or.ke |
| Mexico | Society of Authors and Composers of Mexico | SACM | www.sacm.org.mx |
| New Zealand | Australasian Performing Right Association, Australasian Mechanical Copyright Owners Society | APRA AMCOS | www.apraamcos.co.nz |
| Norway | TONO | N/A | www.tono.no |
| Philippines | Filipino Society of Composers, Authors and Publishers, Inc. | FILSCAP | www.filscap.com.ph |
| Poland | Society of Authors | ZAIKS | www.zaiks.org.pl |
| Portugal | Portuguese Society of Authors | SPA | www.spautores.pt |

| Country | Society's full name | Commonly used acronym | Website |
|---|---|---|---|
| Republic of Ireland | Irish Music Rights Organisation<br>Phonographic Performance Ireland | IMRO<br>PPI | www.imro.ie<br>www.ppimusic.ie |
| Russia | Russian Authors' Society | RAO | www.rao.ru |
| Singapore | Composers and Authors Society of Singapore Ltd. | COMPASS | www.compass.org.sg |
| South Africa | Southern African Music Rights Organization | SAMRO | www.samro.org.za |
| Spain | Spanish Society of Authors and Publishers | SGAE | www.sgae.es |
| Sweden | Swedish Performing Rights Society | STIM | www.stim.se |
| Switzerland | Cooperative Society of Music Authors and Publishers in Switzerland | SUISA | www.suisa.ch |
| The Netherlands | Buma Association, Stemra Foundation | BUMA STEMRA | www.bumastemra.nl |
| Turkey | Musical Work Owners Association of Turkey<br>Musical Work Owners Group | MESAM<br>MSG | www.mesam.org.tr<br>www.msg.org.tr |
| United Kingdom | PPL | PPL | www.ppluk.com/exercisetomusic |
| United States | American Society of Composers, Authors and Publishers<br>Broadcast Music Inc.<br>Society of European Stage Authors and Composers | ASCAP<br><br>BMI<br>SESAC | www.ascap.com<br>www.bmi.com<br>www.sesac.com |

significance when the Games began their modern incarnation in 1896. Music is now part and parcel of all aspects of the Olympic experience.

A basic understanding of concepts such as melody, harmony, and rhythm will put exercise and sport leaders and participants in a good place for all that is to follow in this book. We will be examining such concepts in the illustration and construction of music-related interventions. Figure 1.2 shows how musical works are typically structured and how this structure might relate to exercise or training sessions. The musical technique of syncopation was addressed in some detail, given how challenging it can be for some exercisers or athletes to process highly syncopated rhythms. We also explored some of the key legal considerations in the use of music for both individual and group activities. You now have a solid foundation from which to continue exploring and learning about this fascinating topic.

# 2

# The Science Behind the Music—Performance Connection

*The science of music is an adventure happening all around us right now.*
—Elena Mannes, music writer and award-winning journalist

This chapter provides an overview of the scientific study of music in exercise and sport that serves as an entrée for the chapters that follow. The science is illustrated with examples, and technical terms are fully explained and set in context. A model that practitioners can use as a guiding framework for music interventions is also presented (Karageorghis, 2016).

Of the many scientific disciplines that have addressed the effects of music in the domain of exercise and sport, the three principal ones are psychology, exercise physiology, and biomechanics. My home scientific discipline and that of this book is psychology, which is the study of the human mind and its functions, especially those relating to behavior. Exercise physiology entails the study of responses and adaptations over time to a wide range of physical activities. Among other things, physiologists working in this area have investigated the way musical accompaniment results in more efficient oxygen usage. Biomechanics involves the study of human movement and is particularly relevant to music applications given, for example, the gains in movement efficiency that can be made from moving in time to a beat.

Examples of questions addressed by researchers in each of the three disciplines can be seen in table 2.1. Many studies, however, employ elements of these disciplines in combination given that music can affect us on a number of levels (Bood et al., 2013; Fritz et al., 2013; Loizou & Karageorghis, 2015): an uplifting tune might raise our spirits, speed up our heart rate, and hasten our gait. As we will shortly discover, researchers are often interested in a combination of measures that capture how an individual feels, how his cardiorespiratory system responds to exercise with music, and how well he performs a given task.

In addition to the psychological, physiological, and biomechanical approaches that researchers have taken in recent decades, a number of other approaches have been taken. In neuroscience, these have included the measurement of brain wave activity and blood flow within the brain; in the social sciences, they have included questionnaires, observations, interviews, and focus groups. As alluded to in the quote that opens this chapter, not every aspect of music performance and responsiveness to music can be explained with reference to science; nonetheless, science can often point us in the right direction.

**Table 2.1** Questions Posed by Researchers Investigating Music in Exercise and Sport

| Scientific discipline | Question |
|---|---|
| Psychology | • As we work progressively harder, does music delay the shift in focus from external cues (e.g., our environment) to internal, fatigue-related cues?<br>• If we listen to music before a task, does it promote imagery that is conducive to performance of that task?<br>• When used before sporting competition, can music be used to trigger an optimal mind-set? |
| Physiology | • Can the use of music prolong our ability to sustain intense exercise?<br>• What is the influence of music on physiological arousal during exercise?<br>• Can listening to music after exercise hasten the clearance of lactic acid from the muscles? |
| Biomechanics | • Does moving in time with music promote more efficient movement patterns in aerobic activities?<br>• Can musical accompaniment enhance the stylistic aspects of movement?<br>• What are the neuromechanical processes that allow us to synchronize our movements to a steady beat? |

# WHY CERTAIN TUNES RESONATE WITH US

Among the first people to write about the impact of music on the human psyche were the philosophers of ancient Greece: Aristotle, Plato, Pythagoras, and Socrates. Music was an integral part of their civilization, and these great thinkers considered in some detail how the power of music might be harnessed and what specific qualities of music might be manipulated to alter a person's emotional state. Indeed, much of what we know today about musical scales, pitches, and tuning can be traced back to the writings of these philosophers.

In 350 BC, Aristotle proclaimed that the sound of the flute had healing powers and encouraged his students to engage in daily music making. Such application of music and the playing of instruments in a social sphere gave rise to what has come to be known today as music therapy. Music therapy involves the use of music by a trained professional to achieve therapeutic goals such as improved motor skills, accelerated social development, enhanced thought processes, and increased self-awareness. This is a scientific domain with recent applications to exercise and sport through the use of recuperative music, which is addressed later in this chapter.

Pythagoras is credited with discovering the 12-note chromatic scale; that is, all of the notes in one octave, or from C to C on a piano (see figure

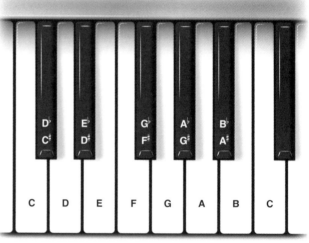

**Figure 2.1** One piano octave. This pattern is repeated six times on a standard piano (i.e., there are seven octaves in total).

2.1). Most contemporary Western musicians and composers borrow from this Pythagorean system of tuning. The system is based on a stack of perfect fifths—that is, a cycle of perfect fifth intervals such as the notes C to G on a piano (see figure 2.1), followed by G to D going from left to right on the keyboard, D to A, and so on, each tuned in the ratio 3:2 (see the sidebar Understanding the Perfect Fifth).

Any sound you hear as a tone is made of regular and evenly spaced waves of air molecules. The closer the waves are to each other, the higher the tone sounds. Because the waves travel at roughly the same speed (the speed of sound, which is

## UNDERSTANDING THE PERFECT FIFTH: A STABLE MUSICAL STAPLE

To familiarize yourself with the concept of the perfect fifth, try singing the first four notes of the popular nursery rhyme "Twinkle, Twinkle, Little Star." The first two notes that you sing in the first word (*Twinkle*) are the root of a scale (e.g., the note C in figure 2.1); the next two notes (the second *Twinkle*) are a perfect fifth above the root (e.g., on the note G if you started on C). The note middle C is tuned to 261.626 Hz, and the G above it—a perfect fifth away—is tuned to 391.995 Hz (the 3:2 ratio). This is thought by musicologists to be the most stable interval, meaning that it is consonant, or sounds pleasant to the ear, because the two notes blend well. It also has the simplest ratio after that of an octave, which is 2:1 (notes C to C in figure 2.1). To familiarize yourself with the concept of the octave, try singing the first two notes of the well-known ballad "Somewhere Over The Rainbow."

340.29 meters per second), waves with a longer wavelength don't arrive at your ears as often or as frequently as shorter waves. This aspect of sound is known as frequency and is measured in hertz (Hz), which is how many wave peaks go by in one second. The shorter the wavelength, the higher the frequency and, thus, the higher the pitch; this means that short waves sound high and long waves sound low. Generally speaking, smaller, shorter instruments, such as the flute, bugle, and violin, make shorter waves and hence higher sounds, whereas larger, longer instruments, such as the bassoon, baritone saxophone, and double bass, make longer waves and lower sounds. Taking an analogy from the animal world, consider the high-pitched shrill of a kingfisher versus the low-frequency rumble of a blue whale.

## How the Brain Responds to Music

An area that is rapidly advancing our understanding of the effects of music is neuroscience. The neuroscience approach centers on examining how music stimulates parts of the brain. One of the main tools of this approach is the functional magnetic resonance imaging (fMRI) scanner, which allows researchers to take moving images of brain activity that track the flow of blood and use of fuel. This technique has revolutionized cognitive science because it enables us to monitor what happens to the brain while it is thinking or responding to stimuli (e.g., sounds).

A leading scientist in this area is Daniel Levitin, author of the best-selling book *This Is Your Brain on Music* (2007). Levitin has examined how our brains turn collections of sounds into the patterns that we recognize as songs, and how these songs influence our emotions. He delivers a compelling argument that our brains have evolved to emphasize musical ability and that this has been integral to our advancement as a species. The central idea underpinning Levitin's work is that the human race is hardwired to engage in music-related activity. By this he means that our brains have evolved to enable the making, processing, and appreciation of music.

Music is quite different from visual art forms in that each composition unfolds over time: sometimes in a predictable way, such as when we listen to a band playing a familiar pop tune; at other times in a highly unpredictable way, such as when we hear a jazz quartet playing an improvisation with periodic changes in rhythmic feel and harmonic progression. Our brains respond differently when our musical expectations are met versus when they are violated.

Generally speaking, a piece of music that violates people's expectations is not particularly effective in an exercise context because it can divert attention from the task at hand by requiring more processing power than a predictable piece does. Think of listening to some of the more edgy compositions of Pink Floyd (unpredictable) versus the chart hits of ABBA (predictable). Through interview data, we know that many exercisers express a preference for familiar, rhythmically regular, and predictable music (Laukka & Quick, 2013; Priest & Karageorghis, 2008). They often add that they would not necessarily wish to listen to their exercise tunes in different life contexts (e.g., when relaxing at home or at a dinner party).

German researchers Stefan Koelsch and Angela Friederici from the Max Planck Institute for Human Cognitive and Brain Sciences are at the forefront of research examining neural responses to music. Their many experiments have shown that the processing of the structure, or syntax, of music occurs in the frontal lobes of both hemispheres of the brain—those associated with higher-order thought processes, planning, and the reining in of animal instincts. Research has demonstrated that, although music and language have independent neural pathways, they share some common neural responses—especially at

birth when the input from the various senses cannot be differentiated fully (Levitin, 2007). An infant might, for example, see the letter P as green, taste her mother's milk in F#, and smell freshly mown grass in rectangles.

The distinctions between neural pathways become evident as babies grow and the neuron cluster that responded in a similar manner to sights, sound, taste, touch, and smell evolves to take more specialized roles. This might explain why musicians are generally highly articulate; their musical activities seem to spill over into their ability to process language (Chan, Ho, & Cheung, 1998). This is true not only of those who came from very well-to-do backgrounds

## MICHELINE OSTERMEYER, OLYMPIC CHAMPION AND CONCERT PIANIST

Research shows that musical training can increase physical coordination and motor skill acquisition. Among the most demanding events in the track and field repertoire are the throws, which require split-second timing and precision footwork. The golden girl of the war-torn 1948 Olympics in London was the French athlete Micheline Ostermeyer. She won gold in the shot put and discus, as well as bronze in the high jump; any combination of just two of these medals would be highly improbable in modern-day track and field.

The unflappable Frenchwoman celebrated her shot put victory with an impromptu recital of Beethoven's *Hammerklavier Sonata*, widely considered to be Beethoven's most demanding composition for solo piano. Following the recital at the French team's headquarters, she told journalists: "Sport taught me to relax, the piano gave me strong biceps and a sense of motion and rhythm." (Bateman, 2008, p. 28). Ostermeyer, who was a niece of the composer Lucien Paroche, retired from athletics two years later to resume her career as a concert pianist. The American novelist John Gardner once said, "The qualities that make a true artist are nearly the same qualities that make a true athlete" (Gardner, 1991, pp. 34-35). To find someone as accomplished as Micheline Ostermeyer in both the arts and athletics is truly remarkable.

AP Photo

Micheline Ostermeyer going for gold in the discus at the 1948 London Olympics.

and are thus likely to have had better educational opportunities, but also of those who grew up in public housing projects or on council estates, such as will.i.am, of the Black Eyed Peas, and Cheryl Cole, formerly of Girls Aloud. In addition to the benefits in processing language, there is emerging evidence that learning a musical instrument from a young age can enhance coordination and the speed of acquiring motor skills (Herholz & Zatorre, 2012; Hyde et al., 2009).

There is a burgeoning body of evidence that the brain grows in response to musical training. We are born with 30 billion nerve cells called neurons that provide a blank canvas for learning, and the complex web of interconnections between neurons is shaped by our experiences. Every childhood event recalled—birthdays, family holidays, playing outside with friends during a school break, or even the first encounter with a new pet—is represented within the physical structure of the brain's neurons and the way they fire when stimulated during these recollections. The implications for exercisers and athletes are that they can associate, over time, a specific piece of music with getting mentally primed to work out or being in the right mind-set of a major competition.

British researcher Daniel Bishop was perhaps the first to shed some light on the neurophysiological impact of music in a sporting context (Bishop, Wright, & Karageorghis, 2014). He placed young tennis players in an fMRI scanner to examine which parts of their brains were stimulated when they listened to music that varied in arousing qualities. Immediately prior to a reaction-time task that had a tennis theme, the players listened to music that differed according to tempo and volume. Bishop's experiment showed that listening to arousing music (i.e., fast and loud) stimulates parts of the primary auditory cortex and the cerebellum (see figure 2.2). These brain regions share the responsibility of processing emotion and governing motor control or movement patterns. Music's cross-stimulation of these regions may be one of the main reasons for its effectiveness as a prime for athletic performance.

Using fMRI enables researchers to pinpoint the effects of different types of music or even music selections on different parts of the brain. For example, if listening to loud rock music increases activity in the cerebellum, it could optimize arousal levels for an athlete wishing to excel in a

power event such as Olympic weightlifting. Mention of this cutting-edge neuroscience research leads nicely into a discussion of the mechanisms that have been advanced by scientists to explain the effects of music in exercise and sport—that is, how music affects performers.

## Music's Impact on Performers

This section explores the range of effects music can have on exercisers and athletes. It places particular emphasis on the underlying mental and physiological processes that account for how music takes effect. It kicks off with a discussion of how music can have a direct influence on aspects of human physiology through the mechanism of entrainment, wherein bodily pulses attune to qualities of the music. The concept of rhythm response concerns the natural tendency to move in sync with a piece of music. The short section on the human nervous system explains how a part of the brain referred to as the "pacemaker" can enable people to execute repetitive movement patterns. The application of music as an attentional distracter during exercise or training is then highlighted, and the key concepts of association and dissociation are introduced.

### Good Vibes

Music can have a direct influence on human physiology. Hearing a lively and up-tempo piece such as "Happy" by Pharrell Williams (160 bpm) as you enter the gym would be expected to elevate your heart rate. Similarly, listening to a slow and serene classical piece as you unwind after a punishing workout should result in a corresponding decrease in heart rate. This is because the autonomic nervous system, which helps to both mobilize the body for action and regulate essential processes such as digestion and breathing, influences the speed of heart and lung action. This process is akin to the way sounds create reciprocal vibrations known as resonance. Think of the way an opera singer can break a wine glass by producing a shrill note of exactly the right frequency. Also, in everyday parlance, we might use the phrase *He's giving me a good vibe* to describe the feeling of comfort with or warmth toward another person.

Researchers have referred to the tendency of biological rhythms such as the heart rate to alter their frequency toward that of a musical pulse as entrainment. A number of other bodily

# MAJOR REGIONS OF THE BRAIN STIMULATED BY MUSIC

- The **parietal lobe** is the upper part of the brain's outer cerebral cortex. It is a junction for sensory information of all kinds, especially that relating to touch, temperature, pain, and movement.

- The **frontal lobe** is perhaps what most separates us from other animals, even our closest relatives such as the chimpanzee. It puts the brakes on our baser instincts and is involved with complex, higher thought processes such as planning and ethical considerations.

- **Broca's area** is responsible for the production of speech and language.

- The **occipital lobe** at the rear of the brain is primarily concerned with vision and related functions.

- The **primary auditory cortex**, situated directly beneath each ear, is the hardware that processes and identifies sounds, establishing basic characteristics such as pitch and volume. We use the primary auditory cortex to identify a note, but the secondary and tertiary cortices to name a tune or link a song with an image.

- The **amygdala** is involved in the processing of emotions such as fear, anger, and pleasure. It is also responsible for determining which memories are stored and where they are stored in the brain.

- The **temporal lobe**, which contains the auditory cortices and language regions such as Broca's area, is also heavily involved with emotion and memory.

- The **reticular activating system**, which we share with all vertebrates including birds, fish, and reptiles, links the brain stem with the cortex—the outer part of the brain. It governs arousal as well as sleep–wake transitions and is thus vital to our survival.

- The **cerebellum** is a region at the base of the brain that assists in the integration of sensory perception and motor control. Given that in our evolution as a species the cerebellum was one of the earliest formed parts of human anatomy, it is also known as the reptilian brain.

- Along with the cerebellum, the **brain stem** is also part of the reptilian brain and sits atop the spinal cord at the very base of the brain. It is a channel and switching center for the nerve connections that govern movement and sensation. It also plays a role in the regulation of essential bodily processes such as breathing and blood circulation.

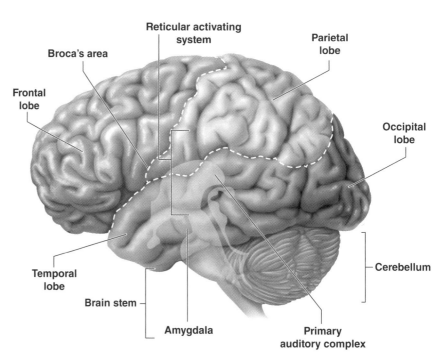

**Figure 2.2** Regions of the brain that neuroscientists have associated with the processing of music.

pulses such as respiration rate and brain waves also entrain to music; in fact, entrainment can be thought of as the rhythmic manifestation of resonance (Leeds, 2010). This is not to say that Jerry Lee Lewis' "Whole Lotta Shakin' Going On," at a rip-roaring 180 bpm, will cause the heart of a resting person to race, although the track does increase heart rate by 5 to 15 bpm in most people. It also has a corresponding effect on breathing rate; at rest, the rate is between 12 and 20 cycles per minute (cpm), and while listening to a very fast piece of music, the rate generally speeds up by 1 to 2 cpm. It is notable that prior to the invention of the metronome, musical tempi were determined with reference to the human heartbeat (Flatischler, 1992).

## Working in Sync

The concept of rhythm response is directly related to that of entrainment. The term refers to the innate human tendency to synchronize movement with musical rhythms. Consider that when you hear a lively tune, you immediately begin to tap your finger, tap your toes, or nod your head in time with the beat. In recent years, the notion of a pacemaker in the brain has been advanced to explain the timing of movements and reactivity to musical rhythm (Schneider et al., 2010). To understand this a little more, let's consider the way the brain governs movement and detects musical stimulation.

The afferent nervous system transmits impulses from the muscles and sense organs to the brain, whereas the efferent nerves send signals to the muscles to bring about movements (see figure 2.3). The idea that underlies the pacemaker is that part of the brain coordinates these afferent and efferent signals. The pacemaker might also enable us to execute repetitive movement patterns (e.g., running) with only the initial command requiring specific attention (Clynes & Walker, 1982); just think of the famous example of a headless chicken continuing to run.

Music can also stimulate parts of the brain that govern arousal and thus prompt a physical response in the listener (Lyttle & Montagne, 1992; Neher, 1962). Work incorporating fMRI scanners has revealed the activation of the cerebellum and parts of the motor cortex (see figure 2.2) when people listen to musical rhythms (Koelsch & Skouras, 2014; Kornysheva et al., 2010; Zatorre

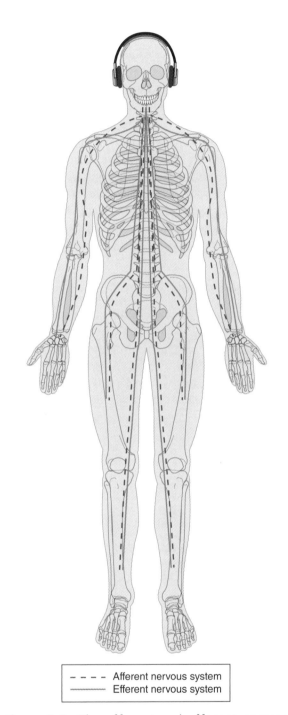

| - - - - | Afferent nervous system |
| ——— | Efferent nervous system |

**Figure 2.3** The afferent and efferent nervous systems.

et al., 1996). These findings indicate a possible location for the brain's proposed pattern generator, although we are sure to learn much more in the next decade when fMRI technology advances sufficiently to enable scientists to assess moving subjects.

Why would it benefit us to coordinate our movements with a musical rhythm? Apart from the fact that it feels compelling and enjoyable, a physiological benefit may also be at play. Running or stationary cycling in time with music has been shown to lower the metabolic cost of the activity by promoting greater movement efficiency (Bacon, Myers, & Karageorghis, 2012; Bood et al., 2013; Terry et al., 2012). Producing movement that is in perfect synchrony with the regular, distinctive beat of a piece of music appears to promote feelings that verge on that of a spiritual experience. Exercisers report intense pleasure from working in time with musical rhythm (Juslin & Laukka, 2004), particularly when they are sharing the experience with others (Molnar-Szakacs & Overy, 2006).

## A Welcome Diversion

One of the key mechanisms that accounts for reductions in the perception of exertion or effort with musical accompaniment is attentional dissociation. Music can encourage people to focus their attention externally toward the sound and thus away from internal fatigue-related sensations. In essence, dissociation concerns focusing outside the body on task-irrelevant information (e.g., the landscape, maintaining a conversation, daydreaming), whereas association concerns focusing inside the body or on task-relevant information (e.g., breathing rate, stride rate, technique).

The afferent nervous system has a limited channel capacity (a concept akin to Internet bandwidth), and so sensory stimuli such as music can inhibit the internal fatigue-related cues associated with physical exertion (Hernández-Peón et al., 1961; Rejeski, 1985). A key point is that the capacity of music to inhibit such cues is greatly reduced at higher physical activity intensities when the signal strength of physiological feedback overwhelms attentional processes (Ekkekakis, 2003; Tenenbaum, 2001).

In recent research, Leighton Jones and I tracked the switch from dissociation to association (see figure 2.4). Our study revealed that the presence

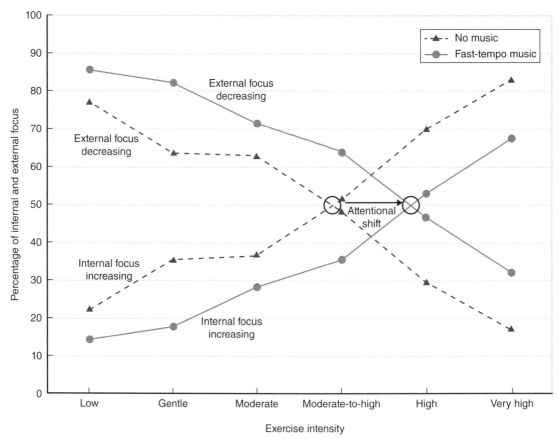

**Figure 2.4**  How exercise intensity influences attentional focus with no music versus fast-tempo music (using data from Karageorghis & Jones, 2014).

Adapted from *Psychology of Sport and Exercise* 15(3), C.I. Karageorghis and L. Jones, "On the stability and relevance of the exercise heart rate-music-tempo preference relationship," 299-310, 2014, with permission from Elsevier.

of music delayed the switch from a dissociative to associative focus at the higher exercise intensities by about 10 percent (Karageorghis & Jones, 2014). This finding reflects the results of many studies that found that the dissociation effect tends to reduce perceived exertion by about 10 percent. Nonetheless, this pattern is most evident at low-to-moderate exercise intensities. At high intensities, an automatic attentional switch from dissociation to association seems to occur. In other words, people are forced to focus inwardly, which may serve as an internal protection mechanism by ensuring that they do not exert themselves to the point of damaging muscles and vital organs.

## Feeling It With Music

Research has shown that music can influence how people feel at all exercise or training intensities—even when working at close to voluntary exhaustion (Hutchinson & Karageorghis, 2013; Karageorghis et al., 2009). An explanation for the influence of music on affect at high exercise intensities is derived from the music–emotion link. European scholars Klaus Scherer (Switzerland)

and Marcel Zentner (Austria) described three routes for emotion induction through the use of music: memory, empathy, and appraisal (Scherer & Zentner, 2001). Memory relates to how music triggers the recollection of an emotive event; empathy concerns the listener's ability to recognize and identify with the emotions expressed by the artist; and appraisal relates to when listeners evaluate the personal significance of an emotion communicated within music with reference to their own well-being.

More recently, Patrick Juslin and Daniel Väst-fjäll from Sweden provided an in-depth account of how music influences human emotions (Juslin & Västfjäll, 2008). Building on the work of Scherer and Zentner, they delved into the notion of emotional contagion—that is, when an exerciser or athlete catches the emotion inherent in a piece of music. A track might express sadness, happiness, sedation, or elation, and the listener has little trouble internalizing the emotion. In the model presented later in this chapter, the music–emotion link is germane to a number of psychological benefits that include affective states, arousal regulation, enjoyment, task-relevant imagery, and self-talk.

## FASHION-CONSCIOUS MIDDLE-DISTANCE STAR ANDREW OSAGIE GETS MENTAL BOOST FROM VERSACE

Andrew Osagie is probably the finest British middle-distance runner since the heady days of Coe, Ovett, and Cram. In the London 2012 Olympics, he made the 800-meter final as the only male Team GB representative to reach a middle-distance final at those Games. His time of 1:43.77 minutes, a new lifetime best, would have won him the gold medal at the preceding three olympiads. During the following year's track season, a new release by the American rap trio Migos caught Osagie's ear. The song title "Versace" was repeated relentlessly in the piece. All that Osagie could hear in the track was a long chorus of "Osagie, Osagie, Osagie,

*To watch a performance of "Versace" and hear the famous Osagie chorus, search "Migos Versace" on YouTube.*

Osagie." In the mix, the word *Versace* sounded just like *Osagie*, and this gave the runner a considerable mental boost. It wasn't long before the track became a staple part of Osagie's pre-race routine. After competing at the 2013 IAAF World Championships in Moscow, where he came in fifth, Osagie revealed to the press: "Everyone was walking past me going 'Osagie, Osagie, Osagie, Osagie,' which was a bit different!"

## Timing of Music Relative to Performance

Much of the research into music in exercise and sport addresses when music is used. The point of application is an important consideration not only for researchers but also for exercisers and athletes. Accordingly, this section explores the application of music pre-activity, during activity, and post-activity. The considerations that feed into music selection in each instance are quite distinct given that exercisers' and athletes' instrumental objectives differ considerably from the pre-activity to the post-activity phase. Prior to a physical task, the central function of music is to create the right mind-set for the individual or group. During activity, the music is used either to distract attention and elevate mood or to function as a rhythmic stimulus that can determine the precise rate of movement. Post-activity, exercisers and athletes who have been participating in high-intensity physical activity (e.g., an all-out interval-type session) can use music to speed up their rate of recovery.

### Pre-Activity

Thirty or so studies have addressed how music can manipulate mind-set prior to physical performance. Remember that in competitive sports in particular, the pre-game mind-set can have a telling influence on performance. Most of the studies examined the impact of stimulative or sedative music and how it enhanced or impaired subsequent performance (Chtourou et al., 2012; Eliakim et al., 2007). This body of work has shown that stimulative music can increase arousal, prompt motivational imagery, and spark both positive self-talk and flow (Bishop, Karageorghis, & Loizou, 2007; Bishop et al., 2014; Pain, Harwood, & Anderson, 2011). Flow is an optimal mental state in which a person is absorbed in the task at hand and functioning on autopilot; coaches often refer to this as being in the zone.

Pre-task music can also be used to manipulate emotional states to influence performance. For example, British researcher Daniel Bishop demonstrated that musically induced emotions influenced athletes' subsequent choice reaction time (CRT) performance (Bishop, Karageorghis,

& Kinrade, 2009). Listening to faster music tempi led to more pleasant and aroused emotional states in 54 young tennis players, whereas higher music intensity (volume) resulted in both higher levels of arousal and faster subsequent CRT performance. The findings of this study demonstrate the music listening–arousal–performance link, although in many competitive situations the use of music in this way has been banned (e.g., during tennis match play).

In an exercise or training context, research groups from both Japan and Israel investigated the effects of pre-task stimulative music on all-out effort on a stationary bike (Eliakim et al., 2007; Yamamoto et al., 2003). Participants in the Japanese study led by Takako Yamamoto heard either slow or fast music for 20 minutes before completing the maximal exercise task. Neither condition influenced performance, which was assessed in terms of power output. The music did, however, influence the neurotransmitter norepinephrine, which is known to play a key role in the fight-or-flight response. The Japanese team concluded that the slower music lowered arousal, whereas the faster music elevated it (Yamamoto et al., 2003).

By way of contrast, the Israeli team led by Michal Eliakim employed only a stimulative music condition that did not produce any ergogenic effect. Nonetheless, the music did raise heart rate immediately before the task, which indicated an elevation in physiological arousal (Eliakim et al., 2007). An issue that clouds our understanding of this research on music and arousal is that we are not always certain of the optimal level of arousal for a given person. Researchers sometimes neglect this important point. Before we know what music to listen to or suggest for others, we need to know what state they want to be in mentally and physically (sometimes our assumptions about this are wrong). Remember the example of super-heavyweight boxer Audley Harrison from chapter 1 and his penchant for Japanese classical music at the Sydney Olympics.

### During Activity

The asynchronous application of music has, by a wide margin, attracted the most interest from researchers; some 100 studies have been published to date. Researchers have used in-task music to stimulate participants during short bouts of high-intensity exercise and demonstrated that they endure longer or work harder in the presence of music when compared to control conditions (see Karageorghis & Priest, 2012a). In a novel approach, British researchers Lee Crust and Peter Clough assessed whether personality traits have a role in moderating responses to music (Crust & Clough, 2006). Their findings revealed associations between the trait of liveliness and rhythm response, and between the trait of sensitivity and the response to the melodic and harmonic properties of music (Karageorghis, Terry, & Lane, 1999).

The majority of studies using low-to-moderate-intensity endurance tasks have shown marked improvements in endurance associated with music use (Lane, Davis, & Devonport, 2011; Yamashita et al., 2006). It is apparent that both preferred music and arbitrarily selected music reduce perceived exertion, although preferred and motivational music has been shown to promote more positive feeling states (Hutchinson & Karageorghis, 2013). Findings relating to RPE generally support the prediction that as we work harder, physiological feedback dominates our attention and wins out over the sensory input provided by music (e.g., Hutchinson et al., 2011; Jones, Karageorghis, & Ekkekakis, 2014; Tenenbaum et al., 2004). Notably, the benefits of music on endurance and perceived exertion appear to be magnified when it is delivered in tandem with video (Barwood et al., 2009; Hutchinson, Karageorghis, & Jones, 2015).

A number of researchers have examined the effects of music on high-intensity endurance tasks (e.g., Hutchinson & Karageorghis, 2013; Nakamura et al., 2010; Tate et al., 2012). The intensity of effort is often expressed as a percentage of maximal oxygen uptake (known as $\dot{V}O_2max$); this represents the maximal volume of oxygen that the body can use per kilogram of body weight per minute. It appears that up to around 75 percent of $\dot{V}O_2max$, music reduces perceived exertion, but its effects are sharply diminished beyond this intensity (e.g., Hutchinson & Karageorghis, 2013; Tenenbaum et al., 2004).

Notwithstanding the consistent finding that even well-selected music does not reduce perceived exertion at very high intensities, it does

appear to make us feel better (e.g., Hutchinson et al., 2011; Karageorghis & Jones, 2014). Music can permeate the affective centers of the brain even at high workloads. In terms of performance measures, music use prolonged the onset of volitional exhaustion (i.e., how hard one chooses to continue under physical duress) in some ergometer trials (e.g., Atkinson, Wilson, & Eubank, 2004; Bharani, Sahu, & Mathew, 2004), although the evidence is contradictory. Some of the studies employing high-intensity tasks showed no performance benefits (e.g., Atan, 2013; Hagen et al., 2013).

Physically untrained people appear to derive greater benefit from music than do those who are trained, regardless of the exercise intensity (see Karageorghis & Priest, 2012a). In particular, music has a more potent effect on perceived exertion and feeling states among the untrained or recreationally active (Hutchinson et al., 2011). Another interesting trend in the literature indicates that when exercise tasks are self-paced, both performance and psychological states appear to be enhanced by the presence of music (e.g., Fritz et al., 2013; Waterhouse, Hudson, & Edwards, 2010). In laboratory experiments, the workload or speed of movement is often controlled very precisely by the researchers, whereas in health clubs and fitness rooms the world over, exercisers can regulate their movements as they wish, choosing to speed up or slow down as the whim takes them. For this reason, studies that involve self-paced movements may be more relevant to real-world settings.

Japanese researcher Makoto Iwanaga proposed that as heart rate increases, people prefer faster and faster music (Iwanaga, 1995). In fact, he suggested that this increasing preference for faster music is in direct proportion to the increasing tempo of the heart rate, which is known as a linear relationship. More recent studies have shown that the relationship between exercise heart rate and preference scores for music tempo takes a rather different shape: essentially, tempi that exceed 140 bpm do not appear to elicit higher music tempo preference scores at high exercise intensities (Karageorghis, Jones, & Low, 2006; Karageorghis, Jones, & Stuart, 2008; Karageorghis et al., 2011). There is a distinct leveling out of music tempo preference when the music is used

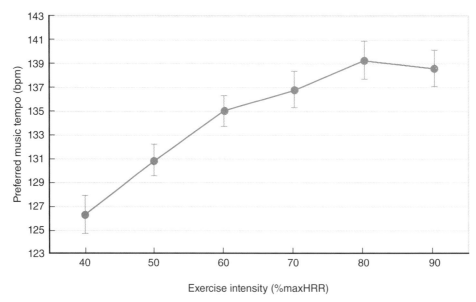

**Figure 2.5** The relationship between preference for music tempo and exercise intensity.

Reprinted from C.I. Karageorghis, L. Jones, D.L. Priest, R.I. Akers, A. Clarke, J.M. Perry, B.T. Reddick, D.T. Bishop, and H.B.T. Lim, 2011, "Revisiting the relationship between exercise heart rate and music tempo preference," *Research Quarterly for Exercise and Sport* 82(2): 274-284, with permission from Taylor & Francis Ltd.

asynchronously (see figure 2.5). In recent studies (e.g., Karageorghis & Jones, 2014), exercise participants reported preferences for a much narrower band of tempi (~120 to ~140 bpm) than was expected (90 to 155 bpm; Karageorghis & Terry, 2009).

People demonstrate a strong tendency to respond to the rhythmic qualities of music. This tendency sometimes results in synchronization between a musical beat and a performer's movements. When movement is consciously performed in time with music, the music is said to be used synchronously. An emerging body of evidence shows the degree to which music with a steady rhythm can enhance the regularity of movement (Bood et al., 2013). The main implication of such research for exercisers and athletes is that some of the chinks in the kinetic chain can be ironed out through the synchronous application of music to relatively simple, repetitive activities such as running and cross-country skiing.

Over the last three decades, many studies have focused on the application of synchronous music (e.g., Bood et al., 2013; Lim et al., 2014; Terry et al., 2012). Such studies have consistently shown that synchronous music yields work-enhancing effects across a broad range of activities that

include bench stepping (Hayakawa et al., 2000), circuit exercises (Karageorghis et al., 2013), callisthenic exercises (Uppal & Datta, 1990), treadmill running (Bood et al., 2013), and 400-meter track running (Simpson & Karageorghis, 2006).

Researchers have suggested that the synchronous use of music increases the efficiency of movement by improving coordination and saving energy (Smoll & Schultz, 1978). New Zealander Catherine Bacon and colleagues examined this suggestion in 2012 (Bacon et al., 2012). The subjects performed a submaximal stationary cycle task and were able to maintain a set intensity at 60 percent of their maximal heart rates using 7.4 percent less oxygen when listening to synchronous music when compared to music that was asynchronous and slightly slower than the movement tempo. This means that exercisers and athletes can be more energy efficient, or achieve the same amount of work with less expended energy, when syncing their movements to a musical beat.

In a recent follow-up study, Singaporean researcher Harry Lim and colleagues examined the degree to which the synchronous application of music reduced the metabolic demands of cycle ergometry at a relatively high intensity (Lim et al., 2014). The physiological data revealed no

## A HAILE IMPRESSIVE PERFORMANCE

A much-cited example of synchronous music having an ergogenic effect dates back to a track and field meet at Birmingham's National Indoor Arena (UK) in February 1998. The out-and-out highlight of the meet was the performance of celebrated distance runner Haile Gebrselassie, who broke Eamonn Coghlan's world indoor record in the 2,000 meters. The Ethiopian star had made a rather unusual request to the race organizers: he wanted his favorite pop song—"Scatman" by Scatman John—to be played during the race. He stormed off from the gun at a furious pace, and the pacemakers were soon left in his wake. The Ethiopian contingent in the crowd went into a frenzy, their passions fueled by the pulsating rhythm of the music. Gebrselassie took more than a second off the existing record finishing in a time of 4 minutes 52.86 seconds. When interviewed by *Athletics Weekly* about the race and his unusual request, he said, "The music gives me a rhythm that fits in with my record pace" (Henderson, 1998, p. 4). Gebrselassie synchronized his stride rate with the beat of the music to achieve a world record. This was the first of many music-fueled record attempts for the doyen of distance running in a remarkable career that spanned 20 years at the top.

© Imago/ZUMAPRESS.com

Prodigious distance runner Haile Gebrselassie had his performances boosted by music on numerous occasions during his 20-year career.

differences in terms of oxygen uptake among synchronous, asynchronous, metronome, and control conditions; however, the task was only six minutes in duration. Efficiency gains may have been apparent if the cyclists had continued to the point of exhaustion. The findings did show that feeling states were more positive in the music conditions, and limb discomfort was lower in the synchronous music and metronome conditions than in the control.

A similar study published in the *Journal of Sport & Exercise Psychology* examined the effects of two synchronous music conditions—one rated as motivating; the other, not—during treadmill walking at 75 percent of maximal heart rate (Karageorghis et al., 2009). The results indicated that the subjects felt more positive right up to the point of voluntary exhaustion during the motivational music condition. Surprisingly, this condition also yielded a 14 percent increase in endurance over a no-music control.

Until fairly recently, there had been no research into the effects of synchronous music on the performance of elite athletes. This prompted Peter Terry, a sport psychologist with an illustrious history of aiding Olympic athletes and teams, to lead a program of research with elite triathletes at the Queensland Academy of Sport in Brisbane, Australia. The triathletes were able to run 19.7 percent longer in synchrony with music regard-

less of how motivational it was. However, mood responses and feeling states were more positive in the presence of motivational music (see figure 2.6). In both music conditions, oxygen consumption was reduced by approximately 1 percent, which meant that running economy had been enhanced.

## Post-Activity

Only a handful of studies have investigated the post-activity application of music. Post-task music has a recuperative role and aids recovery from injury, competition, or exercise or training (Terry & Karageorghis, 2011). Recently, Michal Eliakim of the Hebrew University of Jerusalem and colleagues examined the influence of motivational music during active recovery from high-intensity training (Eliakim et al., 2012, 2013). Active recovery entails engaging in low-intensity continuous activity following exercise or training to aid the

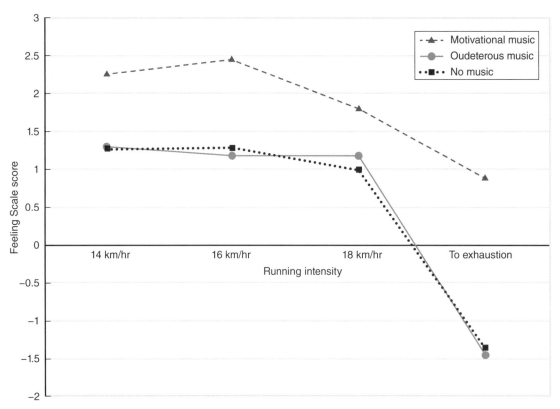

**Figure 2.6** Feeling Scale scores of elite triathletes as a run to exhaustion progressed. *Note:* A brief recovery period occurred between running intensities.

Adapted from *Journal of Science and Medicine in Sport* 15(1), P.C. Terry, C.I. Karageorghis, A. Mecozzi Saha, and S. D'Auria, "Effects of synchronous music on treadmill running among elite triathletes," 52-57, 2012, with permission from Elsevier.

return to a resting state and kick-start the recuperative processes that follow intense work. In the first study, the Israeli researchers found that music led to faster lactate clearance following a treadmill run to exhaustion, which was coupled with lower RPE. In their second study, they isolated the effects of rhythm by using a selection of dance tracks (140 bpm) tested against rhythm-only edits of the same tracks and a no-music control. Both music conditions sped up recovery, and the whole tracks had the best results overall.

Using a passive (static) rather than an active (movement-based) recovery approach, Chinese researchers Li Jing and Wang Xudong played a sedative instrumental piece to aid the recovery of male students for 15 minutes following a stationary cycle trial to exhaustion (Jing & Xudong, 2008). Decreases in heart rate, urinary protein (urinary protein is typically high immediately after exercise or during any other stressful activity), and RPE were greater in the music group than in the no-music control group. Subsequently, Dahi Savitha and colleagues from India showed that slow music hastened the recovery of both heart rate and blood pressure following five minutes of intense treadmill exercise in comparison to both fast music and a no-music control condition (Savitha, Mallikarjuna, & Chythra, 2010).

A study by a group based at Brunel University in the UK progressed further along the research avenue that Jing and Xudong had carved. The group conducted a follow-up study using static recovery but incorporated a brief period of active recovery following a task that involved static cycling to exhaustion (Karageorghis et al., 2014). Using 24 students as subjects, the researchers examined the effects of three conditions: slow, sedative music; fast, stimulative music; and a no-music control. The results showed that in the slow, sedative condition, women's heart rates recovered faster than men's did. Cortisol levels (indicative of stress) were higher in the fast, stimulative condition for both women and men. Measures of feeling states, affective arousal (see figure 2.7), and blood pressure revealed that the slow, sedative condition was associated with superior recovery rates.

Taken together, the findings of the studies presented in this section indicate some initial promise for this line of scientific enquiry and support the use of music for both active and static post-exercise recovery. Nonetheless, much more research is needed to reach firm conclusions.

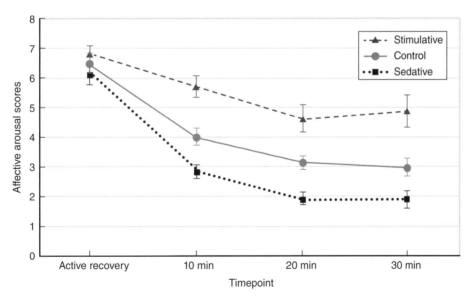

**Figure 2.7**   Changes in affective arousal over time and across music conditions following exhaustive stationary cycle exercise.

Reprinted from C.I. Karageorghis, R.C. Stevens, M. Hamer, A.C. Bruce, and S.T. Pottratz, 2014, "Psychological and psychophysiological effects of recuperative music following exhaustive exercise," *Proceedings of the 2014 British Association of Sport and Exercise Sciences Conference* (Burton on Trent, UK: British Association of Sport and Exercise Sciences).

Courtesy of Sally Trussler, Brunel University London photographer.

Finding music that evokes a relaxation response can aid an athlete's recuperation following heavy training.

# FACTORS INFLUENCING RESPONSES TO MUSIC: A NEW THEORETICAL MODEL

This section describes the latest theoretical model underlying the study and application of music in exercise and sport (Karageorghis, 2016). The model provides a visual framework that describes the way variables relating to music, the listener, and the listening situation interact to determine a range of consequences. The model is based on the literature reviewed earlier in this chapter and contextualizes the interventions presented in parts II and III of this book. The intention is to provide a logical framework to inform music selection for exercise and sport.

## Musical Factors

Attributes of the music are referred to as antecedents because they precede or cause the responses to music. In effect, they are the start of the chain reaction that takes place when an exerciser or athlete is influenced by music. These musical attributes are categorized as intrinsic or extrinsic. Intrinsic qualities refer to the composition of the music, or how it is put together (e.g., melodic and harmonic features, instrumentation, lyrical content); extrinsic qualities refer to how listeners interpret the music and the cultural associations of the music (e.g., how it reminds people of other things). In simpler terms, intrinsic factors are about the way music sounds, and extrinsic factors are about what music means to people.

In terms of intrinsic factors, the rhythmic qualities of music appear to have the strongest influence in an exercise or training context. Based on a wealth of research evidence, our theoretical model predicts that intrinsic factors are more salient than extrinsic factors in determining responses to music (e.g., Crust, 2008; Hutchinson & Karageorghis, 2013; Waterhouse et al., 2010). Therefore, these two sets of factors are arranged in a hierarchical order on the left-hand side of the model (see figure 2.8).

Lyrics also play a salient role by providing affirmations or directing attention toward a particular activity or skill (e.g., "Jump to the beat"). The effect of the semantic information contained in lyrics (i.e., what the lyrics mean) depends not only on the way it is received by the exerciser or athlete but also the relevance of the information to the task at hand. Certain lyrics can prove highly emotive for one athlete, even promote a flow experience, but have no effect whatsoever on another (e.g., Priest & Karageorghis, 2008; Sanchez et al., 2014).

The same piece of music performed with alternative instrumentation can change its influence on exercisers and athletes. Imagine listening to the original orchestral version of the movie theme to *Raiders of the Lost Ark* as a pre-task track in preparation for an American football game. Then envisage hearing the same piece played by a steel band. Notice that much of the emotional power of the composition is lost; it takes on a completely new identity, with new extramusical associations—a Caribbean island vacation perhaps!

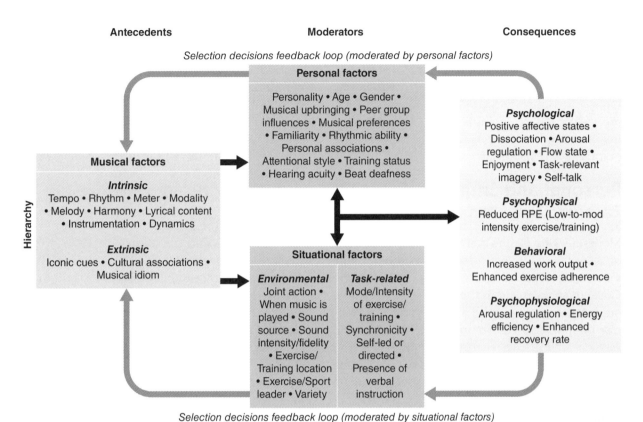

**Figure 2.8**   A theoretical model of the antecedents, moderators, and consequences of music use in exercise and sport.

Reprinted, by permission, from C. Karageorghis, 2016, The scientific application of music in exercise and sport: Towards a new theoretical model. In *Sport and exercise psychology*, 2nd ed., edited by A.M. Lane (London: Routledge), 301.

Musical idiom concerns the stylistic category that a piece of music commonly falls into (e.g., jazz, pop, reggae). This idiomatic criterion is very often overlooked by exercise instructors, who have a tendency to be guided by their own preferences rather than those of their clients (Priest, Karageorghis, & Sharp, 2004).

Among the extrinsic properties of music, iconic cues concern how structural elements of a musical work relate to the tone of certain emotions. For example, fast or loud music may sound lively because of its commonalities with energy and excitement (North & Hargreaves, 2008). Because such cues are grounded in the structure of music, the same music should hold similar iconic meaning for different people. However, the intrinsic properties of music often make an important contribution to iconic cues. As an illustration, the Survivor track "Eye Of The Tiger" was selected for the film *Rocky III* because of its intrinsic properties (e.g., rousing guitar riff

and anthemic chorus), but it developed a strong cultural association with boxing because of its association with an iconic film.

Cultural associations are often created by the mass media and are likely to influence large sections of the population, albeit for a different reason. Consider, for example, the use of Iggy Pop's "Lust For Life" in the Royal Caribbean Cruises Alaska commercials (United States) to engender a sense of adventure and a carefree attitude to life (search "Royal Caribbean Lust For Life" on YouTube). Conversely, students in my first cohort were quick to associate that track with the ritualistic hedonism of their freshman year, because it was indelibly linked with the raucous motion picture *Trainspotting*. The movie opened with a scene in which a juvenile Ewan McGregor charged through the streets of Edinburgh to the strains of Pop's effervescent drum track.

The new theoretical model distinguishes cultural associations from personal associations; the latter relate to people's individual experiences of music. Consider the phenomenon of lovers who have a song they consider *their* song, because it reminds them of the time they first started dating (North & Hargreaves, 2008). Such associations are cultivated at an individual level and may involve the mass media; hence, some overlap with cultural associations occurs.

## Personal and Situational Factors: The Moderators

Moderators are factors that influence the strength of the relationship between a piece of music and a person's response to it (e.g., age and gender). Consequences relate to the main responses and outcomes associated with music use during exercise or sport-related activities (e.g., task-relevant imagery and greater energy efficiency). A reciprocal, or two-way, relationship exists between personal and situational factors, given that, in an exercise or sport context, the music should be functional, or carefully coordinated with the tasks and specifics of the session (Kodzhaspirov, Zaitsev, & Kosarev, 1988). The personal and situational factors are not arranged in a hierarchical order because research evidence to inform any such hierarchy is currently insufficient. The situational factors are subdivided into environmental factors (e.g., the exercise or sport location and how it is organized or set up) and task-related factors (e.g., how the activity is undertaken, such as the intensity of a training session).

Moderators such as personal preferences and attentional style (e.g., associator vs. dissociator) interact with the situational factors to determine exercisers' and athletes' responses to music (Hutchinson & Karageorghis, 2013). For example, an associator who is training to music with a beat that matches her work rate is likely to use the music as a metronome to regulate her movements (task-related factor). As well as dealing with such individual-level responses, our theoretical model also deals with responses to music at a group level (i.e., an environmental factor). Joint action refers to coordinated and synchronized actions performed by a group of people who share common goals (Sebanz, Bekkering, & Knoblich, 2006). Accordingly, if a popular piece results in a surge of enthusiasm in an exercise group (i.e.,

joint action), this surge is likely to have a positive behavioral effect on an individual who may not necessarily express a liking for that piece (i.e., more effort expended). Likewise, if a particular piece is highly preferred by an exercise or sport leader, this preference will have a direct influence on exercise or sport participants through the nonverbal communication of the leader (Priest & Karageorghis, 2008).

The literature also suggests that the rhythm and tempo of music can lead to differential responses depending on the age and personality profiles of the performers and the nature of the task (e.g., Clark, Taylor, & Baker, 2012; Deutsch & Hetland, 2012). In a study completed for the David Lloyd Leisure group in the UK, researchers found that older exercisers (>50 years) generally expressed a preference for slower tempi than their younger counterparts did (Priest et al., 2004). They may need slower tempi to facilitate exercise at a lower work rate than that of their younger counterparts. To select age-congruent music, people need to consider the artist, musical idiom or style, and release date (Karageorghis, Priest et al., 2006). Songs and musical styles that were popular during a person's formative years have a particularly powerful effect owing to the formation of preferences and associations during this time.

In terms of personality influences on music selection (a personal factor), extroverts generally prefer more stimulative music than introverts do (e.g., Eysenck, 1967; McCown et al., 1997). Such music is characterized by a fast tempo, prominent rhythmic features, and exaggerated bass tones; the 2012 international smash hit "Gangnam Style" (130 bpm) by the South Korean artist Psy is a particularly good example of a stimulative track. The melodic and harmonic qualities of music lead to differential responses in listeners depending on their cultural backgrounds and musical upbringings. For example, Westerners typically associate major-scale melodies and harmonies with positive feelings and happiness. Interestingly, in many Eastern cultures (e.g., Arabic and Persian), minor-sounding melodies and harmonies induce a similar response because of cultural differences in musical composition (Levitin, 2007).

Numerous studies have shown that the personal factors of gender and age moderate the response to music during exercise or sport training (e.g.,

Crust, 2008; Karageorghis et al., 2010; Priest et al., 2004). For example, females rate the importance of rhythmic qualities and the danceability of music more highly than males do (Karageorghis et al., 1999). However, males value the importance of cultural associations to a greater extent than their female counterparts do (Karageorghis et al., 1999). Also, males report a preference for exaggerated bass tones, which may relate to the fact that the male voice is generally about one octave lower than the female voice. This difference in voice pitch may account for how sound frequencies are processed by the brain (McCown et al., 1997; Priest & Karageorghis, 2008).

In a study that examined health club members, younger subjects generally rated music as more important to them than their older counterparts did, in addition to preferring contemporary and up-tempo selections (Priest et al., 2004). This finding is consistent with the known role of music in forming a cultural identity during adolescence (Tarrant, North, & Hargreaves, 2001). People in all age groups consider music variety an important factor (Priest et al., 2004); overfamiliarity with music can lead to a decrement in liking (see Berlyne, 1971). Moreover, an athlete's repeated exposure to a piece of music outside of athletic competition can reduce the potency of that piece to engender a particular mind-set in competition (see the sidebar Garth's Mental Preparation With Music in chapter 3, for example).

Personality type (e.g., extrovert vs. introvert), musical upbringing (which goes hand in hand with cultural background), and hearing acuity are likely to moderate a person's response to changes in musical dynamics. For example, an extrovert who grew up listening to heavy metal music and has poor hearing (perhaps as a consequence of attending heavy metal concerts) would be unlikely to find soft music beneficial in the realm of exercise and sport. Coupled with the moderator of hearing acuity is the condition of beat deafness, which afflicts approximately 4 percent of people in North America and Western Europe. This entails not being able to perceive, or hear, the beat in a piece of music (Phillips-Silver & Keller, 2011). The theoretical model predicts that exercisers and athletes with significant hearing loss or beat deafness do not derive major benefits from music use. In the latter case, music may actually reduce the quality of the experience significantly. Instructors should give some latitude to people with beat deafness in exercise-to-music classes, because they will likely struggle to stay with the routine. Such people might be encouraged to make greater use of visual cues as opposed to rhythmic ones (i.e., to follow what they see).

## Consequences of Music Use

The consequences of music use are arranged in the model according to the literature presented earlier in this chapter. The two strongest and most consistent sets of consequences appear first (psychological and psychophysical) followed by behavioral consequences and finally psychophysiological consequences, which are the least consistent. In many studies, the consequences appear to have been experienced in unison; for example, appropriate music use can result in more positive affect coupled with greater work output (e.g., Elliott, Carr, & Savage, 2004; Karageorghis et al., 2009, 2010).

A feedback loop from the consequences back to the music factors influences music selection based on the experienced outcomes. This feedback loop entails reflecting on the consequences of music use with reference to the moderators. Pieces of music that lead to positive consequences (see the right-hand side of figure 2.8) are more likely to be reselected (and vice versa) and promote the selection of similar pieces (e.g., works by the same artist, in the same idiom, or of a similar tempo or rhythmic feel). The converse also holds: a negative consequence of music may lead to the deselection of a particular track or others like it.

A pronounced link occurs between the intrinsic music factors and responses. For example, the temporal, or time-related, aspects of music such as tempo, rhythm, and meter can have a strong influence on arousal. Contrastingly, aspects such as melody and harmony are particularly important in invoking an emotional response (e.g., Juslin, 2009; van der Zwaag, Westerink, & van den Broek, 2011). One of the central predictions of the model is that the influence of music factors on human responses is moderated by a host of personal and situational factors that exercise and sport professionals should consider when selecting music.

## Practical Implications of the Model

The new theoretical model (figure 2.8) details the variables that need to be taken into account when considering exercise and sport participants' responses to music. This section distills the key implications of the model into general recommendations.

Music selected to accompany an exercise or sporting task should be congruent with the participants' personal characteristics, the task, the exercise environment, and desired consequences. The music should be age appropriate and reflect participants' sociocultural backgrounds. The tempo should be selected with exercise or training intensity in mind. Other than when warming up, warming down, or recovering or recuperating, the appropriate band of tempi for the asynchronous application of music appears to be ~120 to ~140 bpm (Karageorghis & Jones, 2014; Karageorghis et al., 2011). Whenever possible, the rhythmic qualities of the music should approximate the motor patterns enacted in the activity (Simpson & Karageorghis, 2006; Leman et al., 2013).

The model has a number of implications that pertain to the application of music during instructor-led exercise or sport training. For example, if verbal instruction is required during the session, the sound should not be so loud as to inhibit participants' hearing and processing of these instructions. The interaction of the task with training status (a personal factor) should also be considered; highly trained exercisers and athletes require less feedback and instruction (McMorris, 2004). Moreover, personal trainers need to be aware of the capacity of music to interfere with their verbal guidance and motivational commentary.

Concerning the consequences of music listening, tracks containing affirmations of exercise or sport or inspirational references to popular culture should be selected to promote task-relevant imagery and self-talk. To maximize positive feeling states, instructors should select music in major keys (e.g., "Talking About" by Conor Maynard) or at least choose music with dark, minor harmonies very carefully (e.g., "Rolling In The Deep" by Adele; Juslin, 2009; van der Zwaag et

al., 2011). Similar oversight needs to be applied to the selection of lyrics, because negative, disempowering lyrics might counteract music that is otherwise motivational (Priest & Karageorghis, 2008; Sanchez et al., 2014). To have a stimulating effect, music should be up-tempo (>120 bpm) and have pronounced rhythmic features. To sedate, a slow tempo (<80 bpm), simple rhythmic structure, regular pulsation, and repetitive tonal patterns based on a limited number of pitch levels have been recommended (Karageorghis & Terry, 2009). Exercise instructors, sport coaches, and participants would benefit from routinely reflecting on and evaluating the consequences of their music listening experiences, and using this process to guide future music selections. This practice is the enactment of the feedback loop, from the consequences to the antecedents in the model in figure 2.8.

A novel finding is that music selection for exercise or sport is concerned with the entire music program—the combination of multiple music selections on a playlist rather than just a series of individual pieces (Priest & Karageorghis, 2008). Compilers of such playlists should consider the congruence of musical pieces that appear in close proximity and aim for variety in terms of the music program; similarly, programs should be suitably varied over time. The earlier review of the literature indicated that when music is self-selected or participants are offered a degree of autonomy in selection, the benefits appear to be magnified (e.g., Barwood et al., 2009; Yamashita et al., 2006).

In a statement released by the British Association of Sport and Exercise Sciences, Karageorghis and colleagues (2012) concluded that, although music is a beneficial accompaniment to exercise or training in most circumstances, it is contraindicated under the following conditions: when it may distract from safety-relevant information (e.g., on public roads); when exercisers or athletes need to focus their full attention on learning a demanding motor skill; and when exercising or training at high intensities that require an associative attentional style (i.e., listening to the body). Music should probably be used as a stimulant only intermittently (i.e., not all the time). This prevents desensitization to its stimulative effects and permits exercisers or athletes to habituate themselves for occasions when they may not be able to use it (e.g., long-distance running events).

Repeated exposure to excessively loud music combined with high-intensity exercise should be avoided because of the potential threat to the structures of the inner ear (Alessio & Hutchinson, 1991). A possible mechanism is that blood flow diverted to the working muscles leaves the 15,400 hair cells in the cochlea more susceptible to damage from high-intensity music (e.g., Nakashima et al., 2003). Research shows that even moderate-intensity activity accompanied by very loud music (>100 dB of sound pressure level, or SPL) can cause temporary hearing loss (Lindgren & Axelsson, 1988). This finding represents an interaction of the personal, environmental, and task-related moderators presented in the model (see figure 2.8).

# SUMMARY

Music has been applied to the field of exercise and sport since ancient times. Modern scientific fields such as psychology, physiology, biomechanics, and neuroscience have cross-fertilized recent advancements in knowledge. Among the mechanisms advanced to account for the effects of music are resonance and entrainment, rhythm response, attentional dissociation, and the music–emotion link. A theoretical model developed in recent years can be used to guide exercise and sport practitioners in their endeavors (Karageorghis, 2016).

Most scientific work in this field has focused on the in-task, asynchronous application of music. The following findings have emerged:

- Music reduces perceived exertion by 10 percent at low-to-moderate intensities of exercise or training, but does not appear to do so beyond the ventilatory threshold.
- Physiological, fatigue-related cues have an overwhelming influence on attentional processes at high exercise intensities (Ekkekakis, 2003; Rejeski, 1985; Tenenbaum, 2001).
- Well-selected music can enhance affect (how people feel) at all exercise intensities (e.g., Hutchinson et al., 2015; Karageorghis et al., 2009).

- Music has a mild ergogenic, or work-enhancing, effect across a range of activities (e.g., Elliott et al., 2004; Lim et al., 2009; Nakamura et al., 2010).
- The relationship between exercise heart rate and preference for music tempo is nonlinear (they do not rise in proportion to each other), and the range of preferred tempi is much narrower than previously thought (~120 to ~140 bpm vs. 90 to 155 bpm; Karageorghis & Terry, 2009).

A small but growing number of studies that have examined the application of synchronous music show that it is associated with an ergogenic effect in long-duration, motorically simple exercise-related tasks (Karageorghis et al., 2009; Terry et al., 2012). Recent evidence suggests that auditory–motor synchronization can promote greater energy efficiency in long-duration tasks, which is possibly one of the key mechanisms underlying the effectiveness and popularity of movement to music (Bacon et al., 2012). In more complex tasks, such as callisthenic and circuit exercises, women appear more adept at coordinating their movements with music and thus derive greater performance-related and psychological benefits than men do (Karageorghis et al., 2010; Michel & Wanner, 1973). The recently emerging body of work addressing the effects of post-task music reveals an array of benefits for both active and passive modes of recovery (e.g., Eliakim et al., 2012, 2013; Savitha et al., 2010).

The new theoretical model (figure 2.8) provides a framework that exercise and sport professionals can use to make well-informed selections and formulate music-related interventions. It provides a bird's-eye view of the subject and places its main emphasis on the interplay between musical factors (antecedents) and personal and situational factors (moderators) to determine a range of consequences that have been observed in the literature. The model suggests that the appraisal of these consequences can guide exercisers, athletes, and practitioners in music selection. Using the content of this chapter as a springboard, the chapters in parts II and III further explore the use of music through a variety of case studies and vivid examples.

# 3

# Assessing Music and Measuring Its Effects

*Nothing else exists but the battle ahead. I put on my earphones and listen to music. It sharpens that sense of flow, removes me further from my surroundings.*

—Rafael Nadal, winner of 14 grand slam
singles titles in tennis

Two big questions that are regularly posed by exercise and sport professionals are "how do I go about selecting music for the people I work with?" and "how do I know whether the music is having the desired effect?" This chapter provides comprehensive answers to these questions along with a broad range of relevant measurement tools. These tools are set in context to help exercise and sport leaders, as well as participants, immediately appreciate where and when to use them. Also, tools that are related to one another are presented in close succession to maintain the flow of the chapter.

In the past, the approach to music choice was often rather haphazard, with the possible exception of group exercise classes for which instructors had some basic training in selecting and sequencing music. I remember participating in radio phone-ins during the pre-iPod era in which callers would tell me they used entire albums with the tracks played back to back as an accompaniment to their training regimes. The radio listeners often associated far more strongly with the mystical qualities of particular artists than to the motivational qualities of individual musical tracks and how they were segued.

One man from Bournemouth (UK) described how he would record Def Leppard albums onto audiocassettes and use these as the sole accompaniment for running sessions in a local park. As I recall, his justification for this selection went something like this:

*I can't imagine running to anything but Def Leppard. . . . I've listened to them almost every day since my late teens. Sometimes when the ballads play, I find myself slowing down a bit, but when an upbeat song like "Rock Of Ages" or "Armageddon It" is blasting through my ears, I put the pedal fully to the metal.*

This statement aptly illustrates how people often select music that could, for the most part, be inappropriate for the type of activity they are engaged in. With modern technologies, our friend from Bournemouth could carefully craft a playlist of the Def Leppard tunes that would be most suited to his optimal stride rate or intended working heart rate. That way, he would maximize the benefits of his playlist.

To take a more structured and scientific approach to the selection of music and to assess its effectiveness in various exercise and sport contexts, we need to employ some specialized tools. This chapter describes some recently developed methods. For the sake of variety, I use the terms *tools, instruments, measures, inventories,* and *questionnaires* interchangeably. Essentially, these all refer to a broad range of assessment methods that can be applied to the selection of music and to the measurement of its perceived effects during and immediately after exercise or training. Accordingly, the chapter is organized into three sections according to how the tools might be used.

The first section presents tools that are useful in the selection of music for exercise and sport, particularly when faced with a large number of tracks to choose. For example, canvassing the opinions of members of a baseball team might result in 100

or more track recommendations. A way to whittle them down to just four or five would be useful. One such tool is the Brunel Music Rating Inventory, which has been used extensively in research projects and applied work throughout the world (e.g., Crust, 2008; Terry et al., 2012; Waterhouse, Hudson, & Edwards, 2010). Other instruments assess the degree to which participants are likely to respond to music-related activities or interventions.

The second section of the chapter presents a wide range of tools to gauge the effectiveness of music in shaping participants' psychological states. These include measures of perceived exertion, affect, state attention, and state motivation (the term *state* means "in the moment"). Practitioners can use this cluster of popular measures

## BMRI-3 AND BASKETBALL BACKBEATS

Deangelo is the long-serving coach of a senior high school basketball team in downtown Minneapolis, USA. Members of the team enjoy having music playing in the background during warm-ups and training drills. They find that it gives them an extra gear and helps them forget about the stresses and strains of lesson time. The players are very particular about what they listen to; they all enjoy urban music forms such as rap, but the particular choices are often a matter of contention and sometimes considerable friction. A music selection that is not favored by one of the dominant personalities on the squad results in the public derision of whoever selected it. Although this takes the form of banter, it can distract to the point that the debate over the music selection takes precedence over the technical elements of team practice.

Deangelo chose to put an end to the disputes and bickering by applying a more systematic approach to music selection. At the beginning and at the midway point of each season, he asks each member of the squad to provide a list of up to five tracks that could be used to accompany training activities. Deangelo screens the players' lists and selects tracks that appear on at least two lists. Moreover, he does not allow tracks with explicit lyrics to make the final cut, mainly for fear of upsetting the board of governors.

The next stage entails a panel of five volunteers from the squad (the composition of this panel is different each time) who sit in a locker room with Deangelo to rate the tracks using the Brunel Music Rating Inventory-3 (BMRI-3). The tracks that appear at least twice on the players' lists are played for about 90 seconds on Deangelo's tablet using a music-streaming service. For training sessions, he chooses 30 or so tracks that attract the highest BMRI-3 scores. Not only is this process democratic and thus reduces the players' bickering to some mild banter, but it also results in choosing the best tracks for their pursuits. The BMRI-3 hones in on individual qualities of music and reveals how motivating they are for given activities. The players' highest-scoring track on the BMRI-3 is "GDFR" by Flo Rida feat. Sage The Gemini and Lookas. It's no wonder Deangelo's team has come to be known locally as "the ballers with the baddest backbeats."

to gauge just how responsive a person is to music per se or even the person's responsiveness to particular styles of music. I have purposefully chosen tools that are relatively easy to administer and interpret; specialist psychometric training is not required to obtain meaningful information if instructions are followed carefully.

The third section presents instruments and schedules of questions that can be used to assess the effectiveness of pieces of music or even entire music programs following an exercise or sport training activity. The results from these instruments might well feed into future music selections (see figure 2.8 in chapter 2) or even help people decide whether to use music at all for particular activities. This batch of instruments includes measures of mood and flow state as well as suggested schedules of questions to facilitate semistructured interviews with participants and focus groups. Some practitioners dissuade participants from using music when they are being instructed in a new skill or when they are working at a very high intensity (e.g., flat-out shuttle running).

# USING PSYCHOMETRICS IN THE FIELD

Given the lack of experience among exercise and sport professionals in administering psychological tests, known as psychometric tests, and the fact that many people find them inaccessible or even mysterious, I devote a few lines to their general use in the field. First and foremost, such tests inspire a wide variety of emotional responses in respondents. These include a sense of respect for the rigor and objectivity of the measurement system, but this goes hand in hand with feelings of unease and suspicion.

Pen-and-paper tests remind exercisers and athletes of school exams, and these memories and associations may not be particularly positive. There is also the question of what the responses will be used for. In many instances in which psychometrics are used (e.g., recruitment), people feel, sometimes rightly, that they are being judged, scrutinized, or "found out" in some way. For all of these reasons, it is important to be extremely up front with clients or athletes about how the data will be used and to allay any concerns regarding confidentiality.

We live in an age in which people have grown wary of releasing any personal information given the ubiquity and incessant nature of marketeering. Indeed, many of my friends have two e-mail addresses—one for their regular daily correspondence and another for commercial organizations, web-based registrations, and social clubs. Without the two addresses, the daily volume of correspondence would simply overwhelm them.

Questionnaires should be demystified from the outset. Participants should be given information that promotes a sense of involvement with the process. Because people often conform to group behaviors, it is normally easier to get a group of exercisers or athletes to complete questionnaires at the same time, which also results in obtaining a large volume of information very quickly. Giving the activity a gamelike feel can motivate respondents to answer the questions honestly.

Given their competitive nature, sportspeople in particular are already motivated by completing tasks that have an objective system of feedback. This can be used to advantage by feeding back the results in a colorful and absorbable format. Athletes often respond warmly to the use of objective tests because it shows that coaches are giving full consideration to their performances and approaching the matter in a scrutinous, scientific manner. With this in mind, I suggest online data-gathering sites.

A variety of services, such as SurveyMonkey (www.surveymonkey.com), provide free and efficient ways to deliver surveys and administer questionnaires. Not only do these services provide a head start on data entry and analysis, but they also inspire participants by letting them use their own devices in a process that is quick and easy. Traditional paper-and-pen approaches may be necessary when software is not available. In my experience, mature coaches and older exercise participants (50 years and older) generally prefer the traditional approach.

# SELECTING MUSIC FOR EXERCISE AND SPORT

This section presents a series of tools that enable exercise and sport professionals to select appropriate music for individuals and groups. The Brunel Music Rating Inventory-3 enables exercisers and athletes to rate the motivational qualities of pieces of music. It can be used to quickly and easily whittle down a large pool of tracks into a more manageable set with strong motivational qualities. The Group Music Selection Tool establishes the musical preferences of a group of exercise participants or athletes. It also sensitizes practitioners to tracks that might be avoided in the construction of playlists.

The Attentional Focusing Questionnaire allows practitioners to gauge the attentional style of those in their charge with reference to association (focusing inwardly and on task-relevant thoughts) and dissociation (focusing outwardly and on task-irrelevant thoughts). Attentional style has a bearing on how people respond to and use music in a wide range of contexts. The Mental Preparation Profile allows coaches to establish an athlete's optimal pre-competition mind-set. Knowledge of this optimal mind-set informs the type of music selections to use in the pre-competition phase. The final tool in this section, the Music

---

## BRUNEL MUSIC RATING INVENTORY-3

The purpose of the Brunel Music Rating Inventory questionnaire is to assess the extent to which the piece of music you are about to hear would motivate you during _____ [*insert activity here; e.g., circuit training*]. For our purposes, the word *motivate* means music that would make you want to pursue _____ [*insert activity here; e.g., circuit training*] with greater intensity, stay with it for longer, or both. As you listen to the piece of music, indicate the extent of your agreement with the six statements by circling *one* of the numbers to the right of each statement. Provide an honest response to each statement. Give the response that best represents your opinion, and avoid dwelling for too long on any single statement.

| | | Strongly disagree | | | | | | Strongly agree |
|---|---|---|---|---|---|---|---|---|
| 1 | The rhythm of this music would motivate me during _____ [*insert activity here*] | 1 | 2 | 3 | 4 | 5 | 6 | 7 |
| 2 | The style of this music (i.e., rock, dance, jazz, hip-hop, etc.) would motivate me during _____ [*insert activity here*] | 1 | 2 | 3 | 4 | 5 | 6 | 7 |
| 3 | The melody (tune) of this music would motivate me during _____ [*insert activity here*] | 1 | 2 | 3 | 4 | 5 | 6 | 7 |
| 4 | The tempo (speed) of this music would motivate me during _____ [*insert activity here*] | 1 | 2 | 3 | 4 | 5 | 6 | 7 |
| 5 | The sound of the instruments used (i.e., guitar, synthesizer, saxophone, etc.) would motivate me during _____ [*insert activity here*] | 1 | 2 | 3 | 4 | 5 | 6 | 7 |
| 6 | The beat of this music would motivate me during _____ [*insert activity here*] | 1 | 2 | 3 | 4 | 5 | 6 | 7 |

### BMRI-3 Scoring Instructions

Add the items for a score between 6 and 42. A score in the range of 36 to 42 indicates high motivational qualities in the piece of music, a score in the range of 24 to 35 indicates moderate motivational qualities, and a score below 24 indicates that the track lacks motivational qualities.

Reprinted, by permission, from C.I. Karageorghis, 2016, The scientific application of music in exercise and sport: Towards a new theoretical model. In *Sport and exercise psychology*, 2nd ed., edited by A.M. Lane (London: Routledge), 283.

Mood-Regulation Scale, assesses the perceived effectiveness of music to regulate exercisers' and athletes' moods.

When I started working in this field, I found no standardized way to select music for exercise and sport-related activities. This led to the development of the Brunel Music Rating Inventory (BMRI), a questionnaire-based instrument that assessed the motivational qualities of music in exercise and sport contexts (Karageorghis, Terry, & Lane, 1999). The structure of the instrument changed over the years as we realized that external music factors such as cultural impact and association could not be measured in a reliable way owing to their inherent subjectivity. The internal qualities of music could, however, be quantified using this questionnaire-based approach.

In addition to using the BMRI-3 scores, an exercise leader or sport professional may want to follow these guidelines when selecting music:

- Music with clear associations to sport or physical activity may prove motivating, although not all exercise participants are motivated by music associated with sport.

- Associations that are unrelated to sport or physical activity may also prove motivating. For example, a theme from a popular movie adventure series (e.g., James Bond or Indiana Jones) may promote the desire to engage in physical activity. Further, lyrics related to strength and perseverance may motivate people to exercise more intensely or for a longer duration, or both (e.g., "Can't Hold Us Down" by Christina Aguilera).

- The musical idiom, date of release, and artist should be allied to the ages and cultural backgrounds of the exercise or sport participants. With very diverse groups, a systematic attempt must be made to vary these factors.

- When selecting music for a predetermined exercise or training intensity, music tempo should be linked to exercise heart rate, particularly during low and high intensities. The ideal tempo range for music used to accompany repetitive and rhythmic exercise is ~120 to ~140 bpm.

- When selecting music for a synchronous application, assess the desired movement rate (e.g., stride rate) and then select music that facilitates either one or two movements per beat. For example, running at 180 strides per minute could be synchronized with music at 90 bpm (e.g., rap, for a stride cycle) or 180 bpm (e.g., hard rock, for each step).

- When selecting music for an individual, the effects of personal associations should be considered. For example, a boxer may have conditioned himself by listening to R. Kelly's "The World's Greatest" prior to fighting. Where possible, exercise and sport practitioners should experiment to form such personal associations and harness their power.

Adapted from C.I. Karageorghis, D.L. Priest, P.C. Terry, L.D. Chatzisarantis, and A.M. Lane, 2006, "Redesign and initial validation of an instrument to assess the motivational qualities of music in exercise: The Brunel Music Rating Inventory-2," *Journal of Sports Sciences* 24(8), 899-909, by permission of Taylor & Francis Ltd.

## Tool for Group Music Selection

Selecting music programs for groups can be difficult because people often hold their dislikes far more ardently than they hold their preferences. Accordingly, it is imperative to select tracks that not only appeal to the majority, but also do not antagonize a significant number of group members. One way to achieve this is to democratize the process and thus give participants a sense of ownership and empowerment. This can be done by seeking a few suggestions from each group member. This method of music selection is not as precise or rigorous as the BMRI-3 method, but it is, nonetheless, a quick-and-dirty way to achieve a similar result.

The Group Music Selection Tool is a means for selecting music for groups and surreptitiously avoiding tracks that are likely to antagonize certain members. Casting an eye over members' responses can reveal information about commonalities. Some tracks or artists may appear repeatedly, and trends may jump out across the responses (e.g., an idiom that appears to resonate with the group or the musical era of the tracks). The suitable tracks section may also bring to light musical styles or artists to avoid. The interesting thing about this exercise is that the tracks some people identify as not motivational will appear on other people's lists of preferred tracks. My advice is to steer clear of tracks that are identified by even a few members of the group as unsuitable

---

## GROUP MUSIC SELECTION TOOL

What would be your three preferred, up-tempo, motivational musical selections to listen to while
_____ [*put the activity and its intensity here;
e.g., doing a hard, continuous conditioning circuit over a short duration*]? Also, which three up-tempo
tracks might be suitable for _____ [*put the
activity and its intensity here; e.g., doing a hard, continuous conditioning circuit over a short duration*],
but not necessarily motivational for you?

**Preferred tracks:**

    1. Title: _____  Artist: _____

    2. Title: _____  Artist: _____

    3. Title: _____  Artist: _____

**Nonpreferred tracks that might also work for this purpose:**

    1. Title: _____  Artist: _____

    2. Title: _____  Artist: _____

    3. Title: _____  Artist: _____

From C.I. Karageorghis, 2017, *Applying music in exercise and sport* (Champaign, IL: Human Kinetics).

---

for the context. Chapter 6 features an example of the Group Music Selection Tool in action.

## Attentional Focusing Questionnaire

Exercise scientists have established that people with different attentional styles respond differently to external distractions such as music, video, and the surrounding environment during an exercise or training session. Attentional style refers to the tendency to focus on task-related cues such as the beating heart, muscular discomfort, or pacing, or the tendency to focus on cues unrelated to the task, such as music, nearby people, or the unfolding landscape. The tendency to focus on task-related cues is known as association, whereas the tendency to focus on cues unrelated to the task or to daydream (or both) is known as dissociation (Stevinson & Biddle, 1999).

The Attentional Focusing Questionnaire (AFQ) is composed of 30 items—11 measure association (e.g., "monitoring specific bodily sensations"), and 12 measure dissociation (e.g., "focusing on the outside environment"). The developers of the AFQ, led by Professor Britton Brewer at Springfield College in Massachusetts, USA, included

a third factor that they termed distress, which was measured using the remaining 7 items (e.g., "wishing the session would end"). The distress factor was included to gauge people's tendencies to focus on distress cues and negative sensations during endurance activities.

Subsequent to the development of the AFQ, other researchers assigned the labels *switcher* and *attentionally flexible* to people with a malleable attentional style (i.e., similar AFQ scores for association and dissociation; Hutchinson & Karageorghis, 2013; Lind, Welch, & Ekkekakis, 2009). This means that they can adapt their attention according to the demands of the situation. For example, many elite athletes tend to associate or focus on regulating their bodies when performing at high intensities. This not only provides a constant source of feedback that enables them to maximize their work output or optimize their effort distribution, but also helps prevent injuries through overexertion.

Those who score highly on the aforementioned distress factor should be actively discouraged from using associative strategies during exercise-related tasks (i.e., they should not focus inwardly). This is because they are likely to negatively interpret the bodily sensations, making them less likely

## LORIS AND THE FACETS OF ATTENTION

Since leaving school, Loris had become a regular gym-goer and fully appreciated the health benefits associated with regular physical activity. She had always found it hard to concentrate in class because her mind would drift to exotic island vacations, earlier episodes in her life, or even her favorite pop group, One Direction, in which she would imagine herself as a backup singer. This tendency to daydream was a habit her teachers had noticed and recorded in her school reports since the days of junior high: "Loris is a pleasant girl who tries hard but oftentimes her attention wanders in class—sometimes it's almost as though she's living in her own little bubble."

Loris actually had a strong tendency to dissociate in almost everything she did. This meant that her mind would drift from the specifics of a task, such as a chemistry experiment or a softball game, to completely unrelated matters or passing distractions. If something really interested Loris, she would be able to focus on it intently and without difficulty—that is, narrow and fixate her attention on all of the relevant details, or fully associate with the task. However, a math teacher droning on or a boring school assembly would lead her to switch off and mentally go elsewhere to find insight and stimulation.

This tendency to drift proved a distinct advantage to Loris each time she visited the gym. In fact, going to the gym every other day was one of the most positive and rewarding aspects of her life. It also provided welcome relief from her full-time job as a cashier in a grocery store, where at least once a day customers would get irate with her for shortchanging them. Whether on the treadmill, elliptical trainer, or cross-country ski machine, Loris would don her over-ear headphones and lose herself in the varied musical contents of her smartphone.

Loris could work at a relatively high intensity—with an exercise heart rate of 150 to 160 bpm—for 25 to 30 minutes, and the music would completely dull the pain. She didn't really care what sort of music it was—it just needed to be loud enough and in her ears! Loris had found an environment and a set of activities in which her tendency to drift mentally could be given free rein and seemed to afford her a distinct advantage. Knowing Loris' gym habits, her boss, Mr. Lubienski, wondered whether switching off the in-store music might result in fewer customers being shortchanged.

to want to participate in that activity in the future. Rather, dissociation was proposed as the optimal attentional strategy for high-distress people. Accordingly, in theory at least, those who score relatively high on the distress and dissociation factors are likely to derive the most benefit from music-related interventions.

## Mental Preparation Profile: A Tool for Athletes

Some athletes are at their best when highly excited and agitated, whereas others need to remain totally calm and composed to perform at their best. Most performers, however, need to strike a happy medium between the states of excitement and calmness. Ultimately, the only reliable way for athletes to determine their optimal activation level is to chart their performance level in relation to their emotional state. Activation level concerns one's level of energy, alertness, and bodily arousal. This influences how athletes think, feel, and behave in those crucial minutes before competition. The Mental Preparation Profile (MPP) is solely for sportspeople as opposed to exercisers.

The MPP leads athletes through a process of retrospection (i.e., thinking about their past experiences) to establish the level of activation

# ATTENTIONAL FOCUSING QUESTIONNAIRE

Please put an X in the space that indicates how much you would engage in each of the following activities during _____ [insert activity here].

| | | Would not do at all | | | | | Would do a lot | |
|---|---|---|---|---|---|---|---|---|
| | | 1 | 2 | 3 | 4 | 5 | 6 | 7 |
| 1 | Letting your mind wander (daydreaming) | | | | | | | |
| 2 | Monitoring specific body sensations (e.g., leg tension, breathing rate) | | | | | | | |
| 3 | Trying to solve problems in your life | | | | | | | |
| 4 | Paying attention to your general level of fatigue | | | | | | | |
| 5 | Focusing on how much you are suffering | | | | | | | |
| 6 | Singing a song in your head | | | | | | | |
| 7 | Focusing on staying loose and relaxed | | | | | | | |
| 8 | Wishing the [include activity here; e.g., run] would end | | | | | | | |
| 9 | Thinking about work, school, social relationships, etc. | | | | | | | |
| 10 | Focusing on your performance goal | | | | | | | |
| 11 | Wondering why you are even [include activity here; e.g., running] in the first place | | | | | | | |
| 12 | Making plans for the future (e.g., a shopping list) | | | | | | | |
| 13 | Getting frustrated at yourself over your performance | | | | | | | |
| 14 | Writing a letter or a paper in your head | | | | | | | |
| 15 | Paying attention to your technique | | | | | | | |
| 16 | Reflecting on past experiences | | | | | | | |
| 17 | Paying attention to your [include activity here; e.g., running] rhythm | | | | | | | |
| 18 | Thinking about how much you want to quit | | | | | | | |
| 19 | Focusing on the surrounding environment | | | | | | | |
| 20 | Thinking about strategy | | | | | | | |
| 21 | Counting (e.g., objects in the environment) | | | | | | | |
| 22 | Monitoring how hard you are working | | | | | | | |
| 23 | Thinking about how much the rest of the [include activity here; e.g., run] will hurt | | | | | | | |
| 24 | Meditating (focusing on a mantra) | | | | | | | |
| 25 | Encouraging yourself to [include activity here; e.g., run] fast | | | | | | | |
| 26 | Trying to ignore all physical sensations | | | | | | | |
| 27 | Concentrating on the [include activity here; e.g., run] | | | | | | | |
| 28 | Wondering whether you will be able to finish the [include activity here; e.g., run] | | | | | | | |
| 29 | Thinking about pleasant images | | | | | | | |
| 30 | Monitoring the time of the [include activity here; e.g., run] | | | | | | | |

## AFQ Scoring Instructions

First add the items from each scale to obtain three scores. Points are assigned depending on where the X is placed (as shown here, where X denotes a score of 4) and then totaled for each subscale.

| | | Would not do at all | | | | | | Would do a lot |
|---|---|---|---|---|---|---|---|---|
| 1 | Letting your mind wander (daydreaming) | | | | X | | | |
| | | 1 | 2 | 3 | 4 | 5 | 6 | 7 |

Association total score = item 2 + item 4 + item 7 + item 10 + item 15 + item 17 + item 20 + item 22 + item 25 + item 27 + item 30

Dissociation total score = item 1 + item 3 + item 6 + item 9 + item 12 + item 14 + item 16 + item 19 + item 21 + item 24 + item 26 + item 29

Distress total score = item 5 + item 8 + item 11 + item 13 + item 18 + item 23 + item 28

Range for Association = 11 to 77

    Low = 11 to 22

    Moderate = 23 to 55

    High = 56 to 77

Range for Dissociation = 12 to 84

    Low = 12 to 24

    Moderate = 25 to 60

    High = 61 to 84

Range for Distress = 7 to 49

    Low = 7 to 14

    Moderate = 15 to 35

    High = 36 to 49

The AFQ allows respondents to endorse both association and dissociation strategies; that is, someone can have high or low scores on both scales. A cognitive index is a combined score for dissociation and association that allows us to ascertain whether the person is a dissociator, associator, or switcher. Use the following set of calculations to establish a cognitive index:

1. Work out the mean (average) of the Association score: the sum of the items divided by 11 (the number of items).
2. Add the mean of the Association score to the sum of the Association score to obtain a range of 12 to 84, identical to the Dissociation range.
3. Subtract the new Association score from the Dissociation score.
4. Add 100 to the score to obtain a Cognitive Index.

## Interpreting the Cognitive Index

A Cognitive Index greater than or equal to 110 = Dissociator
You have a tendency to focus outwardly and on task-irrelevant cues.

A Cognitive Index between 109 and 91 = Attentional Switcher
You have a malleable attention style and are therefore readily able to shift your attention in accord with the demands of the situation.

A Cognitive Index less than or equal to 90 = Associator
You have a tendency to focus inwardly and on task-relevant cues.

*(continued)*

**Attentional Focusing Questionnaire**  *(continued)*

**Stage 1:** Here are the scores entered by David, a recreational runner: Item 1: **6**, Item 2: **5**, Item 3: **5**, Item 4: **5**, Item 5: **5**, Item 6: **5**, Item 7: **6**, Item 8: **5**, Item 9: **6**, Item 10: **7**, Item 11: **2**, Item 12: **5**, Item 13: **4**, Item 14: **2**, Item 15: **6**, Item 16: **6**, Item 17: **6**, Item 18: **4**, Item 19: **6**, Item 20: **6**, Item 21: **2**, Item 22: **7**, Item 23: **3**, Item 24: **5**, Item 25: **6**, Item 26: **2**, Item 27: **5**, Item 28: **6**, Item 29: **2**, Item 30: **6**

**Stage 2:** We need to add together the 11 association item scores (items 2, 4, 7, 10, 15, 17, 20, 22, 25, 27, and 30), so 5 + 5 + 6 + 7 + 6 + 6 + 6 + 7 + 6 + 5 + 6 = 65. It is clear from a brief glance over the scores that they are typically high (closer to 7 than 1), so we are expecting David to be an *associator*, and indeed he is in the "high" category (>56).

**Stage 3:** We do exactly the same for the 12 dissociation item scores (items 1, 3, 6, 9, 12, 14, 16, 19, 21, 24, 26 and 29), which gives us 6 + 5 + 5 + 6 + 5 + 2 + 6 + 6 + 2 + 5 + 2 + 2 = 52. In this case, we see that the responses are less uniform, more irregular. Consequently, David's scores for dissociation put him in the upper part of the "normal" range for this factor (25-60).

**Stage 4:** We follow suit for the seven distress item scores (items 5, 8, 11, 13, 18, 23 and 28), so 5 + 5 + 2 + 4 + 4 + 3 + 6 = 29. David fits into the "normal" range for this factor (15-35).

**Stage 5:** To obtain the cognitive index, which tells us whether David is an associator or dissociator, we need to follow these four steps:
1. We require the mean or average of both the association and dissociation subscales. In our example, the mean for association is calculated by dividing the sum for this factor by the number of items in the factor, so 65 / 11 = 5.91. The same calculation takes place for dissociation, so 52 / 12 = 4.33.
2. Add the mean of association to the sum of scores in the association factor, so 65 + 5.91 = 70.91. Now we can directly compare association and dissociation as they are on the same scale (12-84).
3. Subtract the new association score from the dissociation score, so 52 − 70.91 = −18.91
4. The final step entails adding 100, so −18.91 + 100 = 81.09

**Stage 6:** From our worked example, we can see that David is an associator, because his score is lower than 90.

From C.I. Karageorghis, 2017, *Applying music in exercise and sport* (Champaign, IL: Human Kinetics). Adapted, by permission, from B.W. Brewer, J.L. Van Raalte, and D.E. Linder, 1996, "Attentional focus and endurance performance," *Applied Research in Coaching and Athletics Annual* 11: 1-14.

associated with their best performances. Having established their optimal level, they can make music selections that reflect, or lead them toward, this level. The MPP can also be used to choose tracks that conjure the type of imagery or self-talk that facilitates high-quality performances (e.g., striving to overcome adversity through imagery or affirmations that concern looking for the hero who lies deep within [see "Search For The Hero" by M People]).

When working with a national-level badminton player, I established that the task-related self-statement *flick of the wrist* appeared to work well for her because it encapsulated an aspect of her technique that required greater fluidity. She combined this with the visual image of how a well-timed twist of her racket head could immediately wrong-foot an opponent. The athlete had previously told me that she was a big rock music fan, and so I suggested the early Queen track "Flick Of The Wrist" as a possible addition to her pre-event playlist. I combined this with a new on-court epithet, Racket Queen, that I inserted digitally into her motivational highlight videos; she simply loved the idea of being the ruler of every court over which she presided. The mood and lyrics of the song proved to be especially powerful during her pre-match mental preparation; particularly the lyric concerning how an opponent could be dispatched with a quick flick

# MENTAL PREPARATION PROFILE

Name: _____    Main event: _____

These questions are designed to help you reflect on your competitive experiences in recent seasons and develop your competition preparation plan. This plan may involve the use of a standardized routine, self-statements, or even music tracks, all of which can help you attain your optimal competition mind-set.

a. Think of your best performance in recent seasons and respond to the following:

1. How did you feel just before performing? (Please circle.)

| No determination to achieve goal | 1 | 2 | 3 | 4 | 5 | 6 | 7 | 8 | 9 | 10 | Completely determined |
|---|---|---|---|---|---|---|---|---|---|---|---|
| No physical activation | 1 | 2 | 3 | 4 | 5 | 6 | 7 | 8 | 9 | 10 | Highly physically activated |
| No worries or fears | 1 | 2 | 3 | 4 | 5 | 6 | 7 | 8 | 9 | 10 | Extremely worried or afraid |
| Mentally calm | 1 | 2 | 3 | 4 | 5 | 6 | 7 | 8 | 9 | 10 | Mentally uptight |
| No confidence | 1 | 2 | 3 | 4 | 5 | 6 | 7 | 8 | 9 | 10 | Completely confident |

2. What were you thinking or saying to yourself, or focusing on, just before the competition?

_____

_____

_____

3. What were you thinking or saying to yourself, or focusing on, during the competition?

_____

_____

_____

4. How much were you focused on the process of competing rather than the result of the competition?

_____

_____

_____

b. Think of your worst performance within the last two seasons and respond to the following:

1. How did you feel just before performing?

| No determination to achieve goal | 1 | 2 | 3 | 4 | 5 | 6 | 7 | 8 | 9 | 10 | Completely determined |
|---|---|---|---|---|---|---|---|---|---|---|---|
| No physical activation | 1 | 2 | 3 | 4 | 5 | 6 | 7 | 8 | 9 | 10 | Highly physically activated |
| No worries or fears | 1 | 2 | 3 | 4 | 5 | 6 | 7 | 8 | 9 | 10 | Extremely worried or afraid |
| Mentally calm | 1 | 2 | 3 | 4 | 5 | 6 | 7 | 8 | 9 | 10 | Mentally uptight |
| No confidence | 1 | 2 | 3 | 4 | 5 | 6 | 7 | 8 | 9 | 10 | Completely confident |

2. What were you thinking or saying to yourself, or focusing on, just before the competition?

_____

_____

_____

*(continued)*

3. What were you thinking or saying to yourself, or focusing on, during the competition?

_____

_____

_____

4. How much were you focused on the process of competing rather than the result of the competition?

_____

_____

_____

c. Compare your responses from your best and worst performances, and then respond to the following by indicating how you want to feel in the future before and during a big competition:

1. How do you want to feel just before performing?

| No determination to achieve goal | 1 | 2 | 3 | 4 | 5 | 6 | 7 | 8 | 9 | 10 | Completely determined |
|---|---|---|---|---|---|---|---|---|---|---|---|
| No physical activation | 1 | 2 | 3 | 4 | 5 | 6 | 7 | 8 | 9 | 10 | Highly physically activated |
| No worries or fears | 1 | 2 | 3 | 4 | 5 | 6 | 7 | 8 | 9 | 10 | Extremely worried or afraid |
| Mentally calm | 1 | 2 | 3 | 4 | 5 | 6 | 7 | 8 | 9 | 10 | Mentally uptight |
| No confidence | 1 | 2 | 3 | 4 | 5 | 6 | 7 | 8 | 9 | 10 | Completely confident |

2. What do you want to think or say to yourself, or focus on, just before the competition?

_____

_____

_____

3. What do you want to think or say to yourself, or focus on, during the competition?

_____

_____

_____

4. How much do you want to focus on the process of competing rather than the result of the competition?

_____

_____

_____

5. Now spend a few minutes reflecting carefully on your answers. Think of strategies that you can use to attain your optimal mind-set, and write them down. Use these strategies in your upcoming training sessions, and then gradually introduce them into competitive situations.

_____

_____

_____

_____

From C.I. Karageorghis, 2017, *Applying music in exercise and sport* (Champaign, IL: Human Kinetics). Adapted from T. Orlick, 1986, *Psyching for sport: Mental training for athletes* (Champaign, IL: Human Kinetics), 23-24. Used by permission of Terry Orlick (www .zoneofexcellence.ca).

## GARTH'S MENTAL PREPARATION WITH MUSIC

Garth is a county-level field hockey player in the UK. His sport requires speed, power, and agility coupled with split-second timing and a high degree of accuracy. Despite Garth's considerable talent on the field, from his early years he was given a tough time for his devotion to hockey. He attended an all-boys private school in which rugby union was deemed to be the number one sport. Cricket followed closely, particularly during the spring and summer months, but hockey was very much the poor relation.

The negative reinforcement Garth experienced at school, along with a general predisposition to be a little anxious and uncertain, often led him to experience almost uncontrollable nerves on match days. This was particularly the case on the days of important games such as local derbies and cup ties. Garth's club coach, Melvin, was acutely aware of this tendency and resolved to support him. Melvin knew about the Mental Preparation Profile and figured that this might be a good place to start.

The profile showed Garth and his coach that he was almost always highly determined to succeed and highly activated or aroused. Nonetheless, prior to successful as well as unsuccessful performances, Garth's thought patterns were characterized by self-doubt and a stream of negative images, which generated their own sense of shame and self-recrimination—an endless cycle. After the first few minutes of game play, he would generally be more buoyant, but he realized that in some of the bigger games, his pre-game nerves persisted far too long and affected both the flow of his play and his decision-making processes. Once he had become aware that his mindset was affecting his performance, he became distracted from the game and stuck in a rut. As a central midfielder, Garth's teammates depended on him as a playmaker, so if he wasn't switched on mentally (decisive, quick to respond, and assertive), then every man on the pitch became aware of it.

As part of a package of strategies to address the pre-competition anxiety and turn nervous energy into positive excitement, Garth compiled a playlist that he listened to in the locker room while we was getting ready for the game and mentally preparing. Since his mid-teens, he had been into the Black Eyed Peas; therefore, a couple of their dynamic and uplifting tracks, such as "Let's Get It Started" and "Boom Boom Pow" featured prominently on his playlist. He was also a fan of the rap star Eminem, and so he included the well-known tracks "Lose Yourself" and "Not Afraid." He found that listening to the playlist distracted him from the stream of negative thoughts he usually experienced and imbued him with an inner confidence. Moreover, the music created positive imagery in his mind, prevented him from getting uptight, and promoted positive self-talk—particularly lyrics that emphasize that you get only one chance to make your mark.

Garth also listened to the same Eminem tracks occasionally during training. This enabled him to mentally rehearse the psychological state he wanted to enter before games. However, I cautioned Garth not to listen to his pre-game playlist too often outside of game days, because this would reduce its potency. I wanted him to form a strong and specific association between those tracks and a positive locker room experience.

of the wrist. The lack of structure and niggling doubt that characterized her match preparations in the past had been replaced by thoughts, images, and affirmations that drove her to excel.

Many successful interventions follow the simple principle that affirmative and empowering mental activity reduces the opportunity to worry and fret—people have less time and mental space to fill with negative thoughts and images. It is important to be sure that the athlete buys in to the affirmation, because such affirmations are highly personal. A hook or image may seem perfect, yet the client may reject it for no rational reason. When this happens, adjustments must be made. For this reason and others, it is important to foster a communication climate in which clients feel comfortable speaking honestly about their reservations. Athletes must know that their ideas will be accepted and not met with a harsh response or vindictive criticism. This is especially the case with performers who have worked with a traditional, or old school, autocratic coach.

I have used the MPP on many occasions in scientific experiments and with top-class athletes. Music selected using this method is most often used during a pre-event routine, but it can just as easily be used prior to important training sessions. Having a sense of mental control in the lead-in to competition gives athletes a significant edge that will manifest as superior performance.

Research has shown that thought processes, or cognitions, tend to drive anxiety responses such as butterflies in the stomach and excessive muscular tension (Berkowitz et al., 2007; Eysenck et al., 2007). Therefore, thought-related, or cognitive, anxiety often acts as a catalyst for the unwanted physical symptoms of anxiety. If an athlete starts to have doubts about whether a challenge is within her capabilities, if her self-talk is defeatist, or if her head is full of negative images, then her activation level is likely to be pushed beyond its optimal point.

To reach an optimal level of activation, athletes need to understand their natural responses and be sensitive to their bodily signals. Learning to handle the stresses of competition requires that they learn to read their thought patterns and physical responses, and that they develop the skills for finding their ideal activation levels. Stress management requires excellent self-awareness; athletes who know themselves well can determine the root causes of their anxiety. Using music as a distraction from anxiety before competition can counter phenomena such as choking, which entails excessive focus on the execution of key skills rather than allowing them to flow automatically (Mesagno, Marchant, & Morris, 2009).

From the detail in the sidebar Garth's Mental Preparation With Music, we can gauge that much of the negativity Garth felt was due to historical factors that he simply needed to block from his mind in the pre-game phase. A self-selected playlist proved to be a useful intervention. Music-related interventions and pre-competition soundtracks can form part of a package of measures to optimize athletes' activation levels and curb the negative aspects of anxiety such as defeatist self-talk and mental imagery. Chapter 7 explores how to use the results of the MPP to make music selections and provides examples from the world of sport.

## Music Mood-Regulation Scale

The Music Mood-Regulation Scale (MMRS) was developed by Ruth Hewston, a senior lecturer in education at the University of Worcester in the UK. The MMRS assesses the perceived effectiveness of music to regulate mood in exercise and sport populations. *Mood* is a term used to describe a set of constantly changing feelings that vary in strength and duration.

Moods are formed by clusters of emotions. An emotion has a cause (e.g., the sound of fingernails scraping a blackboard making a person feel uneasy); a mood is an accumulation of emotional responses to daily events that combine to form a current mind-set. This mind-set generally remains until it is altered by events. Moods are perhaps a classic example of the enigmatic nature of psychology: we all experience them and have a strong sense of what they are, yet psychologists have struggled for decades to come up with an all-embracing and universally agreed-on definition.

Method acting is a good way to think about the nature of mood states. Classic method actors such as Dustin Hoffman noticed that a helpful technique for delivering a line the right way was to conjure up the appropriate mood by thinking about a personal memory. Imagine Hoffman sitting in a bar, and the line he has to deliver is "Sure, I'll come over to join you." However, the mood is supposed to be detached and melancholic. The actor learned that recalling an incident from his own life (in this case, of failure or rejection) resulted in his delivering the line just right. It is

# MUSIC MOOD-REGULATION SCALE

Following is a list of items that relate to how music can help you create feelings (e.g., restfulness, liveliness, alertness). Read each item and rate how it applies to you by circling the relevant number: *not at all* (0), *a little* (1), *moderately* (2), *quite a bit* (3), *extremely* (4). Do not dwell on any one item, and provide your dominant response in each case. Make sure that you respond to every item, and please note that there are no right or wrong answers.

| | Not at all | A little | Moderately | Quite a bit | Extremely |
|---|---|---|---|---|---|
| 1. If you need to feel **restful**, how effective is listening to music as a strategy to achieve this feeling? | 0 | 1 | 2 | 3 | 4 |
| 2. If you need to feel **relaxed**, how effective is listening to music as a strategy to achieve this feeling? | 0 | 1 | 2 | 3 | 4 |
| 3. If you need to feel **lively**, how effective is listening to music as a strategy to achieve this feeling? | 0 | 1 | 2 | 3 | 4 |
| 4. If you need to feel **happy**, how effective is listening to music as a strategy to achieve this feeling? | 0 | 1 | 2 | 3 | 4 |
| 5. If you need to feel **energetic**, how effective is listening to music as a strategy to achieve this feeling? | 0 | 1 | 2 | 3 | 4 |
| 6. If you need to feel **contented**, how effective is listening to music as a strategy to achieve this feeling? | 0 | 1 | 2 | 3 | 4 |
| 7. If you need to feel **composed**, how effective is listening to music as a strategy to achieve this feeling? | 0 | 1 | 2 | 3 | 4 |
| 8. If you need to feel **cheerful**, how effective is listening to music as a strategy to achieve this feeling? | 0 | 1 | 2 | 3 | 4 |
| 9. If you need to feel **calm**, how effective is listening to music as a strategy to achieve this feeling? | 0 | 1 | 2 | 3 | 4 |
| 10. If you need to feel **alert**, how effective is listening to music as a strategy to achieve this feeling? | 0 | 1 | 2 | 3 | 4 |
| 11. If you need to feel **active**, how effective is listening to music as a strategy to achieve this feeling? | 0 | 1 | 2 | 3 | 4 |
| 12. If you need to feel **satisfied**, how effective is listening to music as a strategy to achieve this feeling? | 0 | 1 | 2 | 3 | 4 |
| 13. If you are feeling **worried**, how effective is listening to music as a strategy to change this feeling? | 0 | 1 | 2 | 3 | 4 |

*(continued)*

|  | Not at all | A little | Moderately | Quite a bit | Extremely |
|---|---|---|---|---|---|
| 14. If you are feeling **worn out**, how effective is listening to music as a strategy to change this feeling? | 0 | 1 | 2 | 3 | 4 |
| 15. If you are feeling **unhappy**, how effective is listening to music as a strategy to change this feeling? | 0 | 1 | 2 | 3 | 4 |
| 16. If you are feeling **tired**, how effective is listening to music as a strategy to change this feeling? | 0 | 1 | 2 | 3 | 4 |
| 17. If you are feeling **sleepy**, how effective is listening to music as a strategy to change this feeling? | 0 | 1 | 2 | 3 | 4 |
| 18. If you are feeling **panicky**, how effective is listening to music as a strategy to change this feeling? | 0 | 1 | 2 | 3 | 4 |
| 19. If you are feeling **nervous**, how effective is listening to music as a strategy to change this feeling? | 0 | 1 | 2 | 3 | 4 |
| 20. If you are feeling **miserable**, how effective is listening to music as a strategy to change this feeling? | 0 | 1 | 2 | 3 | 4 |
| 21. If you are feeling **exhausted**, how effective is listening to music as a strategy to change this feeling? | 0 | 1 | 2 | 3 | 4 |
| 22. If you are feeling **down-hearted**, how effective is listening to music as a strategy to change this feeling? | 0 | 1 | 2 | 3 | 4 |
| 23. If you are feeling **depressed**, how effective is listening to music as a strategy to change this feeling? | 0 | 1 | 2 | 3 | 4 |
| 24. If you are feeling **bitter**, how effective is listening to music as a strategy to change this feeling? | 0 | 1 | 2 | 3 | 4 |
| 25. If you are feeling **bad tempered**, how effective is listening to music as a strategy to change this feeling? | 0 | 1 | 2 | 3 | 4 |
| 26. If you are feeling **anxious**, how effective is listening to music as a strategy to change this feeling? | 0 | 1 | 2 | 3 | 4 |
| 27. If you are feeling **annoyed**, how effective is listening to music as a strategy to change this feeling? | 0 | 1 | 2 | 3 | 4 |
| 28. If you are feeling **angry**, how effective is listening to music as a strategy to change this feeling? | 0 | 1 | 2 | 3 | 4 |

## Scoring the Music Mood-Regulation Scale

Add items **24**, **25**, **27**, and **28** for an **Anger** score.

Add items **15**, **20**, **22**, and **23** for a **Depression** score.

Add items **14**, **16**, **17**, and **21** for a **Fatigue** score.

Add items **13**, **18**, **19**, and **26** for a **Tension score.**

Add items **1**, **2**, **7**, and **9** for a **Calmness** score.

Add items **4**, **6**, **8**, and **12** for a **Happiness** score.

Add items **3**, **5**, **10**, and **11** for a **Vigor** score.

## Interpreting Your Music Mood-Regulation Scale Score

First turn the raw score you obtained for each factor into a mean score by dividing the raw score by 4 (i.e., dividing by the number of items in each factor). Now examine these means for each of the seven factors in turn. If your mean score for a given factor—say, happiness—is 2 or higher, this suggests that a music-related intervention *is* likely to influence that mood factor. Furthermore, if the score is 3 or higher, we can conclude that the music in question is highly likely to influence the given factor. This approximation should give you a meaningful way to interpret the results.

The MMRS can also help people to identify pieces of music that are likely to promote a particular mood profile (see Selecting Music Using the Amended Music Mood-Regulation Scale). It can also be linked with the earlier Mental Preparation Profile to identify tracks or compile playlists that are likely to promote a certain mind-set. For example, for athletes who feel at their best in a state of high vigor and low tension, depression, anger, fatigue, and confusion, tracks associated with the MMRS vigor items (i.e., lively, energetic, alert, and active) might be used. In my work with athletes, I have used the instrument extensively to identify tracks to achieve a particular pre-performance mind-set, often linking them to their optimal pre-competition mood states. This also gives athletes a sense of control over their mind-sets and helps prevent their pre-competition feelings from being random psychological factors over which they have no control. Typically, we look closely at their music libraries and choose tracks that might be associated with each item.

## Selecting Music Using the Amended Music Mood-Regulation Scale

| | Tracks or pieces of music |
|---|---|
| 1. If you need to feel **restful**, what tracks or pieces of music would you listen to as a strategy to achieve this feeling? | |
| 2. If you need to feel **relaxed**, what tracks or pieces of music would you listen to as a strategy to achieve this feeling? | |
| 3. If you need to feel **lively**, what tracks or pieces of music would you listen to as a strategy to achieve this feeling? | |
| 4. If you need to feel **happy**, what tracks or pieces of music would you listen to as a strategy to achieve this feeling? | |
| 5. If you need to feel **energetic**, what tracks or pieces of music would you listen to as a strategy to achieve this feeling? | |
| 6. If you need to feel **contented**, what tracks or pieces of music would you listen to as a strategy to achieve this feeling? | |
| 7. If you need to feel **composed**, what tracks or pieces of music would you listen to as a strategy to achieve this feeling? | |
| 8. If you need to feel **cheerful**, what tracks or pieces of music would you listen to as a strategy to achieve this feeling? | |

*(continued)*

| | Tracks or pieces of music |
|---|---|
| 9. If you need to feel **calm**, what tracks or pieces of music would you listen to as a strategy to achieve this feeling? | |
| 10. If you need to feel **alert**, what tracks or pieces of music would you listen to as a strategy to achieve this feeling? | |
| 11. If you need to feel **active**, what tracks or pieces of music would you listen to as a strategy to achieve this feeling? | |
| 12. If you need to feel **satisfied**, what tracks or pieces of music would you listen to as a strategy to achieve this feeling? | |
| 13. If you are feeling **worried**, what tracks or pieces of music would you listen to as a strategy to change this feeling? | |
| 14. If you are feeling **worn out**, what tracks or pieces of music would you listen to as a strategy to change this feeling? | |
| 15. If you are feeling **unhappy**, what tracks or pieces of music would you listen to as a strategy to change this feeling? | |
| 16. If you are feeling **tired**, what tracks or pieces of music would you listen to as a strategy to change this feeling? | |
| 17. If you are feeling **sleepy**, what tracks or pieces of music would you listen to as a strategy to change this feeling? | |
| 18. If you are feeling **panicky**, what tracks or pieces of music would you listen to as a strategy to change this feeling? | |
| 19. If you are feeling **nervous**, what tracks or pieces of music would you listen to as a strategy to change this feeling? | |
| 20. If you are feeling **miserable**, what tracks or pieces of music would you listen to as a strategy to change this feeling? | |
| 21. If you are feeling **exhausted**, what tracks or pieces of music would you listen to as a strategy to change this feeling? | |
| 22. If you are feeling **downhearted**, what tracks or pieces of music would you listen to as a strategy to change this feeling? | |
| 23. If you are feeling **depressed**, what tracks or pieces of music would you listen to as a strategy to change this feeling? | |
| 24. If you are feeling **bitter**, what tracks or pieces of music would you listen to as a strategy to change this feeling? | |
| 25. If you are feeling **bad tempered**, what tracks or pieces of music would you listen to as a strategy to change this feeling? | |
| 26. If you are feeling **anxious**, what tracks or pieces of music would you listen to as a strategy to change this feeling? | |
| 27. If you are feeling **annoyed**, what tracks or pieces of music would you listen to as a strategy to change this feeling? | |
| 28. If you are feeling **angry**, what tracks or pieces of music would you listen to as a strategy to change this feeling? | |

From C.I. Karageorghis, 2017, *Applying music in exercise and sport* (Champaign, IL: Human Kinetics).

almost as if Hoffman takes the line and delivers it over the mood in the way that a drink is poured over ice.

The point here is that moods shape our judgments, behaviors, and decision-making processes. In sport and exercise, music is one of the most potent mood-induction and mood-regulation techniques. We can use music to enter a mood state that will allow us to make the right decisions, to engage with others in a mutually productive way, and to focus on solutions and achievements rather than limitations. To reap such benefits, we need to assess the impact of music on mood, and to do this, we need a valid instrument such as the MMRS.

The MMRS has 21 items that assess the extent to which participants use music to alter the mood states of anger, calmness, depression, fatigue, happiness, tension, and vigor. As is the case with the Brunel Mood Scale (BRUMS), which we meet a little later in this chapter, these seven factors stem from the classic Profile of Mood States (POMS) instrument, which sport psychologists have used in recent years to take a snapshot of performers' mood states around competition or to monitor them over an extended period. This tool can be used to sensitize exercise and sport practitioners to the degree that they can use music to regulate mood in situations in which disturbed mood (i.e., a negative mind-set) might be detrimental to performance. Disturbed mood could, for example, entail low levels of vigor coupled with high levels of negative mood factors such as tension and depression.

The California State University academic Robert Thayer and his colleagues proposed that mood regulation entails the raising and lowering of energy levels coupled with reducing tension levels (Thayer, Newman, & McClain, 1994). By extension, successful mood regulation lies in the identification of individual energy and tension levels. Bearing this in mind, the MMRS can easily be used with other measures in this chapter such as the Mental Preparation Profile and the BRUMS, which is presented in the final section of this chapter. Music is a particularly powerful tool for modulating from an unpleasant to a pleasant mood.

The MMRS assesses four unpleasant mood states (anger, depression, fatigue, and tension) and three pleasant mood states (calmness, happiness, and vigor). Each of the seven factors in the MMRS has three items associated with it.

# ASSESSING THE EFFECTS OF MUSIC DURING A TASK

Exercise and sport professionals require tools to assess the effectiveness of their music-related interventions. Following directly from the theoretical and mechanistic aspects of musical responsiveness outlined in the first two chapters, this section addresses the instruments that measure some of the purported benefits of music during a task, as well as the degree to which exercisers and athletes like a given piece. The Rating of Perceived Exertion, or RPE, Scale is often used to measure the degree to which a music intervention reduces the perception of exertion, given that at low-to-moderate work intensities, a musical stimulus can block fatigue-related messages that travel via the afferent nervous system (i.e., from the working muscles and vital organs to the brain). Using Russell's (1980) circumplex model of affect as a point of origin, the Feeling Scale and Felt Arousal Scale can be viewed almost as sister instruments to measure the valence (pleasure vs. displeasure) and arousal (activation vs. deactivation) dimensions of affect, respectively. The music-liking item at the end of this section enables practitioners to measure the degree to which a person likes a specific track for a given exercise- or sport-related task.

## Rating of Perceived Exertion

As explained in chapter 1, the psychophysical effects of music are measured primarily during exercise, but also sometimes during sport training. The most common application is in assessing the perception of physical exertion, or how hard you think you're working. Music provides a distracting stimulus that can reduce our perceptions of exertion at low-to-moderate work intensities. The Borg CR10 Scale (figure 3.1), designed by celebrated Swedish physiologist Gunnar Borg, uses physical signals such as heart rate, breathing rate, and muscle acidosis.

| | | |
|---|---|---|
| 0 | Nothing at all | |
| 0.3 | | |
| 0.5 | Extremely weak | Just noticeable |
| 0.7 | | |
| 1 | Very weak | |
| 1.5 | | |
| 2 | Weak | Light |
| 2.5 | | |
| 3 | Moderate | |
| 4 | | |
| 5 | Strong | Heavy |
| 6 | | |
| 7 | Very strong | |
| 8 | | |
| 9 | | |
| 10 | Extremely strong | "Maximal" |
| 11 | | |
| ✦ | | |
| | | |
| • | Absolute maximum | Highest possible |

**Figure 3.1** Borg's CR10 Scale for the measurement of RPE.

The Borg CR10 Scale® with instruction can be obtained from Dr. Borg (borgperception@telia.com).

The simple concept of the RPE Scale has led to its being used extensively by exercise professionals and coaches to gauge people's perceived levels of intensity during exercise or training on a scale from 0 to 10. A small version of the Borg scale is presented here with kind permission from Dr. Gunnar Borg.

Research shows that RPE can be influenced by phenomena such as the presence of others, environmental conditions (e.g., altitude and humidity), age, and cognitive style (e.g., association vs. dissociation). The general idea is that music should reduce RPE by about 1 unit at low-to-moderate work intensities, which is about 7 on the scale. As highlighted in chapter 2, the effect of music on perceived exertion wanes considerably at high exercise intensities. Music is a particularly effective form of distraction for activities such as treadmill walking, jogging in the park, and recreational swimming. I do not recommend the use of music for any form of physical activity on roads and sidewalks where there is moving traffic, particularly while cycling, in view of important safety considerations (more on this in chapter 4; see also Karageorghis et al., 2012).

## Measuring How People Feel the Music: The Feeling Scale

In exercise science, the RPE Scale has often been used in tandem with the Feeling Scale. Whereas the RPE Scale measures *what* people feel during physical activity, the Feeling Scale measures *how* they feel (Hardy & Rejeski, 1989). It reveals the degree of pleasure or displeasure experienced at any intensity. Such a measure is important in

## FEELING SCALE

While participating in exercise, many people experience changes in mood. Some find exercise pleasurable, whereas others find it unpleasurable. Additionally, feelings may fluctuate across time—that is, a person might feel good and bad a number of times during exercise. Scientists have developed the Feeling Scale to measure such responses.

| | |
|---|---|
| +5 | Very good |
| +4 | |
| +3 | Good |
| +2 | |
| +1 | Fairly good |
| 0 | Neutral |
| −1 | Fairly bad |
| −2 | |
| −3 | Bad |
| −4 | |
| −5 | Very bad |

Reprinted, by permission, from C.J. Hardy and R.J. Rejeski, 1989, "Not what, but how one feels: The measurement of affect during exercise," *Journal of Sport & Exercise Psychology* 11(3): 304-317.

the exercise sphere in particular because it can provide an objective assessment of how someone is feeling during an activity, at a certain intensity, and as a result of a stimulus (e.g., music, video, verbal encouragement).

Much recent research has shown that well-chosen music can enhance affect at all exercise intensities—even very high intensities (e.g., Hutchinson, Karageorghis, & Jones, 2015; Jones, Karageorghis, & Ekkekakis, 2014; Karageorghis & Jones, 2014). Drawing on the analogy with a famous advertising slogan, a well-selected tune appears to reach the parts that other tunes cannot reach. To put a number to this benefit, we could expect a well-chosen track to enhance affect by 2 points; and at high intensities, by 1 point (Hutchinson & Karageorghis, 2013; Hutchinson et al., 2011; Karageorghis et al., 2009). This finding has important implications for those working in the domain of public health. One of the biggest obstacles to engagement in habitual physical

activity is that people find exercise per se to be unpleasurable, particularly at moderate-to-high intensities (Ekkekakis, 2003, 2013). The remaining chapters of this book detail how music can heighten pleasure during exercise and training tasks, and the Feeling Scale can be used to objectively assess people's pleasure ratings in response to pieces of music or even whole music programs (e.g., rock vs. jazz).

Russell's (1980) circumplex model (figure 3.2) is a circle of mood states that resembles a clock face, which is plotted around the intersection, or crossing point, of two bipolar dimensions: one relating to arousal (activation vs. deactivation) and the other relating to affect (pleasure vs. displeasure). The main idea of the circumplex is that each state can be mapped on the circumference of the circle. Accordingly, the states depicted around the model's circumference represent combinations of the two dimensions to varying degrees (Ekkekakis, 2013).

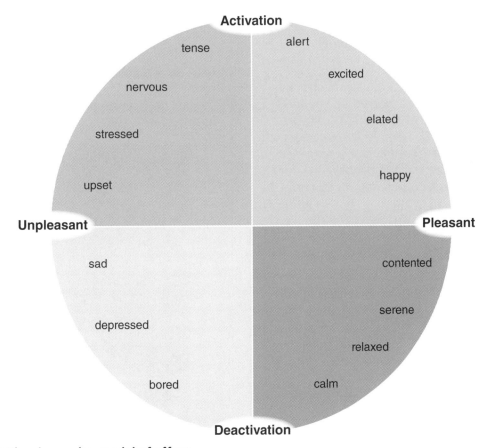

**Figure 3.2 The circumplex model of affect.**

Reprinted from J.A. Russell, 1980, "A circumplex model of affect," *Journal of Personality and Social Psychology* 39(6): 1161-1178, with permission from the American Psychological Association.

## Felt Arousal Scale

A tool that complements the Feeling Scale is the Felt Arousal Scale, which was developed by two European researchers, Sven Sveback and Stephen Murgatroyd. It assesses perceived activation at any point in time—the vertical axis in Russell's circumplex model (see figure 3.2). Why is this aspect important to measure? Many forms of exercise and sporting pursuits are associated with distinct levels of activation. For example, the excitement and high energy characteristic of a Zumba class would be out of place in a yoga class focused on tranquility and a sense of inner calm (see also chapter 5). Similarly, the high level of controlled aggression that embodies the mental state of a blocker in American football is very different from the quietude and stillness required of an archer.

Perceived activation has to do with how wide awake, alert, or energized a person feels, independent of whether that feeling is positive or negative. We learned in the previous section that feelings of positivity and negativity can be tapped by the Feeling Scale, which is why the Felt Arousal Scale and Feeling Scale are often used in tandem. The top half of the Felt Arousal Scale (4 to 6) is for feelings that are above average in arousal. The lower half (1 to 3) is for feelings that are below average. The number 1 represents sleep, and the higher on the scale the person goes, the more awake the person feels. Imagine a state called frantic excitement (remembering that it could be either positive or negative); this feeling would be given the number 6.

## Music Liking

Often, it is necessary to assess the degree to which participants like a piece of music in an exercise-related intervention or experimental trial. The need for an index of liking stems from the fact that we don't always like what we find motivating, and vice versa. There is, of course, a degree of overlap. We may, for example, want to assess the degree to which participants like different pieces over

---

### FELT AROUSAL SCALE

Estimate here how aroused you actually feel. Do this by circling the appropriate number. By *arousal*, we mean how worked up you feel. You might experience high arousal in one of a variety of ways—for example, as excitement, anxiety, or anger. You may also experience low arousal in one of a number of ways—for example, as relaxation, boredom, or calmness.

| 6 | High arousal |
|---|---|
| 5 | |
| 4 | |
| 3 | |
| 2 | |
| 1 | Low arousal |

---

### MUSIC-LIKING ITEM

Rate how much you like this track in the context of _____
[*include the activity and intensity of the activity if relevant*]

| 1 | I do not like it at all |
|---|---|
| 2 | |
| 3 | |
| 4 | |
| 5 | |
| 6 | |
| 7 | |
| 8 | |
| 9 | |
| 10 | I like it very much |

From C.I. Karageorghis, 2017, *Applying music in exercise and sport* (Champaign, IL: Human Kinetics). © Costas I. Karageorghis

a range of exercise or training intensities (Karageorghis & Jones, 2014; Karageorghis, Jones, & Low, 2006; Karageorghis, Jones, & Stuart, 2008; Karageorghis et al., 2011). This can help us get the tempo range right for a given person. The music-liking item has been used in a number of recent studies and can be quickly administered during a task because of its 10-point scale and easy-to-understand verbal anchors.

# ASSESSING THE EFFECTS OF MUSIC AFTER A TASK

Exercise and sport practitioners sometimes want to test the effectiveness of a music intervention immediately after a task. This section presents a variety of tools that enable them to do just that. The Brunel Mood Scale (BRUMS) is a quick-and-easy measure of mood for exercisers and athletes based on six mood factors that have proven particularly popular with practitioners (see, e.g., Terry, 1995). Tammen's (1996) Attentional Focus Scale assesses association and dissociation immediately following a physical task. The Motivation Scale allows exercise and sport professionals to measure the in-the-moment motivation of those in their charge. The Short Flow State Scale assesses the degree to which an exercise or sport participant has experienced the elusive, but much sought-after, state of flow. This section ends with tools and methods to assess the effects of music using observations, semi-structured interviews, and focus groups.

## Brunel Mood Scale

The Brunel Mood Scale, or BRUMS for short, complements the MMRS presented earlier in this chapter, with which it shares a structure that is based on the Profile of Mood States. The main distinction between the BRUMS and the MMRS is that the former is used to assess people's mood, whereas the latter is used to assess how people might use music to regulate their moods. One thing to be aware of from the outset is that people who don't expect a music-related intervention to alter mood (i.e., the person's mind-set) may be better off using the simpler measures such as the Feeling Scale and Felt Arousal Scale.

You might think that it is slightly strange to differentiate between what people feel generally at a given point in time (affect) and the components that merge to form their mind-sets (moods). There has actually been a fierce debate among scholars regarding the distinctions among terms such as *affect, mood,* and *emotion,* which you can follow in the psychology literature (Beedie, Terry, & Lane, 2005; Ekkekakis, 2013). This debate also touches on the limitations of using instruments such as the BRUMS to moderately elevate affect, rather than to alter a prevailing mind-set.

Case study 1 in chapter 6 illustrates how the BRUMS can be used to monitor mood state and assess the influence of a physical conditioning program with music on psychological state. Keep in mind that the BRUMS should be used for self-assessment; exercise and sport professionals should encourage this, perhaps by suggesting that participants complete the instrument once a week on the same day of the week and at the same time of day (e.g., every Wednesday at 2:00 pm).

In the sport context, mood profiling is often used to identify mood states associated with peak performances. In this regard, the BRUMS is similar to the Mental Preparation Profile presented earlier. Once the optimal mood state has been charted, it can serve as a target for future competitions. In exercise and sport training, an alternative application of mood profiling is to assess responses to various training loads. Such profiles can help people avoid overtraining, staleness, and injury. Profiles are also a good indicator of people's general psychological state and thus well worth completing on a weekly basis. Bear in mind that there is diurnal variation in mood (i.e., it changes through the course of a day) and so it is important to measure mood at the same time of day if taking weekly measures; this enables one to compare like with like.

## Measuring Attentional Focus

Sometimes we want to find out how someone is focusing at a given point in time during a specific type and intensity of activity. Vance Tammen from Concordia University in California developed a single-item bipolar attention scale to measure the degree of association or dissociation an exerciser or athlete experiences during an activity. You may recall from the sidebar Loris and the Facets of Attention that association refers to an internal focus, whereas dissociation refers to an external focus, or daydreaming.

# BRUNEL MOOD SCALE (BRUMS)

Following is a list of words that describe feelings. Please read each one carefully. Then mark the answer that best describes how you feel right now. Make sure that you respond to every item.

| Mood items | Not at all | A little | Moderately | Quite a bit | Extremely |
|---|---|---|---|---|---|
| 1. Panicky | 0 | 1 | 2 | 3 | 4 |
| 2. Lively | 0 | 1 | 2 | 3 | 4 |
| 3. Confused | 0 | 1 | 2 | 3 | 4 |
| 4. Worn out | 0 | 1 | 2 | 3 | 4 |
| 5. Depressed | 0 | 1 | 2 | 3 | 4 |
| 6. Downhearted | 0 | 1 | 2 | 3 | 4 |
| 7. Annoyed | 0 | 1 | 2 | 3 | 4 |
| 8. Exhausted | 0 | 1 | 2 | 3 | 4 |
| 9. Mixed-up | 0 | 1 | 2 | 3 | 4 |
| 10. Sleepy | 0 | 1 | 2 | 3 | 4 |
| 11. Bitter | 0 | 1 | 2 | 3 | 4 |
| 12. Unhappy | 0 | 1 | 2 | 3 | 4 |
| 13. Anxious | 0 | 1 | 2 | 3 | 4 |
| 14. Worried | 0 | 1 | 2 | 3 | 4 |
| 15. Energetic | 0 | 1 | 2 | 3 | 4 |
| 16. Miserable | 0 | 1 | 2 | 3 | 4 |
| 17. Muddled | 0 | 1 | 2 | 3 | 4 |
| 18. Nervous | 0 | 1 | 2 | 3 | 4 |
| 19. Angry | 0 | 1 | 2 | 3 | 4 |
| 20. Active | 0 | 1 | 2 | 3 | 4 |
| 21. Tired | 0 | 1 | 2 | 3 | 4 |
| 22. Bad tempered | 0 | 1 | 2 | 3 | 4 |
| 23. Alert | 0 | 1 | 2 | 3 | 4 |
| 24. Uncertain | 0 | 1 | 2 | 3 | 4 |

## Scoring the BRUMS

Add items **1**, **13**, **14**, and **18** for a **Tension** score.

Add items **5**, **6**, **12**, and **16** for a **Depression** score.

Add items **7**, **11**, **19**, and **22** for an **Anger** score.

Add items **2**, **15**, **20**, and **23** for a **Vigor** score.

Add items **4**, **8**, **10**, and **21** for a **Fatigue** score.

Add items **3**, **9**, **17**, and **24** for a **Confusion** score.

## Interpreting Your Mood Profile

First, turn the raw score you obtained into what is known as a standard score. This has a range of 1 to 100, and can be interpreted in the same way as a percentage score. So if you are an athlete and your tension score corresponds with a standard score of 58 (see table 3.1), you are 8 percent tenser than the average athlete (50 percent). Similarly, if your standard score for fatigue is 43, you are 7 percent less fatigued than the average athlete (50 percent). Read across from your raw score to the standard scores. The scores in table 3.2 are applicable to people who exercise but are not athletes, so be sure to select the correct table.

**Table 3.1** BRUMS Standard Scores for Adult Athletes

| Raw score | Tension | Depression | Anger | Vigor | Fatigue | Confusion |
|---|---|---|---|---|---|---|
| 0 | 38 | 45 | 45 | 28 | 40 | 43 |
| 1 | 40 | 49 | 48 | 31 | 43 | 46 |
| 2 | 43 | 53 | 52 | 34 | 46 | 50 |
| 3 | 45 | 57 | 55 | 36 | 48 | 53 |
| 4 | 48 | 62 | 58 | 39 | 51 | 57 |
| 5 | 50 | 66 | 62 | 42 | 53 | 60 |
| 6 | 53 | 70 | 65 | 44 | 56 | 64 |
| 7 | 56 | 75 | 68 | 47 | 59 | 67 |
| 8 | 58 | 79 | 72 | 50 | 61 | 71 |
| 9 | 61 | 83 | 75 | 52 | 64 | 75 |
| 10 | 63 | 88 | 78 | 55 | 67 | 78 |
| 11 | 66 | 92 | 82 | 57 | 69 | 82 |
| 12 | 68 | 96 | 85 | 60 | 72 | 85 |
| 13 | 71 | 101 | 88 | 63 | 74 | 89 |
| 14 | 73 | 105 | 92 | 65 | 77 | 92 |
| 15 | 76 | 109 | 95 | 68 | 80 | 96 |
| 16 | 79 | 114 | 98 | 71 | 82 | 99 |

**Table 3.2** BRUMS Standard Scores for Adults (Suitable for Exercisers)

| Raw Score | Tension | Depression | Anger | Vigor | Fatigue | Confusion |
|---|---|---|---|---|---|---|
| 0 | 42 | 43 | 44 | 34 | 38 | 42 |
| 1 | 46 | 47 | 48 | 36 | 40 | 45 |
| 2 | 49 | 50 | 51 | 39 | 42 | 48 |
| 3 | 53 | 54 | 54 | 42 | 45 | 51 |
| 4 | 57 | 57 | 58 | 45 | 47 | 55 |
| 5 | 61 | 60 | 61 | 47 | 49 | 58 |
| 6 | 65 | 64 | 64 | 50 | 51 | 61 |
| 7 | 69 | 67 | 67 | 53 | 54 | 64 |
| 8 | 72 | 71 | 71 | 55 | 56 | 68 |
| 9 | 76 | 74 | 74 | 58 | 58 | 71 |
| 10 | 80 | 77 | 77 | 61 | 61 | 74 |
| 11 | 84 | 81 | 81 | 64 | 63 | 77 |
| 12 | 88 | 84 | 84 | 66 | 65 | 81 |
| 13 | 92 | 88 | 87 | 69 | 67 | 84 |
| 14 | 96 | 91 | 90 | 72 | 70 | 87 |
| 15 | 99 | 94 | 94 | 75 | 72 | 91 |
| 16 | 103 | 98 | 97 | 77 | 74 | 94 |

(continued)

**Brunel Mood Scale** *(continued)*

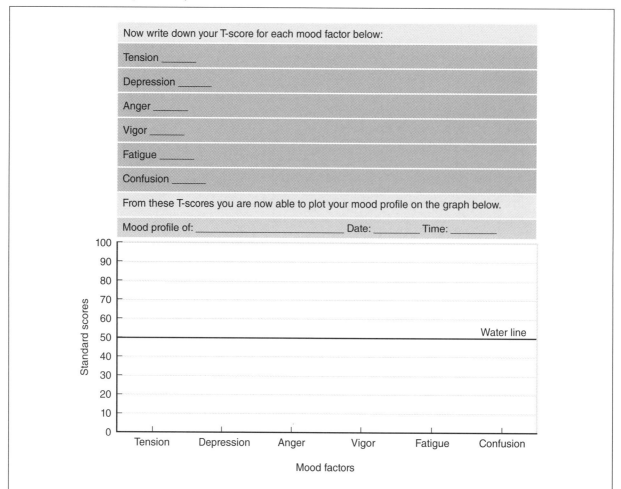

Now write down your T-score for each mood factor below:

Tension _____

Depression _____

Anger _____

Vigor _____

Fatigue _____

Confusion _____

From these T-scores you are now able to plot your mood profile on the graph below.

Mood profile of: _____ Date: _____ Time: _____

From C.I. Karageorghis, 2017, *Applying music in exercise and sport* (Champaign, IL: Human Kinetics). © 2003 Peter C. Terry and Andrew M. Lane. From P.C. Terry, A.M. Lane, H.J. Lane, and L. Keohane, 1999, "Development and validation of a mood measure for adolescents," *Journal of Sports Sciences* 17: 861-872.

Like the RPE Scale and the Feeling Scale, this is a quick and easy-to-use tool that assesses how an environmental stimulus, such as music or video, affects a person's attentional focus. At low-to-moderate intensities of exercise or training, music has a relatively strong influence on attentional focus—as much as 20 percent—but at high workloads in excess of ventilatory threshold (when breathing gets labored), this is reduced to just 0 to 5 percent.

An exercise instructor might use the Attentional Focus Scale to gauge how different styles of music influence the focus of class members. Similarly, a coach could use the Attentional Focus Scale to find out precisely the work intensity at which music is likely to be ineffective as a dissociative tool for a given athlete. For maximal effect, the scale should be administered immediately after an exercise or training session. Alternatively, it can be administered between short bouts of

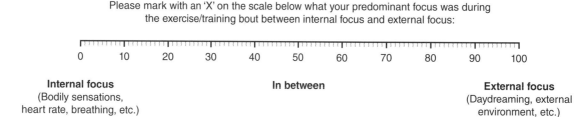

Please mark with an 'X' on the scale below what your predominant focus was during the exercise/training bout between internal focus and external focus:

exercise or training intervals (e.g., between 100-meter intervals during a swimming session).

### Interpreting the Attentional Focus Scale Score

It is very much a case of "X marks the spot" with the Attentional Focus Scale: we can tell at a glance the degree of association or dissociation. Research has shown that at low exercise or training intensities, people have a tendency to dissociate (right-hand side of the scale), at moderate intensities they have a tendency to attend in accordance with their dominant attentional style (as can be determined by the Attentional Focusing Questionnaire, or AFQ). At high exercise intensities, everyone has a tendency to associate (left-hand side of the scale; see Hutchinson & Karageorghis, 2013).

## Measuring Motivation in the Moment

In the psychology literature, countless questionnaires assess motivation—either general motivation or the motivation to engage in specific pursuits such as watching TV or engaging in physical activity. To gauge the response to a music selection, it is sometimes handy to have a quick and easy-to-use scale rather than an extended inventory of items that take a long time to complete. In my research, I have found the Motivation Scale,

developed by Professor Gershon Tenenbaum and his colleagues at Florida State University, USA, to be particularly useful.

Similar to Borg's CR10 Scale, the Motivation Scale is an 11-point scale that ranges from 0 (*Not at all motivated*) to 10 (*Extremely motivated*). And similar to the BRUMS, it is based on how people are feeling right now, which makes it particularly appropriate for assessing the influence a piece of music has on an individual. It provides a gestalt, or overall estimation, of how motivated a person feels at any point in time. The lack of sophistication of this scale is largely outweighed by its ease of use.

## Getting Into the Zone With Music

On occasion, we wish to assess how absorbed someone is in an activity that is accompanied by music. In the psychology literature, a state of complete absorption, in which nothing else seems to matter, is known as a flow state. We saw in the opening quote of this chapter how music helps tennis legend Rafael Nadal enter flow. During a flow experience, exercisers and athletes lose self-consciousness and become one with the activity in which they are engaged. This creates an intrinsically rewarding or highly enjoyable state that many coaches refer to as being in the zone.

---

## MOTIVATION SCALE INSTRUCTIONS

Motivation refers to how much you want to keep going (persistence) and the extent to which you want to push yourself to work harder (effort).

Use this scale from 0 to 10, in which 0 means *Not motivated at all* (i.e., you are not at all motivated to keep going or to work hard) and 10 means *Extremely motivated* (i.e., you are extremely motivated to keep going or to work hard).

Try to appraise your feelings of motivation as honestly as possible. Don't underestimate them, but don't overestimate them either. It is your own feelings of motivation that are important, not how they compare to other people's. What other people think is not important either. Look at the scale and the expressions, and then choose a number.

### Motivation

From C.I. Karageorghis, 2017, *Applying music in exercise and sport* (Champaign, IL: Human Kinetics).

This state is associated with a peak experience and, often, with superior sport performances.

Susan Jackson from Brisbane, Australia, and her colleagues Robert Eklund and Andrew Martin developed a range of instruments that assess facets of flow (Jackson, Eklund, & Martin, 2004). One of the easiest to use is the Short Flow State Scale, which has just nine items. The items address each of the nine dimensions of flow (see table 3.3; Jackson & Csikszentmihalyi, 1999). Given the highly transient or even elusive nature of flow, this scale should be administered immediately after an activity, while the memory of it is fresh in the participant's mind.

## Assessing the Effects of Music Using Observations, Interviews, and Focus Groups

In addition to the broad array of scientific instruments presented earlier, other assessment tools are available. Those who do not want to overload clients or athletes with measurement tools can assess using observations, structured sets of questions, or group discussions. Such approaches can also be supplemented by good old-fashioned note taking. From my experiences as a sport psychologist, I can assure you that taking notes on what athletes are doing or reporting creates a good impression; it shows that you are switched on, thinking ahead, and taking their views seriously.

Most of the instruments addressed thus far yield simple numerical scores. Although, for the most part, such instruments provide valid information on a range of music-related phenomena quickly and easily, a great deal of detail that can be found by observing or listening to people is often lost in numbers. Indeed, there has been a long-running scientific debate regarding the relative merits of quantitative and qualitative methods; in psychology, qualitative methods are very much the new kid on the block. In the music area, the consensus is that a combination of quantitative and qualitative methods (numbers, in vivo observations, and words) provides the most comprehensive understanding of people's motivations, preferences, and responses.

The observation, semi-structured interview, and focus group approaches discussed in this section are much more time-consuming than the earlier-presented surveys and questionnaires. Nonetheless, they yield rich information to help

**Table 3.3**   Nine Dimensions of Flow

| Flow dimension | Description |
| --- | --- |
| Challenge–skills balance | Known as the golden rule of flow, this refers to a match between the challenge of the task or situation and the skills the performer brings to it. |
| Action–awareness merging | This occurs when performers feel at one with the movements they are performing. |
| Clear goals | Performers know exactly what they need to do to achieve their goals during an activity. |
| Unambiguous feedback | The feedback performers receive about their performances facilitates the pursuit of their goals. |
| Concentration on the task at hand | Performers are focused on everything that is relevant to the activity. |
| Sense of control | Performers have a strong sense of control over aspects of their performances that lie within their control (e.g., performance accuracy). |
| Loss of self-consciousness | Concern for the self disappears in a flow state, and the performer experiences an absence of worries and negative thoughts. |
| Transformation of time | Flow frees the performer from the pressures of time; time seems to either speed up or slow down. |
| Autotelic experience | *Autotelic* means "an end in itself"; flow is an intrinsically rewarding and enjoyable experience involving full personal involvement without undue focus on the outcome (e.g., winning or losing). |

# SHORT FLOW STATE SCALE

Please answer the following questions in relation to your experience in the activity you have just completed. These questions relate to the thoughts and feelings you may have experienced while taking part. There are no right or wrong answers. Think about how you felt during the activity, and answer the questions using the rating scale. For each question circle the number that best matches your experience.

1. I feel I am competent enough to meet the high demands of the situation.

| Strongly disagree | Disagree | Neither agree nor disagree | Agree | Strongly agree |
|---|---|---|---|---|
| 1 | 2 | 3 | 4 | 5 |

2. I do things spontaneously and automatically without having to think.

| Strongly disagree | Disagree | Neither agree nor disagree | Agree | Strongly agree |
|---|---|---|---|---|
| 1 | 2 | 3 | 4 | 5 |

3. I have a strong sense of what I want to do.

| Strongly disagree | Disagree | Neither agree nor disagree | Agree | Strongly agree |
|---|---|---|---|---|
| 1 | 2 | 3 | 4 | 5 |

4. I have a good idea while I am performing about how well I am doing.

| Strongly disagree | Disagree | Neither agree nor disagree | Agree | Strongly agree |
|---|---|---|---|---|
| 1 | 2 | 3 | 4 | 5 |

5. I am completely focused on the task at hand.

| Strongly disagree | Disagree | Neither agree nor disagree | Agree | Strongly agree |
|---|---|---|---|---|
| 1 | 2 | 3 | 4 | 5 |

6. I have a sense of complete control over what I am engaged in.

| Strongly disagree | Disagree | Neither agree nor disagree | Agree | Strongly agree |
|---|---|---|---|---|
| 1 | 2 | 3 | 4 | 5 |

7. Time passes in a way that is rather different to how it normally passes.

| Strongly disagree | Disagree | Neither agree nor disagree | Agree | Strongly agree |
|---|---|---|---|---|
| 1 | 2 | 3 | 4 | 5 |

8. I find the experience to be truly rewarding.

| Strongly disagree | Disagree | Neither agree nor disagree | Agree | Strongly agree |
|---|---|---|---|---|
| 1 | 2 | 3 | 4 | 5 |

9. While engaged in the task, I am not concerned about what others might think of me.

| Strongly disagree | Disagree | Neither agree nor disagree | Agree | Strongly agree |
|---|---|---|---|---|
| 1 | 2 | 3 | 4 | 5 |

*(continued)*

**Short Flow State Scale** *(continued)*

### Scoring and Interpreting the Short Flow State Scale

There is one item for each of nine flow dimensions represented in the short scales (e.g., challenge–skills balance, clear goals). The item scores represent each dimension of flow. To obtain a flow state score, simply add the nine items and then divide by 9. A mean score between 1.0 and 3.5 means that you did not enter a flow state during the activity. If your score is between 3.6 and 4.4, you achieved a moderate degree of flow. A score of 4.5 and higher indicates a high degree of flow, or complete absorption in the task.

Flow items 1-5 are reprinted with permission from Mind Garden, Inc. (www.mindgarden.com). Flow items 6-9 were composed by the author and are based upon the content of the original Short Flow State Scale.

evaluate how people feel about music in exercise or sport and how to go about enhancing the experience of any music-related activity. Analysis of the responses is sure to provide significant insights that will enhance the services provided.

## Structured Observation of Individuals and Groups

Observation is a commonly applied approach of qualitative researchers and can reveal a great deal about how people respond to music across a wide range of environments. When I am asked to design playlists for marketing campaigns or compilation albums, I often spend time in the trendiest nightclubs in town observing how people respond to a range of recently released, or sometimes about-to-be released, tracks. I also like to observe how specific mixes, or combinations of tracks, influence people either in getting onto the dance floor or in becoming more animated on the dance floor. Such observations provide excellent clues as to how people may respond to this new music in the domain of exercise and sport, and they also keep me up-to-date on what people are listening to.

When conducting observations, it is best to blend into the environment so that people feel comfortable and behave normally. Taking notes is fine, but avoid looking at people during note taking because this can make them feel uncomfortable. During my nightclub observations, I carry a small notepad and pen in the inside pocket of my jacket and often sit in the chill-out zone or at the bar to make my notes. Avoid using cameras because they can alter how people behave by

making them self-conscious or even anxious. In some venues, you may be able to access security camera videos to gauge how people are responding to a music program. People tend not to be so conscious of security cameras, unless, of course, they are intent on committing a crime!

In such observations, I never record people's names or take notes that might identify a given person. In vivo observation in this context is all about the relationship between the music and the people. You might record whether people's facial expressions change in response to a particular track, whether they move faster, whether they are mouthing the lyrics, or whether one subgroup responds differently from another subgroup (e.g., males vs. females or teenagers vs. twentysomethings). Figure 3.3 can help with observations; feel free to adapt it to your needs.

The semi-structured interview schedule and focus group schedule can be used as supplements to your observations, or separately. Again, feel free to adapt the items to your needs and to use supplementary questions that allow you to delve deeper into the subject matter. Find a quiet room in your wellness center or sport club where you are unlikely to be disturbed. For an individual interview, set chairs at 45-degree angles to each other, so that the interviewee does not feel stared at the whole time and has a choice of looking at you or looking elsewhere. For a focus group session, set participants' chairs in a horseshoe and your chair facing theirs. It is advisable to digitally record the interviews or focus group sessions so that you can transcribe or analyze later what was said and how it was said to arrive at meaningful conclusions about people's experiences with

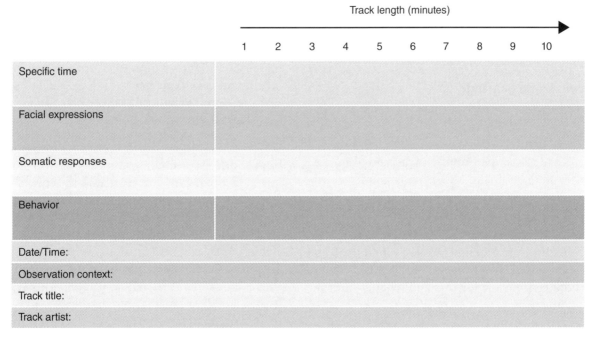

**Figure 3.3**  Music listening observation tool (M-LOT) for exercise and sport.

From C.I. Karageorghis, 2017, *Applying music in exercise and sport* (Champaign, IL: Human Kinetics).

music. During both individual interviews and focus groups, it is fine to take notes so that you can reflect later on a particularly hot topic or the way something was said.

**Semi-Structured Interview Schedule**

1. You have been _____ [*write the activity here; e.g., running*] with an MP3 player delivering musical accompaniment; what did you think of the music?

2. Did the music have any effect at all on how you were feeling?

3. Did the music have any effect at all on what you were thinking?

4. Did the music have any effect at all on what you did (i.e., how you performed)?

5. You used the music for the duration of your activity. Do you believe the music had the same effect on what you were doing throughout the session?

6. Do you believe the music had the same effect on how you were feeling throughout the session?

7. How well did you feel the music was coordinated with the task?

8. How would it have felt to perform the activity you did today without music? How might the experience have been different?

9. Describe the music that is best for you in a high-intensity task.

10. Were there any negative or unhelpful effects from listening to the music today?

11. What suggestions do you have to improve the music program for the future? Do you have any tracks or playlists that you would like to suggest? Why do you believe these are particularly effective?

When an interview veers off topic, gentle probing from the interviewer can reveal some real gems about people's experiences with music. Use the preceding questions as a guiding framework and adapt them to suit different individuals and circumstances. Do not be afraid of gaps in the conversation. Give your interviewees plenty of space to express themselves, and encourage them to talk through your body language (nodding occasionally, showing understanding and empathy). Providing short summaries of what they've said can ensure that you have understood them. This also demonstrates that you are fully attentive and interested in what they have to say. Follow up with gentle probing questions to encourage respondents to elaborate, expand on, and more fully describe their answers.

**Focus Group Schedule**

1. Consider the type of music that is appropriate to accompany _____ [*write the activity here; e.g., a cross-training class*]. Discuss in the group which type of music would be fitting and why. A good way to do this is to imagine participating in the various sections of the class.

2. In what ways might the music affect the feelings (e.g., emotions or moods) of an exerciser? What aspects of the music would be responsible for this and what might the effects be?

3. Do you believe the music would influence thought patterns and mental activity during the class?

4. How and to what extent might the music influence the behavior of class members? Are there both positive and negative aspects to this influence?

5. If music exerts an effect, do you believe it would be experienced in the same manner throughout the class (i.e., during the warm-up, in the main section, and during the cool-down)?

6. In shorter, more intense efforts during the class, such as high knees on the spot, do you believe the role of music would be different? Would its importance decrease or increase? Should we select the same kinds of music for different activities during the class?

7. What might exercisers' experiences be in a class without music—for example, if the PA system broke down halfway through the class? Do you believe this would affect class members' performances in any way?

8. To what extent is listening to music during a class unhelpful or negative?

9. How might we balance the different needs of class members in selecting music to accompany the class?

10. What do you feel about the music variety? How often should the music program change?

11. How might we improve group music programs? Do you have track or playlist suggestions? Why would these be good for the class?

These questions are intended to provide a framework for a focus group discussion. Each question is presented in turn, and the role of the facilitator (i.e., you) is to respond to the answers by probing and providing direction when necessary. You might have noticed that this process of elaboration is present in the way the questions are phrased. Encourage participants to pause and think about their answers and reflections while using all of their imaginative faculties to envisage the music-related scenarios they are describing.

# SUMMARY

In the past, a relatively haphazard approach characterized the selection of music in exercise and sport contexts. This approach has perhaps restricted the benefits that many athletes and exercisers derived from music, but also led to scientific studies whose findings were inconclusive (for reviews, see Karageorghis, 2016; Karageorghis & Terry, 1997; Terry & Karageorghis, 2011). As explored in chapter 2, when those who prescribe music consider a range of musical qualities, personal factors, and situational factors, a variety of benefits are likely to ensue. This chapter addressed, in practical terms, how these factors might be embraced in music selection processes and how music choices and playlists might be evaluated. We encountered tools that can be used to select music, to assess how effective music is during an activity, and to determine how people feel immediately after an activity involving music.

Tools such as the Brunel Music Rating Inventory-3 and Music Mood-Regulation Scale allow for large pools of tracks to be whittled down to coherent playlists for groups, teams, or individuals. The Music Mood-Regulation Scale also has a supplementary version that enables people to select tracks that are likely to regulate specific aspects of mood (e.g., liveliness or calmness). Athletes who want to select music to help create an optimal pre-competition mind-set can use the Mental Preparation Profile; an example of its application in field hockey appears in the sidebar Garth's Mental Preparation With Music. The Attentional Focusing Questionnaire allows practitioners to assess the attentional style of those in their charge. It can help them establish whether individuals are associators, dissociators, or switchers (i.e., have a flexible attentional style).

Four tools facilitate an assessment of the effects of music during exercise activities or sport training—the Rating of Perceived Exertion (RPE) Scale, the Feeling Scale, the Felt Arousal Scale, and a music-liking item. All have been used to complement each other in scientific studies (e.g., Hutchinson & Karageorghis, 2013; Karageorghis & Jones, 2014; Karageorghis et al., 2013). The RPE Scale has been particularly popular in exercise science labs the world over; well-selected music is typically associated with a reduction in RPE scores of ~12 percent. This is a phenomenon that you might explore with your athletes or exercisers. Although the RPE Scale is useful in assessing *what* people feel during physical activity, the Feeling Scale is helpful in assessing *how* they feel. Research has shown consistently that well-selected music can color the interpretation

of fatigue, even at high exercise intensities (e.g., Hutchinson & Karageorghis, 2013; Jones et al., 2014). The Felt Arousal Scale provides a window into how activated a person feels when exposed to a piece of music, whereas the music-liking item gives us a gestalt, or overall liking, score for a piece of music.

Tools that might be used after a task to assess the psychological influence of a single piece of music or a playlist include a measure of general mind-set, the Brunel Mood Scale (BRUMS), and two quick-to-administer measures of state attention and motivation, respectively. The state attention measure complements the Attentional Focusing Questionnaire particularly well; the former provides a snapshot index of attention, whereas the latter assesses attentional style. The Short Flow State Scale facilitates a post-task assessment of flow—an optimal psychological state often associated with peak performance. Sample questions for use during individual interviews and focus groups in relation to a music program were presented. The responses elicited by these questions can inform the compilation of playlists. My intention is that you choose from among these measures based on the people you are working with and the nature of the task. Almost all of the measures discussed in this chapter reappear in later chapters, in which we explore further how they might be applied in the field.

# Summary Points for Part I

1. Music has been used as an ergogenic, or work-enhancing, aid throughout human history and across many cultures because of its energizing, unifying, and motivating qualities.

2. To select music effectively for exercise and sport environments, we need to consider the musical characteristics of a piece, the performer's musical preferences and cultural background, the performer's goals, the setting, and the nature and intensity of the task.

3. The anaerobic threshold, which signifies the transition to high-intensity exercise, is a critical point in terms of the efficacy of music in reducing perceived exertion: music can reduce perceived exertion by around 10 percent below this threshold. Well-selected music can, however, enhance affect (how good a person feels) at workloads that exceed the anaerobic threshold.

4. In the selection of music for exercise and sport, we can draw on a theory and accompanying model (see figure 2.8) that embraces music-related factors, personal and situational moderators, and a range of outcomes.

5. From among the range of musical characteristics, rhythm, harmony, and lyrics are the most important for exercise and sport professionals to focus on.

6. Music affects the experience of exercise and sport participants in several ways, including distracting from the common symptoms of fatigue, promoting enjoyment, regulating arousal levels, prompting task-specific imagery, and serving as a metronome that regulates movement.

7. Music has a role to play in helping people prepare and recover from intense work during exercise, sports training, and competition.

8. In the asynchronous application of music, the relationship between exercise heart rate and preference for music tempo is nonlinear, and there is a narrow range of preferred tempi from ~120 to ~140 bpm. Increasing the tempo beyond this range does not appear to increase the psychological benefits to exercisers or athletes.

9. Using measurement tools is a good tactic to underpin music selections and to assess the responses of exercisers and athletes (e.g., Brunel Music Rating Inventory-3, Music Mood-Regulation Scale, Feeling Scale, Short Flow State Scale).

10. Music selection in the field of exercise and sport is certainly an art as well as a science; it relies on experience, instinct, and creativity, as well as scientific theory and data.

# PART II

# Using Music to Enhance Exercise and Workouts

Part II provides comprehensive coverage of the application of music in the exercise context. Similar to the other two parts of this book, the material is organized into three chapters. Chapter 4 deals with the use of music in individual exercise sessions, such as those that take place at home or in a park. It begins by considering the pre-workout phase and how music can be used to create an appropriate mind-set for a bout of physical activity—for example, as a type of prime. It also addresses how extramusical associations can be exploited to mentally prep people for exercise. The chapter discusses warm-up and flexibility routines and the role music can play in enhancing the experience of such activities. Many people like to use music as a rousing stimulus during strength-based workouts such as core and dynamic strength training; therefore, relevant music applications are presented. A lengthy section explores the selection of music for cardiorespiratory workouts that include running, indoor cycling, and using popular exercise machines (e.g., step mills, elliptical trainers, and rowing ergometers). The chapter ends with guidance on the use of music in the context of personal training and during the cool-down phase of a workout.

Chapter 5 explores music applications in group-based exercise, beginning with a brief overview of how class-based exercise to music evolved into the multiplicity of forms used today. A section is devoted to classes that use choreographed movements such as dance aerobics, BodyCombat, and Zumba, followed by a discussion of classes and group activities that involve the use of asynchronous, or background, music. Such classes include circuit training, Boxercise, and Pilates.

Chapter 6 presents two in-depth case studies—one about individual exercise and one about group exercise—to illustrate the principles addressed in the preceding two chapters. The first case study is about Sophie, a fortysomething mother of three with a passion for music, who wants to rekindle the exercise habit. Sophie seeks the advice of a lifestyle coach, who puts her on a music-fueled journey toward rediscovering the svelte physique of her college years. The second case study concerns Marino, a young and enthusiastic exercise-to-music instructor, who initially alienates his class members through inappropriate personal music choices, and then finds novel means by which to re-engage them.

# 4

# Individual Exercise and Workouts

*I think I should have no other mortal wants, if I could always have plenty of music. It seems to infuse strength into my limbs, and ideas into my brain. Life seems to go on without effort, when I am filled with music.*

—George Eliot (1819-1880), from *The Mill on the Floss*

It is perhaps in the realm of exercise that music-related interventions have had the most profound impact over the last four decades. It is almost the exception nowadays for people to conduct their daily exercise routine without musical accompaniment. From the lone jogger in a park to highly choreographed group exercise classes, music seems to play a seminal role in people's physical activity regimens.

This chapter explores how to optimize music selections for individuals who are working out in a variety of exercise modalities that include flexibility-, strength-, and aerobic-based activities such as running and stationary cycling. Parallels across exercise modalities are highlighted. Particular emphasis is given to the motivational role of music in promoting exercise adherence in Western populations. Keep in mind that when personal music devices or exercise machines are used, participants should use their own headphones or in-ear phones to maintain good hygiene.

## PRE-WORKOUT PREPARATION

The hustle and bustle of working life places an almost endless array of demands on us, and this is coupled with infinite choices in how we use our leisure time. A corporate boss asks for work to be returned by mid-afternoon, which precludes a lunchtime walk, or an impromptu meeting with colleagues after hours interferes with a Zumba class. Many of us grapple with conflicting demands such as these on a daily basis. It says something about human nature that the pull toward lifestyle-negative behaviors such as sitting in a stuffy office all day, eating fast food over a desk, and going for an all-night drinking session with friends from work is often far stronger than the pull toward lifestyle-positive behaviors such as following a balanced diet, taking regular breaks, and exercising. So why is that?

Although it is not exactly a conspiracy, marketers have a huge investment in compelling us to engage in behaviors and purchase products that we don't really need or want. Their transmissions harness our emotions and learning from a very young age. Most kids would choose the latest version of Xbox over a new soccer ball, which reflects the power of slick TV advertising rather than a disdain for kicking a ball around in the park. The result of this type of persuasion is less physical activity for kids—playing in the park cannot be easily monetized.

Marketers are keenly aware of a tendency called social proof, a phenomenon in which people respond to demands placed on them in a social environment to garner the approval of those around them. For example, by skipping the lunchtime walk, a worker can meet the boss' mid-afternoon deadline, which might lead to a promotion down the line. These decisions are also about immediate gratification. As a species we are not good at deferring gratification; we tend to go for quick wins at the expense of long-term contentment.

Activities such as regular daily exercise are intrinsically rewarding and beneficial to our long-term well-being. Unfortunately, they are often lost among the confusion of demands we face each day and the blitz by marketers encouraging us to drink beer, smoke cigarettes, gamble online, eat fatty foods, and play video games—all things we don't need or necessarily want.

## Music as a Prime

To overcome the almost overwhelming array of potentially negative external forces that inhibit progress toward their goals, people require tight routines, considerable self-discipline, and regular social support. Music can play a critical role by forming part of a routine and creating a mind-set associated with exercise and physical activity. Research shows that music can have a priming effect, meaning that it can activate the mind automatically (i.e., without conscious effort) and increase the motivation to exercise and take part in physical activity (e.g., Goerlich et al., 2012; Loizou & Karageorghis, 2015; Loizou, Karageorghis, & Bishop, 2014). Music can help elevate us; it can be a bridge to our higher purposes and goals.

Perhaps unsurprisingly, priming is a psychological technique popularized and refined by people in marketing. Back in the mid-1950s, market researcher James Vicary contrived an intriguing experiment in which the phrases *Drink Coca-Cola* and *Eat popcorn* were flashed on movie screens for just 0.03 seconds during the first half of movies (Vicary, 1957, cited in Radford, 2007). The viewers were not consciously aware of these visual primes (they appeared for too short a time to be registered), but they apparently led to an 18 percent increase in sales of Coca-Cola, and a whopping 58 percent increase in sales of popcorn during the interval.

Considerable controversy surrounded Vicary's claims and persists to the present day, but U.S. government legislators were quick to prevent companies from using such techniques to promote the purchase of consumer products. Despite the ban, similar techniques—now applied with a staggering degree of sophistication—are used routinely by advertisers. Apparently, the priming police have no teeth!

Research has demonstrated that people are largely unaware of the processes underlying their perceptions, pursuits, and behaviors (Levesque & Pelletier, 2003). Given that such processes play a pivotal role in health-related behaviors, taking some control over them through the measured application of pre-exercise music can create a pattern of thoughts and feelings that lead to the initiation of exercise-related behaviors. Music activates the emotional and movement-related segments of the brain such as the amygdala, temporal lobe, and cerebellum (see figure 2.2 in chapter 2) and can therefore greatly facilitate the mental preparation for exercise.

Scientists maintain that music has a particularly strong influence on the brain's unconscious processes (e.g., Levitin & Tirovolas, 2009; Scherer & Zentner, 2001). As noted in chapter 2, studies investigating high-intensity exercise have shown that well-selected music can enhance how people generally feel (affect), although it has little influence on their perceived exertion (RPE; Hutchinson & Karageorghis, 2013; Karageorghis et al. 2009). To a degree, such findings support the notion that the brain processes music at a subcortical, or automatic, level without conscious effort. It is precisely this apparent lack of a need for conscious processing that can make music an ideal form of prime for people who want to create an exercise habit. We do not have to think very much for music to influence our behaviors or feelings.

As discussed in chapter 2, both stimulative and calming music can prepare people mentally for exercise. Stimulating music can promote the entrainment of brain waves, the heartbeat, and the breathing rate, whereas calming music with strong extramusical associations can conjure the right type of mental imagery or thought processes (e.g.,

## DARREN'S OLYMPIC MARATHON DREAMS

Darren is a recreational runner with big ambitions. He was an above-average cross-country runner at school but stopped running when he began his first job as a motorcycle courier in London. Darren found it particularly hard to motivate himself to go out for a run on cold and dank winter evenings; it was much easier to sit back on the sofa with a can of lager and enjoy whatever was on TV. The lack of physical activity during the winter months soon spilled over into the summer, and like many boys in their late teens, Darren drifted into some rather undesirable habits: late nights, too many burgers and chips, binge drinking with his friends on the weekends, and precious little exercise.

Darren had an interest in movies. Through his film club, he watched Hugh Hudson's classic *Chariots of Fire* for the first time. He loved the heroic imagery that characterized the movie as well as Vangelis' uplifting soundtrack. After almost a year of being a courier, Darren took a close look at himself and didn't like what he saw. He resolved that it was time to reinitiate his running routine. He hooked up with an old acquaintance from school, who was a halfway-decent athlete, and they ran together or went to the gym four or five times a week. The improvement in Darren's fitness and waistline was dramatic.

Near the end of October, when it was chilly outside and the nights were closing in, Darren felt his motivation diminishing, but he recalled the positive influence of the *Chariots of Fire* theme. Now, whenever Darren feels his motivation flagging, he plays the familiar theme on his iPod docking station at a high intensity while he stretches. At the same time, he imagines himself running against the Kenyan athletes in the closing stages of the Olympic marathon. In three or four minutes, he is fully primed and ready to head out the door.

heroic images, thoughts of overcoming adversity, motion-related thoughts). Table 4.1 lists examples of musical works that function particularly well as preparatory tracks for physical activity programs. The tracks are arranged in three categories: those that are intrinsically stimulating (i.e., upbeat and energetic), those that are relatively slow in tempo but have strong extramusical associations, and those that both are stimulating *and* have strong extramusical associations.

Situations and circumstances will determine which category in table 4.1 you might wish to dip into for a pre-exercise track (consider also the theoretical model in figure 2.8). The first category, intrinsically stimulating, works particularly well for diverse groups of exercisers who do not necessarily have common cultural reference points (e.g., a physiotherapy rehabilitation class with a mix of age groups and ethnicities).

The second category, slow tempo with strong extramusical associations, would serve individ-uals or small groups of exercisers with common cultural reference points (e.g., they enjoy similar movies, have similar musical tastes, frequent the same social venues). The key consideration is that the exerciser(s) do not require a great deal of bodily activation but more mental stimulation, perhaps as a precursor to engaging in a stretching, yoga, or Pilates session. Older people and intro-verts tend not to like highly stimulative music; therefore, the second category might be ideal for them. This is a general rule that certainly does not hold in all instances; if you happen to be work-ing with a 74-year-old grandma who's into Led Zeppelin played at high amplitude, you'd better pander to her tastes!

The third category is for individuals or groups with common cultural points of reference who are about to engage in vigorous and demanding physical activity (e.g., a high-intensity run or a step class). Here the goal is to activate or stimulate both the mind and body to a high degree. Younger

**Table 4.1** Pre-Exercise Tracks: Intrinsically Stimulating, Slow Tempo With Strong Extramusical Associations, and Intrinsically Stimulating With Strong Extramusical Associations

| | Track title | Artist(s) or composer | Tempo (bpm) | Genre |
|---|---|---|---|---|
| **Intrinsically stimulating** | Firework | Katy Perry | 124 | Disco rock |
| | Do It Right | Martin Solveig feat. Tkay Maidza | 125 | Dance |
| | María | Ricky Martin | 127 | Latin pop |
| | Shut Up And Dance | Walk the Moon | 128 | Pop rock |
| | Dare (La La La) | Shakira | 144 | Dance |
| **Slow tempo with strong extramusical associations** | You Raise Me Up | Josh Groban | 59 | Inspirational |
| | I Believe I Can Fly | R. Kelly | 60 | R&B |
| | Flying Without Wings | Westlife | 72 | Pop |
| | One Moment In Time | Whitney Houston | 78 | Pop/soul |
| | Going The Distance (Theme from *Rocky*) | Bill Conti | 91 | Orchestral |
| **Intrinsically stimulating with strong extramusical associations** | Eye Of The Tiger | Survivor | 109 | Hard rock |
| | *Raider's March* (theme music from the Indiana Jones movies) | John Williams | 128 | Classical/soundtrack |
| | Don't Look Down | Martin Garrix feat. Usher | 128 | Progressive house |
| | Let's Get Loud | Jennifer Lopez | 131 | Salsa |
| | Don't Stop Me Now | Queen | 158 | Rock |

*Note:* All of these tracks can be located on YouTube.

and more extroverted exercisers tend to report a preference for more stimulative music as well. You might wonder why there is no fourth category of slow-tempo music without extramusical associations (i.e., sedative music). Well, we know from research, and to a certain degree common sense, that such a category has no meaningful role to play in preparing people for exercise (Karageorghis & Priest, 2012a). It can, however, play a role in preparing people for sport (see chapter 7).

## Warm-Up and Flexibility Routines

Before engaging in any form of strenuous physical activity, people should raise their heart rates gradually to fully prepare the musculoskeletal system for what is to come. To apply the principle of entrainment (see chapter 2), exercisers and athletes can use music to elevate the heart rate in a smooth and gradual transition from the sedate

state to the highly active state. The principles of extramusical associations can also be applied liberally during warm-up and flexibility routines, particularly with slower music selections.

The typical stages of a warm-up for exercise are active stretching (gentle, movement based); a brief aerobic activity to get the blood flowing, raise core temperature, and elevate the heart rate (e.g., jogging, cycling, or skipping); and some deeper stretching, perhaps holding stretches for six to eight seconds (also known as static stretching). Thereafter, some forms of exercise routine, such as dance-based classes, use ballistic stretches (e.g., swinging each leg from side to side while holding on to a bar). In designated flexibility sessions, some instructors use passive stretching, in which stretches are held with slight manual pressure from a partner to increase the range of motion.

My purpose here is not to detail the many types of warm-up and flexibility routines; numerous texts provide extensive coverage (e.g., Michael

Alter's excellent *Science of Flexibility*). Rather, my intention is to address music selection considerations for warm-up and flexibility routines. Table 4.2 lists these considerations with reference to some of the key components of music introduced in chapter 1. Because passive stretching involves constant communication and physical interaction with a partner as well as a focus on holding what

**Table 4.2**   Music Considerations for Warm-Up and Flexibility

| Music components | Active stretching | Aerobic activity | Static stretching | Ballistic stretching | Passive stretching |
|---|---|---|---|---|---|
| Melody | Not too busy; creates a feel-good vibe | Melody of secondary importance to rhythmic qualities, yet still uplifting | Gentle melody and not too intricate | Melodically simple with positive feel | Long, sustained notes, avoiding complexity and musical conversations |
| Harmony | Gives a sense of optimism and positive energy | In the major mode without complex harmonic progressions | Warm harmonies that avoid rapid progressions | Gives a sense of dynamism and verve | Warm, sustained harmonies avoiding complexity and rapid progressions |
| Rhythm | Simple structure with lack of syncopation | Clearly discernible beat with syncopation that complements the rhythm of the activity | Gentle rhythm with a lack of syncopation and no strong beat | More dynamic rhythm that is syncopated and energizes | Very gentle rhythm with an absence of syncopation |
| Tempo (bpm) | 90-110 | 100-120 | 90-110 | 100-120 | 80-100 |
| Meter | Does not require a strong meter; gentle pulsation is sufficient | Meter needs to be clearly extractable to direct movement patterns | No need for strong meter—just enough to keep the heart rate suitably elevated | A strong meter is necessary to direct movement and energize the listener | Gentle pulsations without strongly identifiable meter |
| Lyrics | Gentle and inspiring to entice the exerciser into the routine | Raise the spirits and sit comfortably within the music's rhythmic structure | Not of central importance, but should blend with the nature of the task | Reinforce the nature of the activity and activate the listener | Instrumental music preferable, or lyrics that are not clearly identifiable to discourage syntactic processing |
| Timbre | Warm sound that draws the person in to the activity (e.g., piano, strings, smooth voice) | Predominance of rhythm section instruments to direct movement (e.g., bass guitar and percussion) | Blend of instruments to create low-tempo, warm soundscape | Resurgence of rhythm section to direct movements and uplift the listener | Warm, resonant, and soothing sounds, perhaps orchestral, that fade into the background |
| Dynamics and volume | Limited dynamic range and low volume (60 dBA) | Broader dynamic range and moderate volume (65 dBA) | Limited dynamic range and low volume (60 dBA) | High-end dynamics and moderate-to-high volume (70 dBA) | Low-end dynamics and very low volume (55 dBA) |

can be somewhat unusual positions, the music for this activity is intentionally the least stimulating and most ambient (e.g., has the lowest volume). Passive stretching is typically not used prior to vigorous exercise routines; it might be used afterward or as a stand-alone session.

Having examined some of the key considerations for warm-up and flexibility, table 4.3 gives five examples of tracks for each of the five activities detailed in table 4.2. It is important to remember that the music is not intended to have

an ergogenic, or work-enhancing, effect during warm-up and flexibility routings. Rather, its purpose is to help exercisers prepare physically and mentally for the more vigorous forms of activity that typically follow.

Nonetheless, for some people, stretching- and flexibility-related activities are the mainstay of their physical activity programs and can be also conducted synchronously. In such instances, greater emphasis should be placed on the regularity and strength of the beat of the music, to

**Table 4.3**   Tracks for Warm-Up and Flexibility

| | Track | Artist(s) or composer | Tempo (bpm) | Genre |
|---|---|---|---|---|
| **Active stretching (aerobic activity)** | Roar | Katy Perry | 90 | Pop |
| | As | George Michael with Mary J. Blige | 93 | Pop/R&B |
| | Girl On Fire | Alicia Keys | 93 | Pop/R&B |
| | Suddenly I See | KT Tunstall | 100 | Pop rock |
| | Liberian Girl | Michael Jackson | 105 | Pop |
| | Work From Home | Fifth Harmony feat. Ty Dolla $ign | 105 | Pop |
| | Downtown | Macklemore & Ryan Lewis | 110 | Hip-hop/funk pop |
| | The Way I Are | Timbaland feat. Keri Hilson | 115 | Hip-hop |
| | Sugar | Maroon 5 | 120 | Disco/pop |
| | Rather Be | Clean Bandit | 121 | House |
| **Static stretching** | Hold My Hand | Michael Jackson feat. Akon | 90 | R&B |
| | Read All About It, pt. III | Emeli Sandé | 98 | R&B |
| | Sweet Home Alabama | Lynyrd Skynyrd | 99 | Southern rock |
| | She Will Be Loved | Maroon 5 | 102 | Pop rock |
| | Set Fire To The Rain | Adele | 109 | Pop |
| **Ballistic stretching** | Breathe And Stop | Q-Tip | 100 | Hip-hop |
| | Bounce | Timbaland feat. Missy Elliott and Justin Timberlake | 100 | Hip-hop |
| | Focus | Ariana Grande | 100 | Pop |
| | Work It | Missy Elliott | 102 | Hip-hop |
| | Men In Black | Will Smith | 108 | Hip-hop |
| **Passive stretching** | Porcelain | Moby | 96 | Ambient pop |
| | Experience | Ludovico Einaudi | 93 | Classical |
| | Return To Innocence | Enigma | 88 | New age |
| | American Beauty | Thomas Newman | 85 | Classical |
| | Coming Home | Röyksopp | 80 | Ambient pop |

*Note:* All of these tracks can be located on YouTube.

clearly define the segments of the stretching or flexibility routine (see the sidebar Yoga Goes Pop in chapter 5).

# STRENGTH-BASED WORKOUTS

In surveys and interview-based work done with exercisers, it is striking how much the rock genre—and hard rock in particular—comes up as a favored accompaniment for strength-based workouts. The more intense variants of hip-hop are a very close second. That is certainly not to say that rock and hip-hop provide the ideal accompaniment for everyone who weight trains. The apparent predominance of these genres might be far more reflective of the types of people who either hang out in gyms or publish survey results online for weight training devotees.

Many people, however, engage in strength-based workouts in other locations, such as in their own homes, on beaches, and in their local parks. These exercise venues may not be so strongly associated with hard rock and hip-hop. The gym may attract certain personality types, and these types express a preference for music that is quite aggressive (such music is associated with male gym users in particular). Suffice it to say that many genres beyond rock and hip-hop work perfectly well for strength-based routines (more on this later).

Because research into how music affects strength performance is minimal, the recommendations in this section are based on the dozen or so published studies that exist in tandem with interview-based and anecdotal evidence (e.g., examinations of strength training and bodybuilding websites). Given that strength-based workouts are predominantly anaerobic and engage large sections of the musculature in high-intensity efforts, the music does require a strong arousing, or psych-up, element for many people, but this is not essential. A hulking, extroverted male in his 30s is likely to be driven by the deafening roar and crashing guitars of Iron Maiden, whereas a petite and introverted female in her 60s might prefer the more soothing sound of Vivaldi's later orchestral works, not least because their goals and self-perceptions would be entirely different.

Much depends on the preferred mind-set when working out. Young go-getters and ardent goal-setters invariably express a desire for more external stimulation during their weights workouts than do people in their parents' generation. People in middle or old age may not want to push hard, but just go through the motions for a safe and pain-free workout that allows them to function optimally. Given the high-intensity nature of strength training, research shows that music has a bigger role to play before lifting—as a type of psychomotor stimulant—than it does while lifting. In fact, people lifting relatively heavy weights (e.g., in excess of 70 percent of 1-repetition max) find attending to music while lifting to be challenging. Most of the benefit from music comes between sets when they are recovering and mentally preparing for the next set.

Weight training using synchronous music is also challenging because as people tire, their movement rate invariably slows down for the last few reps and they immediately go out of sync with the beat. Nonetheless, when working out with light weights and emphasizing high repetitions (e.g., 20 to 25 reps), it is relatively easy to use music in a synchronous mode, and the ideal tempo range tends to be 110 to 145 bpm. A great deal of commercially recorded music is available in this range, so it is easy to find music to suit.

As an interesting add-on, the performance of slow sets can be achieved by completing half a repetition (e.g., the flexion stage of a biceps curl) over two measures, or bars, of music at the lower end of the 110 to 145 bpm tempo range. This means, for example, completing an entire biceps curl in 16 musical beats with 8 beats to flex the elbow joints and 8 beats to extend them. The idea behind slow sets is that slowing the movement rate and applying tension over a greater duration promotes new muscle growth. Because music serves a metronomic function, it can be used just as easily to regulate slow movement as it can to maintain fast movement. Music can also be used to emphasize either the concentric or eccentric phase of a movement through completion of that phase over eight musical beats (two bars) with the opposing phase over four musical beats (one bar). Various mathematical combinations are possible depending on the desired emphasis (e.g., two beats for concentric and six beats for eccentric).

## Core Strength

*Core strength* is a popular term that captures a broad range of strength-related activities. During my days as an athlete, coaches talked a great deal about the importance of abdominal strength and back strength; on occasion, they would also mention poise, posture, and stability. Nowadays, all of this appears to come under the umbrella of core strength. The primary muscles involved in developing core strength are the diaphragm (breathing muscle), transversus abdominis, internal obliques, multifidus, quadratus lumborum, and pelvic floor. The action of these muscles contracting together on the contents of the abdominal cavity (i.e., the internal organs) provides support to the spine and pelvis during physical exercise (see figure 4.1).

I do not wish to enter into a discussion here regarding the pros and cons of core strength training and how it compares to more general exercise modes such as walking and swimming. As I write these lines, the scientific evidence of whether core training confers significant benefits in terms of greater power output, reduced risk of injury, superior health maintenance, and so forth, remains mixed, at best. In some gyms that I visit in the United Kingdom, United States, and Australia, one might be forgiven for believing that core training is a type of new age religion—such is the reverence with which gym instructors and personal trainers speak of it. Throughout this chapter, my intention is to provide guidelines on music selection for physical activities. I leave it for others to question how exercise programs should be constructed, what the balance of activities within such programs should be, and what the long-term health benefits might be.

Core strength exercises are conducted using isotonic, isokinetic, and isometric muscular contractions (see the sidebar Types of Muscular Contractions Used in Strength Training for explanations). If you're not familiar with these types of contractions, familiarize yourself with them, because they pertain to a greater or lesser extent to each form of strength training. It should be noted, however, that core muscles can *only*

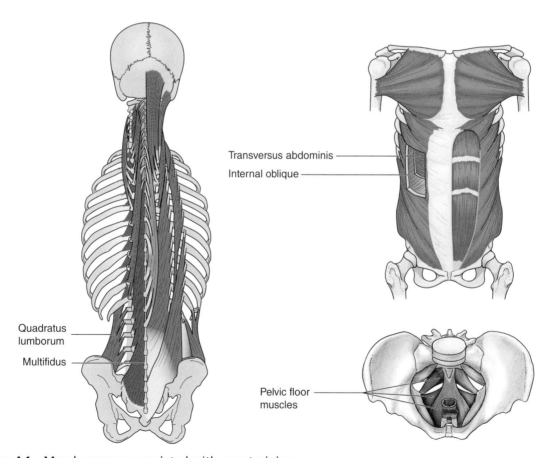

Transversus abdominis
Internal oblique

Quadratus lumborum
Multifidus

Pelvic floor muscles

**Figure 4.1** Muscle groups associated with core training.

# TYPES OF MUSCULAR CONTRACTIONS USED IN STRENGTH TRAINING

**Isotonic**  In an isotonic contraction, tension remains unchanged while muscle length changes. Performing an incline sit-up at a constant speed is a good example. The two types of isotonic contractions are concentric and eccentric. During concentric contraction (e.g., lifting upward in the sit-up movement), the muscle tension rises to meet the resistance (gravity, in this instance) and then remains the same as the muscle shortens. During eccentric contraction (e.g., the descending part of the sit-up), the muscle lengthens because the resistance is greater than the force produced by the muscle.

**Isokinetic**  An isokinetic muscle contraction is one in which the muscle contracts and shortens at a constant rate. This type of contraction requires special training equipment that increases the load in response to the muscle contraction speeding up, and vice versa (e.g., Exerbotics). The benefit of this mode of training is that the muscle gains strength evenly throughout the range of movement. Thus, isokinetic training is one of the fastest ways to increase muscle strength. For this reason, exercises involving isokinetic contractions are often the mainstay of physical rehabilitation programs.

**Isometric**  An isometric contraction is one in which the joint angle and muscle length do not change during contraction. Isometric exercises are done in static positions, rather than being dynamic through a range of motion. Good examples of isometric exercises that develop core strength are the plank (figure 4.2) and the abdominal bridge (lying on the back with knees bent and raising the hips to create a straight line from knees to shoulders).

**Figure 4.2**  The plank is a commonly-used core strength exercise that entails an isometric contraction.

contract isometrically, whereas core strength exercises can involve all three types of contractions. The type of muscular contractions and the rate of movement involved in an exercise have a bearing on the optimal music selection for it.

Core training requires the maintenance of good form, a predominant internal (associative) focus, and strong kinesthetic awareness. Kinesthesia is the sense that detects bodily position, weight, or the movement of muscles, tendons, and joints. Accordingly, music that is loud and highly distractive is not the ideal accompaniment for such training. Rather, the music needs to complement the nature of the activity and the type of mental state that will optimize performance (see figure 2.8).

No genres are especially conducive to core strength training, albeit highly arousing genres, such as heavy metal and speed garage, are generally to be avoided. Because core training is generally not conducted at a high movement rate given the emphasis on strict form and breathing patterns, music of a moderate tempo is ideal, particularly if trying to sync movements to the beat. The optimal tempo range is ~105 to ~125 bpm, and the tempo should match the expected heart rate when working out asynchronously (i.e., the music is in the background). If a person achieves a relatively high working heart rate during core strength work (e.g., 140 to 160 bpm), then music at the top end of that tempo range would be most desirable (possibly as high as 130 bpm).

The ideal music for core strength training would have a simple melodic and harmonic structure (not too distracting or mentally challenging), a steady but not strong beat, a lack of syncopation, lyrics that reinforce the nature of the activity but are not too obtrusive, a rhythm section–based timbre with warmth (not harshness), a limited dynamic range, and moderate volume. Some people might refer to this as middle-of-the-road music—in the background, not too distracting, and with some rhythmic cues and lyrical affirmations.

That said, for people who are associators (see the discussion of the Attentional Focusing Questionnaire in chapter 3), I do not recommend the use of music for core training. Because their dominant attentional style is conducive to the nature of such training activities, music could be disruptive. Table 4.4 contains a selection of sample tracks, going across the recommended tempo range and from a range of genres, that are suitable for core strength training. As with all of the guidelines in this book, use the principles and examples to construct playlists that are suited to the demographic profile, musical predilections, and personalities of your clients (or yourself; see figure 2.8).

## Dynamic Strength Training

Dynamic strength training (see also Power-Based Sports in chapter 7), which entails both isotonic and isokinetic contractions, involves the lengthening or shortening of a muscle during a contraction. This type of training takes many forms, including stage training, circuit training, pyramid training, breakdown training, negative training, slow training, powerlifting, and supersets (see the glossary for definitions). Essentially, these differ in terms of how much is lifted, how much recovery is taken, how fast the weight is lifted, which part of the contraction is emphasized (concentric or eccentric), and the kind of strength development that ensues.

For example, pyramid training entails decreasing the number of reps in consecutive sets of an exercise while at the same time increasing the weight. Once at the top of the pyramid (e.g., three reps at a weight equivalent to 90 percent of 1-repetition max), the exerciser descends the pyramid by decreasing the weight and increasing the number of repetitions in each set. This is an intense routine that can promote the development of both muscular endurance and absolute

**Table 4.4** Tracks for Core Strength Training

| Track | Artist(s) | Tempo (bpm) | Genre |
|---|---|---|---|
| Hip Hop Hooray | Naughty by Nature | 100 | Hip-hop |
| It's Time | Imagine Dragons | 105 | Alternative rock |
| Just The Way You Are (Amazing) | Bruno Mars | 110 | Pop |
| Payphone | Maroon 5 feat. Wiz Khalifa | 112 | Pop |
| Breaking News | Michael Jackson | 113 | Pop |
| Clothes Off | Gym Class Heroes | 115 | Rap rock |
| We Are Young | Fun | 116 | Pop |
| Stronger (What Doesn't Kill You) | Kelly Clarkson | 116 | Pop rock |
| Don't Stop The Music | Rihanna | 122 | Dance-pop |
| Telephone | Lady Gaga | 122 | Pop/R&B |
| Hideaway | Kiesza | 124 | Deep house |
| Me Too | Meghan Trainor | 124 | Pop |
| Starships | Nicki Minaj | 125 | Europop |
| La La La | Naughty Boy feat. Sam Smith | 125 | R&B |
| Stronger | Clean Bandit | 125 | Dance/synthpop |

*Note:* All of these tracks can be located on YouTube.

strength. As with all of the training techniques mentioned in this book, pyramid training has many permutations (e.g., ascending, descending, double wave loads); you can find out more about them in training manuals (e.g., Nick Tumminello's *Strength Training for Fat Loss*).

By contrast, supersets, popular among bodybuilders, require the exerciser to perform two or three different exercises, one immediately after the other, followed by a recovery period before repeating the superset. This is most often for the same muscle group (e.g., pec deck followed by decline bench press, followed by seated incline press), but it can be for different muscle groups (e.g., agonist coupled with antagonist; leg extension followed by hamstring curl). Leading trainers advocate this approach for building muscle mass because the time under tension (TUT) for each muscle group can be increased.

When selecting music, people need to consider the specific demands of each type of workout and how music may facilitate or even impede the performance of the task at hand. For very intense workouts that draw on every sinew in the body, music can certainly be an unwanted distraction beyond preparing mentally for the workout or aiding recovery afterward. For lower-intensity workouts, such as circuit training, music can be fully integrated and even used to regulate the activity (see the section Circuit Training in chapter 5).

Music during dynamic strength training should reflect the type of mind-set that will likely lead to a fulfilling and productive session. It should also reflect the vigorous and high-intensity nature of the activity. Outside of exercise classes, which are addressed comprehensively in chapter 5, dynamic strength training is seldom conducted in a synchronous mode, and so the asynchronous application of music is emphasized here.

A couple of primary considerations when choosing music during dynamic strength training are the expected heart rate (to determine an appropriate tempo) and the lyrical affirmations of the songs. A secondary consideration is the harmonic content of the music. Our research shows that people performing dynamic strength training prefer darker harmonies, rather than the lighter, warmer harmonic textures of music that might be used for running or recuperating. Hard-edged music genres such as rock and gangsta rap are often espoused by strength training devotees (Priest & Karageorghis, 2008).

Perhaps the negatively valenced nature of such music reflects the physical pain that can be experienced and the slightly masochistic mind-set needed to prevail in intense resistance training. This expressed preference might also mirror the musical tastes and personalities of people who enjoy conducting their workouts in gyms. Keep in mind that links between musical genres and particular activities are not set in stone. Several decades from now, weight trainers will be using different music genres, although they are likely to have some similarities with those currently in vogue (i.e., aggressive, rousing, anti-establishment).

During dynamic strength activities that entail intermittent periods of recovery, heart rate rarely exceeds 70 to 80 percent of maximum. It is usually around 50 to 60 percent of max, unless very heavy weights are lifted, in which case it shoots up during the lift and recovers quickly immediately afterward. The relatively low expected heart rates during such training suggest that a tempo range of 110 to 130 bpm would be ideal. Studies correlating music tempo preference with exercise heart rate during dynamic strength training have yet to be conducted, but an optimal range of 110 to 130 bpm is expected given the research on other forms of physical activity such as walking, running, and cycling, wherein music is applied asynchronously (see chapter 2) (Karageorghis & Jones, 2014; Karageorghis, Jones, & Low, 2006; Karageorghis, Jones, & Stuart, 2008; Karageorghis et al., 2011).

On the basis of anecdotal evidence, I suggest that going below this theoretically optimal range is fine as long as the music is rhythmically busy and has the right sort of lyrical content (Priest & Karageorghis, 2008). The music does not regulate weight training routines as much as it inspires people with its lyrical content (e.g., Karageorghis et al., 2013; Priest & Karageorghis, 2008). For dynamic strength training, the messages conveyed by the music need to promote and reinforce the nature of the activity. Alternatively, they need to bolster self-esteem, self-confidence, or both.

The favorite songs of iron pumpers tend to carry messages of strength (e.g., "Harder, Better, Faster, Stronger" by Daft Punk), power (e.g., "The Power" by Snap!), dominance (e.g., "Mama Said Knock You Out" by LL Cool J), gritty determination (e.g., "Not Letting Go" by Tinie Tempah feat. Jess Glynne), aggression (e.g., "Fistful Of Steel" by Rage Against the Machine), rebellion (e.g., "Fight The Power" by Public Enemy), and sexual prowess (e.g., "Sexy And I Know It" by LMFAO). In many hard rock/heavy metal and hip-hop tracks, you can find almost all of these lyrical strands in abundance. These musical idioms appear to reinforce and almost symbolize the mind-set of the modern-day lifter. Table 4.5 contains some of the all-time favorite tracks reported by the lifting brigade on their websites and in their online forums. You can see that this list has much more to do with swagger and a rebellious attitude than any particular rhythmic quality.

In addition to the static and dynamic varieties, there is a third category of strength training known as explosive strength training. This is used predominantly in preparation for a range of sports that require explosive actions such as sprinting and jumping (e.g., American football, basketball,

**Table 4.5**   Popular Tracks for Dynamic Strength Training

| Track | Artist(s) | Tempo (bpm) | Genre | Brief analysis |
|---|---|---|---|---|
| Bait | Wale | 68 | Hip-hop | This track has a slow underlying tempo but quite a pulsating and complex rhythm sitting above it; this gives a sense of dynamism. The lyrics repeat the word *work* and thus reinforce the fact that high levels of physical exertion are called for. |
| Iron Man | Black Sabbath | 74 | Heavy metal | This song oozes machismo and has a simple structure. The theme is a fictional Iron Man who spreads fear in all around him. The link to men pumping iron does not require a great leap of imagination. |
| Power | Kanye West feat. Dwele | 77 | Hip-hop | This aggressive rap is laced with expletives and underscored by a highly syncopated drum pattern. The lyrics center on a dystopia in which one man yields all the power. Clearly, lifters like to imagine themselves as the power brokers of the gym. |
| Black Dog | Led Zeppelin | ~82 (not an even tempo) | Hard rock | This track has an uneven rhythmic structure, but it carries a strong message. The lyrics center on bodily movement and perspiration—a perfect combination for the business end of a weights workout. Jimmy Page's improvisational magic on the electric guitar is a highly uplifting feature. |
| Don't Push Me | 50 Cent feat. Lloyd Banks and Eminem | 86 | Hip-hop | The rhythmic accompaniment is quite disorientating, while the rap includes the work of two of the finest exponents of the art—50 Cent and Eminem. The content is highly adult in nature and places lifters at the hub of a gangsta's paradise in which they rule the roost. |
| Fight Music | D12 | 89 | Hip-hop | This track is heavy on hostility and majors on the intent to do harm to others. It places the listener in a dark mood through its highly explicit lyrics. As well as being popular among those who weight train, the track could work equally well for a boxer about to enter the ring. |

| Track | Artist(s) | Tempo (bpm) | Genre | Brief analysis |
|---|---|---|---|---|
| Back In Black | AC/DC | 91 | Rock | This heavy metal classic is characterized by crashing guitars and a screaming vocal delivery by Brian Johnson. The motivational apex of the track is a hard-core, bluesy guitar solo that comes in at around 2 minutes. The solo makes a welcome return during the outro. |
| Rip This Joint | The Rolling Stones | 98 | Rock 'n' roll | You're taken on an auditory roller-coaster ride with this one. This lively and energetic song gets the toes tapping and the heart pumping. The lyrics don't have anything particularly to do with working out but contain many colorful American cultural references. |
| Mama Said Knock You Out | LL Cool J | 102 | Hip-hop | It is apposite that on the music video, LL Cool J performs the track from the center of a boxing ring. It's a quintessential hip-hop beat with a defiant and totally self-affirming lyric. A nuanced aspect of the piece that enhances its appeal is the skillful emphasis on words such as *boom, move,* and *blastin,* to fill them with greater significance. |
| Time 4 Sum Aksion | Redman | 103 | Hip-hop | A pulsating rhythm and affirmative lyric greet the listener. This is a power-packed track that elicits a super-high level of activation. The juxtaposition of gangsta jive with a boxing theme imbues the track with a hard edge. A line about knocking gold teeth loose is particularly evocative. |
| Fight The Power | Public Enemy | 106 | Hip-hop | A classic from the annals of hip-hop, this track is all about fighting the establishment. There's a funky rhythmic underlay and empowering lyrics that serve as an ideal complement to dynamic strength training. The track is essentially about the American civil rights movement, but its central message is universally appealing. |
| Highway To Hell | AC/DC | 116 | Rock | The track opens with a catchy guitar riff coupled with a strong backbeat. Lyrically, the piece is uplifting in tone despite the rather negative title that is repeated during the refrain. I imagine that lifters who enjoy this track in the gym would find it equally conducive to a long-distance road trip. It is a standard on music-for-driving compilations, after all. |
| For Whom The Bell Tolls | Metallica | 118 | Heavy metal | This track has a slightly menacing feel about it, and the sense of imminent danger is perpetuated by an extended intro. The title is borrowed from the writings of the English poet and cleric John Donne. The bell is a funeral bell, and so this is a dark musical work through and through. |
| Everlong | Foo Fighters | 158 | Rock | This song is characterized by a blistering tempo and the use of power chords on the electric guitar. The energy seems to build gradually, and the central message is about living in the moment. The notion of immersion in the here and now is germane to getting the most out of a weights workout. |

*Note:* All of these tracks can be located on YouTube.

# *JYMMIN*: A NEAT COMBINATION OF *JAMMIN* AND *GYMMIN*

Most of us know how gratifying it can be to work out and listen to some great tunes while doing so. The music can help us get optimally psyched, making the workout a sheer delight rather than physical drudgery. Some of us might also know how wonderful it is to play a musical instrument to express our innermost emotions or relieve the stresses and strains of the day. Well, imagine combining both into one—workout machines that make music! That's exactly what German scientist Thomas Fritz and his colleagues did in creating a music-inspired form of exercise known as Jymmin (Fritz et al., 2013).

The research team rigged up three commonly used exercise machines—a tower for underarm pull-downs, a stair stepper, and an abdominal trainer—to music composition software. The result was a machine that allowed exercisers to use their movements to create original musical compositions in real time that played at a constant 130 bpm. Exercisers would have the feeling that they caused the emerging symphony of sound with their muscle contractions. Not only did the researchers design this musical multigym; they also went on to test it to see whether it worked.

Sixty-one volunteers were placed in groups of three and asked to select their favorite exercise machine. They worked out for three 6-minute sessions. In one of the sessions, they made music together using the rigged composition software. The following two sessions functioned as controls: in one they listened to background music and in another they performed 10-second bursts of isometric movements accompanied by background music. The three groups of volunteers exercised at their chosen rate, and they gave a rating of perceived exertion (see chapter 3) after each session. During each exercise bout, the research team monitored the type of muscle contraction employed and how much oxygen was used.

In 53 of the 61 volunteers, RPE scores were lower when they were making the movement-generated music compared to listening to a similar musical composition in the background (control conditions; see figure 4.3). The pattern of movement also changed: when listening to music in the

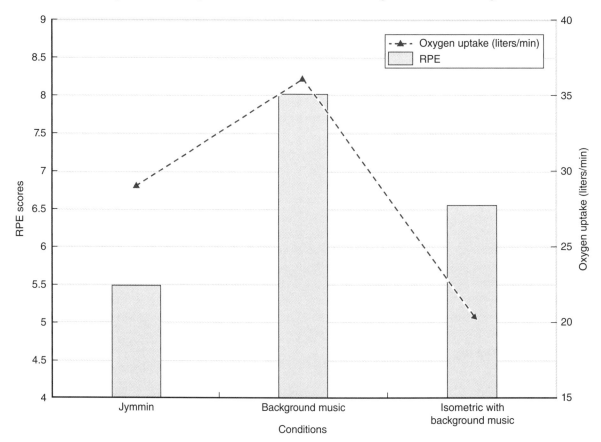

**Figure 4.3**  RPE scores and oxygen uptake in the jymmin, background music, and isometric conditions.

background, volunteers moved in a highly repetitive manner; when jymmin, they used a greater proportion of isometric contractions to generate music that they perhaps found pleasurable.

Although the total force applied to the exercise machine did not differ across the three conditions, the experimental subjects used less oxygen in the music-making session compared to the background music session (see figure 4.3), meaning that their metabolic expenditure was lower. Interestingly, the strong effect that jymmin had in reducing perceived exertion led the researchers to conclude that this could not be accounted for solely by the reduction in metabolic expenditure. It could be due to emotional processes associated with musical creativity.

It also seems plausible that the greater proportion of isometric contractions, and thus fewer repetitions recorded during the music-making, or jymmin, session, may have been the result of participants wanting to fully engage with their bandmates!

---

track and field) and is therefore mentioned in chapter 7. In terms of musical accompaniment, there are no significant differences in music selection between dynamic strength training and explosive strength training. Nonetheless, lyrics that affirm speed of movement, power, bounce, explosiveness, and so on, will add to the potency of music used to accompany explosive strength training.

# CARDIORESPIRATORY WORKOUTS

When people select their own music for exercise, it's most often for cardiorespiratory workouts. The long-duration, repetitive, and monotonous nature of such workouts almost predisposes them to musical accompaniment. This section kicks off with extensive coverage of the activity that has attracted the most interest from researchers and music technologists: running. Three popular cardiorespiratory machines found in local gyms are then examined—namely, the step mill, Versa-Climber, and exercise stepper. Walking programs set to music have become increasingly popular in recent years. Because such programs are at the vanguard of public health initiatives, this activity is duly examined through the prism of public health. Indoor stationary cycling follows, the highly rhythmic nature of which makes it particularly well suited to the application of synchronous music. The use of music for road cycling is not recommended for safety reasons. The final three sections cover music applications with elliptical trainers (XTrainers), rowing ergometers,

and arm ergometers. Rowing presents particular challenges for exercise professionals wanting to use musical accompaniment, and the nuances of this activity are explored.

## Running

Running is perhaps the physical activity that most popularized the use of music for individual exercise and led the manufacturers of music-playing devices to create ever lighter and more ergonomically designed units. This trend began in the late 1970s with the Sony Walkman (13.7 oz, or 388 g) and continues in the present day with the iPod Shuffle (0.4 oz, or 12.5 g). To assist runners in their music selections, dozens of websites provide playlists or music composed specifically for runners (see examples in table 4.6).

There are subtle differences between music for running outdoors and music for running indoors on a treadmill. One of the main differences is that using music synchronously on a treadmill is far more challenging; people often find themselves having to readjust their stride every few minutes to stay in sync with the beat. Similarly, remaining in sync with music when running into a strong headwind or up a hill is also challenging.

### Outdoor Running

The first thing to highlight about outdoor running is that *I do not recommend the use of music on roads and sidewalks.* Runners need to be fully tuned in to the environment to ensure their safety, and music can be an all-too-dangerous distraction. I hope to never hear of another runner who has been critically injured as a result of becoming intoxicated by

**Table 4.6**  Websites Offering Playlists for Runners

| Company name (country) | Website | Services offered |
|---|---|---|
| run2rhythm (Australia) | www.run2r.com | Specially composed running music suitable for auditory–motor synchronization |
| Jiwok (France) | www.jiwok.com | Segued MP3 files from your own music library or the Jiwok library with coach voice-over |
| AudioFuel (UK) | www.audiofuel.co.uk | Specially composed running music with coach voice-over to promote synchronous use |
| jog.fm (USA) | http://jog.fm | Mixes well-known tracks and classical pieces into playlists for distance running at various speeds |
| JogTunes (USA) | www.jogtunes.com | Allows you to create playlists based on your target running pace; ideal for auditory–motor synchronization |
| RockMyRun (USA) | www.rockmyrun.com | DJ mixes of well-known tracks that contour the physical demands of runs of various lengths and intensities |
| 8tracks (USA) | http://8tracks.com/#explore/workout | Free music-streaming service with playlists designed by people and not algorithms; wide range of mixes for a variety of workout modes |
| Spotify Running (Sweden) | www.spotify.com/running/ | A streaming service that generates playlists based on music preferences and desired stride rate to promote auditory–motor synchronization |
| Running Mixes (USA) | www.runningmixes.com | DJ mixes of predominantly electronic dance music of 40 to 60 minutes in duration that encourage syncing stride rate to a tempo of 180 bpm |

music and losing track of time and space. Music is such a powerful stimulus that it should never be used on roads and sidewalks. During road events in which traffic has been blocked from the course and the organizers permit the use of personal listening devices, it is fine. However, even in this instance, the volume should be at a level that does not place runners at risk of colliding with others. It happens . . . a lot.

Music is best used in wide open spaces where there are no vehicles to run people down or people to collide with—on cross-country trails, on long sandy beaches, in parks. People who live in urban areas should not use music players at night, because this places them at heightened risk, particularly females. Notwithstanding the various safety recommendations, being in an open space, basking in the splendor of nature, and having this experience augmented by a fitting musical backdrop can create a movie moment.

Research has shown that runners derive the most benefit from music when their performance

levels begin to dip or plateau; that is when they are most in need of a boost. To date, exercise participants have seldom used music in this differentiated way, which is a method for applying scientific findings to bolster workout performances. For example, someone running 5 miles (8 km), a typical distance for a recreational run on a Sunday morning, who uses asynchronous music over the last half of the run might expect to lower the finishing time by 30 to 50 seconds (e.g., Edworthy & Waring, 2006; Ghaderi, Rahimi, & Ali Azarbayjani, 2009; Nethery, 2002). This differentiated music use is particularly effective for elevating performance levels because it provides an extra push when most needed.

There has been an ongoing debate between those who support the use of music during running and running purists who claim that music distracts from the pleasure of running and should be avoided. My view is that there is merit on both sides of the argument. A few years ago, however, I was asked to argue the case for using music

---

# THE CASE FOR AND AGAINST RUNNING WITH MUSIC

The Case For (the author)

- Many modern-day runners rarely take a step without their headphones on.
- Music can make running feel easier at low-to-moderate intensities, and research shows that it reduces the perception of how hard the person is running by about 10 percent.
- Music elevates positive aspects of mood and so can be used as part of the mental preparation process for a run.
- Some runners need music far more than other runners do; dissociators (people who have a tendency to look for external distractions) will actively seek it to distract them from the boredom and pain associated with running.
- Many people would probably not be runners if it were not for music heightening the experience.
- Serious runners tend to be associators, which means that they focus intently on internal cues such as breathing, heart rate, and muscular tension; this type of person tends not to derive as much benefit from music.
- Good research evidence shows that music can help people enter a flow state during running, which is an immersive and highly pleasurable experience.
- Music can be part of a holistic running experience and not necessarily detached from it or a detriment to it.

The Case Against (Dr. Jim Denison, University of Alberta, Canada)

- Being aware of the surroundings is an elemental part of running.
- Listening to music can remove the person from the other sounds that running produces, such as breathing and foot strike, which are essential cues, providing feedback on effort level.
- Running while listening to music removes the person from the environment, which presents a safety issue (can't hear cars, thunder in the distance, people coming up from behind, etc.).
- Runners can become dependent on music; eventually, they can lose the sense of what motivates them, such as the energized feeling they get during a run.
- It is not the case that every recreational runner views running as a means to an end and finds it boring, and so needs music to get through it.
- Many people enjoy running and being present in the sensation of moving; people don't have to be elite athletes to be in tune with their bodies.
- The ability to be at peace and calm is something we've lost in our culture in favor of multitasking.
- Listening to music—or podcasts or audio books—while running is a form of multitasking; it keeps people too plugged in and prevents them from enjoying the experience.

Adapted from Adam Bean, "Running with music," *Runner's World*, December 1, 2010. Copyrighted 2016. Rodale, Inc. 120027:0216AT

---

during running in opposition to the esteemed writer and erstwhile distance runner Jim Denison (author of *Bannister and Beyond: The Mystique of the Four-Minute Mile,* among many other running-related books). The sidebar The Case For and Against Running With Music presents a summary of the case.

Some athletes tell me that when they are running outdoors, the visual environment is so captivating that they do not like to use music; they tend to save it for treadmill running, where there is little environmental distraction. Whether using music outdoors or in, the ideal tempo range for its synchronous application is 75 to 95 bpm if taking a stride cycle per beat, or 150 to 190 bpm if taking a step per beat. For asynchronous use, a tempo range of ~110 to ~150 bpm provides a sufficient level of stimulation, with the lower end of the range (110 to 124 bpm) for low-intensity running, the middle of the range (125 to 134 bpm) for moderate-intensity running, and the top of the range (135 to 150 bpm) for high-intensity running (Karageorghis & Jones, 2014; Karageorghis et al., 2008; Karageorghis, Jones et al., 2006, 2011).

## Treadmill Running

During indoor running on a treadmill, the environment is often not particularly distracting or pleasurable, and one can quickly grow tired of looking at the photos of well-oiled bodybuilders from yesteryear that adorn the gym walls. The incessant sound of the treadmill, that horrid whir (multiplied by 10 if running alongside others), is also rather off-putting. There is more reason to use music in this environment, and many people

choose to combine music with video to maximize the distraction.

It is considerably safer to use music on a treadmill, where there is no risk of getting knocked over or mugged. In this environment, people can exercise safely and truly lose themselves in music. Most gyms provide integrated entertainment systems for which people need only bring a set of headphones to plug in. Research has shown that watching music videos while treadmill running results in greater dissociation, lower RPE, and more positive affective states than listening to music alone (Hutchinson, Karageorghis, & Jones, 2015; see figure 4.4). For exercisers who are interested in performance outcomes and want to work hard rather than be entertained, the combination of music and video can be a little too immersing.

Music can be used synchronously or asynchronously on the treadmill. However, people using it synchronously will occasionally need to adjust their stride to the music or lean on the treadmill

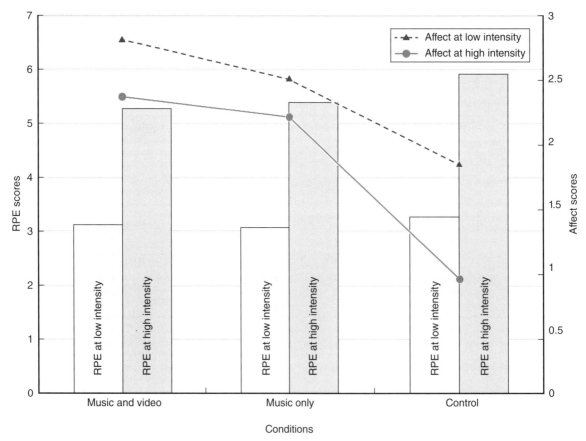

**Figure 4.4** Effects of music and video on ratings of perceived exertion (RPE) and affect (feeling states) at low and high intensities of treadmill running.

supports and then resync their stride. The factors of belt speed, leg length, and preferred stride length make getting the combination of music, (wo)man, and machine working together as one a tough mathematical challenge! As long as the stride pattern is adjusted slightly periodically, there is absolutely no problem. I have produced many playlists for runners in my career, and table 4.7 contains my all-time running favorites. Notice that each song has an association with running, some more so than others.

## Step Mill

The step mill is an exercise machine that looks much like an escalator and challenges exercisers with a rotating staircase that can be set at a speed of their choice. Given the way it functions, it can almost be grouped under treadmill running in terms of music applications, although the demands on the upper thighs are far greater and, for the uninitiated exerciser, can induce fatigue quite rapidly. Given the emphasis that the step

**Table 4.7** The Author's All-Time Favorite Running Tracks

| Track | Artist(s) | Tempo (bpm) | Genre | Running phase |
|---|---|---|---|---|
| *Chariots of Fire* | Vangelis | 68 | Film score | Mental preparation |
| Ready To Run | Dixie Chicks | 99 | Country | Mental preparation |
| Running On Sunshine | Jesus Jackson | 100 | Urban soul | Warm-up |
| Running Up That Hill | Kate Bush | 108 | Rock/new wave | Low intensity |
| Runaway | Linkin Park | 109 | Hard rock | Low intensity |
| Running With The Night | Lionel Richie | 120 | Pop | Low intensity |
| Run, Baby, Run | Sheryl Crow | 124 | Alternative rock | Low intensity |
| Run To You | Bryan Adams | 126 | Rock | Moderate intensity |
| Run The World (Girls) | Beyoncé | 127 | Pop | Moderate intensity |
| Where Are We Runnin | Lenny Kravitz | 130 | Rock | Moderate intensity |
| I Don't Wanna Stop | Ozzy Osbourne | 138 | Heavy metal | High intensity |
| Runnin' (Lose It All) | Naughty Boy feat. Beyoncé and Arrow Benjamin | 140 | UK garage | High intensity |
| I Ran | A Flock of Seagulls | 146 | Rock | High intensity |
| Born To Run | Bruce Springsteen | 148 | Rock | High intensity |
| Run-Around | Blues Traveler | 152 | Blues rock | Very high intensity |
| Runaway | Bon Jovi | 153 | Heavy metal | Very high intensity |
| Run Run Run | Celeste Buckingham | 162 | Pop | Very high intensity |
| Run With The Wolves | Prodigy | 166 | Alternative rock | Very high intensity |
| I Start To Run | White Denim | 168 | Progressive rock | Very high intensity |
| Running Free | Iron Maiden | 170 | Heavy metal | Very high intensity |
| Footloose | Kenny Loggins | 174 | Pop rock | Very high intensity |
| Move Your Feet | Junior Senior | 119 | Dance | Cool-down |
| Run On | Moby | 97 | Electronica | Cool-down |
| The Distance | Cake | 92 | Alternative rock | Cool-down |
| Waterfalls | TLC | 86 | R&B | Post-run recuperation |

*Note:* All of these tracks can be located on YouTube.

mill places on the thighs and gluteal muscles, it is popular among women. It can also provide a vigorous cardiorespiratory workout.

It is slightly easier to use music in the synchronous mode on the step mill than it is on the treadmill, particularly for people who know the speed at which they are going to be stepping and can thus select music with the appropriate beats per minute. The reason it is easier is that there is no point at which both feet are off the surface of the machine and so there is less variability in the movement pattern. Tracks with relevant lyrical affirmations for the step mill allude to climbing, ascending, rising, and so on, such as "Ain't No Mountain High Enough" by Diana Ross, "Keep On Rising" by Ian Carey, and "Up And Up" by Coldplay. A website with a broad array of relevant suggestions is www.climbingandrunning.com/songs-about-mountains-everest.

## VersaClimbers

The VersaClimber machine is a close cousin of the step mill. This is a total-body, nonimpact vertical trainer that can provide an intense cardiorespiratory workout. These machines have proven popular with exercisers and athletes alike. All of the major muscle groups are engaged by the VersaClimber, and the user can set the level of resistance. This activity lends itself particularly well to the synchronous application of music, particularly because the exerciser can determine the precise rate of movement using a built-in pulley system. This is unlike treadmills and step mills, which are motorized.

Because a strong beat, or meter, is recommended for a whole-body activity of this nature, commercial dance or disco music with a powerful four-to-the-bar rhythm works particularly well. Similar to running, the tempo range 110 to 150 bpm works well, depending on how hard the person wants to work. Because the VersaClimber provides essentially a climbing activity, as does the step mill, tracks whose lyrics allude to climbing activities can provide an extra mental boost. From the repository of dance and disco music, good examples include "The Only Way Is Up" by Yazz and the Plastic Population, "Rise Up" by Yves LaRock, and "Strut Your Funky Stuff (Get Up, Stand Up)" by Frantique.

## Exercise Stepper

The step machine is an item of cardiorespiratory equipment that was hugely popular in the 1980s and 1990s—particularly as a home exercise machine. Its popularity has certainly dwindled during the first part of the 21st century. It could be referred to as a forebear of the VersaClimber, but only the legs work while the hands grip foam-covered handlebars. Exercise steppers have two foot platforms connected to a set of hydraulic pistons that keep the platforms above the floor and facilitate the up–down stepping motion.

The stepper lends itself to the synchronous application of music given its regular and rhythmic nature. The movement rate can vary anywhere from 36 steps per minute (low intensity at two floors per minute) to 72 steps per minute (very high intensity at six floors per minute). Doubling the step rate results in a music tempo range of 72 to 144 bpm, which is quite broad, although most stepper workouts are conducted in the narrower range of 45 to 60 steps per minute, which corresponds with the tempo range of 90 to 120 bpm.

Music selection considerations for exercise steppers are identical to those for the VersaClimber. Nonetheless, step-related lyrics might be used periodically over a strong four-to-the-beat rhythm. Suitable tracks include "Step On" by Happy Mondays, "Follow The Step" by Rachel Row, and "Mind Ur Step" by Dennis Ferrer feat. Janelle Kroll. Stepping works well with both synchronous and asynchronous applications of music.

## Walking Programs

Walking is one of the main forms of exercise that professionals in the fields of medicine, health, and exercise have promoted to increase physical activity in developed countries. It is widely acknowledged that sustained walking sessions of a minimum of 30 minutes per day, five days a week are associated with a range of health benefits that include reducing the chances of cancer, type 2 diabetes, heart disease, anxiety, and depression.

Typical walking interventions include encouraging people to walk to work or to get off the bus a stop early. Remember that the first lightweight personal music device was named the Walkman.

It is no coincidence that walking is an activity that best lends itself to music-related interventions—in particular, the application of synchronous music.

For most people, a natural pace is 120 steps per minute (spm) plus or minus 5 spm. The significant health benefits come from walking at a brisk pace, which for most people is in the range of 130 to

## LISA, THE MUSICALLY POWERED GP REFERRAL SCHEME INSTRUCTOR

General practitioner (GP) referral schemes are hugely popular in the UK as a way to encourage people with relatively sedentary or unhealthy lifestyles to be more physically active. Through a network of organizations collaborating at a local level, GPs can refer their patients to gymnasiums that employ suitably qualified exercise instructors. The instructors assess the patient's physical fitness, prescribe a suitable exercise program (often for 12 weeks), and monitor the patient's progress, providing interim and end-of-scheme reports to the GP. The idea is that this process will kick-start a more physically active lifestyle and arm patients with the tools they need to prevent the diseases associated with a sedentary lifestyle. On a national level, the investment in exercise-based programs is intended to lessen the financial burden on the UK National Health Service in terms of drug prescriptions, surgeries, and hospital care.

Lisa works on one such scheme in Newport in South Wales. She has a strong background in exercise to music and so is well versed in harnessing the power of music to bring about health benefits for previously inactive people. It was noticeable to Lisa just how reluctant people in her city were about using their local health and exercise facilities. Whether it was the cost of membership, the perceived need to be seen in the designer gymwear, or the fear of being evaluated negatively by others, she wasn't sure. What she did know was that the city had some great riverscapes (being located close to the banks of the River Usk) and beautiful countryside with rolling hills that relatively few members of the 300,000-strong population of the city used for exercise.

Bringing her knowledge of exercise-to-music classes and the natural resources at her disposal together, Lisa promoted walking-to-music programs for patients who were previously inactive or did not express a strong desire to undergo indoor instructor-led exercise programs. At first, patients were a little nonplussed as to why Lisa was questioning them about what they had on their iPods, but they soon understood the considerable benefits of synchronous walking. Most started their regimens at around 120 strides per minute (spm) with tracks such as "Le Freak" by Generation Disco and "The One And Only" by Chesney Hawkes.

Each week Lisa encouraged the use of ever-so-slightly faster tracks so that by the end of the 12-week program, some patients were speed walking comfortably for 30 to 40 minutes at around 140 spm accompanied by tracks such as "Don't Stop" (The Outhere Brothers) and "Honey Honey" (ABBA). The best part was that they were thoroughly immersed in the walking experience and fully enjoying their daily bouts of exercise. An unexpected benefit of the intervention was that Lisa's tutees started to recognize each other on the towpaths. They would acknowledge each other when their paths crossed, much as bus drivers do. This provided a subtle yet powerful form of social support. Other instructors saw the benefits of Lisa's systematic approach to music-based walking programs. She was asked to provide seminars in her region so that other exercise professionals could tap the power of music in their ongoing fight against inactivity.

150 spm. To move from the comfortable rate of 120 spm to the brisk rate of 130 to 150 spm, synchronous music can serve a metronomic function to regulate walking cadence. Small increases in spm from week to week (e.g., 1 to 2), make the increase in exercise intensity virtually imperceptible: people work harder and feel just as good (Karageorghis et al., 2009; Leman et al., 2013).

A strong body of scientific research has emerged in recent years to support the promotion of walking that is synchronized to music. One of the key messages from this research is that music lifts people's moods and reduces the perception of exertion (e.g., Franêk, van Noorden, & Režný, 2014; Leman et al., 2013). The combination of enhanced cadence with a more positive mood and lower RPE provides the basis for a compelling argument for the promotion of walking programs set to music.

Several online companies offer music-based walking programs; among these are www.work outmusic.com, https://walk.jog.fm, and www .djsteveboy.com/podrunner.html. Simply selecting tracks with the appropriate beats per minute, as described earlier, can lead to bespoke music playlists that accommodate anyone's musical tastes. Some websites even provide software that enables people to arrange their music libraries in accordance with their bpm (or other musical characteristics), which then makes syncing a great deal easier (e.g., www.beatunes.com).

## Stationary Cycling

One of the safest and most popular activities involving the use of music is stationary cycling. Even the most poorly equipped gyms around the world have at least one stationary cycle. Moreover, many people invest in one for home use, although these mostly end up as rusting relics in yard sales. Similar to running on roads and sidewalks, I do not recommend using music at all for outdoor cycling—it is too dangerous. This is why this section on cycling concerns purely the indoor variety. Moreover, the recommendations here pertain in equal measure to conventional and recumbent cycling, both of which are popular indoors.

Indoor cycling is self-paced and so there is little room for variation in technique. Given that commercial cycling machines provide a digital reading

for revolutions per minute (rpm), it is the perfect activity for the synchronous application of music. This is perhaps why so much of the scientific research into auditory–motor synchronization has employed cycle ergometers (e.g., Anshel & Marisi, 1978; Bacon, Myers, & Karageorghis, 2012; Lim et al., 2014). Stationary cycling also works well with asynchronous, or background, music, but people are more likely to maximize their physiological gains with synchronous music.

As a starting point, for exercise purposes, the viable range on most cycle ergometers is 40 to 120 rpm. To apply music synchronously, instructors should work out the rpm they want their clients to cycle at, and then double this number to establish the appropriate music tempo. For example, for a client who cycles at 65 rpm, the appropriate tempo would be 130 bpm, which is in line with a broad range of modern dance tracks. At high pedal cadences (e.g., beyond 80 rpm), it is easier to take

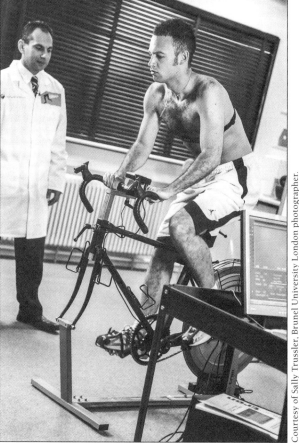

Courtesy of Sally Trussler, Brunel University London photographer.

**Many scientific studies have shown how music can enhance stationary cycling performance.**

one pedal revolution per musical beat, so there is no need to double the beats per minute. Given that high pedal cadences are also often associated with higher exercise intensities, taking one pedal revolution per beat makes for less information processing, which is advantageous given the narrowing of attention that occurs during such high intensities (see chapter 2). In addition, finding a sufficient number of suitable tracks at very high tempi to facilitate a semi-revolution of the pedals per beat is often challenging.

Table 4.8 lists tracks that facilitate synchronous cycling at various pedal cadences—all the way from warm-ups to what highly conditioned exercisers might produce at full speed. In terms of asynchronous music, good scientific evidence suggests that the optimal tempo range is ~115 to ~145 bpm: 115 to 124 bpm is appropriate for low intensities; 125 to 134 bpm for moderate intensities; and 135 to 145 bpm for high intensities (Karageorghis et al., 2008, 2011).

## Elliptical Trainers (XTrainers)

Elliptical trainers, or XTrainers, as they are also referred to, are a relatively recent development in exercise machines. They provide whole-body, low-impact cardiorespiratory workouts by simulating climbing, walking, or running. Users can set the resistance in accordance with the intensity of workout they require. Elliptical trainers are one of the safest modes of indoor exercise from an injury-prevention perspective and lend themselves to the synchronous application of music. Asynchronous music is fine, too, particularly when using the trainer for an interval workout with high- and low-intensity components.

Music selection considerations for the elliptical trainer are very similar to those for other items of exercise equipment discussed in this chapter (e.g., VersaClimber). It provides a whole-body activity that requires music with a strong beat and thus an easily extractable meter to allow the exerciser to achieve a high level of synchronization. The possible movement rate is 30 to 70 rpm, and the typical movement rate for a workout would be close to 40 to 60 rpm. By doubling the rpm, we can expect a music tempo range of 80 to 120 bpm to work best in terms of facilitating synchronization, with one semi-revolution taken per beat. Alongside the rhythmic elements, catchy and relatively simple melodies, bright and uplifting harmonies (particularly for women who are high responders in this regard; Karageorghis et al., 2010), lyrical affirmations, and relevant extramusical associations are other key considerations. I have not included a section for cross-country ski machines to avoid repetition, but the music selection considerations are identical to those for elliptical trainers.

**Table 4.8** Synchronous Application of Music to Stationary Cycling

| Track | Artist(s) | Tempo (bpm) | Genre | Cycle cadence (rpm) |
|---|---|---|---|---|
| Flashing Lights | Kanye West feat. Dwele | 91 | Hip-hop | 45.5 |
| Ruby | Kaiser Chiefs | 93 | Rock | 46.5 |
| Faith | George Michael | 96 | Pop | 48 |
| Burning Heart | Survivor | 98 | Rock | 49 |
| Levels | Nick Jonas | 102 | Electropop | 51 |
| Valerie | Mark Ronson feat. Amy Winehouse | 106 | R&B | 53 |
| I Want To Break Free | Queen | 112 | Pop rock | 56 |
| Can't Stop The Feeling | Justin Timberlake | 113 | Disco/pop | 56.5 |
| The Way You Make Me Feel | Michael Jackson | 114 | Pop | 57 |
| Billie Jean | Michael Jackson | 117 | Pop | 58.5 |

*(continued)*

Table 4.8 *(continued)*

| Track | Artist(s) | Tempo (bpm) | Genre | Cycle cadence (rpm) |
|---|---|---|---|---|
| Good Life | Inner City | 121 | Dance | 60.5 |
| Celebration | Kool & the Gang | 122 | Disco | 61 |
| Wake Me Up | Avicii | 125 | Dance | 62.5 |
| Reflections | Jacob Plant feat. Example | 126 | House | 63 |
| Work Hard Play Hard | Tiësto | 128 | House | 64 |
| Instant Replay | Dan Hartman | 129 | Disco | 64.5 |
| Boom Boom Pow | Black Eyed Peas | 130 | Hip-house | 65 |
| Tour de France | Kraftwerk | 134 | Electronic | 67 |
| Move On Up | Curtis Mayfield | 136 | Funk soul | 68 |
| I Drove All Night | Bandido | 138 | Dance | 69 |
| Feel Good Inc. | Gorillaz | 139 | Alternative rock | 69.5 |
| The Road | Alistair Griffin feat. Kimberley Walsh | 140 | Pop rock | 70 |
| Chase This Light | Jimmy Eat World | 141 | Alternative rock | 70.5 |
| The Heat Is On | Glenn Frey | 144 | Pop rock | 72 |
| Rockerfeller Skank | Fatboy Slim | 145 | Big beat | 72.5 |
| Dancing In The Dark | Bruce Springsteen | 148 | Rock | 74 |
| Sex On Fire | Kings of Leon | 152 | Alternative rock | 76 |
| One Way Or Another | Blondie | 161 | Punk rock | 80.5 |
| Lonely Boy | The Black Keys | 165 | Blues rock | 82.5 |
| What A Wonderful World | Joey Ramone | 168 | Punk rock | 84 |
| **One pedal revolution per musical beat (for higher cycle cadences)** | | | | |
| Boombastic | Shaggy | 84 | Reggae | 84 |
| Bitter Sweet Symphony | The Verve | 86 | Alternative rock | 86 |
| Burn | Ellie Goulding | 88 | Synthpop | 88 |
| Dangerous | David Guetta feat. Sam Martin | 92 | Electropop | 92 |
| Next To Me | Emeli Sandé | 95 | R&B | 95 |
| Independent Women Part I | Destiny's Child | 98 | R&B | 98 |
| Dreamers | Rizzle Kicks | 100 | Alternative hip-hop | 100 |
| 22 | Taylor Swift | 104 | Pop | 104 |
| Troublemaker | Olly Murs feat. Flo Rida | 106 | Pop | 106 |
| Bangarang | Skrillex feat. Sirah | 109 | Electro house | 109 |
| Fun | Pitbull feat. Chris Brown | 114 | Hip-hop | 114 |
| Candy | Robbie Williams | 116 | Pop | 116 |

*Note:* Where there is an odd-numbered tempo, this will not be reflected in a half of a revolution per minute on cycle ergometer display, which only displays whole numbers. Following the music tempo, and not the displayed revolutions, to direct pedal movements will result in pedaling at the desired rate. All tracks can be located on YouTube.

## Rowing Ergometers

The use of music in rowing has attracted a fair bit of scientific interest given what a grueling and monotonous activity it can be (Rendi, Szabo, & Szabó, 2008; Scott et al., 1999). Long before any scientific research had been conducted, both the Greeks and the Romans understood the benefits of having drummers on rowing boats, a practice that continues to the present day in the sport of dragon boat racing. Modern rowing boats have facilities for audio equipment, and music is often used in training; nonetheless, it is with the rowing ergometer that most people have experienced the benefits of music firsthand. Rowing is a relatively complex motor skill in which the work, or drive, phase is not equal to the recovery phase; the ratio of work to recovery is approximately 1:2. This raises the issue of where the strong beat should fall in the music: at the beginning of the drive phase, when the arms are extended, or at the beginning of the recovery phase, when the arms are flexed. Experts have a variety of opinions on this; some even suggest that music should be especially composed for rowing (Mann, 2004).

It is quite tricky to sync music to rowing given the activity's technical demands and inherent irregularity in terms of work and recovery phases. To use it synchronously, completing a stroke in each musical bar (four beats in common time) is the best way to go. If we take a music tempo of 128 bpm and divide it by four to get the number of bars (32), we end up with the common work rate of 32 strokes per minute. A tempo of 124 bpm gives 31 strokes per minute, whereas a tempo of 132 bpm gives 33 strokes per minute. This is an easy way to more or less synchronize the work rate with music if you know the desired stroke rate. To use the music asynchronously, which is the more common approach, a range of ~110 to ~145 bpm works well, with 110 to 124 bpm for low intensity, 125 to 134 for moderate intensity, and 135 to 145 for high intensity. The lyrical and harmonic and melodic qualities of the music should emulate those for other aerobic activities such as running and cycling.

## Arm Ergometers

Arm ergometers, also known as handbikes, are often used by disabled or injured exercisers to create a safe, low-impact cardiorespiratory workout. They consist of two handles and in most

Arm ergometers facilitate the application of synchronous music.

# MUSIC MAKING AS EXERCISE?

At the London 2012 pre-Olympic Congress, I met Mark Richardson, prodigious drummer of the Britrock band Skunk Anansie. I'd had a keen interest in his band since the mid-1990s because their lead vocalist, Skin (aka Deborah Dyer), hailed from the part of South London in which I grew up. The focal point of a captivating symposium titled The Science of Drumming: Enhancing Physical and Psychological Well-Being involved Richardson engaging in a novel demonstration of physiological responses to an incremental drumming task.

The strong rock beat started steadily at 100 bpm and progressed in 10 bpm steps until the point of voluntary exhaustion, or aerobic capacity, at which point Richardson was rocking out at 190 bpm—about the same tempo as "I'll Be There For You" by The Rembrandts (think *Friends* TV theme tune). Richardson wore a face mask to measure gas exchange, and his oxygen expenditure and heart rate were displayed on a giant screen just behind him. He achieved a peak heart rate of 183 bpm, and his oxygen consumption peaked at 4.1 L/min, which is analogous to that of an elite sprinter. Work by British researcher Marcus Smith and his colleagues, organizers of the symposium, has shown that during the average stage performance, drummers can burn 650 calories per hour and reach heart rates close to their age-predicted max!

Mark Richardson from Britrock band Skunk Anansie managed to reach $\dot{V}O_2$max on his drumkit.

The demonstration highlighted the point that playing an instrument such as the drums can have significant benefits for health and well-being, as well as a host of social and intellectual benefits (although neighbors might not always agree). In regard to the social and intellectual benefits, drummers often have to interact with other band members, and their job is to hold the groove together. Speeding up or slowing down, even just a little, will lead to some irate bandmates. Also, drumming uses all four limbs, often working independently of each other to produce complex rhythmic patterns; this requires the engagement of regions of the brain such as the parietal lobe and temporal lobe (see figure 2.2, chapter 2). Drummers are particularly adept at accessing and integrating competing information from the left and right brain hemispheres.

Like me, Richardson had been playing in loud bands from a young age, and during his teens and twenties did not wear earplugs; it was just not done. At the end of the symposium, I asked how the high physiological load imposed by drumming coupled with the high volumes to which drummers were routinely exposed affected their hearing. Richardson made the public confession that he suffered with tinnitus as a consequence of his exposure to loud music and was now "super careful" in his professional endeavors, to limit his exposure to very loud sounds. He advised that all musicians and DJs playing in concert venues wear earplugs. The same "sound advice" applies in equal measure to exercise professionals.

cases a seat; the object is to crank the handles in full circles using the hands in much the same way as turning the pedals on a bike with the feet. The exercise engages both flexors and extensors around the shoulders, scapulae, and elbows. It is common to rotate the arms in a forward motion, but some models facilitate backward revolutions. It is also possible to use such ergometers with a single arm. The principles pertaining to music selection for arm ergometers are the same as those for cycle ergometers (see also table 4.8), although the potential range for work rate is slightly narrower in arm ergometry at 40 to 80 rpm. This is yet another exercise activity that lends itself well to the synchronous application of music. Doubling the rpm results in a music tempo range of 80 to 160 bpm. For some arm-specific lyrical affirmations, try "Crank It Up" by David Guetta, "Arms" by Christina Perri, and "Hands All Over" by Maroon 5.

# USING MUSIC IN PERSONAL TRAINING

Because personal training involves human interaction, the use of music needs to be carefully considered. By necessity, personal training involves a constant stream of two-way communication between the trainer and the client. Because of this, music can disrupt the flow of this interaction and prevent some of the trainer's form- and motivation-related messages from getting through.

If ambient music is used as a backdrop to personal training, it needs to be set at a low volume so as not to block important communications. All of the other principles that have been detailed thus far in this book regarding marrying music with a specific type of activity (see, for example, chapter 2) can be adhered to with this important volume consideration in mind.

At times during a personal training session, the client works out independently, perhaps when jogging a lap of a sport field or completing a cardiorespiratory component using an elliptical trainer. In such instances, the use of individual tracks (or mini-playlists) that are personally meaningful and motivating, as well as conducive to the activity, can work well. Again, the volume should be moderated so the client can hear any instructions or motivational comments from the instructor. Research shows that the motivation an exerciser derives from an exercise leader can exceed that derived from a music program (Patton, 1991). In sum, there is a fine balance to be struck between the guidance and motivation provided by the trainer and the stimulation provided by the music. Trainers can also demonstrate their expertise and offer enhanced perceived value to clients by asking them about their music preferences and helping them prepare their own playlists for solo sessions. This is a practice that most people can do, but perhaps lack the motivation or time for; those who struggle to get down to the gym at all are highly unlikely to spend an hour creating an exercise playlist! However, because this seemingly idle activity may make all the difference in helping a person adhere to training over the long term, it is a false economy to forgo it.

# COOL-DOWN

Music use is a great way to round out a workout and ease the heart rate back down toward resting levels. Key selection considerations are the tempo, lyrics, and harmonic content. The essential goal of cool-down music is to leave the exerciser feeling calm, refreshed, revitalized, and ready for whatever lies ahead. Such music does not necessarily need to have strong physical activity or sporting associations. It does, however, need to have a soothing and feel-good flavor to have the desired effect. The selections might also speak to people's self-esteem, or how they feel about themselves, to give them a small mental boost.

Given that one of the main goals of cool-down music is to gradually return exercise heart rate to resting levels using the principle of entrainment (see chapter 2), the tempo and rhythmic qualities of such music require careful consideration. Depending on the type of activity, the heart rate following the conditioning elements of a workout is likely to be in the range ~120 to ~140 bpm, perhaps higher if working at a relatively high-intensity activity. The cool-down music needs to gradually bring the heart rate down; starting from ~115 bpm and progressing down to ~80 bpm generally works well.

A heart rate lower than ~80 bpm will likely cause a person to feel sleepy rather than re-energized! Nonetheless, when using relaxation techniques such as meditation or progressive muscular relaxation at the end of workout sessions, slower tempi, in the range 60-80 bpm, can be helpful. Cool-down music should not be rhythmically busy—even at a slow tempo—so in this instance rap does not work well. Yes, rap generally has a slow tempo, but its rhythmic complexity invariably has a stimulating effect on mind and body. Gentle pop, slow country rock, new age, and ambient music can work well for this purpose.

The lyrics of cool-down music should be smooth, soothing, and nonaggressive, and the pieces should be melodically simple. Messages that reinforce target feelings—calmness, refreshment, revitalization—are helpful for inducing the desired mind-set. In the final stages of cool-down or during mental relaxation exercises, lyrics might not be required. Gentle instrumental music can provide a moment for self-reflection and contemplation before getting on with the next part of the day.

The harmonic content of cool-down music needs to be predicated on consonance and major harmony or a subtle blend of major and minor harmonies. It doesn't need to be too sugary, but it does need to induce a positively valenced and calming mental state. In chapter 3 we learned about the circumplex model of affect (figure 3.2). If we attach cool-down music to that model, the music choices would be placed in the middle of the bottom-right quadrant, the quadrant James Russell labeled relaxation (Russell, 1980). Table 4.9 provides some music selections for cool-downs.

# SUMMARY

This chapter examined how music can be applied to a range of individual exercise activities. The examples embody the theoretical principles outlined in chapter 2 (see figure 2.8); musical qualities are considered in light of a host of personal factors and situational demands. The desired mind-set for a range of exercise-related activities and intensities has proved pivotal in providing music recommendations; low-arousal activities such as passive stretching require music that is relatively slow and calming, whereas high-intensity weight training requires faster and more stimulative music. Although music recommendations have a scientific premise, because music is an art form, exercise professionals need to carefully consider exercisers' personal tastes and aesthetics.

In some situations the use of music is not advised, such as when running or cycling on roads and sidewalks, and during periods of verbal communication in personal training. The use of high-volume music during exercise (>85 dBA) is also not advised, because this can lead to hearing damage over time. Moreover, instructors should think carefully about protecting their ears with earplugs, particularly when leading large classes, which are characterized by the blare of loud music. Numerous exercise activities are conducive to the application of synchronous music, including VersaClimbing, walking, XTraining,

**Table 4.9**  Music Selections for Cool-Downs

| Track | Artist(s) | Tempo (bpm) | Genre |
|---|---|---|---|
| Zoom | Fat Larry's Band | 105 | Modern soul |
| How Ya Doin'? | Little Mix feat. Missy Elliott | 101 | Pop |
| Perfect | One Direction | 100 | Pop rock |
| Hold On, We're Going Home | Drake feat. Majid Jordan | 100 | R&B |
| Lovely Day | Bill Withers | 98 | R&B |
| One | Mary J. Blige & U2 | 93 | R&B |
| Everybody's Free (To Wear Sunscreen) | Baz Luhrmann | 91 | Spoken word |
| If I Were A Boy | Beyoncé | 90 | Pop |
| We Have All The Time In The World | Louis Armstrong | 89 | Jazz |
| Don't Know Why | Norah Jones | 88 | Jazz/pop |
| Everything Is Everything | Gabriel Garzón-Montano | 86 | R&B |
| Empire State Of Mind | Jay-Z feat. Alicia Keys | 87 | Hip-hop |
| You're Beautiful | James Blunt | 83 | Folk rock |
| The Air That I Breathe | The Hollies | 82 | Pop |
| Hello | Adele | 79 | Pop |
| Crimson | Morcheeba | 77 | Alternative rock |
| One Love | Bob Marley | 76 | Reggae |
| Ribbon In The Sky | Stevie Wonder | 69 | R&B |
| You And I | One Direction | 66 | Pop |

*Note:* All of these tracks can be located on YouTube.

stationary cycling, and arm ergometry. The less movement variation there is in a particular type of exercise, the easier it is to apply music in a synchronous mode.

All forms of individual exercise lend themselves to the use of asynchronous music: guidelines for tempo, lyrics, and harmonic and melodic content are provided in table 4.2. Music can be used to prime people for an exercise program, lead people from a relatively sedate state to an active state during the warm-up, and do the converse during the cool-down. The arousing qualities of music are particularly salient between high-intensity bouts of activity such as weight training. The lyrical content of music is also important in this type of training because it provides exercisers with strong affirmations (see table 4.5).

Despite the desire of the English novelist George Eliot to always have music (see the opening quote to this chapter), exercise professionals are well advised not to use music in every session. Experiencing exercise bouts or components without music can result in a different type of pleasure—as we learned from Jim Denison (see the sidebar The Case For and Against Running With Music). Moreover, repeated exposure to a stimulus can lessen its effect over time. A balance of two exercise sessions with music to one session without is a good rule of thumb for exercise professionals.

# 5

# Group Exercise and Workouts

*We're still living with the old paradigm of age as an arch. That's the old metaphor: You're born, you peak at midlife, and decline into decrepitude. A more appropriate metaphor for aging is a staircase. The upward ascension of the human spirit, bringing us into wisdom, wholeness, and authenticity.*

—Jane Fonda, actress, writer, activist, and fitness guru

Group exercise with musical accompaniment took off in a big way during the late 1970s and went stratospheric during the 1980s. At the vanguard of this new workout trend was the celebrated Hollywood actress Jane Fonda. She realized that there was something captivating about bringing people together to exercise in sync with a musical beat—whatever their age. Fonda also knew how to package exercise to music and sell it on a grand scale. There can't be many women over 45 who don't have a Jane Fonda VHS cassette hidden away somewhere in the attic!

It became apparent that exercise-to-music classes were much more rewarding than exercising on one's own or in a group but without music—particularly for people who struggle to stick to exercise routines. The music was a kind of environmental adhesive that brought people together not only in time and space, but also at a deeper, primal level. Moving together to music is imprinted in our DNA. In most languages, the word for music and dance is the same. This tells

us much about how closely entwined music and movement were in the evolution of the human species. When we move in time with others in response to a piece of music, the neurons in the brain fire in time with the music and our movements. At a group level, it appears that even our neurology is in sync!

The dance-based classes that were popular in the 1970s and 1980s sowed the seeds for many variations such as step, aqua, BodyPump, Body-Combat, and Zumba, proving every bit as popular in the decades that followed. Each permutation dreamed up by entrepreneurs such as Les Mills has served up the same engaging music–exercise recipe under a new guise that stimulates sales and public interest. Music has also been applied to other forms of group exercise such as circuit training, spinning, yoga, and Pilates. The exercise-to-music revolution has evolved hand in hand with our newfound ability to manage and mix music digitally.

The first half of this chapter addresses music selection for choreographed classes (e.g., step and aqua aerobics); the second half addresses classes or group activities in which music is predominantly in the background or applied asynchronously (e.g., circuits and Pilates). Interestingly, activities that have used background music for many decades are now morphing into new forms that coordinate movement with music (see the sidebar Yoga Goes Pop).

## YOGA GOES POP

When Rebecca Russell-Turner was at school, she hated physical education lessons with an abiding passion. She longed for something she could do to keep fit that would be both fun and noncompetitive. Years later, when Rebecca worked as a personal assistant for American actor Woody Harrelson in the West End of London, she noticed how he practiced yoga to get "into the zone," as he called it, before going on stage. "Woody really inspired me, as the yoga gave him courage, calmness, and composure," she recalled. Rebecca gave Bikram yoga a try and immediately got bitten by the bug. Thereafter, during a cold and soggy January night, she decided to book a flight from London to Goa (India), in search of some sunshine and a little adventure. Over the three months that followed, she learned the intricacies of Ashtanga yoga and became a full-fledged yoga teacher.

Russell-Turner led a bohemian lifestyle in East London and became part of a broader creative community that included designers, poets, painters, stylists, producers, and musicians. Drawing on her array of artistic skills, in 2013 she launched a new exercise concept: Pop Yoga—that is, yoga coordinated with pop music to promote synchronization and a sense of flow. "Pop Yoga has the magic mix of music, people, movement, and an atmosphere associated with a positive energy," she says. "The people of London

work extraordinarily long hours, endure incessant traffic jams, and have a daily need to de-stress. Pop Yoga allows them to balance mind and body, enhance their fitness, and realign their posture. A fun experience in a supportive environment is at the very core of Pop Yoga."

So Londoners can now charge their chakras to Chaka Khan, breathe with Bronski Beat, and stretch to the Stranglers. Pop music combined with dynamic yoga brings people together and has proven so popular that Russell-Turner plans to franchise the concept with four versions of the class (see table 5.1) under the name Yung Club (www.yung.club). The classes have become a totally immersive experience with an eclectic music mix, aromatherapy scents, relaxation through touch, and colorful projections on the walls. The word *yoga* means "unity," and Russell-Turner's goal is to unite music, yoga, breathing, and meditation to address the challenges faced by modern-day city dwellers. The key

Courtesy of Pop Yoga.

Pop Yoga creates an immersive experience that can charge the chakras of stressed-out city dwellers.

**Table 5.1** Four Types of Pop Yoga Classes

| Class | Type of activity | Typical music choice | Brief analysis |
|---|---|---|---|
| Sensuality | Movements that put yogis in touch with their sensuality with an emphasis on a breathing pattern that emulates rolling waves | Love To Love You Baby by Donna Summer | This track oozes sensuality and magnifies the goals of the class. |
| Elegance | Stretching exercises that emphasize postural strength, stability, and self-confidence | Fire by Kasabian | A reverberating and slightly haunting lyrical track sits on a driving blues-rock beat. The lyrics have a strong self-affirming quality. |
| Connect | Class members are coordinated in a way that promotes a sense of group cohesion and togetherness | Loaded by Primal Scream | An infectious funky groove implores people to move in unison; although the lyrics are sparse, they spread the love. |
| Kicks | The class with the most leg exercises that is also the most physically demanding; entails forward and backward rolling movements as well as headstands | Space Oddity by David Bowie | The slightly disorientating nature of the Kicks class is aptly reflected in Bowie's allegorical homage to the space race. |

*Note:* All of these tracks can be located on YouTube.

message is that yoga is not just for hippies, vegans, and contortionists; it can benefit almost everyone. And when combined with music, it is the perfect antidote to a long, hard day in the urban jungle.

# CLASSES WITH CHOREOGRAPHED MOVEMENTS

This section addresses group exercise formats that use choreographed movements to music applied synchronously (for the most part). Choreographed classes began with dance aerobics, and virtually all exercise-to-music classes that followed, as well as those included here, are offshoots of dance aerobics.

The popular formats of LBT (legs, bums, and tums) and step aerobics are outlined next. We dip into the history of step aerobics to detail the innovation of American Gin Miller, which was prompted by a knee injury she was keen to overcome.

Aqua aerobics follows, a format that is especially popular among elderly people, the obese, and women in the pre- or post-natal phase. The main reason for this is that the water bears body weight, making the exercise routine far less stressful on the joints than land-based alternatives.

Two of the Les Mills formats are then presented: BodyPump and BodyCombat. Music is provided for these classes under license, and therefore, personal playlists cannot be used. The final section covers the exercise-to-music phenomenon that is Zumba, which is rendered distinct by the multicultural music programs employed by its devotees.

# Dance Aerobics

Dance aerobics is the archetypal exercise-to-music class that provided the building blocks for many, if not all, of the classes and activities that follow in this chapter. The term *aerobics* can be traced back to 1968 and the groundbreaking work of Kenneth Cooper and Colonel Pauline Potts, both of the U.S. Air Force. They constructed a program of aerobic exercise based on running, walking, swimming, and cycling to enhance the physical conditioning of NASA astronauts. Cooper's many books inspired the adoption of a range of exercise techniques by American dance instructors. Within one decade—the 1970s—Cooper's notion of aerobics and aspects of modern dance were melded into what has come to be known today as dance aerobics. Dance aerobics is an instructor-led activity that provides a fun and safe environment in which to enhance all aspects of physical fitness (flexibility, muscular strength, and cardiorespiratory endurance).

The use of music was critical in getting people who had previously led relatively sedentary lives to become habitually active. Also, a class structure for exercise provides social support, clear guidance from a qualified instructor, and a regular time commitment. Each of these aspects greatly influences how people adhere to a physical activity program (Biddle, Mutrie, & Gorely, 2015). From the outset of a dance aerobics class, the music brings people together in time and space. It locks them together as a unit, helps them forget about their troubles, and immerses them in the here and now. Although this book is not focused on choreography (see, e.g., the text *Exercise to Music* by Debbie Lawrence), we explore briefly how the demands of choreography influence an instructor's music selections and how they are segued to optimize the delivery of a class.

Choreography entails a great deal of beat counting to know what to do, when to do it, and how to express different parts of a musical composition through movement patterns. Dance aerobics instructors are taught to think in terms of 32-beat blocks of music when developing their choreography. Thirty-two beats is the same as eight musical bars of four beats each (common time). In much popular music, an eight-bar segment corresponds with the length of half a verse or half a chorus, and

therefore, the blocks can correspond directly with distinct parts of a song (see figure 1.2 in chapter 1). Music most appropriate for dance aerobics has a regular and fairly predictable rhythmic structure, a clearly discernible meter to enable the class to stay in time, uplifting harmonies, and motivational lyrics (e.g., "Come on let's work"), and is allied to the cultural background or preferences of the class. It provides a rhythmic structure and makes people feel good – in themselves and about themselves. Music that is rhythmically disjointed or that has lyrics that offend certain members of the class is not going to have the desired effect (see case study 2 in chapter 6).

Instructors need to think about segueing tracks or mixing a music program much as DJs do to create the right kind of atmosphere in a nightclub. The tracks should correspond with sections of the class such as warm-up (slow tempo), high intensity (fast tempo), and core strength (medium tempo). Clusters of tracks, or "mini-sets," as I like to call them, can then be created for each class segment (see table 5.2). To address the coherence of the music program, instructors should listen carefully to beat patterns (not just the tempi) of tracks in a mini-set to ensure that they are rhythmically similar (e.g., dubstep followed by dubstep, acid house followed by acid house). Moreover, where possible, tracks from the same artist should be grouped together or tracks should be linked thematically (e.g., two tracks from a well-known movie played back to back). Exploiting class members' cultural associations and surprising them with creativity and musical acumen are sure to place a given instructor's sessions at the top of their lists.

## LBT

LBT stands for legs, bums, and tums. This is a variant or even an integral part of regular dance aerobics classes that targets these areas of the body. In its full form, LBT is a concentrated 45-minute workout that appears to have particular appeal to women. This may be because many women have a genetic predisposition to accumulate fat in these regions of the body and view LBT as a way to address this. As well as being a popular studio-based activity, LBT workouts can also easily take place at home; all that's needed is a mat and great music to help break through the

**Table 5.2**   Dance Aerobics Class Playlist With Contemporary Music Selections

| Track | Artist(s) | Tempo (bpm) | Class segment |
|---|---|---|---|
| **Mini-set 1** | | | |
| Fancy | Iggy Azalea | 93 | Warm-up |
| Sugah Daddy | D'Angelo and the Vanguard | 93 | |
| Move With You | Jacob Banks | 95 | |
| **Mini-set 2** | | | |
| Uptown Funk | Mark Ronson feat. Bruno Mars | 115 | Low intensity |
| Treasure | Bruno Mars | 116 | |
| Hey Boy | Take That | 120 | |
| **Mini-set 3** | | | |
| Vibe Out | GotSome feat. Wiley | 128 | Moderate intensity |
| Cool | Alesso feat. Roy English | 128 | |
| Weird People | Little Mix | 128 | |
| **Mini-set 4** | | | |
| Break Free | Ariana Grande feat. Zedd | 130 | High intensity |
| All About That Bass | Meghan Trainor | 134 | |
| Lips Are Moving | Meghan Trainor | 139 | |
| **Mini-set 5** | | | |
| Gecko | Oliver Heldens & Becky Hill | 125 | Core strength |
| Pushing On | Oliver $ & Jimi Jules | 122 | |
| Go All Night | Gorgon City feat. Jennifer Hudson | 121 | |
| **Mini-set 6** | | | |
| I'm Not The Only One | Sam Smith | 83 | Cool-down and recuperation |
| Let It Be | Labrinth | 81 | |
| Thinking Out Loud | Ed Sheeran | 79 | |

*Note:* All of these tracks can be located on YouTube.

pain barrier. The class begins with a low-impact aerobic warm-up, followed by a series of exercises to isolate the lower limb and gluteal muscles, usually through squats and lunges. High reps are performed and free weights as well as ankle and wrist straps can be used to increase the intensity. The second half of the class is spent working on the floor and targets the abdominal and gluteal muscles. The class is rounded off with a cool-down and thorough stretch.

The music recommendations for core strength training (see chapter 4) and dance aerobics in this chapter apply in broad terms to LBT. Given the high number of repetitions involved in LBT, beat regularity without breaks, speeding up, or slowing down is a central consideration, because it is an endurance activity rather than a strength workout per se. Most rock music has considerable rhythmic variation and does not lend itself particularly well to the relentless regularity demanded by an LBT class. Far better are dance-related or earlier disco tracks in common time (4/4) with a strong beat in the tempo range of ~105 to ~125 bpm. The tempo can be varied in line with the desired rate of movement, although this range is generally easy to work with and easy to find tracks for. The following tracks can imbue an LBT session with lyrical affirmations: "She's Got The Power" by Stan Bush, "Bom Bom" by Sam and the Womp, and "Bootylicious" by Destiny's Child.

## Step Aerobics

Step aerobics is a group exercise class that is a derivative of dance aerobics and distinguished from other forms of aerobic exercise by its use of an elevated platform (the step). The sporting equipment company Reebok is closely associated with step aerobics and manufactures the steps, which can be height adjusted to meet individual needs. Step aerobics classes are offered at almost all gyms and fitness centers that have group exercise programs. American Gin Miller developed step aerobics in the late 1980s following a knee injury. She was advised by an orthopedic doctor to step up and down on a milk crate to strengthen the muscles supporting the knee. An infusion of creativity during the long and arduous rehabilitation process led her to develop the first step program. Miller then worked with Reebok to turn step into a global fitness phenomenon with many spinoffs (see http://ginmillerfitness.com).

Step choreography is based on 32 beats in a set, as described in the dance aerobics section of this chapter. Advanced step classes incorporate several dance elements such as turns, mambos, and stops. The principles associated with compiling the music program for step are almost identical to those for dance aerobics with some notable exceptions. First, because a 32-beat step routine is often performed on one side of the body and then mirrored by the other side, track length becomes more of an issue. If two tracks have different rhythmic qualities and the instructor is halfway through a sequence when the track transition takes place, this can be quite off-putting for the class. So it is important to think carefully about tracks lengths to ensure that discrete routines and their repeats on the opposite side of the body can be coordinated with a single track.

Another consideration for step aerobics is the fact that the action of stepping on and off the step has a significant time requirement. Therefore, using relatively fast tempi (e.g., >130 bpm) can be both disorientating and demotivating for beginners. This is because their brains are working hard to master the motor programs required, but the music compels them to perform the movements at a speed for which they are not yet ready. This can create anxiety, resulting in falling off the step, knocking it over because of a lack of motor control, or even twisting an ankle. The optimal music tempo in the main part of the class tends to be in the range of ~120 to ~130 bpm. Finally, step choreography has a very strong four-to-the-bar feel (e.g., step up right foot, step up left foot, step down right foot, step down left foot). Accordingly, this needs to be reflected in the rhythmic qualities of each track, with four quarter beats to the bar, an easily extractable meter, and no speeding up or slowing down of the tempo within a track. For a wide variety of step music programs, go to www.powermusic.com, www.fitnessav.ca, or www.fitstore.be/en/music/.

## Aqua Aerobics

Exercising in water comes naturally to many, be it at a Floridian beach resort, in an Italian lake, or even at the humble local public pool. The water helps bear body weight, and this comparative lack of stress on the joints creates feelings of liberation and security. Aqua aerobics, another derivative of dance aerobics, entails the performance of instructor-led aerobic exercise in the shallow end of a swimming pool. It is a type of resistance training with a primary focus on aerobic endurance and all-round strength development. This exercise modality is popular with the elderly, who are more prone to arthritis, osteoporosis, and weak joints. It is also popular with obese people and women who are in the pre- or post-natal phase. Aqua aerobics is a particularly safe form of exercise and is associated with an enjoyable atmosphere.

From a physiological standpoint, a benefit of aqua aerobics is the cooling effect the water has on the body. The average temperature of a community pool is around 80°F (26.7°C). This temperature forces the body to burn calories to maintain homeostasis while the water helps to limit the buildup of lactic acid in the muscles. Moreover, the heart does not beat as fast during a water-based activity as it does during an equivalent activity on land. Given what we know about the relationship between exercise heart rate and preference for music tempo (see chapter 2), this has a bearing on the tempi selected. Coupled with this is the fact that movements are resisted by the water, which means that they are not as fast or fluid as similar movements performed on land.

For an aqua aerobics music program, the speaker system should be relatively close to the participants (10 to 20 m) and should deliver a punchy, high-fidelity sound. The acoustics in swimming pools can be challenging. Given that water is one of the most effective reflectors of sound, pool ceilings are high, and the wall-to-wall tiling creates an echo effect, sound bounces around in the pool environment. Moreover, pool-related sounds such as splashing, breathing, and bubbling can easily obscure a musical beat when music is used in a synchronous way. At the heart of a successful aqua aerobics class is a good sound system. Do not cut corners!

Aqua aerobics instructors should consider the age range and musical predilections of the people attending the class. To maintain variety in the examples presented in this book, I focus on older people with reference to aqua aerobics. Older people generally do not like loud, fast, or aggressive music (Priest, Karageorghis, & Sharp, 2004). It is advisable to use a mix of old and new selections with an emphasis on rhythmic music dating from the formative years of attendees. It is relatively easy to find chart successes of the distant past using almanacs or websites and pick out tracks for an aqua aerobics class (see a sample playlist in table 5.3). I maintain a database for this purpose so that I can build it up over time and don't need to retrace my steps.

**Table 5.3**  Tracks for Elderly Participants in an Aqua Aerobics Class

| Track | Artist(s) | Year | Genre | Tempo (bpm) |
|---|---|---|---|---|
| At The Hop | Danny & the Juniors | 1957 | Rock 'n' roll | 95 |
| Blue Suede Shoes | Elvis Presley | 1956 | Rockabilly | 96 |
| Walk On By | Dionne Warwick | 1964 | R&B | 99 |
| In The Midnight Hour | Wilson Pickett | 1965 | Soul | 112 |
| Ob-La-Di, Ob-La-Da | The Beatles | 1968 | Pop | 113 |
| Summer In The City | The Lovin' Spoonful | 1966 | Pop | 113 |
| He's The Greatest Dancer | Sister Sledge | 1979 | Disco | 113 |
| Mustang Sally | Wilson Pickett | 1966 | Soul | 115 |
| Respect | Aretha Franklin | 1967 | R&B | 116 |
| Young Hearts Run Free | Candi Staton | 1976 | R&B | 116 |
| I Will Survive | Gloria Gaynor | 1978 | Disco | 116 |
| Stop! In The Name Of Love | The Supremes | 1965 | R&B | 117 |
| Heaven Must Be Missing An Angel | Tavares | 1976 | Disco | 117 |
| Yakety Yak | The Coasters | 1958 | Rock 'n' roll | 122 |
| Sugar Sugar | The Archies | 1969 | Pop | 122 |
| Ticket To Ride | The Beatles | 1965 | Rock | 124 |
| Daydream Believer | The Monkees | 1967 | Pop rock | 125 |
| Do Wah Diddy Diddy | Manfred Mann | 1963 | Pop rock | 126 |
| Oh, Pretty Woman | Roy Orbison | 1964 | Rock | 127 |
| My Guy | Mary Wells | 1964 | Soul | 127 |
| Twist And Shout | The Beatles | 1964 | Rock 'n' roll | 128 |
| Dance To The Music | Sly & the Family Stone | 1968 | Soul-funk | 129 |
| The Loco-Motion | Little Eva | 1962 | Pop | 130 |
| School Days | Chuck Berry | 1957 | Rock 'n' roll | 130 |
| I'm Into Something Good | Herman's Hermits | 1964 | Pop | 135 |

*Note:* All of these tracks can be located on YouTube.

Aqua aerobics provide a fun group-exercise activity that is popular with older people.

In terms of music tempo, given the resistance of the water, the relatively slow body movements, and lower exercise heart rates, the optimal range is ~100 to ~130 bpm. The warm-up and cool-down components of the class should use the lower end of this range (~100 to ~110 bpm), and the physiologically most demanding elements—generally the middle section of the class—should use the higher end (~120 to ~130 bpm). Including choreographed elements that demand tempi outside of this range is fine; the range is a guideline to use while keeping the overarching biomechanical and physiological demands of this activity in mind.

The many forms of water-based exercise set to music include aqua Zumba, Hydrorider, water yoga, and aqua jogging. The principles detailed in this section along with those detailed for the land-based versions of such activities can be considered in combination. The key principle to grasp is that the resistance generated by the water slows things down, and so the choice of music tempi needs to reflect this, particularly in the synchronous application of music.

## BodyPump

BodyPump is a weight-based group fitness program launched by Les Mills International in 1991 and now practiced in more than 10,000 gyms and health clubs around the world. Spin-offs of BodyPump are known collectively as group resistance classes. The idea behind BodyPump was to draw more men into aerobic exercise studios; thus, it places a particular emphasis on developing muscular endurance and a svelte, well-toned physique. There is a homogenized format to the classes in that they are pre-choreographed, with the accompanying music provided under license by Les Mills. Thus, a similar experience can be had at BodyPump classes around the world (a little bit like McDonald's, only healthier!).

The classes are 60 minutes long and contain eight muscle-group-specific music tracks along with a warm-up track and cool-down track. The music is purported to create a "musical journey" that propels participants through the workout. The tracks are normally cover versions or remixes of chart hits, but there is also a strong rock element to the playlists to attract male participants. To meet the demands of time-poor city dwellers, 45-minute and 30-minute variants of the class have been developed, the latter of which is known as BodyPump Express. Music for these classes comes from a set menu, and new music programs are released every quarter. A variety of music programs is available from the Les Mills catalog; instructors should consider carefully the demographics of their classes when selecting music programs.

The music programs have a standardized format. The tracks are mixed to allow for 32-count, or 32-beat, phrasing, and they vary in tempo in accordance with the type of movement they are accompanying. With the exception of the warm-up and cool-down tracks, BodyPump routines are performed in a synchronous mode. The tracks are directed at warm-up, legs or squats, chest, back, triceps, biceps, lunges, shoulders, abdominals, and a cool-down that includes a variety of stretches. Between tracks are brief intervals for stretching the muscle groups just exercised, changing weights, and explaining the next exercise.

## BodyCombat

BodyCombat is another popular Les Mills format that involves high-intensity martial arts–based workouts set to high-tempo music. Billed as the "empowering group fitness cardio workout where you are totally unleashed," these classes draw on a broad range of disciplines that include karate,

boxing, taekwondo, tai chi, and muay thai. A new routine and accompanying playlist (see table 5.4) is produced quarterly to keep things fresh. The fact that music is provided for these classes under license again leaves little scope for prescription—instructors use what they're given. Nonetheless, if you're developing a martial arts–based class of your own and not calling it BodyCombat, which is a registered trademark, consider spicing up your playlist by incorporating some fight-related tracks such as "Kung Fu Fighting" by Carl Douglas, "Fighter" by Christina Aguilera, and "Fight For This Love" by Cheryl Cole.

## Zumba

The flamboyant grandchild of dance aerobics, Zumba is, quite simply, the biggest exercise phenomenon of the last decade. As I write these lines, its onward march seems almost unstoppable. The concept was developed in the 1990s by a Columbian, Beto Perez, who one day happened to forget his cassette tape of aerobics music for a class he was teaching. He returned to his car and listened to cassettes of traditional salsa and merengue music for a few minutes before teaching the class on the fly with the Latin grooves as an

**Table 5.4** Playlist From a Les Mills BodyCombat Class

| Track | Artist(s) | Tempo (bpm) | Workout component |
|---|---|---|---|
| I Knew You Were Trouble [DRM remix edit] | Girls Only | 144 | Warm-up |
| Everything About You [Danceboy remix edit] | SupaHit | 144 | Warm-up |
| Danger Zone | International Outlaw | 145 | Warm-up |
| Be The One | Hixxy, Sy and Unknown | 176 | Intervals |
| A Warrior's Call | Volbeat | 146 | Active recovery |
| Bright Like The Sun | Sy and Unknown feat. Kirsten Joy | 170 | Intervals |
| Danger Zone | KDrew | 144 | Active recovery |
| Lost In Space | The Original Movies Orchestra | 163 | Muscular endurance |
| Falling From The Sky | Hixxy, Dave Castellano and Fat Steve | 175 | Muscular endurance |
| Do Or Die | Flux Pavilion feat. Childish Gambino | 145 | Muscular endurance |
| Fleurs Du Mal | Sarah Brightman | 97 | Cool-down |

*Note:* All of these tracks can be located on YouTube.

accompaniment. It proved a hugely successful formula, so he exported it to the United States and launched Zumba in 2001. An estimated 14 million people take weekly Zumba classes in over 140,000 locations across almost 200 countries. Now that's what you might call high-impact aerobics!

Zumba classes use a wide variety of music from the Americas, the West Indies, and Spain that includes salsa, merengue, mambo, flamenco, cha cha cha, reggaeton, soca, samba, hip-hop, and tango. In musical terms, Zumba provides one of the most diverse selections of styles, and perhaps this is one of the secrets of its success. The music programs are pre-packaged or can be formulated using a menu of tracks that instructors can use as the inspiration for their own choreography. An advantage of Zumba is the huge variety of programs and instructional DVDs to choose from

(see www.zumba.com/en-US/trainings). Given the diversity of styles used in Zumba music programs, there is also considerable diversity in terms of the tempi—much more so than in any other class covered in this chapter. The reason for this is that the diverse styles also have diverse subdivisions of the beat. This means that a style in a relatively slow tempo (e.g., 95 to 105 bpm) such as samba can feel extremely fast. Similarly, a classic reggae number with a characteristic skank (a strong emphasis on the second and fourth beats of the bar) can feel slower than its underlying tempo. The main message here is to consider both tempo *and* meter very carefully in devising Zumba choreography.

The numerous variations of the Zumba format include Zumba Kids for youngsters and Zumba Gold for seniors. Instructors should therefore select music programs that are age appropriate.

## RAVING ABOUT RUNNING AND FITNESS

Clubercise is the new workout craze sweeping the UK, and one of its most colorful formats is the Fitness Rave. The hedonistic 1990s are back with a vengeance, but there's not even the hint of narcotics in the air; the only type of high craved by these ravers is the one derived from exercise-induced endorphins! The first event of this type took place in The Vaults beneath London's Waterloo Station, with DJs spinning the decks, three instructors on stage, and a hoard of 1990s club scene devotees donning neon outfits and holding glow sticks.

Fitness Rave events are the brainchild of fitness innovator Shara Tochia, a Londoner who is determined to make exercise fun and more accessible: "People simply love fitness classes that are entertaining and the gimmicks that go with them—you almost forget that you're exercising!" (personal communication, April 1, 2014). The high-energy class lasts for an hour and entails a combination of cardio, interval training, and conditioning components. It's all set to old-school dance classics such as "Gonna Make You Sweat" and "I Like To Move It," which means that the revelers burn up to 500 calories while having a complete blast (see the sample playlist in table 5.5).

**Table 5.5**   1990s Playlist From the Fitness Rave

| Track | Artist(s) | Tempo (bpm) | Style | Workout segment |
|---|---|---|---|---|
| No Diggity | Blackstreet feat. Dr. Dre, Queen Pen | 89 | R&B | Stretching |
| Ready Or Not | Fugees | 89 | Hip-hop | Stretching |
| Gettin' Jiggy Wit It | Will Smith | 108 | Hip-hop | Aerobic warm-up |
| The Power | Snap! | 109 | Hip-house | Aerobic warm-up |
| Gonna Make You Sweat (Everybody Dance Now) | C+C Music Factory feat. Freedom Williams | 113 | Dance-pop | Aerobic warm-up |

| Track | Artist(s) | Tempo (bpm) | Style | Workout segment |
|---|---|---|---|---|
| Groove Is In The Heart | Deee-Lite | 120 | Dance-pop | Cardio training (low intensity) |
| I Like To Move It | Reel 2 Real | 123 | Dance | Cardio training (low intensity) |
| Rhythm Is A Dancer | Snap! | 125 | Eurodance | Cardio training (low intensity) |
| I See You Baby (Fatboy Slim edit) | Groove Armada | 130 | Big beat | Cardio training (moderate intensity) |
| Whoomp (There It Is) | Tag Team | 130 | Hip-hop | Cardio training (moderate intensity) |
| Ooh Aah . . . Just A Little Bit | Gina G | 131 | Eurodance | Interval training (high intensity) |
| Keep On Jumpin' | The Lisa Marie Experience | 132 | House | Interval training (high intensity) |
| Mr. Vain | Culture Beat | 133 | Eurodance | Interval training (high intensity) |
| No Limit | 2 Unlimited | 141 | Eurodance | Interval training (very high intensity) |
| Pure Shores | All Saints | 101 | Pop | Cool-down |
| Lifted | Lighthouse Family | 97 | Pop | Cool-down |
| Hero | Mariah Carey | 60 | R&B | Final stretch-out |

*Note:* All of these tracks can be located on YouTube.

Shara explained some of the additional benefits associated with such fitness events: "They have an air of nostalgia about them and are something that you can easily do with friends." Professional women in the age range of 20 to 40 have been rushing to get a piece of the action. Perhaps the appeal of the events is best summed up by one of the participants, Georgina Spenceley from Harlow in Essex: "It was the perfect combination of a fun workout, neon outfits and my favorite 90s floor-fillers. With glow sticks highlighting our every move, it was a nonstop underground fitness party" (Waterlow, 2013).

A similar craze sweeping the UK is the Electric Run, in which glow-in-the-dark, spandex-wearing, neon-covered runners take hold of glow-stick paraphernalia to run and dance their way through a 5 km course. Once they cross the finish line, there is a

*Courtesy of Shara Tochia.*

With thumping 90s dance tracks, neon outfits, and flashing lights, the Fitness Rave evokes youthful memories in its devotees.

tub-thumping dance party with a live DJ. Moreover, the Electric Run has inspired a recent spinoff, the Cosmic Run, in which after-hours athletes are sprayed with glow-in-the-dark powder as they progress through the course. Even if they don't like the throbbing electronic dance music that greets them at the finish, at least it's a good way to stay safe during their evening run.

Moreover, a consideration for all of the Zumba classes is that, given the degree of syncopation in Latin music (e.g., salsa), music programs should have the least amount of syncopation for inexperienced participants, so they can most easily feel where the first beat of the bar lies. In addition, given the complexities of some of the rhythms that are popular in Zumba classes, exercise leaders can help participants by emphasizing vocally and through their movement patterns where the first beat of the bar lies. This improves exercisers' senses of rhythm and keeps the movement patterns in check.

# CLASSES AND GROUP ACTIVITIES WITH ASYNCHRONOUS MUSIC

This section addresses popular classes and group activities that apply asynchronous, or background, music. Circuit training is particularly close to my heart because I have run a weekly circuit training class for over 25 years. The nature of circuit training is thoroughly explained, and a sample playlist that draws from the musical eras of the last quarter century is provided. Rock music works particularly well for the instructor-led stationary cycling workout known as spinning. Boxercise was developed and popularized by one of my former students, Andy Wake. It entails boxing-related cross-training and so employs a boxing-themed playlist to instill the desired mind-set. The rapidly advancing Pilates is a mind–body program that is best accompanied by soft and uncomplicated music. A related physical activity is yoga, whose main goal is to help participants achieve a sense of well-being and inner calm. Music that accompanies yoga needs to support this objective, but some yogis are thoroughly opposed to the use of music in their classes. The section ends with an examination of music use in tai chi, a martial art grounded in the Taoist and Buddhist faiths.

## Circuit Training

Circuit training has grown considerably in popularity recently because it is an intense workout that can deliver relatively fast results in anaerobic endurance, muscle tone, and cardiorespiratory fitness. As the name *circuit* suggests, exercises and activities are organized in a circular formation; people exercise at each station for a set period (e.g., 25 seconds) before recovering for a set period (e.g., 20 seconds) and moving to the next station during the recovery. Once all of the stations have been completed (i.e., the circuit is completed), there is a longer period of recovery (normally two to five minutes). A typical workout consists of three or four circuits of 15 to 20 stations.

Circuit training is a hybrid fitness activity that includes muscular endurance, strength, mobility, plyometric, and speed components. Some instructors include coordination activities (e.g., skipping drills over plastic hurdles) to encourage participants to think while under physical stress. Given the repetitive and almost regimented nature of a circuit, people generally love to have music playing in the background. Even highly-trained participants express a preference for music. The activity is usually performed to asynchronous music, although lab-based research showed that coordinating circuit exercises with music in a synchronous manner particularly benefitted women in terms of the number of repetitions completed and how positive they felt (see figure 5.1 for performance data) (Karageorghis et al., 2010).

Interestingly, the men in this research appeared to derive no performance benefit from synchronous music when the two music conditions (motivational and oudeterous) were compared to a bleeping metronome that served as a control. In explaining their findings, the authors reflected on the experiences males and females have with music during their formative years. They explained that girls are more likely to engage in movement to music-based activities and demonstrate a greater desire to engage in dance-related activity (Karageorghis et al., 2010). The findings also showed that women were, on the whole, more adept than their male counterparts at keeping in sync with the musical beat. Despite the potential benefits for women that this study demonstrates, the mix of activities in a real-life circuit and their physical demands means that the use of asynchronous music generally works best.

There are opportunities for synchronization during parts of a circuit, but this is often done

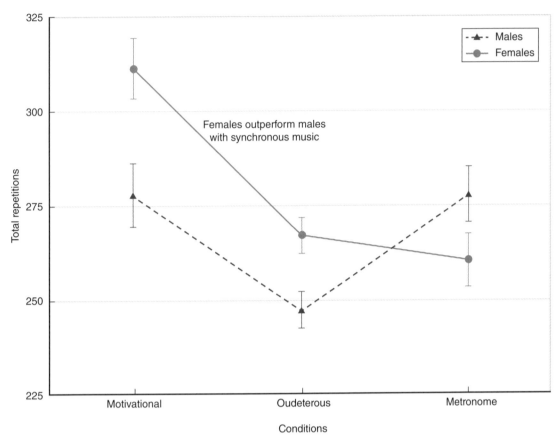

**Figure 5.1** Gender differences in circuit training performance accompanied by synchronous music (motivational and oudeterous) and a metronome control.

Adapted from *Psychology of Sport and Exercise* 11(6), C.I. Karageorghis, D.L. Priest, L.S. Williams, R.M. Hirani, K.M. Lannon, and B.J. Bates, "Ergogenic and psychological effects of synchronous music during circuit-type exercise," 551-559, 2010, with permission from Elsevier.

on an ad hoc basis. For example, if an exerciser is performing bench dips, the background music is playing at 140 bpm, and her dipping rate is 35 reps per minute, she can either flex or extend the elbow joint with each two beats of music in 4/4 time to sync with it. There are musical ways to boost a circuits class. First, the music should be motivational and uplifting (see chapter 2 and the discussion of the BMRI-3 in chapter 3) and in a tempo range of 120 to 145 bpm. Second, the lower end of that tempo range should be used for the first circuit and gradually be built up toward the top end of the range for the final circuit, when the class needs the most stimulation. Taking this principle a step further, music may not be used at all for the first circuit and introduced in the second circuit. Third, a soundtrack for a circuits class can punctuate work and recovery periods. This can be done by having periods of silence for the recovery periods to signal when people need to stop and move to the next station, or by including bleeps on the soundtrack—perhaps a high-pitched bleep to start and a low-pitched bleep to stop.

As an unassuming undergraduate, my first scientific research into the effects of music on human performance entailed examining how stimulative and sedative music programs influenced the number of repetitions performed. The stimulative music produced superior performance levels when compared to sedative music and a no-music control (Karageorghis, 1991). Since that time, I have used music for a Monday night circuits class at my university. During the last 25 years, I have compiled many playlists (at least one a term) and have often asked participants for selections that I subsequently incorporate. For table 5.6, I have trawled through these playlists from the last quarter century to produce my all-time circuits

**Table 5.6**   Playlist for Circuit Training

| Track | Artist(s) | Year | Tempo (bpm) | Class component and musical era |
|-------|-----------|------|-------------|--------------------------------|
| I'm Every Woman | Whitney Houston | 1992 | 119 | Circuit 1 (1990-1995) |
| Groove Is In The Heart | Deee-Lite | 1990 | 119 | |
| Now That We Found Love | Heavy D & The Boyz feat. Aaron Hall | 1991 | 120 | |
| Two Can Play That Game | Bobby Brown | 1994 | 120 | |
| Shout (It Out) | Louchie Lou & Michie One | 1993 | 120 | |
| Don't Call Me Baby | Madison Avenue | 2000 | 125 | Circuit 2 (1996-2001) |
| When The Going Gets Tough | Boyzone | 1999 | 128 | |
| It's Like That | Run-D.M.C. vs. Jason Nevins | 1998 | 129 | |
| Freed From Desire | Gala | 1997 | 129 | |
| Don't Stop Movin' | Livin' Joy | 1996 | 130 | |
| Mercy | Duffy | 2008 | 130 | Circuit 3 (2002-2008) |
| Shut Up And Drive | Rihanna | 2007 | 133 | |
| Jump | Girls Aloud | 2003 | 135 | |
| What You Waiting For? | Gwen Stefani | 2004 | 136 | |
| Heaven | DJ Sammy & Yanou feat. Do | 2002 | 138 | |
| Ex's & Oh's | Elle King | 2015 | 140 | Circuit 4 (2009-2015) |
| The Story Of Us | Taylor Swift | 2011 | 140 | |
| Put It Down (Clean) | Brandy feat. Chris Brown | 2012 | 141 | |
| How Low | Ludacris | 2010 | 144 | |
| Can't Hold Us | Macklemore & Ryan Lewis feat. Ray Dalton | 2011 | 146 | |

*Note:* All of these tracks can be located on YouTube.

playlist. Each mini-set (i.e., tracks for a single circuit) uses music from a distinct musical era to give the playlist greater coherence.

## Spinning

Spinning is an instructor-led stationary cycling workout that uses both synchronous and asynchronous music. In its generic form, it is known as an indoor cycling class, but I use the far more commonly known term *spinning* here. This low-impact workout can be very high intensity: participants expend up to 1,000 calories per session! Given the low-impact and low-weight-bearing nature of spinning, it can supplement other high-impact cardio workouts such as road running, and it is a particularly good form of exercise for people with joint problems (under appropriate medical supervision). The class is generally 40 to 60 minutes long, and the participants decide how much resistance to add and how fast to pedal, with guidance from the instructor. The movements in the class reflect those of a cycling road race, with sprint sections, hill climbs, and free-wheeling recovery stints that are analogous to downhill coasting.

The music is generally in the background because class members cycle at different rates, although from time to time, they sync with the music and each other. For example, the instructor might lead the group to cycle in synchrony to resemble the efficiency of a peloton, with each cyclist adjusting the pedal resistance to suit. Two distinct side effects of spinning, particularly during the first few weeks of participation, are pain in the quadriceps, which are worked relentlessly, and saddle soreness. Therefore, it helps to have fairly loud music to dull the pain (75 to 80 dBA—the same volume as city traffic heard from inside a car). Also, given the whir of the bikes, a high-quality speaker system is a must. The music tempo needs to match working heart rate, and a range of ~115 to ~145 bpm works well. The music should have strong stimulative qualities—particularly for the "belly" of the workout—and powerful lyrical messages to spur people on when the workout starts to hurt.

Rock selections can work well for spinning because any rhythmic irregularities (e.g., changes in tempo) do not offset a choreographed routine. For a heavy-duty session, participants can rock out to "Can't Get Enough" by Bad Company, "Face The Pain" by Stem, and "Back For More" by Five Finger Death Punch. The numerous websites offering music programs across genres for spinning include http://spinningmusic.word press.com, www.spinning.com/en/webshop/ products/23/music_cds, and http://8tracks.com/# explore/spinning.

## Boxercise

Back in the early 1990s, I had a pint-sized and rather charismatic student from Ponteland in Northumberland (UK) named Andy Wake. He was

Courtesy of Amber Wallace.

Founder of Boxercise Andy Wake puts one of his protégés through her paces.

a talented all-round athlete who was particularly well known for his achievements at the national level in the pole vault as a Great Britain representative with a personal best of 5.10 meters. Unfortunately, a persistent back injury ended Wake's promising pole-vaulting career. He deferred to his second sporting passion, boxing, to make a living. Although clearly a veritable adrenaline junkie, Wake was not intent on shuffling around a ring getting punchdrunk; his vision was to take what he'd learned through years of boxing training and his college education to create an entirely new exercise format. Thus, Boxercise was born.

It's been over 20 years since Wake graduated from his course in sport sciences. Since then, the Boxercise format has literally taken the world by storm (see www.boxercise.co.uk), spreading to over 30 countries and practiced by more than 2 million people. The retention rates are extremely high (~80 percent from year to year), which may be the result of participants having regular individual instruction within the class format. Boxercise is a form of cross-training accompanied by loud and pulsating asynchronous music: "The key aspect is a heavy beat and some sort of relationship with the fight game," Wake says (personal communication, May 20, 2014). Accordingly, the playlists often have strong boxing themes; tracks from the *Rocky* series (starring Sylvester Stallone) and the movie *Ali* (starring Will Smith) feature prominently (see the sample playlist in table 5.7). Recently, Wake developed an iPhone Boxercise app that dubs a bell-like sound over a playlist to signal work and rest periods.

Boxercise classes do not have a set format like the Les Mills classes described earlier; rather, they can incorporate many training components and vary according to the specialty and personality of the instructor. Boxing-style circuits is one of the favorite formats; circuit stations include activities such as focus pads, punch bags, skipping, and medicine ball throws. Wake reveals that "Focus pads are the closest you'll ever get to actually hitting anyone in class!" (personal communication, May 20, 2014). Boxercise is a great way to let off steam and get superfit, as well as to develop eye–hand coordination, balance, and split-second timing. And with the new iPhone app, it's "seconds out, round 2."

## Pilates

Pilates is a physical fitness system developed in the early 20th century by Joseph Pilates—a physical-culturist from Mönchengladbach in Germany. It is very popular in the West and can help people build flexibility, muscle strength, and endurance in all of the major muscle groups. Pilates places particular emphasis on spinal and pelvic alignment, breathing patterns, a strong core, and coordination and balance. Exercises can be modified in terms of difficulty, and intensity can be increased over time as the body adapts to the system. Many elite athletes such as Tiger Woods (golf) and Sanya Richards-Ross (track and field) use Pilates as a central part of their conditioning programs.

Pilates is very much a mind–body system of conditioning. Its originator actually named it ontology, given the strong emphasis on controlling the musculature. Because the mind-set of Pilates is one of inner calm and internal focus toward the center of the body (centering), music that detracts from this (e.g., loud punk rock) is certainly not advisable. The music that best complements Pilates is akin to that described in chapter 4 for passive stretching (see table 4.3). It needs to be at a low volume, melodically and rhythmically simple without a strong pulse, preferably instrumental, and with a warm and soothing ambiance. Contemporary artists who produce music that fits this description include Ludovico Einaudi (Italy), Röyksopp (Norway), Amethystium (Norway), and Enigma (Germany).

## Yoga

Yoga is a set of physical, mental, and spiritual practices or disciplines that originated in ancient India. The underlying philosophy relates to attaining a state of permanent peace of mind to experience one's true self, and it embraces relaxation, meditation, proper breathing, and a good diet, in addition to exercise. Various traditions of yoga are found in Hinduism, Buddhism, and Jainism; the commonality is the goal of transcending the physical form. Gurus such as Swami Vivekananda, who brought yoga to the West in the late 19th century, initiated a trend that perhaps reached its apex in the early 1990s. There are about 20

**Table 5.7** Popular Tracks From Boxercise Classes

| Track | Artist(s) or Composer | Tempo (bpm) | Brief analysis |
|-------|----------------------|-------------|----------------|
| Take You Back | Frank Stallone | 75 | A sparse and evocative vocal-harmony track that was written and performed by Sly's younger brother, Frank, for the singing corner scene in the original *Rocky* movie (1976). |
| It's A Fight | Three 6 Mafia | 82 | An aggressive rap tune that captures the essence of the fight game and provides a stream of verbal cues for boxercisers. It talks of hitting an opponent with the left and then the right, almost providing the instructions of an imaginary second. |
| Going The Distance | Bill Conti | 91 | An instrumental piece that resembles a Bach fugue in the early stages and then launches into an incredibly uplifting melodic section to fully prime pugilists for action. |
| Gonna Fly Now (Theme From *Rocky*) | Rocky Orchestra | 96 | One of the most inspiring pieces of music of all time that accompanies the warm-up and gets everyone pumped up for the tough workout to come. |
| Eye Of The Tiger | Survivor | 108 | A staple of all Boxercise classes and consistently voted the most motivational workout song of all time in media polls; defined by the stirring lyrics and guitar stabs that come at you like sonic punches. |
| Keep It Up | Snap! | 109 | Snap recreated some of the magic of their 1990 international smash hit "The Power" with this track for *Rocky V*; it feels like the same rhythmic backdrop. |
| Go For It | Joey B Ellis AKA MC Breeze feat. Tynetta Hare | 110 | Sounds particularly good when mixed with "Keep It Up"; the two tracks complement each other in rhythmic style as well as in their brazen attitude. |
| How You Like Me Now? | The Heavy | 110 | A track from the hit movie *The Fighter* that has an infectious funky groove and builds the intensity toward a giant wall of sound in the closing stages. |
| Living In America | James Brown | 114 | This tune from *Rocky III* takes the pointer on the funkometer into the red zone—the Godfather of Soul at his glorious best. |
| Hearts On Fire | John Cafferty | 136 | A rock track used for a *Rocky IV* training montage (in Siberia) to drive a cardiovascular system that is already working at full capacity. The lyrics address the desire to excel and the passion that rages within. |
| The Final Bell | Bill Conti | 159 | A rousing instrumental piece for that last big push during a workout. It brings into sharp focus how the extra effort can pay big dividends. |
| The World's Greatest | R. Kelly | 96 | A highly inspiring track that is at an ideal tempo for a cool-down and has well-established associations with boxing through its prominent use in the movie *Ali*. |

*Note:* There is a distinct lack of these well-known boxing-themed tracks in the tempo range of 115 to 135 bpm. Hopefully, Bill Conti will read this book and address the omission when writing the film score for any future spinoff of the *Rocky* film series! All of the tracks in this table can be located on YouTube.

forms of yoga, but the form most practiced in the West is hatha yoga, during which exercise heart rate rarely rises above 100 bpm (Hagins, Moore, & Rundle, 2007). This form is derived from Hinduism and focuses on developing physical and mental strength.

Some of the main reported benefits of yoga are a deep sense of well-being and inner calm, superior function of the internal organs, enhanced circulation, and improved posture. Scientific evidence comparing the long-term benefits of mind–body forms of exercise such as yoga and Pilates to those of other popular forms of exercise such as swimming, running, and dance aerobics is largely lacking. Nonetheless, given that yoga is a low-impact and low-intensity form of physical activity—regardless of people's views on its purported spiritual and psychological benefits—it carries the strong likelihood of promoting health and perhaps longevity. In a similar vein to Pilates, music plays a subordinate role in yoga, and some teachers are resistant to it.

> Sound is there to reveal silence. When the music stops, there's still so much song: the sound of your breath, the beating of your heart, the cacophony of nature and humanity outside the studio. Sometimes music can mask the more subtle sounds that bring us closer to our inner rhythms. (Karl Erb, former San Francisco–based yoga instructor; Charnas, 2007)

If not appropriate to the moment, and not experienced in its totality, music can be intrusive. In this case, its many gifts can go to waste.

For those who want to use music in yoga classes, a vast array is commercially available. Such music more or less follows the criteria detailed in relation to exercise forms such as passive stretching (see table 4.3 in chapter 4) and Pilates. Good places to start are www.yogi-tunes.com and www.myyogaonline.com/music. Because yoga is derived from ancient Indian culture, some instructors use Indian classical music as an accompaniment to their classes. Such music is particularly expressive and predicated on a different type of tuning to the Pythagorean system used in Western music (see chapter 2). Specifically, just-intonation tuning can facilitate smaller gaps in pitch between the notes in a scale. This can heighten the expressiveness of the music, which is largely improvised,

and have an absorbing and meditative quality (think background music in a traditional Indian restaurant and you're halfway there).

## Tai Chi

Tai chi is a Chinese martial art whose origins can be traced to the traditions of Taoist and Buddhist monasteries in the 12th century. Nowadays, it is practiced in the East and West as a mind–body form of exercise that is gentle on the body. Tai chi is typified by slow and highly controlled movements that replicate animal movements (e.g., white crane spreads its wings) with a concurrent focus on bodily sensations. It is particularly popular among older people because it is thought to promote functional stability, flexibility, and longevity. Some instructors describe tai chi as "meditation in motion," but it could just as easily be described as "medication in motion" given its numerous health benefits.

Similar to Pilates and yoga, music is not an essential aspect of a tai chi class, but it can heighten and enrich the experience for some people when played in the background. Some tai chi instructors use Chinese classical music as an accompaniment for their classes (see www.last.fm/tag/tai+chi). Such music is built on the pentatonic scale (think of the evocative sound created when you play only the five black keys on a piano). Slow music that uses the pentatonic scale has a soothing and calming effect. It can supplement both the gentle nature of the activity and the internal body-focused attention that tai chi requires. If Chinese classical music is not your bag, the gentle ambient pop and classical music recommendations for Pilates and yoga (~80 to ~100 bpm) work nearly as well. Just keep the volume turned down low.

## SUMMARY

There are two broad forms of group exercise with music—one that entails moves that are choreographed to music and another in which music is played in the background. These applications relate directly to the synchronous and asynchronous uses of music described in chapter 1. Some forms of group exercise such as circuit training and spinning can involve both applications, and

**Table 5.8**  Summary of Group Exercise Class Characteristics

| Class | Synchronous vs. asynchronous music application | Compulsory music programs | Participants mirror instructor | Predominant attendees | Tempo range (bpm) |
|---|---|---|---|---|---|
| Dance aerobics | Synchronous | No | Yes | Females | 90-150 |
| LBT | Synchronous | No | Yes | Females | 105-125 |
| Step aerobics | Synchronous | No | Yes | Females | 115-130 |
| Aqua aerobics | Synchronous | No | Yes | Both genders | 100-130 |
| Bodypump | Both | Yes | Yes | Both genders | 100-140 |
| BodyCombat | Both | Yes | Yes | Both genders | 90-180 |
| Zumba | Synchronous | Yes | Yes | Females | 80-180 |
| Circuit training | Asynchronous | No | No | Both genders | 120-145 |
| Spinning | Asynchronous | No | Yes | Both genders | 115-145 |
| Boxercise | Asynchronous | No | No | Both genders | 75-160 |
| Pilates | Asynchronous | No | Yes | Both genders | 80-100 |
| Yoga | Asynchronous | No | Yes | Females | 80-100 |
| Tai chi | Asynchronous | No | Yes | Both genders | 80-100 |

even choreographed classes often use music asynchronously for the warm-up and cool-down phases. The music is ideally loud (~75 dBA, the volume of city traffic) for some group activities such as LBT and spinning, whereas for other activities, such as Pilates and tai chi, it plays a far more supplementary role and thus requires a relatively low volume. The key characteristics of group exercise classes in relation to music selection are summarized in table 5.8.

Although this text is not about choreography (another crucial aspect of dance-based classes), instructors need to plan carefully to ensure that the music facilitates participants' choreographed moves. Specific rhythmic patterns or melodic figures may inspire certain movements; nonetheless, the basic structure of a music program in terms of track lengths, tempi, and the energy of the music must be given careful consideration. For example, reaching the end of the 55 minutes designated for a class and still playing thumping dance music at 130 bpm rather than a slower, rejuvenating-type track may not enable participants to depart with the desired mind-set (i.e., calm and revitalized). Instructors should also use volume and the dynamics within tracks to create a crescendo when the greatest amount

of physical exertion is required. Thereafter, the mood of the music should lighten toward the end of the session with soft, slow selections. Similar to a musical performance, the first and last tracks played during an exercise program hold special significance. Skillful exercise instructors create a coherent whole, with music and choreography that optimizes the experience of the class (see the sidebar Yoga Goes Pop). A group exercise class can be considered a type of musical journey.

This chapter covers only the most popular forms of group exercise. Because emerging classes such as bootcamp, Metafit, and Piloxing bear a close resemblance to the classes or activities covered, the music selection principles for those classes or activities can be applied. Those covered have a number of commonalities (e.g., the need to analyze expected heart rate or movement rate when selecting music). In all classes or activities, instructors need to consider variety in the music program. They should survey their clients (see case study 2 in chapter 6) and keep abreast of new releases. The much-loved and sorely missed BBC Radio 1 DJ, John Peel (UK), was once asked by a journalist why he never took days off. "There's so much music in the world," he said, "and so little time."

# 6

# Exercise Case Studies and Playlists

*Musical training is a more potent instrument than any other, because rhythm and harmony find their way into the inward places of the soul, on which they mightily fasten, imparting grace, and making the soul of him who is rightly educated graceful, or of him who is ill-educated ungraceful.*

—Socrates, from Book 3 of Plato's *Republic*

This chapter presents two detailed case studies—one on individual exercise and one on group exercise—to help exercise practitioners take the main principles from the chapters in this part and apply them to their own endeavors. The case studies are broadly based on real people and cover a range of contexts and music applications. The intent here is to encourage reflection on the dynamics of the situation, the nature of the people involved, the thought processes that underlie music selection, and some of the key consequences of music listening.

## CASE STUDY 1: SOPHIE, MOTHER OF THREE, WANTS TO REKINDLE THE EXERCISE HABIT

### Introduction and Background

Sophie had been a vivacious cheerleader during her college days. Now in her mid-40s, after raising three sons who were all in their late teens, she had lost confidence in her appearance and with it some of her self-esteem. During her younger days, Sophie had had a svelte body and could eat what she wanted without adding extra inches to her waistline. Now it seemed that she had only to look at a candy bar to feel bloated and unattractive.

Before cheerleading, Sophie had studied ballet, jazz, and tap at a local dance academy. As a result, Sophie had developed a good sense of rhythm and was particularly well coordinated; she still enjoyed the liberating feeling of kicking off her shoes and dancing to her favorite tunes by 1980s icons like Duran Duran, Madonna, Journey, and Bon Jovi. Most of the time, this happened in the sunroom while the kids were at school.

An acrimonious divorce from Mick, her husband of 17 years, had taken its toll on Sophie. He was a successful stockbroker who had maintained a privileged lifestyle for his wife and children but didn't seem to love or even like them most of the time. Since the divorce, Sophie had gotten into the habit of comfort eating either cookies or ice cream, particularly late at night in front of the TV. Despite her best intentions, she rarely made it for a workout at the neighborhood YMCA, which was just a 10-minute walk away.

Sophie resolved to do something about all of this. She knew that she had a toned, lean physique underneath the accumulation of fat and wanted to show the world, and herself, the persona of a more confident and self-assured woman. Most of all, she didn't want to let herself feel beaten by the failure of her marriage; she wanted to do something positive to reclaim control of her life.

Throughout her life the pleasurable associations that Sophie made with any form of physical activity involved music in some way—in dance classes, in cheerleading, at the local Y, and even dancing wildly around the sunroom at home. Since the birth of her children, what Sophie had lacked most was a systematic and structured approach to exercise. She knew that if she could embed her program into a regular routine and set it to music, she would stand a good chance of sticking to it. To facilitate this, Sophie went to see a local lifestyle coach, Pam Walters, in search of some ideas and a little inspiration.

## Consultation With the Lifestyle Coach

Pam was warm, receptive, and understanding; having raised two kids herself, she knew about the main barriers to habitual physical activity and so she readily empathized with Sophie. The pair began by talking about Sophie's background, some of the perceived roadblocks in her life, and her hopes, dreams, and aspirations. They went on to discuss in some detail the structure of Sophie's typical week: the times she drove the kids to their various activities, when she did shopping and housework, social events with family friends, and so on. Pam proposed that, to fully embed exercise into her routine, Sophie would need to find 90-minute windows for sessions outside of the home (e.g., at the local YMCA) and 60-minute windows for sessions at home. These windows would give her sufficient time for getting changed, traveling, and showering.

The pair reached the conclusion that Sophie could schedule one session at home every Monday during the midmorning and attend classes at the local Y on Tuesdays and Thursdays during the late afternoon, with a possible further class early on Saturday mornings, just before the weekly grocery shop. Pam advised Sophie to inform family and friends about these four slots of "me time" so that

people did not phone or make demands on her during these times. Pam said, "Think of it like an appointment with the doctor or dentist, a part of your day that's owned and no one can tamper with." Pam also explained that once people understood Sophie's general pattern of activity, they would be less likely to make demands on her during those times. This neat trick took advantage of psychological principles such as expectancy and reinforcement.

## Designing the Program

The pair went on to discuss the types of activities that appealed to Sophie and would fuel her interest in physical activity into the foreseeable future. Sophie mentioned music again and again as the most prominent feature of any physical activity she had engaged in during the past—whether by accident or by design. It was also evident that Sophie loved 1980s pop acts and their contemporary reincarnations such as Lady Gaga, Maroon 5, and Rihanna. Engaging with this music reconnected her with the experience of being young and aspirational; it created a world full of freedom and possibility.

Given Sophie's expressed love of music and the central role it played in her life, Pam decided to use a tool she found online—a modified version of the Music Mood-Regulation Scale (see chapter 3) to identify pieces of music that would regulate aspects of Sophie's mood (see figure 6.1). If Sophie wanted to feel contented, she would listen to the rather appropriately titled "Song For Sophie" by Aura Dione; to feel more alert, she would listen to "Boom Boom Pow" by the Black Eyed Peas; and to alleviate feelings of anxiety, she would listen to Bobby McFerrin's classic "Don't Worry, Be Happy."

The consultation then turned to how music could be more effectively intertwined with Sophie's workouts to make them fun and appealing. Moving in time to music, or synchronously, was something Sophie highlighted as particularly pleasurable. The types of activities she identified as working best involve rhythmic movement and mimicking music's ebb and flow through movement.

The pair viewed the schedule of classes at the local Y online and considered the activities that Sophie might like. For the home-based session on Mondays, they decided on a 1980s music dance

| | **Tracks/pieces of music** |
|---|---|
| 1. If you need to feel **restful**, what tracks or pieces of music would you listen to as a strategy to achieve this feeling? | *Return to Innocence by Enigma* |
| 2. If you need to feel **relaxed**, what tracks or pieces of music would you listen to as a strategy to achieve this feeling? | *Songbird by Eva Cassidy* |
| 3. If you need to feel **lively**, what tracks or pieces of music would you listen to as a strategy to achieve this feeling? | *Cheerleader (Felix Jaehn Video Edit) by OMI* |
| 4. If you need to feel **happy**, what tracks or pieces of music would you listen to as a strategy to achieve this feeling? | *I'm Coming Out by Diana Ross* |
| 5. If you need to feel **energetic**, what tracks or pieces of music would you listen to as a strategy to achieve this feeling? | *Jump by Van Halen* |
| 6. If you need to feel **contented**, what tracks or pieces of music would you listen to as a strategy to achieve this feeling? | *Song For Sophie (I Hope She Flies) by Aura Dione* |
| 7. If you need to feel **composed**, what tracks or pieces of music would you listen to as a strategy to achieve this feeling? | *I Can See Clearly Now by Jimmy Cliff* |
| 8. If you need to feel **cheerful**, what tracks or pieces of music would you listen to as a strategy to achieve this feeling? | *Happy Days Theme Song by Charles Fox* |
| 9. If you need to feel **calm**, what tracks or pieces of music would you listen to as a strategy to achieve this feeling? | *Paint The Night With Stars by Enya* |
| 10. If you need to feel **alert**, what tracks or pieces of music would you listen to as a strategy to achieve this feeling? | *Boom Boom Pow by the Black Eyed Peas* |
| 11. If you need to feel **active**, what tracks or pieces of music would you listen to as a strategy to achieve this feeling? | *I'm So Excited by the Pointer Sisters* |
| 12. If you are feeling **satisfied**, what tracks or pieces of music would you listen to as a strategy to achieve this feeling? | *What A Wonderful World by Louis Armstrong* |
| 13. If you are feeling **worried**, what tracks or pieces of music would you listen to as a strategy to change this feeling? | *Not Afraid by Eminem* |
| 14. If you are feeling **worn out**, what tracks or pieces of music would you listen to as a strategy to change this feeling? | *Super Trouper by Abba* |
| 15. If you are feeling **unhappy**, what tracks or pieces of music would you listen to as a strategy to change this feeling? | *Don't Let The Sun Go Down On Me by Elton John and George Michael* |
| 16. If you are feeling **tired**, what tracks or pieces of music would you listen to as a strategy to change this feeling? | *We Built This City by Starship* |
| 17. If you are feeling **sleepy**, what tracks or pieces of music would you listen to as a strategy to change this feeling? | *We Are Never Getting Back Together by Taylor Swift* |
| 18. If you are feel **panicky**, what tracks or pieces of music would you listen to as a strategy to change this feeling? | *One Day I'll Fly Away by Randy Crawford* |
| 19. If you are feel **nervous**, what tracks or pieces of music would you listen to as a strategy to change this feeling? | *I Knew You Were Waiting by Aretha Franklin and George Michael* |
| 20. If you are feeling **miserable**, what tracks or pieces of music would you listen to as a strategy to change this feeling? | *Feeling Good by Michael Bublé* |
| 21. If you are feeling **exhausted**, what tracks or pieces of music would you listen to as a strategy to change this feeling? | *High Energy by Evelyn Thomas* |
| 22. If you are feeling **downhearted**, what tracks or pieces of music would you listen to as a strategy to change this feeling? | *The Only Way Is Up by Yazz* |
| 23. If you are feeling **depressed**, what tracks or pieces of music would you listen to as a strategy to change this feeling? | *Big Girl (You Are Beautiful) by Mika* |
| 24. If you are feeling **bitter**, what tracks or pieces of music would you listen to as a strategy to change this feeling? | *Man In The Mirror by Michael Jackson* |
| 25. If you are feeling **bad tempered**, what tracks or pieces of music would you listen to as a strategy to change this feeling? | *Arthur's Theme (Best That You Can Be) by Christopher Cross* |
| 26. If you are feeling **anxious**, what tracks or pieces of music would you listen to as a strategy to change this feeling? | *Don't Worry, Be Happy by Bobby McFerrin* |
| 27. If you are feeling **annoyed**, what tracks or pieces of music would you listen to as a strategy to change this feeling? | *Peace by Sabrina Johnston* |
| 28. If you are feeling **angry**, what tracks or pieces of music would you listen to as a strategy to change this feeling? | *Poker Face by Lady Gaga* |

**Figure 6.1** Sophie's selections using the Amended Music Mood-Regulation Scale.

aerobic workout delivered via DVD. Sophie had a state-of-the-art home entertainment system with a projector that she could put to good use; she would only need to buy an exercise mat, some ankle weights, and a few dumbbells. She also had plenty of 1980s music-based workout DVDs in the attic, many of which she was given by friends for Christmas or birthdays, but had never even taken out of their cellophane wrappers. Sophie agreed to audition the DVDs every Monday to find out which ones appealed to her the most.

At the times Sophie was available, the Y offered Pilates on Tuesdays, Zumba on Thursdays, and step aerobics on Saturdays. These classes appealed to Sophie for different reasons—much-needed postural improvements, the zing of Latin dance routines, as well as the burn and sense of achievement from gut-wrenching workouts (see the overview of Sophie's weekly timetable in table 6.1). All she had to do now was try to stick to it.

Pam rounded off the session by asking Sophie to complete a Brunel Mood Scale (BRUMS for short; see chapter 3), with reference to how she was feeling during the past week. The BRUMS complemented the Music Mood-Regulation Scale particularly well and provided Pam with a useful snapshot of how Sophie was feeling. That initial profile suggested relatively high levels of tension, depression, and confusion coupled with low levels of vigor. Pam suggested that Sophie complete the profile once weekly, on the same day of the week and at about the same time of day as their consultation, using an online mood profiling website (www.moodprofiling.com). Pam could use this to assess the profiles and advise Sophie accordingly—for example, if she needed to take a day off from exercise because of excessively high levels of fatigue.

## Executing the Program

In the first few weeks, it wasn't at all easy for Sophie. As well as having to find the time in her busy schedule of running a household and looking after three demanding teenagers, the workouts were causing her muscles to ache, and simply finding the motivation to do each session proved a real challenge. At times she was hobbling around with sore quads feeling frailer and older than before. Her difficulties were reflected in her BRUMS profile from week 1, which showed a steep elevation in fatigue coupled with relatively high depression scores (see figure 6.2). What was notable in this profile was a reduction in her tension scores; this may have been attributable to the nervous energy she expended during her new workout routine. Nonetheless, Pam advised Sophie to drop Saturday morning's step class in weeks 2 and 3, so that she would have sufficient time to recover and re-energize.

As the weeks progressed, Sophie gradually got into a groove (almost literally) and began to look forward to her regular workout sessions—even the grueling step class on Saturday mornings. She focused on the music, to the point of anticipating the sounds she would be hearing later in the day when she exercised. The hardest part was getting herself out the front door to go to the Y, especially given that she didn't like the way she looked and felt self-conscious. To this end, she learned a new trick: she would put on her iPod and listen to 1980s workout tunes while getting ready to leave the house and packing her workout bag. Some of the tunes subconsciously ministered to her wounded body image, such as Madonna's "Vogue," which emphasizes how beauty is where *you* find it and should not be determined by others.

**Table 6.1**  Overview of Sophie's Weekly Routine

|  | Sunday | Monday | Tuesday | Wednesday | Thursday | Friday | Saturday |
|---|---|---|---|---|---|---|---|
| **Morning** | Sleep in, R&R | Home workout | Housework | Household paperwork | Housework | Hair and nail salon | Step aerobics at YMCA |
| **Afternoon** | Visitors or visiting | Housework | Pilates at YMCA | Sporting events with sons | Zumba at YMCA | Coffee with friends | Sporting events with sons |
| **Evening** | Family time | Family time | Family time | Girls' night out | Family time | Family time | Family time |

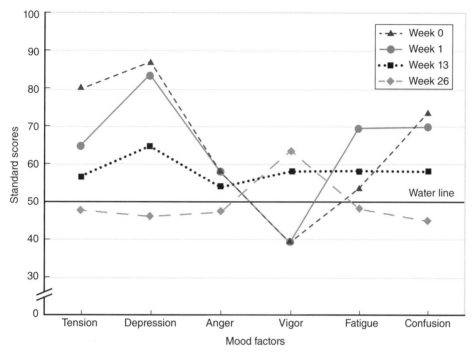

**Figure 6.2**   Sophie's mood profile for weeks 0, 1, 13, and 26.

She sometimes found herself floating and lost in the music, particularly during the Monday and Thursday sessions, which had a strong choreographic component. When in the thrall of the music, Sophie found that she was unaware of the problems associated with the breakdown of her marriage and transported into a different space in which she was not trying to judge, analyze, and solve problems but just experience the living moment. After three months of the program, Sophie's weekly BRUMS profiles showed a definite shift toward greater positivity (see figure 6.2). Her depression levels had come down, she rarely felt tense or uptight anymore, and her vigor scores were rising in tandem with a decline in her levels of fatigue.

Without being aware of it, Sophie was selecting musical pieces by strong female role models, especially women who had been mistreated by men but were unbowed, such as Tina Turner. "The Best" had a positive, affirmative message and a visceral pumping bass line that kept her legs moving toward the Y. In "The Best," Turner sings about a superlative romantic partner, but in Sophie's mind, Turner was singing about her and how she was overcoming the big challenges in her life—not by getting mired in bitterness

and vengefulness, but by elevating herself from a bad situation that was not of her making. She wasn't trying to get mad or even; she just wanted to move forward toward brighter days. It was no longer about him, but about her.

Most of the tracks Sophie favored had a throbbing, regular rhythm that recalled the marching bands that took the field on game days when she was a football cheerleader in college. For the same reason, she liked tracks with a prominent drumbeat such as "Nothing's Gonna Stop Us Now" by Starship and "Walk This Way" by Run-D.M.C. feat. Aerosmith.

To keep things interesting, Sophie created her own 1980s soundtrack for her 45-minute Monday morning routine (see table 6.2) and recounted her cheerleading days to create a punishing home workout routine for herself. On occasion, she would bend the rules regarding the musical epoch to throw in more contemporary tracks highly associated with cheerleading, such as Gwen Stefani's brash and catchy "Hollaback Girl." She met Lindy, who had also dabbled in cheerleading back in the 1980s, at the Y, and they would sometimes go to each other's houses to share a workout and a cup of freshly ground coffee while putting the world to rights. Lindy had been through two

**Table 6.2**  Sophie's Home Workout 1980s Soundtrack

| Track | Artist(s) | Tempo (bpm) | Style | Workout segment |
|-------|-----------|-------------|-------|-----------------|
| Nothing's Gonna Stop Us Now | Starship | 96 | Rock | Mental preparation |
| Hangin' Tough | New Kids on the Block | 92 | Pop | Active stretching |
| Walk This Way | Run-D.M.C. feat. Aerosmith | 107 | Rap rock | Aerobic warm-up |
| Express Yourself | Madonna | 120 | Dance-pop | Cardio training (low intensity) |
| Physical | Olivia Newton-John | 124 | Pop disco | Cardio training (moderate intensity) |
| Sweet Child O' Mine | Guns N' Roses | 127 | Hard rock | Cardio training (moderate intensity) |
| Jump | Van Halen | 131 | Synth rock | Interval training (high intensity) |
| Sisters Are Doin' It For Themselves | Eurythmics and Aretha Franklin | 137 | Pop rock | Interval training (high intensity) |
| Hungry Like The Wolf | Duran Duran | 130 | Dance rock | Strength training |
| Pump Up The Jam | Technotronic feat. Ya Kid K | 125 | Hip-house | Strength training |
| Livin' On A Prayer | Bon Jovi | 123 | Rock | Core stability |
| Don't Stop Believin' | Journey | 119 | Rock | Core stability |
| Cherish | Kool & the Gang | 95 | Pop | Cool-down, revitalization |

*Note:* All of these tracks can be located on YouTube.

marriages, and so she provided Sophie with tremendous social support. Their workout visits met a number of Sophie's psychological needs—understanding, empathy, and companionship. Research shows that social losses are the main triggers for depression, whereas social support is one of the very best cures (Amato, 2000).

Sophie and Lindy cultivated their friendship online by sending each other workout tunes using YouTube links and devising sessions for each other. This brought in a game-playing element that was rewarding and kept them focused. Both increased their adherence because they felt that if they missed a workout, they wouldn't be letting just themselves down. At the Y, the management regularly changed the schedule of classes or instructors, which provided Sophie with appropriate balance and variety. She made lots of new friends there too and looked forward to going as much for a good chat with other moms as for the workout.

## Program Review

Six months down the line, Sophie arranged another meeting with Pam, the lifestyle coach, and proudly reported her progress. She had made a bunch of new friends that changed her entire perspective on life and opened her eyes to a new reality. More specifically, Sophie had lost nearly 10 pounds (4.5 kg), gone down a dress size, was more even tempered with her kids (she realized that she had been taking much of her frustration out on them), and felt that she had generally got her mojo back. Pam pointed to her latest weekly BRUMS profile online, which told a very similar story: a high vigor score coupled with low scores on each of the negative mood factors (see figure 6.2).

Pam knew that to create a lasting lifestyle change, going beyond the six-month point was absolutely crucial. The pair addressed this new

Sophie enjoys a home workout.

challenge of keeping things fresh by devoting most of their time to discussing variations in the exercise program that would maintain the interest and appeal. This involved picking up some new music via Spotify for the Monday morning sessions and, once a fortnight, driving to a smaller gym that had a dance class that Sophie particularly enjoyed (the instructor had impeccable taste in music). Sophie had found out about the class by occasionally trying out new gyms, an adventurous approach that resulted from her increased sense of self-confidence.

Lifestyle coach Pam and Sophie also discussed how she could combine the program with better eating habits. Sophie now felt so good about herself that she had not felt the need to comfort eat as much. When she did go out for a meal with the girls, she looked forward to and enjoyed the desserts much more than she had when bingeing on them at home; plus, she always managed to work off the calories (and more besides) on the dance floor afterward. Much of the excess weight from her waist and hips had melted off during this

period, and she hadn't felt so good physically and emotionally since her college days.

Sophie confessed that on the rare occasion she had felt the sudden urge to comfort eat, she would go into the sunroom and put on a wild track at high volume, as a type of distraction, such as "TV Dinners" by ZZ Top. In particular, the lyric about TV dinners making one feel "rough" would put her off another munching session in front of the box. And the music selection often drew such derision from her teenage sons that her yearning for cookies would quickly dissipate. Supplanting the late-night munchies with a blast of the long-bearded fellas from Texas made her feel far more in control of her emotions than ever before. Sophie used this technique rather instinctively, but it is based on behavioral learning principles; psychologists who apply such principles might use terms such as *substitution* or *counterconditioning*. Regardless of the term, cutting down on comfort eating was a pillar of Sophie's program, and the fact that she managed to achieve this in a sustainable way was truly commendable.

# CASE STUDY 2: AMBITIOUS EXERCISE-TO-MUSIC INSTRUCTOR MARINO SUPERCHARGES HIS CLASSES

## Introduction and Background

Marino had studied physical education in college, but decided in the middle of his sophomore year that he did not want to go into teaching. His first teaching placement in a downtown high school had reminded him just how abrasive and disrespectful kids could be. Beyond this, he wanted a work schedule that could be more self-governed, as opposed to one governed by the sound of a bell. Having thought long and hard about what to do with his life, Marino decided to take some professional courses to become an exercise-to-music instructor.

During his senior year, Marino completed courses in a wide variety of exercise-to-music classes (e.g., LBT, step, Zumba) and passed each with flying colors. His career plan was to spend 10 to 15 years as an exercise instructor and then to make a transition into wellness center management. He certainly did not want to be teaching 20 classes a week into his 40s, and so a progression into management seemed like a fruitful long-term plan. For Marino, keeping fit and taking pride in his physical appearance was just a fringe benefit of his favorite hobby.

After graduating from college, Marino spent six months traveling around Europe before embarking on his professional life as an exercise-to-music instructor. The time away gave him a good opportunity to broaden his horizons, learn a little more about world history, and even brush up on the French he hadn't practiced since his school days. Moreover, through socializing with other travelers, he learned a great deal about Europe's dance music scene, which had previously been a musical blind spot for him. In particular, Marino became quite an expert in the music of David Guetta (France), Avicii (Sweden), and Disclosure (UK). He began inwardly compiling a repository of up-tempo selections he could use when leading exercise classes back in the States.

## Starting Work as an Instructor

On returning to his home city of Cincinnati, Ohio, Marino felt re-energized and couldn't wait to start work as an instructor. He decided to try freelancing in the clubs around the city center that catered predominantly to office workers. His typical day involved an early-morning class before people went to work, an "hour of power" at lunchtime, and one or two classes in the early evening. These classes were interspersed with some personal training, mostly for local housewives and executives working in finance or law.

Marino had grown up in the Over-the-Rhine district, a cultural melting pot and one of the most socially deprived areas of Cincinnati. In the summer of 2001, when Marino was just a kid, he witnessed three days of race riots that devastated his neighborhood. Despite his Hispanic roots, most of Marino's close friends were African American, and from a young age, he had been a true hip-hop aficionado. He had tracked the evolution of urban music from the days of Run-D.M.C. and LL Cool J while in elementary school, through Dr. Dre, Eminem, and Tupac, to Jay-Z, Drake, and Kanye West, his contemporary music heroes. Accordingly, it was no surprise that Marino's class soundtracks had a strong urban flavor. In fact, passersby could easily have mistaken the classes for serial urban music conventions.

## Rapcentric Playlist

Marino meticulously selected the tracks according to their rhythmic qualities and tempi (beats per minute). He paid less attention to the lyrics, which on occasion eulogized gun crime, drug trafficking, and the degradation of women. Marino was so keyed in to the rhythms of the music that he paid little attention to what the artists were saying—and most rap lyrics were delivered at a machine-gun pace anyway. He was of course aware of the themes covered in the music, but he thought that, in its totality, the music was fairly innocuous in the context of exercise.

In the early months of Marino's career, his classes were brimming with exercisers of all shapes and sizes. They were inspired in equal measure by Marino's engaging teaching style and boundless enthusiasm. Moreover, his choreography was universally praised, because it made for a mentally stimulating as well as physically challenging workout. Initially, Marino changed his routines and the accompanying playlists on a regular basis to keep things fresh, even drawing on his newfound knowledge of European dance music. Nonetheless, over the course of a few months, people began edging away from his classes. Many returned to the more conventional exercise routines of well-established instructors, and some dropped out of exercise classes altogether.

Cincinnatians are known to be a rather conservative bunch, and protestant evangelicalism has strong roots in the city. Marino's classes attracted a broad cross-section of the public. Like him, many enjoyed hip-hop and listened to it regularly, but others were not quite so keen. Some took offense at the lyrics when they listened closely and realized the negative messages they contained. Because Marino was such a charismatic instructor and an all-around nice guy, they did not voice their concerns to him. For some, the vulgarity of hip-hop was balanced out, to a degree, by the relative gentility of European dance tracks. Over time, however, people simply drifted away in dribs and drabs and did not continue to recommend Marino's classes to their friends and colleagues. With an eye on the bottom line, the managers of the clubs where Marino taught were acutely aware of the gradual hemorrhaging of attendees.

One of the managers saw huge potential in Marino. Lataesha had worked in the fitness industry for many years, first as an aerobics instructor and, after completing a part-time master's degree in business administration, as the manager of one of the largest and swankiest clubs in town. Marino had a great deal of respect for Lataesha and was only too pleased to meet with her when he received an e-mail from her administrative assistant. As a committed Christian, Lataesha was clued in to some of the issues surrounding Marino's classes. In fact, many of the comments received anonymously from club members spelled it out: "Marino's classes are great but his music sucks—it's full of profanities and I can't bear to listen to it anymore" or "I think that Marino is one of your best instructors, but I am not too sure about his music choices. . . . he could probably make better selections for the type of folks who come to his classes."

## Democratizing the Music Selection

Marino had not considered that urban music might offend the people who attended his classes. He thought that perhaps his routines were too highly choreographed or that the dropouts represented natural depletion in such classes, and that this was a cyclical process. Being new to the job and relatively naive, he did not consider the broad range of factors that influence people's attendance at classes, especially the music.

The problem of participant attrition in Marino's classes could be fixed relatively easily. If he could find music programs that both he and his clients liked, that should start to entice people back. He spoke with a few of the regular attendees and asked for music suggestions. One of the exercisers, an intern from a local marketing company, suggested that he create a Facebook page for his clients and ask for suggestions of artists and tracks. After all, most people who attended his classes were of the Facebook generation. Marino went back to his apartment and did exactly that. He made good use of the Group Music Selection Tool (see chapter 3) to identify preferred tracks and also tracks that were not preferred but would work for the purposes of his classes. Marino wanted to avoid tracks that people felt a strong aversion to, and he knew that this would be a good way to identify them.

Word soon got around about the new Facebook page, and suggestions began to flood in. Marino was almost overwhelmed. People suggested everything from rock gospel to melodic death metal. Interestingly, some people who hadn't attended for a few weeks or even months also readily chimed in with their views. At first, Marino didn't know what to do with the abundance of suggested tracks and artists. Instinctively, he knew that much of the music suggested was wholly unsuitable for choreographed exercise classes (e.g., Pink Floyd's progressive rock album *Ummagumma*), and some he absolutely abhorred (e.g., Justin Bieber's album *Purpose*). Such dirges were taking Marino to a place he certainly didn't want to go!

## Constructing the Music Program

Marino decided to create a chart of all of the suggestions from Facebook as a basis for a series of new music programs to accompany his classes (see table 6.3). He grouped tracks from similar genres; within the genres, if the same artist appeared more than once, he placed the relevant tracks next to each other. In the genre clusters,

**Table 6.3**  Track Suggestions by People Attending Marino's Classes

| Track | Year | Artist(s) | Tempo (bpm) | Yes, No, Maybe |
|---|---|---|---|---|
| Jumpin', Jumpin' | 1999 | Destiny's Child | 89 | Yes (such an energizing lyric) |
| If I Were A Boy | 2008 | Beyoncé | 90 | No (just doesn't work for this context) |
| Love On Top | 2011 | Beyoncé | 94 | Maybe (quite an uplifting song but too slow) |
| Single Ladies (Put A Ring On It) | 2008 | Beyoncé | 97 | Yes (absolutely buzzing track) |
| Crazy In Love | 2003 | Beyoncé feat. Jay-Z | 100 | Yes (fantastic for dance-based routines) |
| Run The World (Girls) | 2011 | Beyoncé | 127 | No (not sufficient regularity in the beat) |
| Diva | 2009 | Beyoncé | 74 | No (too slow, doesn't cut it) |
| 7/11 | 2014 | Beyoncé | 68 | No (slow and rhythmically irregular) |
| Wish You Were Here | 1975 | Pink Floyd | 60 | No (my people won't relate to it) |
| We Are The Champions | 1977 | Queen | 64 | Maybe (good associations suitable for the end of a class) |
| I Want To Break Free | 1984 | Queen | 109 | Yes (guitar solo raises hairs on the back of my neck) |
| Under Pressure | 1981 | Queen | 113 | Maybe (people want to forget about their pressures in class) |
| One Vision | 1985 | Queen | 120 | Yes (unifying track with lots of verve) |
| Don't Stop Me Now | 1979 | Queen | 157 | Yes (gets people revved up to the max) |
| How You Remind Me | 2001 | Nickelback | 86 | Maybe (may not create the right ambiance) |
| Can't Stop | 2003 | Red Hot Chili Peppers | 92 | No (wrong rhythmic feel for my routines) |
| My House | 2015 | Flo Rida | 94 | Maybe (beat not ideal) |
| Get Right | 2005 | Jennifer Lopez | 97 | Yes (intoxicating melodic figure) |
| Play | 2001 | Jennifer Lopez | 105 | Yes (great rhythmic feel for the warm-up) |
| On The Floor | 2011 | Jennifer Lopez feat. Pitbull | 130 | Yes (checks all the boxes) |
| Timber | 2013 | Pitbull feat. Ke$ha | 130 | Maybe (country feel might be tough to link with other tracks) |

| Track | Year | Artist(s) | Tempo (bpm) | Yes, No, Maybe |
|-------|------|-----------|-------------|----------------|
| Feel This Moment | 2013 | Pitbull feat. Christina Aguilera | 136 | Yes (high-energy track) |
| Bad Man | 2016 | Pitbull feat. Robin Thicke, Joe Perry, and Travis Barker | 120 | Maybe (could fit into a mid-tempo Pitbull mini-set) |
| Fireball | 2014 | Pitbull feat. John Ryan | 123 | Yes (checks all the boxes) |
| Shake | 2005 | Ying Yang Twins feat. Pitbull | 118 | No (too stop-start) |
| Holy Grail | 2013 | Jay-Z feat. Justin Timberlake | 73 | No (too slow, offensive rap lyrics) |
| Mirrors | 2013 | Justin Timberlake | 77 | No (difficult to mix with another track rhythmically) |
| Carry Out | 2010 | Timbaland feat. Justin Timberlake | 99 | Yes (great percussion track) |
| Señorita | 2003 | Justin Timberlake | 98 | Yes (incredible Latin vamp going on) |
| Rock Your Body | 2003 | Justin Timberlake | 104 | Yes (simply perfect) |
| Take Back The Night | 2013 | Justin Timberlake | 108 | Yes (superb backbeat, catchy lyrics) |
| Like I Love You | 2002 | Justin Timberlake | 115 | Yes (catchy syncopated groove that sucks you in) |
| SexyBack | 2006 | Justin Timberlake feat. Timbaland | 117 | Yes (wonderful synth vamp) |
| Dancing Queen | 1976 | ABBA | 101 | Yes (this one's a guaranteed floor filler at parties, so will work well) |
| Paradise City | 1988 | Guns N' Roses | 99 | No (too slow and anthemic for this purpose) |
| Time Of My Life | 1987 | Bill Medley and Jennifer Warnes | 107 | Maybe (people like the tune, but it's just not quite right for class) |
| Purple Haze | 1967 | Jimi Hendrix | 110 | No (sounds good for my parents' generation) |
| Walk This Way | 1986 | Run-D.M.C. feat. Aerosmith | 106 | Yes (very strong rhythmically and an old-school fave) |
| Eye Of The Tiger | 1982 | Survivor | 109 | Maybe (perhaps too much of a cliché) |
| Stayin' Alive | 1977 | Bee Gees | 104 | Yes (has a solid groove and people love it) |
| Caught Up | 2004 | Usher | 110 | Yes (great lyrics and backbeat) |
| Good Kisser | 2014 | Usher | 97 | No (lyrics are inappropriate and lacks energy early on) |
| OMG | 2010 | Usher feat. will.i.am | 130 | Maybe (something slightly irritating about the backing track) |

*(continued)*

Table 6.3 *(continued)*

| Track | Year | Artist(s) | Tempo (bpm) | Yes, No, Maybe |
|---|---|---|---|---|
| Yeah! | 2004 | Usher feat. Lil Jon and Ludacris | 105 | Yes (what an amazing groove) |
| Take A Bow | 2008 | Rihanna | 82 | Maybe (on the slow side but might work for cool-down) |
| Diamonds | 2012 | Rihanna | 92 | Yes (perfect for cool-down) |
| In The Dark | 2015 | Rihanna feat. Justin Bieber | 85 | No (far too dreary) |
| Monster | 2013 | Eminem feat. Rihanna | 110 | Yes (two very popular artists) |
| Stay | 2013 | Rihanna feat. Mikky Ekko | 112 | No (creates the wrong mood altogether) |
| Blurred Lines | 2013 | Robin Thicke feat. T.I. and Pharrell Williams | 120 | Maybe (the track's had a lot of bad press) |
| Happy | 2013 | Pharrell Williams | 80 | Yes (feel-good track of 2014, gets people in the right mood) |
| Gust Of Wind | 2014 | Pharrell Williams | 100 | Yes (funky groove that's ideal for warm-up) |
| Drop It Like It's Hot (Radio Edit) | 2004 | Snoop Dogg feat. Pharrell Williams | 92 | Maybe (slow tempo but could work for warm-up) |
| Thrift Shop | 2012 | Macklemore & Ryan Lewis feat. Wanz | 95 | No (could easily cause offense) |
| Can't Hold Us | 2011 | Macklemore & Ryan Lewis feat. Ray Dalton | 144 | No (difficult to link with any other track) |
| Bad | 1987 | Michael Jackson | 113 | Yes (just an amazing synth bass line) |
| Black Or White | 1991 | Michael Jackson | 115 | Yes (oozes with energy and makes you want to dance) |
| Billie Jean | 1982 | Michael Jackson | 117 | Yes (the hook and bass line are so energetic) |
| Off The Wall | 1979 | Michael Jackson | 119 | Yes (the lyrics are all about having a great time) |
| Don't Stop 'Til You Get Enough | 1979 | Michael Jackson | 119 | Yes (Jackson is the ultimate groove-meister) |
| Beat It | 1982 | Michael Jackson | 139 | Maybe (very fast track so hard to link with others) |
| Easy Love | 2015 | Sigala | 124 | Maybe (could link to a Michael Jackson theme) |
| I Will Survive | 1978 | Gloria Gaynor | 116 | Yes (dance floor classic with empowering lyrics) |
| Smells Like Teen Spirit | 1991 | Nirvana | 118 | No (wrong feel: angry track rather than having a positive vibe) |
| Baba O'Riley | 1971 | The Who | 116 | No (irregular beat) |
| I Heard It Through The Grapevine | 1968 | Marvin Gaye | 118 | Maybe (quite an old track but will be familiar to all) |

| Track | Year | Artist(s) | Tempo (bpm) | Yes, No, Maybe |
|---|---|---|---|---|
| Don't Stop Believing | 1981 | Journey | 118 | Yes (great track to raise spirits toward the end of a workout) |
| Fade To Black | 1984 | Metallica | 143 | No (slightly unnerving feel; unsuitable) |
| Bad Romance | 2009 | Lady Gaga | 119 | No (feels like it's been overplayed) |
| Just Dance | 2008 | Lady Gaga feat. Colby O'Donis | 119 | Yes (the ladies in the group absolutely love this one) |
| Poker Face | 2008 | Lady Gaga | 119 | Yes (sits really well with other Gaga tracks) |
| Telephone | 2010 | Lady Gaga feat. Beyoncé | 122 | Yes (one of Gaga's finest) |
| Born This Way | 2011 | Lady Gaga | 124 | Yes (electrifying track with uplifting lyrics) |
| Applause | 2013 | Lady Gaga | 140 | Yes (perfect for the hardest part of the routine) |
| The Edge Of Glory | 2011 | Lady Gaga | 126 | Yes (plays to people's fantasy side) |
| Wrecking Ball | 2013 | Miley Cyrus | 60 | No (too slow; doesn't work well for any part of the class) |
| We Can't Stop | 2013 | Miley Cyrus | 80 | Maybe (could work as part of a cool-down sequence) |
| Lolita | 2013 | Leah LaBelle | 120 | Maybe (lyrics slightly risqué) |
| Groove Is In The Heart [video version] | 1990 | Deee-Lite | 120 | Yes (instantly recognizable floor filler) |
| Wind It Up | 2006 | Gwen Stefani | 120 | Yes (plenty of affirmations here) |
| Yummy | 2007 | Gwen Stefani | 124 | No (some explicit lyrics) |
| What You Waiting For? (Clean) | 2004 | Gwen Stefani | 135 | Yes (strong beat; pumps people up) |
| No | 2016 | Meghan Trainor | 93 | Has a great hook but hard to link with other Meghan Trainor tunes |
| Better When I'm Dancin' | 2015 | Meghan Trainor | 128 | Yes (really easy to choreograph moves to) |
| My Future Husband | 2015 | Meghan Trainor | 158 | Maybe (much weaker than her first couple of hits) |
| I Feel Love | 1977 | Donna Summer | 125 | Yes (electrifying groove from the outset that builds and intensifies) |
| Lose Control | 2005 | Missy Elliott feat. Ciara and Fatman Scoop | 126 | No (too stop-start for aerobics) |
| Hold On | 2013 | NERVO | 127 | Yes (this checks a lot of the boxes) |
| YMCA | 1978 | Village People | 126 | Yes (makes the group feel a little more united) |
| It's Not Right But It's Okay | 1999 | Whitney Houston | 128 | No (a bit light and rhythm is patchy) |

*(continued)*

Table 6.3 *(continued)*

| Track | Year | Artist(s) | Tempo (bpm) | Yes, No, Maybe |
|---|---|---|---|---|
| Acapella | 2010 | Kelis | 128 | Yes (thumping beat and engaging lyric) |
| Moves Like Jagger | 2011 | Maroon 5 feat. Christina Aguilera | 128 | Yes (all-around great exercise tune) |
| You Shook Me All Night Long | 1980 | AC/DC | 129 | Maybe (a little risqué for my people) |
| Baby | 2010 | Justin Bieber feat. Ludacris | 129 | Maybe (I hate it, but some people love it) |
| Since U Been Gone | 2004 | Kelly Clarkson | 130 | Maybe (energetic but nondescript) |
| It Feels So Good | 1998 | Sonique | 134 | Maybe (anthemic, uplifting tune) |
| (I Can't Get No) Satisfaction | 1965 | The Rolling Stones | 136 | No (my great uncle used to sing this one) |
| Paint It, Black | 1966 | The Rolling Stones | 158 | No (doesn't fit well) |
| Radioactive | 2013 | Imagine Dragons | 136 | No (drifts in and out, doesn't sit in a groove) |
| Scream & Shout | 2013 | will.i.am & Britney Spears | 130 | Yes (infectious with strong affirmations) |
| Toxic | 2004 | Britney Spears | 143 | Yes (another favorite with the ladies) |
| Streets Of Philadelphia | 1994 | Bruce Springsteen | 93 | No (too somber) |
| Born In The U.S.A. | 1984 | Bruce Springsteen | 121 | Maybe (raucous blue collar stuff) |
| Born To Be Wild | 1968 | Steppenwolf | 145 | Yes (this has a killer lick) |
| I'm A Believer | 1966 | The Monkees | 160 | Maybe (certainly has the feel-good factor) |
| Great Balls Of Fire | 1957 | Jerry Lee Lewis | 160 | No (would stick out like a sore thumb) |
| The Trooper | 1983 | Iron Maiden | 160 | No (a bit manic) |
| Kashmir | 1975 | Led Zeppelin | 83 | No (tempo doesn't work well for my routines) |
| Paranoid | 1970 | Black Sabbath | 164 | No (this track is manic and hard to coordinate dance movements with) |
| Closer | 1994 | Nine Inch Nails | 90 | No (far, far too rude) |
| La Tortura | 2005 | Shakira feat. Alejandro Sanz | 100 | Maybe (but the other Shakira tracks near this tempo are better) |
| Hips Don't Lie | 2006 | Shakira feat. Wyclef Jean | 100 | Yes (the ladies absolutely love this one) |
| Whenever, Wherever | 2001 | Shakira | 108 | Yes (sits well with the preceding track) |
| Can't Remember To Forget You | 2014 | Shakira feat. Rihanna | 139 | No (hard to link this with other suggestions) |
| Hero | 2001 | Enrique Iglesias | 76 | Maybe (a little trite, even for a cooldown) |
| Bailamos | 1999 | Enrique Iglesias | 124 | Maybe (energetic and catchy Latin track) |

*Note:* All of these tracks can be located on YouTube.

he ranked the tracks by tempo (see column 4) to determine what part of a class they might be most suitable for (e.g., warm-up, low intensity, high intensity, abs, cool-down). In the final column, Marino made a judgment regarding the overall suitability of the tracks (yes, no, or maybe). He knew that he would need to include at least some of the maybes to satisfy the people who attended his classes, reflecting a degree of compromise between his own musical predilections and those of the class. He also tried to briefly justify his rating of each track.

Eventually, Marino came up with a workable solution to meet his own aesthetic needs, satisfy his clients, and provide the right sort of rhythmic structure for the content of his classes (see table 6.4 for a dance aerobics class sample playlist). He informed his Facebook followers that he had

**Table 6.4**  Playlist From One of Marino's Dance Aerobic Classes

| Track | Artist(s) | Tempo (bpm) | Class segment |
|---|---|---|---|
| **Mini-set 1: Pharrell Williams mix** | | | |
| Happy | Pharrell Williams | 80 | Warm-up |
| Drop It Like It's Hot (Radio Edit) | Snoop Dogg feat. Pharrell Williams | 92 | |
| **Mini-set 2: Shakira mix** | | | |
| Hips Don't Lie | Shakira feat. Wyclef Jean | 100 | Low intensity |
| Whenever, Wherever | Shakira | 108 | |
| **Mini-set 3: Michael Jackson mix** | | | |
| Black Or White | Michael Jackson | 115 | Low-to-moderate intensity |
| Billie Jean | Michael Jackson | 117 | |
| Off The Wall | Michael Jackson | 119 | |
| Don't Stop 'Til You Get Enough | Michael Jackson | 119 | |
| **Mini-set 4: Lady Gaga mix** | | | |
| Telephone | Lady Gaga feat. Beyoncé | 122 | Moderate intensity |
| Born This Way | Lady Gaga | 124 | |
| The Edge Of Glory | Lady Gaga | 126 | |
| **Mini-set 5: Pitbull mix** | | | |
| On The Floor | Jennifer Lopez feat. Pitbull | 130 | High intensity |
| Timber | Pitbull feat. Ke$ha | 130 | |
| Feel This Moment | Pitbull feat. Christina Aguilera | 136 | |
| **Mini-set 6: Justin Timberlake mix** | | | |
| SexyBack | Justin Timberlake feat. Timbaland | 117 | Core strength |
| Like I Love You | Justin Timberlake | 115 | |
| Take Back The Night | Justin Timberlake | 108 | |
| Rock Your Body | Justin Timberlake | 104 | |
| **Mini-set 7: Rihanna mix** | | | |
| Diamonds | Rihanna | 92 | Cool-down, active |
| Take A Bow | Rihanna | 82 | Cool-down, stretch |

*Note:* All of these tracks can be located on YouTube.

constructed a series of new playlists that embraced many of the tracks they had suggested. Over the weeks that followed, Marino's clients began to return to his classes, partly out of curiosity and partly because they felt empowered by the sense of agency that came from having their say. Not only did many of the former participants who had dropped out make a welcome return, but they even brought friends and family members along!

## Evaluating the Music Programs

Marino had learned a fair amount about psychological measures during his days as a physical education student. He knew that he could use this knowledge to evaluate how people in his classes were receiving his music programs. He had also come to the realization that simply showing an interest in how people feel tends to generate a positive response. Marino selected two measures to chart people's feeling states and motivation at the end of the classes: the Feeling Scale and the Motivation Scale (see chapter 3). He created a simple online survey using www.surveymonkey

.com and encouraged exercisers to complete the survey at the end of class using their smartphones or tablets.

The two-item survey, which participants completed just before the new music program, was used as a baseline, and then readministered every two or three weeks. The benefits associated with this went beyond showing Marino how effective the music was. It got people thinking about how they were feeling and put them completely in touch with their overall exercise experience. This enabled them to get more out of their workout and to readjust the typical mind-set of worrying about the next appointment or rushing home to start dinner.

The results of the online survey over the first couple of months of the new music program showed an overall improvement in affect (how people generally felt emotionally) of 2.4 points and an increase in state motivation scores of 2.1 (see figure 6.3). Being quite a provocative and sassy character, Marino often found humorous ways to report the survey results to his classes.

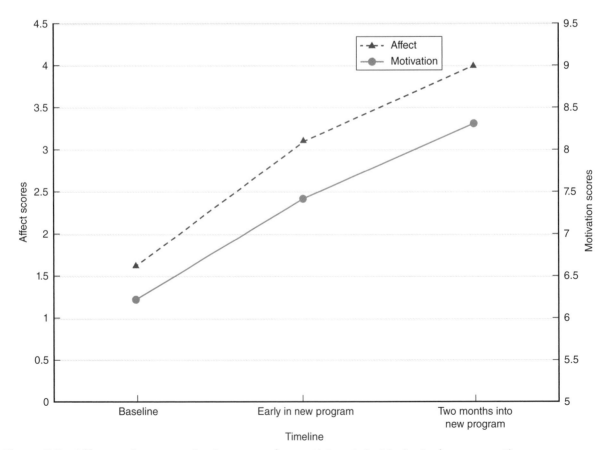

**Figure 6.3** Affect and state motivation scores for participants in Marino's classes over time.

He sometimes chided participants by telling them that they had let their moods slip a tenth in the last week and so they needed to be "extra happy" this time around!

## The Hottest Ticket in Town

Marino's aerobics classes became one of the hottest tickets in town, and he was even nominated for Instructor of the Year by members of Lataesha's club. Everyone wanted to go to a class in which they could share their favorite workout tracks with everyone else. It was like going to a nightclub and having their requests played by the DJ. Marino revealed the identity of the member who selected a track at the start of each class, which cultivated considerable debate among his followers. Occasionally, he would use the polling feature of Facebook to stage a mini-vote on the way the tracks were mixed or juxtaposed, or to choose a feature artist for the month. Knowing that they had some say in the music program gave people a real buzz. Also, it was much easier for Marino to defend music selected by class attendees.

The playlists that Marino used to use had been sanitized. He became far more conscious of and sensitive to people's beliefs and what is acceptable for broadcast in a public space. In doing this, he came to understand how important people's religious and political affiliations are in determining their tastes in cultural products such as music. Although gangsta rap is played in many American nightclubs, people choose to visit them for that style of music; they do not necessarily choose to go to an exercise class to hear this style of music. Important though it is, the music is an adjunct to the class, whereas in a nightclub, it is the focal point, the raison d'être.

In fact, the easiest way to classify nightclubs is by the type of music they play, and consumers base their choices on this information. When choosing a gym or instructor, musical accompaniment is not as apparent. Marino also found that he could still incorporate his favorite hip-hop selections by using radio edits or even splicing the tracks on his laptop using simple, free editing software such as Audacity. In this way, he was able

Marino is all smiles, having rejuvenated his classes with new music programs.

to retain the pulsating rhythms and breakbeats that contributed to the motivational qualities of his music programs, without some of the darker lyrical themes that detracted from them.

Being an innovator in the group exercise space and taking inspiration from some of his hip-hop heroes, Marino occasionally spun his own rhymes. He used a catchy Run-D.M.C. backbeat that personified the uplifting vibe of old-school rap. This added a new dimension to the classes that completely set Marino aside from his fellow instructors—he was an exercise teacher and a music artist all rolled up into one. Marino's raps had a positive energy and were intended to motivate, entertain, and amuse rather than to protest, deride, and offend:

> *Step, slide, shuffle, and glide,*
>
> *I've got the groove in my feet*
>
> *I'm a one-of-a-kind*
>
> *Raise your arms in the air*
>
> *Gimme a smile*
>
> *Let's rock to the beat in a superfresh style!*

## Marino's Lessons Learned

Several important principles guided Marino's shift in music selection. One was listening to what people wanted and carefully considering and justifying all suggestions rather than imposing his own musical preferences. Another was providing the exercisers with a sense of autonomy in terms of what was played; this gave them far greater governance and ownership of the playlists. Marino often gave verbal credit to the person who selected a track, which added to the fun and strengthened his rapport with the classes. He would report mood- and motivation-related scores verbally in class and graphically via social media. This made participants more engaged with their psychological as well as physical well-being. Further, he used social media to truly democratize the selection process and give the group a sense of ownership and empowerment. Finally, Marino realized just how one man's meat can be another man's poison, and that music he deemed entirely acceptable could be viewed in an entirely different light by many class participants.

In reaching these decisions, Marino understood that groups act as groups rather than as a collection of individuals. Classes take on a group identity and display preferences that often lean toward the conservative. For this reason, he needed a different mind-set when approaching music selection for a group. He learned to think on behalf of the collective rather than maintaining a "this is the music that I like so it's the music we're going to have" approach. He also learned that there was no use searching for an eclectic mix that represents all the tastes in the room. Doing so almost invariably results in everyone disliking a substantial segment of the program. Satisfying as many people as possible without offending any individual is a principle that holds for classes in virtually any field. In practice, this means that playlists for groups should probably be somewhat safer than those for individuals.

# Summary Points for Part II

1. Music has a key role to play in improving public health by making physical activity feel more enjoyable and thereby promoting higher levels of adherence.

2. In the synchronous application of music, its rhythmic qualities should match those of the task and be relatively easy for the performer to process, so that the audible can be made visible.

3. Music can impair safety when used in potentially dangerous environments such as on public roads or walkways. For example, music should not be used when out cycling on the roads or running on sidewalks. It can be so intoxicating that exercisers or athletes risk placing themselves in danger.

4. In strength training, contraction speed needs to be carefully considered to optimize music selection. During very intense workouts with weights, music can be an unwanted distraction, although it can serve psych-up and recuperative functions.

5. The movement patterns involved in the full gamut of exercise machines are central to the selection of music applied synchronously. Chapter 4 provides tempo range guidelines.

6. The experience of certain exercise classes can be heightened through the selection of music programs that are directly linked to the content of the class (e.g., boxing-themed music for Boxercise).

7. Surveying exercisers and democratizing the selection process is a good way to enhance the relevance of playlists, heighten empowerment, and increase group motivation.

8. The judicious use of music has considerable potential to promote adherence in group exercise settings given the unity, enjoyment, and motivation it creates when shared among members of a group.

9. Fitness activities with music that are highly successful appear to emphasize easy-to-learn choreography (particularly in the early stages of learning), catchy rhythms, uplifting harmonies, and the frequent changing of the music program to maintain exercisers' interest (e.g., Zumba).

10. Thought should be given to constructing playlists as a whole and to how they segue to ensure the continuity of musical features between tracks (e.g., rhythm and tempo) and the themes that connect them (e.g., a particular musical era).

# PART III

# Using Music to Enhance Sport Training and Performance

Part III addresses using music in the area of sport training and performance. A key focus is how music can be used to help athletes work longer and harder or attain a mind-set associated with peak performance. Chapter 7 covers the use of music in individual sport training and performance. This mirrors the approach of chapter 4, which addressed individual exercise. Applying music effectively to individual sports requires an understanding of their technical demands. This is why chapter 7 opens with a classification of sport skills. A broad range of sports are clustered according to the skills and technical competencies they demand—that is, sports with common characteristics (e.g., racket sports) are grouped together. The chapter also provides a detailed exposition of music applications in a range of sport clusters that includes serve-and-return, endurance-based, power-based, combat, and aiming and shooting sports.

In chapter 8, the focus turns to team sport training and performance; thus, team dynamics and, in particular, team cohesion are key considerations. As in chapter 7, sports with common characteristics (e.g., high-contact field sports)

are clustered. The thinking underlying this is that principles that guide music selection in, say, American football, are similar to those that guide selection in related sports such as rugby and Australian rules football. The chapter covers activities as diverse as paddle sports, bat-and-ball sports, and court-based ball games.

The final chapter of this book, chapter 9, presents two sport-specific case studies. The first deals with an individual sport (long-distance running); the second, with a team sport (American football). The individual sport case study shines a light on Australian runner Frieda and the music-related methods she employs to improve her performances. The team sport case study follows the plight of a West Coast high school American football team. The players seem to be distracted by social media and lack a common purpose; also, their performance levels have dipped to an all-time low. Coach Anderson hires sport psychologist Dr. Arnold Byford to work with the team. Arnold's interventions, including cleverly integrating music, help to turn the team's fortunes around.

# 7

# Individual Sport Training and Performance

*The 2012 Olympics was insane. The crowds were wild, the atmosphere was electric, and Sean Paul was on all the time. I loved the track "Hold On"; I felt hyped whenever I heard it, so I'd always play it on my headphones when I was getting ready for a race. It must have worked because I won another three gold medals and confirmed myself as a living legend to the world.*

—Usain Bolt, six-time Olympic gold medalist (sprints)

Success in individual sports has almost as much to do with the right mental approach as with superior physical conditioning or an abundance of motor skills. At the elite level in particular, the differences between athletes in terms of speed or technique are truly miniscule; it is all about who can keep their nerve when the spotlight shines brightly on them. Success also has much to do with performance consistency. Although athletes may not produce their best in every competition, the most successful can perform at around 92 to 98 percent of their best week in and week out. As legendary American sprinter Michael Johnson put it to the press after his win at the 1997 World Athletics Championships, "I'm good when I'm good and I'm good when I'm bad." This chapter illustrates how music can play a role in both optimizing athletes' mind-sets and promoting greater consistency in training and competition.

Including a section on every individual sport is clearly not feasible—each would probably require its own chapter. Thus, we need a workable structure from which to explore music applications. All sports can be grouped into categories and classified with reference to a common set of char-acteristics, as summarized in table 7.1. Consider the popular racket sports of tennis, squash, and badminton. All involve sequences of serial skills (i.e., a series of very different movements required to succeed, such as service, forehand, backhand, and overhead smash), and the skills are open (i.e., the playing environment changes because of the need to respond to an opponent). Also, games are externally paced because, other than when serving, players have to return the ball or shuttlecock as struck by the opponent. Moreover, all of these sports require an even blend of movement-related (motor) and decision-making (cognitive) skills coupled with whole-body (gross) and delicate (fine) movement patterns.

Golf is an excellent sport for illustrating the span of the gross–fine skill continuum. Long drive competitions that take place on a driving range represent a gross motor skill akin to a javelin throw (i.e., speed and distance are the key features). On the other hand, holing a downhill putt on a fast green is all about feel and touch because hardly any movement is required.

Popular individual sports such as archery, darts, and target shooting involve discrete skills

**Table 7.1**  Classifying Sport Skills

| Skill dimension | Type of skill | Key features | Examples from sport |
|---|---|---|---|
| Open–closed continuum | Closed | Predictable environment | High dive<br>Archery<br>Serve in squash |
| | Open | Unpredictable environment | Sailing<br>Judo<br>Return of service in tennis |
| Internally or externally paced | Internal | Performer determines speed and starting point | Serve in tennis<br>Throw in darts<br>Bunker shot in golf |
| | External | Environment (e.g., opponent) determines the rate | Saving a penalty in soccer<br>Taking a slip catch in cricket<br>Making a rebound in basketball |
| Discrete, serial, or continuous | Discrete | Distinct beginning and end | Throwing a dart<br>Performing the power snatch in weightlifting<br>Tee shot in golf |
| | Serial | Discrete actions linked | Rhythmic gymnastics routine<br>Triple jump<br>Boxing punch combinations |
| | Continuous | No distinct beginning or end | Cross-country skiing<br>Track cycling<br>Single skull rowing |
| Motor–cognitive continuum | Motor | Decision making minimized and motor control maximized | High jump<br>50-meter front crawl (swimming)<br>Triathlon |
| | Cognitive | Decision making maximized and motor control minimized | Cox in rowing<br>Clay pigeon shooting<br>Curling |
| Gross–fine continuum | Gross | Engagement of large-muscle groups with little need for mental processing | Putting the shot<br>100-meter sprinting<br>Flying 200-meter cycle time trial |
| | Fine | Limited use of the musculature but high reliance on accuracy or timing | Snooker<br>Drawing a wood in indoor carpet bowls<br>Target shooting |

(i.e., the same movement is performed repeatedly), the skills required are closed (i.e., the playing environment remains relatively consistent and predictable over time), and performance is self-paced (i.e., the performer does not react or respond to the movements of others). In addition, these sports are predominantly motoric because very little decision making is involved; rather, fine movement patterns are necessary for success. Table 7.2 shows every possible combination of the four skill dimensions (24 altogether) along with the cluster of individual sports associated with each. Hard as I tried, I couldn't find individual sports to represent every combination of skill dimensions. If you can think of a popular sport that is closed, serial, cognitive, and gross in nature, let me know!

The sport groupings in this chapter are not based exclusively on the skill classifications (see tables 7.1 and 7.2); some additional factors have

**Table 7.2**  Skill Dimensions and Clusters of Sports

| | | | | |
|---|---|---|---|---|
| **Discrete** | Open | Cognitive | Fine | Billiards, boccia, curling, pool, snooker |
| | | | Gross | N/A |
| | | Motor | Fine | Bowls, croquet |
| | | | Gross | Golf driving |
| | Closed | Cognitive | Fine | Darts, golf putting |
| | | | Gross | Badminton serve, handball serve, squash serve, tennis serve |
| | | Motor | Fine | Archery, target shooting, tenpin bowling |
| | | | Gross | Discus throw, hammer throw, powerlifting, shot put, weightlifting |
| **Serial** | Open | Cognitive | Fine | Dressage, horse racing (steeplechase), motorcycling, motor racing, sailing, show jumping |
| | | | Gross | Aikido, boxing, fencing, judo, jujitsu, karate, kendo, kung fu, mixed martial arts, rock climbing, taekwondo, wrestling |
| | | Motor | Fine | Hang gliding, parachuting, paragliding, parascending |
| | | | Gross | Badminton, racquetball, squash, steeplechase, surfing, table tennis, tennis, waterskiing, windsurfing |
| | Closed | Cognitive | Fine | Clay pigeon shooting, single luge, skeleton |
| | | | Gross | N/A |
| | | Motor | Fine | Skateboarding, water-ski jumping |
| | | | Gross | Artistic gymnastics, diving, downhill skiing, high jump, figure skating, javelin throw, long jump, pole vault, rhythmic gymnastics, ski jumping, slalom skiing, snowboarding, sprinting, swimming, trampolining, triple jump |
| **Continuous** | Open | Cognitive | Fine | Horse racing (flat) |
| | | | Gross | N/A |
| | | Motor | Fine | N/A |
| | | | Gross | Arm wrestling, BMX biking, canoeing, cross-country skiing, duathlon, kayaking, middle- and long-distance wheelchair racing, mountain biking, road cycling, speed skating, triathlon |
| | Closed | Cognitive | Fine | Rapid-fire pistol shooting |
| | | | Gross | N/A |
| | | Motor | Fine | N/A |
| | | | Gross | Middle- and long-distance running, single scull rowing, track cycling, short-distance wheelchair racing |

N/A = not applicable.

been taken into consideration to ensure that the clusters are meaningful in practice. Consider, as an example, sports in which the main function of music is to psych up athletes before powerful and explosive performances. The triple jump is a serial skill and weightlifting is a discrete skill, yet they are presented in the power-based sport section because both require a relatively high level of pre-task psychomotor arousal for optimal performance. Along similar lines, aerial and water-based sports are grouped together because the role of music is essentially similar in these sports (i.e., pre-task). A further commonality among these sports is the level of anxiety associated with competing in an environment with significant challenges and hazards. Sports are grouped for other reasons, also. For example, some are played with similar implements (e.g., rackets), some involve combat (i.e., individuals play directly against each other), some entail physical contact, and some take place in similar performance spaces (e.g., luge and skeleton).

The reason for grouping sports according to their skill-related, physical, and mental demands is to avoid repetition, leaving space to explore the music application principles in greater depth. Individual sports that are hugely popular and have significant music cultures (e.g., boxing and snooker) are covered more fully in sidebars.

Following much deliberation, I chose not to include equine sports in this chapter. The effect, if any, music has on animals is a highly debatable topic. I have observed that some horses are highly responsive to noise, which is how music selections may well be interpreted. In a recent TV interview, William Haggas, a leading British racehorse trainer, was asked whether he played music to his horses, to which he replied, "Only local radio! Noise is actually good, makes 'em relax; it's sudden noise they can't cope with."

The influence of the rider is, for the most part, subordinate to the horse's movements; like a Swiss watch, there are a great number of moving parts! For this reason, it is tricky to tease out the influence of music on equine performance. Having said that, music could be used pre-task to ease the considerable and understandable anxiety some riders feel. Like many other mammals we interact with, horses are incredibly sensitive to our moods and outward expressions. Accordingly, riders' nerves can greatly affect their mounts. In this way, music might exert an indirect influence on equine psychology. Those involved in sports such as horse racing and show jumping may extract key principles from this chapter that apply to their personal needs and mental preparation.

Within each cluster of sports, a broad range of music applications is possible (e.g., psych-up music, asynchronous music for training, recuperative music), although each has a distinct emphasis (e.g., ego-affirming lyrics in combat sports). Athletes and coaches should choose the music applications pertaining to the cluster related to their sports and use them accordingly. However, some music applications may be uniquely relevant for a given person; consider a young golfer with self-esteem issues who may benefit from ego-affirming lyrics even though he does not typically engage in direct combat with opponents. These music selection principles apply in equal measure to team sports, which are addressed in chapter 8. Keep in mind that some team sport applications might be useful for individuals, and vice versa for individuals on teams. Also, many scenarios in team sports emphasize the individual. Baseball, for example, is like a team and individual sport wrapped up into one.

Building on the classifications in table 7.1, the next step entails grouping sports into meaningful clusters (see table 7.2). This clustering greatly

## THE ROYAL PHILHARMONIC'S HORSEPLAY

A few years back, I was called by a BBC radio station in relation to a special horse race at the Kempton Park racecourse in the west of London. It was decided that, as part of a series of Best of British celebrations, the Royal Philharmonic Orchestra (RPO) would accompany the race and have the performance piped along the entire 1 mile and 3 furlong course via loudspeakers, for the delectation of man and beast alike. I was asked to give my scientific perspective on the type of music that would most likely aid the horses' running performance. In light of no substantive scientific evidence, I flippantly suggested "whip-hop." Rather predictably, perhaps, the RPO went with Rossini's *William Tell Overture* (think theme music to *The Lone Ranger*) played at what their director duly described as a "galloping rhythm."

# MAE THE FORCE BE WITH YOU

Musical icon Vanessa-Mae created one of the most striking examples of a sport–music crossover when she competed in the 2014 Sochi Winter Olympics. A child prodigy on the violin, she joined the Royal College of Music in London at the age of 11, just six years after taking up the instrument. Interestingly, an even earlier passion eventually blossomed into an Olympic odyssey. She took up skiing at the tender age of four and had resolved to be an Olympian from her teenage years.

Vanessa-Mae's earlier attempts to represent Thailand in the 2002 Salt Lake City Games had been thwarted by citizenship issues. Yet her commitment to go the distance bore fruit in 2014. She made it to the Games in the slalom and giant slalom classifications using her Thai father's surname of Vanakorn. Leading out a largest-ever Thai contingent of two winter Olympians, Vanessa-Mae chose to compete only in the giant slalom, where she finished last of the 67 who completed the course (there were 90 starters), and nearly a minute behind gold medalist Tina Maze of Slovenia after two runs.

Although Vanessa-Mae did not perhaps exude the poise and athleticism of the elite skiers, she executed her turns with a certain grace that endeared her to the watching millions and made her something of a sound-bite on the evening news. There was a strange parallel between the way she slid and carved her way to and fro across the giant slalom course and the rhythmical way she draws her bow back and forth across her half-million-dollar 1761 Guadagnini violin. A further commonality between these two seemingly contrasting endeavors may be the opportunity they provide to take a risk. "I was the only child, I was climbing trees. . . . and there is a side of me that likes risks, and I took risks also with my music, I have always enjoyed risks," she said (Folley, 2014).

The epilogue to this story is that Vanessa-Mae's qualification for the Sochi Olympics was called into question and then placed under severe scrutiny. Apparently smitten by her celebrity, skiing officials in Krvavec, Slovenia, acquiesced in the rigging of a series of races, run in close succession, that allowed the Britain-born musician to amass a sufficient number of points to qualify for the Games. The Fédération Internationale de Ski (FIS) slapped a four-year participation ban on Vanessa-Mae, who subsequently took her case to the Court of Arbitration for Sport (CAS) in Lausanne, Switzerland. The CAS papers (see www.tas-cas.org/en/index.html) reveal that one of the competitions was listed as the Thai Junior National Championships despite the fact that only one participant, Vanessa-Mae, had Thai citizenship, and she was 35 years old. The points from the competitions held in Krvavec were duly annulled, and so Vanessa-Mae's participation in Sochi was not officially recognized. Nonetheless, she was cleared of any personal wrongdoing, and the four-year FIS ban was lifted, allowing her to contemplate a second Olympic appearance in Pyeongchang, South Korea.

Vanessa-Mae: Musical prodigy or sporting wannabe?

facilitates the assignment of music-related interventions given the commonalities in terms of skill requirements within each cluster.

# SERVE-AND-RETURN SPORTS: BADMINTON, RACQUETBALL, SQUASH, TABLE TENNIS, TENNIS

All serve-and-return sports have similar characteristics and so cleave together particularly well when we consider potential music applications. In terms of the classifications presented in table 7.1, the skills involved are serial, open, externally paced (with the exception of the service, which is internally paced), and a combination of motoric and cognitive, as well as gross (e.g., large leg movements) and fine (e.g., small wrist movements). Additional commonalities are that such sports are combative (i.e., involved direct competition against an opponent) and require excellent eye–hand coordination.

As with the majority of individual sports, the role of music in serve-and-return sports is to prepare athletes mentally prior to competition, to aid their relaxation post-competition, and to accompany the more physically arduous aspects of the training such as shuttle runs and resistance training (see chapter 4 for examples). Far and away the most important application is mental preparation for competition. In this group of sports, competition is often as much mental as it is physical or tactical. The greatest exponents, such as Serena Williams (USA, tennis), Nick Matthew (UK, squash), and Ratchanok Intanon (Thailand, badminton), have a certain aura about them. They are somehow able to demonstrate their mastery and assert their authority even before a single ball

Andy Murray is well known for his use of music to ease pre-match nerves.

Leon Neal/AFP/Getty Images

or shuttlecock has been struck. Music can help sportspeople reinforce their public personas or attitudes through their courtside demeanor and social interactions.

In the early part of his tennis career, British number one Andy Murray was famous for using the music of the American hip-hop collective the Black Eyed Peas both before and during competition. In those days, the tennis authorities had not yet banned personal listening devices on court. In 2007, a 19-year-old Murray told British journalists: "I listen to my iPod as I walk on. If I'm winning, I'll listen to the same song, that's like a good luck thing—usually the Black Eyed Peas' 'Let's Get It Started'" (Daily Mirror, 2007). In more recent years, now that music use is permitted only before players go on court, the 2012 Olympic champion uses music in a more structured way:

*I always listen to music before I go out on court, but for me, it's important that it's fairly relaxing. With the nerves and excitement, you don't want to get the adrenaline flowing too much before you get out on court. It's about focusing and conserving energy and making sure you are ready to go at the right time. (The Hits, 2013)*

Table 7.3 shows Murray's playlist from the 2013 season. It includes a number of fairly slow and sedate tracks such as "Further" by Longview and "All Summer Long" by Kid Rock.

When athletes are practicing decision-making or cognitive skills, music can be an unnecessary distraction. The risk is that the primary task (e.g., stroke-related decision making) may be diminished by the secondary task of listening to music. The quick reactions essential in sports such as racquetball, table tennis, and squash are likely to be impeded by blaring music. The exponents of serve-and-return sports listen intently for the sound of contact between the ball and the opponent's racket, hand, or paddle so that they can plan a return shot. An added issue is that many of these sports take place in large concrete buildings with wooden floors, resulting in sound reverberations that make the listening experience far from optimal.

With all that said, research shows that listening to low-intensity music (<65 dBA) while performing very well-learned decision-making skills is unlikely to influence the quality of the execution of such skills (Ünal et al., 2013). A repeated cross-court hitting drill in tennis (from forehand to backhand) is unlikely to be disrupted by low-intensity music playing at the side of the court. The use of music is certainly inadvisable if a coach is delivering instructions during the drill. In serve-and-return sports, well-selected music is best used during self-directed, repetitive, and mundane activities. It can make such activities feel pleasurable rather than laborious.

**Table 7.3**   Murray's 2013 Pre-Match Playlist (Courtesy of Spotify)

| Track | Artist(s) | Tempo (bpm) | Genre |
|---|---|---|---|
| Further | Longview | 77 | Indie rock |
| Jack & Diane | John Mellencamp | 104 | Heartland rock |
| Small Town | John Mellencamp | 123 | Heartland rock |
| Drunk | Ed Sheeran | 100 | Pop |
| You Need Me, I Don't Need You | Ed Sheeran | 103 | Alternative hip-hop |
| You're Never Over | Eminem | 82 | Hip-hop |
| Blurred Lines | Robin Thicke feat. T.I., Pharrell Williams | 120 | R&B |
| Maggie May | Rod Stewart | 129 | Folk rock |
| All Summer Long | Kid Rock | 103 | Country rock |

*Note:* All of these tracks can be located on YouTube.

# ENDURANCE-BASED SPORTS: CANOEING, CROSS-COUNTRY SKIING, CYCLING, DUATHLON, KAYAKING, RACEWALKING, ROWING, RUNNING, SWIMMING, TRIATHLON

Athletes in long-duration motoric sports can benefit from music in the pre-competition phase and also as part of their recuperation process (see the sidebar Amelia's Trepidation for the Triathlon). Perhaps the greatest benefit is from in-task music applied during training sessions. Here music can serve the function of blocking pain or elevating mood when used asynchronously, and maintaining a given work rate or enhancing efficiency when used synchronously (see chapter 2). Some endurance athletes, such as double Olympic gold medalist Mo Farah, use music whenever they can in search of a marginal gain. They might use it to mentally prepare for a race, regulate a tough training session, or relax.

*For the hours leading up to the race I try to keep things as normal as possible. Every athlete has a routine they like to stick to. I like to shave my head—to feel my scalp smooth, the refreshing sense of slapping cold water over it. Then I'll listen to some tunes. Depending on my mood, it'll be some Tupac or maybe Dizzee Rascal. If I want something a bit more chilled, I'll put on some Somali music. (Farah, 2013)*

Mo Farah (2012 Olympic gold medalist over 5,000 and 10,000 meters)

Over the last two decades, music has been integrated into many large-scale sporting events. One of the most successful fusions of sport and music has been the Run to the Beat series of musical half marathons that have taken place in London and mainland Europe (see the sidebar The Run to the Beat Phenomenon). The genesis of Run to the Beat was prompted by the banning of personal music devices in the 2007 New York City Marathon. It led to vociferous objections from competitors and,

without a dedicated music police, the ban was almost impossible to enforce. The strong reaction of runners revealed the integral part music played in their competitive experience, which prompted many race organizers around the world to place either live or pre-recorded music stations on running courses. A number of long-established mass participation events such as the Philadelphia Marathon (U.S.) and the Great North Run (UK) have placed live bands along their routes to give runners a boost. However, the music has generally not been systematically selected for its motivational qualities.

A music application specific to such long-duration sports is the differentiated use of music, which entails the use of music for segments of an activity (often when it is most needed) rather than from start to finish. This application is based on the idea that the beneficial effects of music (see chapter 2) wane with continued listening, but exposure to music when a person experiences fatigue or boredom can sustain or enhance work output at a time when it might otherwise dip. A wealth of research evidence supports the differentiated use of music (e.g., Bigliassi et al., 2014; Lim, 2012; Lim et al., 2009). For example, Singaporean researcher and salsa dancer Harry Lim demonstrated that, when music was introduced for the second half of a 10-km (6.2-mile) cycle time trial, affective valence (i.e., how good the subjects felt) remained relatively stable compared to when music was played throughout, in the first half only, and not at all (see figure 7.1 on page 160). Lim used the 11-point Feeling Scale to measure affective valence (see chapter 3).

Over the last decade, advances in underwater MP3 technology have led to the popularization of music use in swimming. This sport demands a regular motor pattern and highly rhythmic limb movements and breathing patterns. Rhythmic music can help swimmers set a good rhythm while also distracting them from the monotony of grinding out repetitive lengths in the pool. In partnership with Speedo, my group sought to measure the psychological and ergogenic (work-enhancing) effects of music in an all-out 200-meter freestyle task (Karageorghis et al., 2013). We found that both motivational ("Sexy And I Know It" by LMFAO) and oudeterous ("Howl" by Florence and the Machine) tracks enhanced swimmers'

## AMELIA'S TREPIDATION FOR THE TRIATHLON

While I was working with Amelia, an international triathlete, she expressed a deep-seated fear of the physical demands of the Ironman event. The Ironman is a grueling physical challenge that entails a 2.4-mile (3.9 km) swim that is followed by a 112-mile (180 km) cycle race, and capped off by a marathon run of 26.2 miles (42 km). Any one of these elements in isolation would be beyond the ability of most mere mortals. Amelia was habituated to the Olympic-distance triathlon, which is much shorter (1.5 km [0.9 mile] swim, 40 km [25 mile] ride, 10 km [6.2 mile] run), and so the prospect of the Ironman event filled her with trepidation; she simply didn't know whether she had the mettle to get through it. To overcome her anxieties, as part of a mental preparation program, Amelia used "The Climb" by Miley Cyrus, which encapsulated the "continue through the pain barrier" mentality that she needed to adopt. Despite the leisurely rock tempo and an unlikely choice of artist, the Hannah Montana star spelled out the required mind-set in lucid terms:

*I can almost see it*

*That dream I am dreaming*

*But there's a voice inside my head saying*

*"You'll never reach it"*

*Every step I'm taking*

*Every move I make feels*

*Lost with no direction*

*My faith is shaking*

*But I gotta keep trying*

*Gotta keep my head held high*

The lyrics of the song resonated with the triathlete, and the uplifting guitar-led refrain and strong backbeat gave her the hard edge she needed to grapple with this extreme challenge. Although not without some pain and anguish, Amelia's first Ironman was a relative success. She managed to complete it unbowed and in one piece, albeit only 32nd out of 39 women who started. Much like the surfer who craves the next giant wave, Amelia immediately commenced preparations for her second Ironman, which she was determined to complete in a much faster time.

perceptions of state motivation and time trial performance when compared to a no-music control (see figure 7.2). This suggests that, during all-out efforts, athletes may tune in only to the rhythmic qualities of music (Terry et al., 2012). Athletes in all rhythmic endurance sports (e.g., cross-country skiing, rowing, running) can benefit from music, and a strong body of scientific evidence (for reviews, see Karageorghis, 2016; Karageorghis & Priest, 2012a, 2012b) has inspired new types of sporting events (see the sidebar The Run to the Beat Phenomenon).

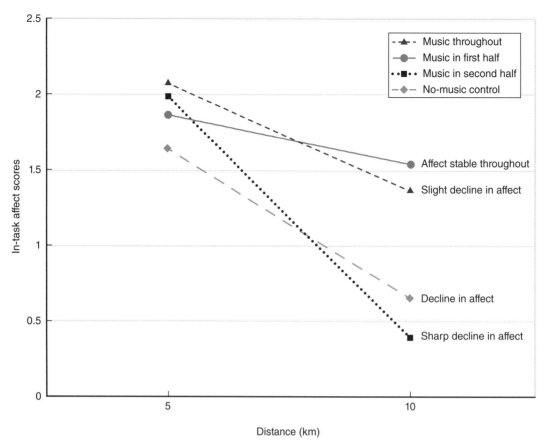

**Figure 7.1** The influence of differentiated music use on in-task affect.

Adapted, by permission, from H.B.T. Lim, 2012, "Effects of varied music applications in cycle ergometry." Unpublished doctoral thesis, Brunel University London, UK.

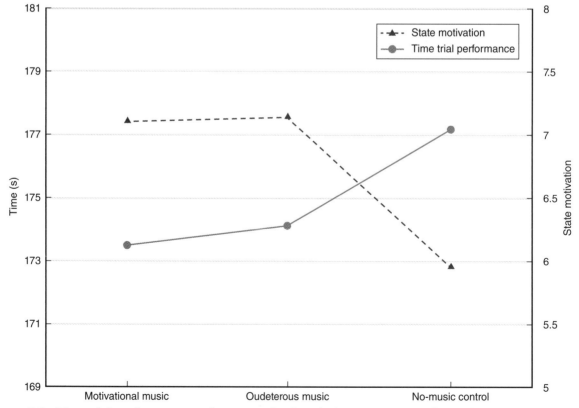

**Figure 7.2** Time trial performance and state motivation during a 200-meter freestyle task.

Adapted from *Psychology of Sport and Exercise* 14(4), C.I. Karageorghis, J.C. Hutchinson, L. Jones, H.L. Farmer, M.S. Ayhan, R.C. Wilson, J. Rance, C.J. Hepworth, and S.G. Bailey, "Psychological, psychophysical, and ergogenic effects of music in swimming," 560-568, 2013, with permission from Elsevier.

# THE RUN TO THE BEAT PHENOMENON

The International Management Group (IMG), which organized the Run to the Beat series of half marathons, adopted the mission to take a more systematic approach to music delivery and the experience of spectators at mass participation events. They identified a clear gap in the market given that London did not have a half marathon event and there were no events nationally or internationally in which live bands and DJs lined the entire course.

In the fall of 2007, the erstwhile managing director of mass participation sports at IMG, Nick Rusling, stumbled across some of my research on an Australian website. He assumed that I was based south of the equator and e-mailed me in the hope that we might arrange an early-morning conference call. It transpired that, at the time, I was living on the same road as IMG's offices in Chiswick, West London. We began to plan the first event, which took place in the London Borough of Greenwich on Sunday, October 5, 2008. The intention underlying Run to the Beat events was to select music that matched the physiological demands of the event as well as the demographic profiles and music preferences of participants (see Karageorghis, 2014). We determined participants' profiles and preferences via a portal on the event's website (www.runtothebeat.co.uk).

When preparing the music programs (see, e.g., table 7.4), we had difficulty selecting music as a type of pacemaker with which runners could synchronize their stride rates. The event attracts runners with a vast range of running abilities and body types, and the varying topography leads to considerable variation in stride-rate frequency. Nonetheless, my goal was to select music with regular rhythmic qualities and avoid irregular or highly syncopated rhythms (see chapter 1). I also applied the principles outlined in chapter 2 to increase the motivational intensity of the music as runners progressed through the course. Moreover, bands were positioned strategically on hilly parts of the course, where the physiological demands on runners were heightened.

**Table 7.4** Set List From the Closing Stages of the 2010 Run to the Beat Event

| Track | Artist(s) | Tempo (bpm) | Genre |
|---|---|---|---|
| Day 'N' Nite | Kid Cudi vs. Crookers | 130 | Dubstep/dance |
| Stay | Sash | 134 | Dance |
| Sunrise | Angel City | 135 | Dance |
| Raindrops (Encore Une Fois) | Sash feat. Stunt | 138 | Dance |
| Heaven | DJ Sammy & Yanou feat. Do | 138 | Dance |
| The Boys Of Summer | DJ Sammy | 145 | Dance |
| Run To The Beat | Radiola | 130 | Pop |

*Note:* All of these tracks can be located on YouTube.

The demographic information that we collated from the event website showed that, in complete contrast to most mass participation events, the participants were predominantly female (there was a 2:3 male-to-female ratio). Interestingly, our data also revealed that, for the majority of participants, it was their first half marathon; the inclusion of scientifically selected music had proven an inspiration for them to set a competitive goal and get active. The event gathered considerable momentum: there were 7,252 finishers in 2008, 9,082 finishers in 2009, and over 11,000 finishers in 2010, which was the final year of my involvement as a consultant.

Run to the Beat attracted some notable local acts that included North London singer-songwriter Radiola, who performed the event's eponymous theme tune in 2009. This was composed using a brief that I prepared and distributed to songwriters in an open competition. In 2010, South London–based grime star Tinie Tempah gave a rousing performance as the headline act on the main stage

*(continued)*

**The Run to the Beat Phenomenon**    *(continued)*

next to the famous O2 Arena. His appearance brought a huge number of additional spectators, which created a carnival-like atmosphere. Also, Bhangra-influenced hip-hop group Panjabi Hit Squad, representing West London, gave repeat performances year after year. It was notable that the band's lead vocalist used improvisational techniques to interact with fatiguing runners and provide well-received encouragement.

Run to the Beat has had many positive outcomes, not the least of which is that it has encouraged many people to take up habitual physical activity with the pleasurable stimulus that well-selected music can provide. It has raised large sums for a wide variety of charities; for example, over £400,000 ($550,000) for the charity Leukaemia and Lymphoma Research in the first year alone. Different strands of the community have come together (musicians, business leaders, local residents, charity fund-raisers, elite athletes, and recreational runners), and London now has a new half marathon, which may provide a stepping-stone to its famous counterpart, the London Marathon.

*Run to the rhythm, run to the beat, keep your feet moving, and pound that street!*

(Run to the Beat marketing slogan)

Courtesy of International Management Group (IMG) Mass Participation Events.

---

# SUBJECTIVELY SCORED SPORTS WITH AN ARTISTIC COMPONENT: FIGURE SKATING, HIGH DIVING, GYMNASTICS, TRAMPOLINING

Sound scientific evidence supports the notion that subjectively scored sports are more anxiety inducing than objectively scored ones (e.g., Woodman & Hardy, 2003; Zell & Krizan, 2014). In subjectively scored sports, judges rate the quality of individual athletes' movement patterns and decide who wins and who loses. These judges have their own hobbyhorses, idiosyncrasies, and biases. Some sports in this category, such as figure skating and rhythmic gymnastics, involve performances carefully choreographed to music. The purpose of this section is not to address aesthetic considerations (i.e., the worth of one musical work over another and the associated artistic interpretations); rather, it is to consider the role music might have in the preparation phase immediately before competition.

For athletes competing in sports without musical accompaniment such as high diving and trampolining, pre-event music can be a useful antidote to anxiety. It can also deliver a minor ego boost and facilitate mental rehearsal. In this regard, music functions in the same way as it does in many of the sports in this chapter that require serial, closed, motor, and gross skills (e.g., the long and triple jumps). The main difference, however, is the subjectivity of the scoring process and the havoc this can wreak on athletes' thought processes. Essentially, the pre-event music should take an athlete's mind off the outcome of the event and onto the processes that will facilitate a successful performance. To this end, a steady beat, warm harmonies, and strong lyrical affirmations are important considerations. Good examples include the boisterous Jamaican dancehall track "Ravin" by Popcaan. This song was used to great effect by British gymnast Louis Smith in London 2012, where he won a silver medal on the pommel horse. In a similar vein, the oft-used "Lose Yourself" by Eminem (see also the sidebar Garth's Mental Preparation With Music in chapter 3) was deployed by American trampolinist Savannah Vinsant at the London Games, where she made it to the finals. The lines about losing yourself in the music and the intensity of the moment particularly helped Vinsant, the youngest competitor in the field, to fully immerse herself in the here and now.

Athletes in subjectively scored sports often visualize their performances in real time and in first person (i.e., looking through their own eyes) and concurrently use auditory imagery to reproduce the music in their mind's ear. The senses are blended to create a close-to-life performance that is technically perfect but without any physical energy expended. This is a useful way to prime for a figure skating or rhythmic gymnastics routine. Indeed, the Japanese figure skater Yuzuru Hanyu used visual and auditory imagery in his pre-event routine on course to a gold-medal-winning performance at the 2014 Sochi Winter Olympic Games.

Yusuke Nakanishi/AFLO/Icon Sportswire

Japanese figure skater Yuzuru Hanyu uses both visual and auditory imagery as an integral part of his pre-event routine.

# POWER-BASED SPORTS: DISCUS THROW, HAMMER THROW, HIGH JUMP, JAVELIN THROW, LONG JUMP, POLE VAULT, POWERLIFTING, SHOT PUT, SPEED SKATING, SPRINTING AND HURDLING, SWIMMING (UP TO 100 METERS), TRIPLE JUMP, WEIGHTLIFTING

For single, highly motoric efforts such as the long jump, hammer throw, and clean-and-jerk in weightlifting, music is no longer permitted in the arena. Not only have sporting authorities wised up to the performance-enhancing effects of music, but they are also conscious of athletes obtaining feedback from coaches via headphones and radio receivers. Accordingly, the role of music in power-based sports is to prepare the athlete mentally during the lead-in phase prior to entering the arena for competition. Music can be used during this phase to ease the journey to the venue, while hanging around at the venue before the event, and for the warm-up outside of the stadium or venue. For some, it is also used as a backdrop to explosive strength training, which entails exerting a maximal amount of force in the shortest possible time. For training routines involving Olympic lifts (e.g., power clean, snatch balance), plyometric drills, and kettlebell workouts, rousing and rambunctious music selections are recommended (see examples in table 4.5). This section focuses on music for power-based athletes' pre-competition phase.

Although competitors differ in personality and optimal pre-competition mood state, power events demand a maximal burst of movement and typically require a certain type of attitude. It is not enough simply to be highly energetic, or "aroused," as psychologists put it. That energy must be channeled rather than simply floating about in the form of jittery nerves. Indeed, many

power athletes lose before they even leave the locker room because they expend so much nervous energy contemplating their performance. This can easily result in muscle tension and an increased chance of soft tissue injury.

Arguably, the ability to regulate arousal is more salient for power athletes than for any other athletes; they must peak fast and late. Music can facilitate this process by providing a soothing distraction in the hours leading up to the event and by helping to "flick the switch" when a surge of adrenaline and intensity is required (see the sidebar Just What is Michael Phelps Listening To?). In terms of attitude, power athletes need to be unfettered, single-minded, and truly fearless. Any doubts about ability or the enormity of the task can prove fatal. This type of certainty can be aided by lyrics and an identification with the performer and his or her emotions. Consider the affinity expressed by British track athlete Dina Asher-Smith (see Foreword) for the American R&B star, Beyoncé—the no-stone-left-unturned approach of the singer mirrors the athlete's approach to competitive excellence. Music can also exert a powerful influence on an athlete's body language—that most crucial of competitive weapons.

Multiple world record–holder Usain Bolt (Jamaica) expressed a penchant for the music of dancehall artist and teenage friend Vybz Kartel: "Vybz Kartel is my favorite artist. He's a good lyricist. I listen to all his music—it's fun" (Stubbs, 2012). Bolt is well known for apparently switching off and having fun right up until he appears on the starting line and prepares to sink into his blocks. He claims that he can't bear to think about the race until about one minute before the gun goes off. This is Bolt's very personal way of dealing with the pressure of being the fastest man on earth, and music forms part of an overall strategy that many casual observers might interpret as a carefree attitude. In terms of peaking fast and late, Bolt is certainly an expert. Later in this section, we explore the pre-event music and mind-set of a very different type of power athlete, the British 400-meter hurdler Dai Greene.

## Dai Hard Music

Performance tracks are pieces of music that are written, produced, and recorded for a given

## JUST WHAT IS MICHAEL PHELPS LISTENING TO?

American swimmer Michael Phelps is the most decorated Olympian in history. He claimed six gold medals at the 2004 Athens Games, surpassing even that feat with an unprecedented haul of eight gold medals at the 2008 Beijing Games, before capping his career with four golds and two silvers in London 2012. Phelps is an avid music listener when in his pre-competition bubble, using his iPod until about two minutes before swimming. One of the most frequently asked questions on Olympic-related blogs over the last three olympiads was "Just what is Michael Phelps listening to?" Well, his playlist includes mostly rap and hip-hop sounds, with artists such as Jay-Z, Young Jeezy, and Eminem featuring prominently. "I'm Me" by Lil' Wayne was on his pre-race playlist in Beijing and London, which includes a line about being the best and knowing the game so well that he could be officiating it. There is an eminent and gladiatorial slant to his selections, which befits an Olympian of such towering frame and fame. One wonders what he will be listening to in Rio at his fifth Olympic Games.

athlete or team, sometimes in preparation for a major competition such as the Olympic Games or a world cup. The following section details the preparation and application of a performance track for the British track and field athlete, Dai Greene. The account of how the project unfolded illustrates the key principles and highlights points of interest for any readers—be they sport professionals or musicians—who might wish to engage in a similar project.

In preparation for the London 2012 olympiad, I was given a music-and-sport assignment that went beyond the run-of-the-mill playlists for events or athlete training. Early in the year, I was invited to meet with the performance team of Red Bull, the sponsors of World, European, and Commonwealth 400-meter hurdles champion Dai Greene. Since winning gold in emphatic style at the Daegu World Championships the previous year, Dai's Olympic preparations had been hampered by knee surgery and a string of minor injuries. Red Bull wanted to provide the star athlete with an extra boost, something to give him a psychological edge in advance of the Games that were to take place on his home soil.

The folks at Red Bull had read about previous work I'd done in this domain, in particular with Run to the Beat, and requested that I work with Dai Greene and his favorite producer, Redlight, on what they branded the Performance Track Project. The entire project would be filmed and later turned into a documentary (see http://goo

.gl/nvJTf). We also agreed that the performance track would be made freely available to the general public as an MP3 download. The project comprised the following three phases:

Phase 1: Psychological screening of Dai Greene

Phase 2: Construction of the performance track with Redlight

Phase 3: Implementation and media dissemination

### Phase 1: Psychological Screening of Dai Greene

Dai came to visit me at Brunel University London with an entourage that included a film crew and his management team. I had asked him to bring along a wide selection of the tracks he had used in the past as part of his pre-event routine. Dai's playlist had a distinctly urban flavor, with American artists such as Snoop Dogg, Jay-Z, and Tupac Shakur at the fore. We talked in some detail about his formative musical background and experiences, growing up as he did in the small village of Felinfoel near Llanelli in Wales.

I tried to get a clear idea of the musical works that appealed to Dai and why—what was in his musical DNA? In those crucial minutes before the call-up at major track and field championships, the music must bring about the desired mindset. I decided to use a semi-structured interview approach (see Semi-Structured Interview Questions in the Performance Track Project) and

Courtesy of Sally Trussler, Brunel University London photographer.

Usain Bolt, the world's fastest man, is known to enjoy the music of his teenage friend Vybz Kartel.

the following battery of psychometric tests to establish the details of Dai's optimal state of mind immediately before a race. Some of these tests are discussed in chapter 3.

- Terry Orlick's Mental Preparation Profile (MPP) to ascertain Dai's optimal pre-competition state (see chapter 3)
- The Brunel Music Rating Inventory-3 (BMRI-3) to gauge how motivating Dai found a number of tracks that he commonly listened to (see chapter 3)
- Rainer Martens and colleagues' Sport Competition Anxiety Test (SCAT) to gauge Dai's typical level of pre-competition anxiety (for a copy of the SCAT, see pp. 105-106 of *Inside Sport Psychology*, Human Kinetics, 2011)

- Peter Terry and Andrew Lane's Brunel Mood Scale (BRUMS), which is a shortened and sport-specific version of the widely used Profile of Mood States (see chapter 3)
- Oliver P. John's (Berkeley Personality Lab) Big Five Inventory, which assesses five major personality traits: extraversion, agreeableness, conscientiousness, neuroticism, and openness (this test should be administered and interpreted by a trained psychologist)

### Semi-Structured Interview Questions in the Performance Track Project

1. What are your earliest memories of music?
2. How musical was your family while you were growing up? What were the musical tastes of your siblings, friends, and parents?

3. Can you name a few tracks from your child-hood that really stick in your mind?

4. Have you ever played a musical instrument?

5. What sort of music do you like and dislike generally? Let's rate a few tracks using the Brunel Music Rating Inventory-3.

6. Does it matter to you which artist(s) is/are performing a song? Who are your favorite artists?

7. To what extent do you use music in your training and competitive routines?

8. What sort of music do you use? Name a couple of pieces and describe why you use them and how they generally make you feel.

9. Do you use music for any other purpose outside of sport?

10. Describe your pre-event routine from the morning of the race onward.

11. What is going through your mind in the final minutes before you compete? What sort of images do you see? How do you see yourself? How would you describe your energy levels?

12. In your event, what kinds of restrictions are placed on your use of music?

13. Is there any way you would like to enhance your pre-competition state?

14. How do you think music might help in your pre-event routine?

    *Note:* These questions can be easily adapted to create an interview for any sportsperson.

Following the psychological screening, we spent time in the laboratory conducting a further battery of tests to gauge how Dai responded to different types of music across a range of motor tasks (e.g., treadmill running, cycle ergometry, handgrip dynamometry). We talked generally about the Welshman's preparation for the Games during this time. I even shared a few Edwin Moses anecdotes with him, such as the time when Moses was asked by a young journalist whether he was worried about all of the up-and-coming 400-meter hurdlers: "The other guys are so far behind, I don't even know what they look like" was his audacious response.

Delving into Dai's music library and trying to understand exactly what made him tick, I realized what the musical properties of the performance track would need to be in order to optimize his pre-race mind-set and imbue him with a strong sense of control. Many people in the music business have suggested to me that you can see peoples' personalities simply by delving into their music collections, and some scientific evidence is emerging to back this up (Chamorro-Premuzic & Furnham, 2007; Park et al., 2013). I had the results of the Big Five Personality Inventory to help me with Dai's music collection.

Dai is quite an introverted and soft-spoken character. At his core is a steely determination to be the best in the world, and he takes a meticulous approach to preparing for competition. His optimal pre-race mood is unlike that of many of the athletes I have worked with. It was typified by low vigor and moderate levels of fatigue; it was quite a low-energy state, almost bordering on the lethargic. Elite track and field athletes are permitted to use music at major championships only up to about 20 minutes before the event. I visited the Olympic stadium in East London to get a feel for the warm-up track, how long it would take to get from there to the main stadium via the athletes' passage, and the majesty of Dai's competition environment.

The athletes' warm-up is punctuated by two call-ups. Call-up 1 is to the side of the warm-up track, and call-up 2 is beneath the grandstand that runs parallel to the home straight in the Olympic stadium. There is also a prayer room adjacent to the call-up 2 area. Personal listening devices need to be left with coaches at the warm-up track and are not permitted in the main arena. Twenty minutes before the start, Dai is visualizing the race and trying not to expend too much mental or bodily energy. Table 7.5 provides a summary of the notes I made regarding the potential qualities of the performance track with reference to the factors in the theoretical model presented in chapter 2 (figure 2.8).

## Phase 2: Construction of the Performance Track With Redlight

The English summer of 2012 will be remembered for its almost two and a half months of continuous rain. However, on the day I met producer Redlight at the Red Bull Studios in London, it was unusually bright and sunny. Redlight insisted on wearing sunglasses and sported a full face of designer stubble. We started chatting about the project over a cup of tea, and he was rather inquisitive,

**Table 7.5** Potential Qualities of Dai Greene's Performance Track

| Musical factors | Personal factors | Situational factors |
|---|---|---|
| "I enjoy music with a strong bass line." | "I grew up on chart music, Radio 1, and cheesy pop." | "I listen to music on my headphones on the morning of a race." |
| "I particularly like American rap music like Tupac and Jay-Z." | "I really dislike cheesy pop music for performance purposes." | "I enjoy using music during my warm-up because I can block out any distractions." |
| "The music needs to be quite stimulative, but not too much." | "The music needs to make me feel strong and determined." | "I can use the music only up until the first call, as thereafter I have to hand my personal stereo over to my coach." |
| "I like a sense of aggression in my music because that reflects my approach to the race." | "Ultimately, I need to be in a fairly calm state of mind before I compete because my event is very technical and mentally as well as physically demanding." | "There is a long gap—perhaps as long as 20 minutes—between warming up and competing; therefore, that last track before I go to the second call room is of critical importance." |
| "The music needs to have a steady rhythm because my event requires a steady rhythm to clear the hurdles fluidly." | "The last thing I listen to tends to reverberate in my mind and set the tone for what's to come." | "There is a massive opportunity for me here [London Olympic Games], and I need that extra 1 percent for my performance using the power of music." |

stopping me to ask the meaning of almost every psychological term I used.

Working with someone like me was a rather unusual addition to the creative process for Redlight. An enigmatic character, Redlight was wary of how the project output might be perceived and what it might do for his street cred: "Cos man, I can imagine seeing myself on YouTube in 10 years' time with this wacky scientist bloke [pointing at me] and thinking What the hell am I doing?" He had good reason to be self-conscious; throughout that day our every move and utterance was documented by not only the regular film crew from Gammafilm but also a team from BBC News (for release the same night) and a photographer hired by Red Bull. It was the equivalent of creating art in a fishbowl.

Redlight and I discussed the desired properties and potential rhythmic feel of the track. He played me a series of samples and rhythm tracks he had prepared as a starting point and stimulus for discussion. I explained to him that I was a music graduate as well as a psychologist, and that I

understood the process of music production. Redlight told me that "musicians know how to play tunes, but what I do is completely different." That soon became evident as we began working on the track with Redlight at the mixing desk and me by his side, chiming in with the occasional comment. There was very little playing of instruments other than some melodic figures that he added into the mix using a keyboard module.

By mid-afternoon, when Dai joined us in the studio, Redlight had the skeleton of a track down (bass line, rhythm track, melodic figure) and was playing it at an ear-splitting volume through the studio monitors. The time spent with Dai was possibly the most fulfilling during the creative process. He told us precisely how the fledgling track related to his musical predilections—what he liked and what he didn't like. The rhythmic track had a strong groove but was not too lively. Dai wanted some sparse lyrical content—we hadn't quite gotten that far on the first day of recording.

Redlight was taking it all in, and by the time the work with Dai was done, he showed invigorated enthusiasm. He realized precisely how the track would fit in to Dai's preparation and just how important music was in the hotbed of competition: "I think that athletics is not far from my industry—it's all about pushing yourself. . . . No one is there to push you along. In athletics you've gotta get your mind on that one goal, which is winning." The day ended with interviews from each of us that later featured in a BBC news item on music and sport (see http://goo.gl/ecdwD0).

## Phase 3: Implementation and Media Dissemination

Red Bull sent me the performance track—now known as "Talk To The Drum"—for feedback (see the sidebar The Author's Feedback to Redlight on the First Version of the Performance Track). I subsequently learned from Dai that he "absolutely loved it." Accordingly, Dai began to use the track as part of his pre-race routine to develop an affinity for it in preparation for the Olympic Games. Notably, a couple of weeks later, Dai smashed his personal best for the 400-meter hurdles in Paris

with a time of 47.84 seconds, a time that ranked him second in the world.

During this final phase, my main role was to present the project to the world's media. I was to tell the story of how the project unfolded, emphasize its uniqueness, and explain the brand significance of Red Bull's partnership with Dai. There was massive media interest in the project that spanned TV, radio, and print (see, e.g., http://goo.gl/IIlXtO). Most journalists were interested to know how far science had advanced in using music in the sport and exercise domain. Their interest was compounded by the fact that UK Athletics head coach Charles van Commenee had appointed Dai as Team GB athletics captain.

This was a role Dai was to fill with considerable aplomb. He provided inspirational leadership throughout the Games, and his pep talk to the British track and field athletes led them to one of their best-ever medal hauls. Dai had some niggles while progressing through the rounds of the 400-meter hurdles and was ideally placed in the final having been given lane 3. We had long

## THE AUTHOR'S FEEDBACK TO REDLIGHT ON THE FIRST VERSION OF THE PERFORMANCE TRACK

- The general architecture of the track is wholly appropriate, and the way the percussion comes in and out in waves is particularly effective.

- The repeated use of "hey" in the main rhythmic pattern quickly becomes irritating. It's too repetitive and could be used more sparingly.

- Rhythmically, the introduction is strong and builds energy, but the initial vocals are indiscernible. This may or may not matter to Dai.

- The main melodic hook is almost whimsical and does not seem to inspire action—but Dai might love it, so you would need to check with him. I also don't like the instrumentation of the melodic hook—it gives the track quite an ambient feel, whereas it would be preferable to have a timbre (sound) that was more energizing (e.g., synth brass or orchestra hits).

- There are some excellent affirmations in the track, although I am not sure that "wind up your body" is the best affirmation to give a 400-meter hurdler before competition. This lyric is common to music of West Indian derivation but does not work well in this particular context.

- The ending is a tad too sudden. Perhaps structure it a little better or use a fade out.

- The tempo feels about right at 126 bpm, and the rhythms are not too busy, which will help Dai stay focused and preserve energy before he heads for the second call-up room at the Olympic stadium.

To listen to a recording of the performance, search "Redlight Talk To The Drum" on YouTube.

believed that the main threat would come from Javier Culson of Puerto Rico, who was leading the world rankings and had narrowly beaten Dai at the Crystal Palace Grand Prix a few weeks earlier. Nonetheless, it was an old master of the event, Félix Sánchez (Dominican Republic), who, at the ripe old age of 34, enjoyed a swansong to clinch his second Olympic gold in emphatic style. Despite the injury woes, Dai held himself together and finished fourth in the final and later contributed to Team GB's fourth-place finish in the final of the 4 × 400-meter relay.

At 26 years of age, Dai was young enough to plan at least one more Olympic campaign. Who knows? If he endures as long as his rival Sánchez, he may have two more campaigns. As I write these lines, Rio 2016 is beckoning for Dai, but I am not sure how accomplished Redlight is with a samba beat!

# ICE TRACK SPORTS: LUGE, SKELETON

Luge and skeleton bobsled are winter sports that have the commonality of requiring serial, closed, cognitive, and fine motor skills. Music use is not permitted during these sports; athletes must use auditory feedback to get the line of travel down the ice-covered track just right. Nonetheless, a particular function for music in these sports is as a backdrop to mentally rehearsing hurtling down the track. Athletes know quite precisely the time it takes to complete the course at various venues, and a piece of music with a corresponding duration can enable them to peg specific segments of the course to sections of the music. This makes the temporal, or time-related, aspect of the mental rehearsal much more accurate.

After about a dozen attempts at imagining the track run while listening to the piece of music, the athlete may be able to conjure vivid images of the course simply from hearing the music. Psychologists refer to this process as classical conditioning—that is, a response is prompted by a stimulus (i.e., the piece of music) that is paired with an unconditioned response (i.e., visualizing the luge track). After repeated pairing of the music with the mental rehearsal, simply hearing the music will prompt the imagery (i.e., a conditioned response). Ultimately, the music is a way to enhance performance consistency.

## "THE YARNOLD" REACHES DIZZEE HEIGHTS IN SOCHI 2014

British skeleton bobsled athlete Elizabeth Yarnold made an emphatic Olympic debut at the 2014 Winter Olympic Games in Sochi, where she won the gold medal by a gaping 0.97 seconds ahead of the well-established Noelle Pikus-Pace of the United States. What made Yarnold's performance remarkable was that she had the fastest slide on each of the four runs and set new track records on her first and third runs. Yarnold, who notably wrote her university dissertation on mental toughness, appears to have two very distinct personas on and off the ice. Outside of skeleton bob, her favorite hobbies are knitting and listening to *The Archers* on the radio (a sedate and traditional serial drama about village life in England). When she is in competition, preparing mentally between rounds, she dances around to grime music to get pumped up and becomes "The Yarnold"—a ferocious and highly focused competitor. In this guise, her favorite artists include Wiley, Giggs, and Dizzee Rascal (Wiley even follows her on Twitter). The context-specific application of music enables Yarnold to flip from one persona to another—a type of Jekyll and Hyde effect with a happier outcome than that experienced by Robert Louis Stevenson's infamous character.

# COMBAT SPORTS: AIKIDO, ARM WRESTLING, BOXING, FENCING, JUDO, JUJITSU, KARATE, KENDO, KUNG FU, MIXED MARTIAL ARTS, TAEKWONDO, THAI BOXING, WRESTLING

Combat sports generally require serial, open, cognitive, and gross skills. A notable exception is the sport of arm wrestling, which requires continuous, open, motor, and gross skills (the goal is to pin the opponent's arm to the table and so little decision making is involved relative to the other combat sports). Many participants in combat sports use music to prepare psychologically for competition. In fact, the concept of walk-on music, now a staple across so many sports, has its origins in the vaudevillian entrances of boxers and wrestlers. The line between sport and entertainment has become increasingly blurred to the extent that a theatrical element is now expected in almost every spectator sport.

There are notable distinctions among the combat sports, given that the martial arts are predicated on a philosophy that espouses centering, mental calmness, highly controlled aggression, and mindfulness. For this reason, many martial artists either do not use music at all or employ music that is more soothing or meditative than the music employed by boxers and wrestlers. Boxers and wrestlers routinely use rousing walk-on music to signal their entry into the ring. Some martial artists favor music that alludes to the Eastern cultures identified with these sports.

In chapter 5, a number of boxing-related tracks were provided for an exercise or training context (see table 5.7). Given the strong extramusical associations inspired by these tracks, they serve well for boxers in training just as well as they do for boxercisers. The soundtrack that boxers and wrestlers use to enter the ring can have a decisive influence on how they feel about themselves and how they are perceived by spectators and the press. The music has a gladiatorial air about it and serves to affirm athletes' status, bolster their egos, and prime them for the task at hand.

One of the most famous walk-on tracks in boxing is former WBO middleweight and super-middleweight champion Chris Eubank's "The Best" by Tina Turner. The unashamedly eccentric and bombastic Eubank would pose and posture before vaulting over the top rope of the ring in emphatic style. In the welterweight division, 50 Cent was a favorite artist of Floyd Mayweather Jr., who used "I'll Whip Ya Head Boy" to signal his intentions to rival Zab Judah. Among the heavyweights, former world champion Wladimir Klitschko is well known for his use of "Can't Stop" by the Red Hot Chili Peppers, a guitar-led track that is hugely energizing and affirming in its lyrical content (in particular, about winning big).

In professional wrestling, the much-celebrated Steve Austin was famous for entering the ring to the chilling metal instrumental "Stone Cold Steve Austin," a performance track composed especially for him. Austin's long-time rival Hulk Hogan thundered in with "Real American," a song that is said to represent "America and real American heroes." Hulk's persona as the ultimate face for the crowd to rally behind was perfectly in keeping with this song. In all cases, the primary purpose of the music is to say "Hey, people, here I am; I am a badass, pumped up to the max, and ready for action!"

# AERIAL AND WATER-BASED SPORTS: HANG GLIDING, PARACHUTING, PARAGLIDING, SAILING, SKYDIVING, SURFING, WATERSKIING, WINDSURFING

Aerial and water-based sports can be hugely exhilarating, but at the same time quite anxiety provoking. The central function of music in such sports is to calm athletes so they can visualize the skills they need to execute in competition. The adrenaline rushes tend to be prompted by the environment—its exhilarations and inherent hazards. Aerial sports do not have a well-established music culture, although surfing has a rich one. For music to have a calming or anxiety-reducing effect, the entrainment principles detailed in chapter 2 come into play.

Calming music for aerial and water-based sports ideally has a tempo in the range of 75 to 95 bpm, given that the heart will be racing considerably faster than this prior to parachuting or waterskiing. The music should also have a warm and comforting harmonic structure, a simple melody, and a positive message in the lyrics. It may also conjure some event-specific imagery. In sports such as hang gliding and paragliding, a track such as "I'm Like A Bird" by Nelly Furtado, at 90 bpm, is a particularly good example for the pre-competition phase, as is "If I Had A Boat" by Lyle Lovett, at 92 bpm, for sailing.

Few sports can lay claim to having inspired so much music as surfing. In fact, in the early to mid-1960s, the American billboard charts were blitzed by the surf rock phenomenon, with acts such as the Beach Boys and the Del-Tones at the fore. The upshot is that a wealth of material, both vintage and contemporary, is available for the aspiring surfer to use in a pre-event routine. Choices will relate to cultural background: surfers in Cornwall, UK, have very different tastes from those of surfers in Orange County, California, who in turn differ from surfers on the Sunshine Coast of Australia. An important note to add is that surfers tend to be fairly extroverted characters and score highly on sensation-seeking scales. This means that despite the ever-present risk of a wipeout, they often express a preference for more upbeat selections in the pre-competition phase such as "Surfin' Safari" (159 bpm) and "Surfin' U.S.A." by the Beach Boys (158 bpm) rather than downbeat tracks such as "Rumble" by Link Wray & His Ray Men (87 bpm) and "Slow Jabroni" by Surfer Blood (85 bpm).

# MOTOR SPORTS: MOTOR RACING, MOTORCYCLE RACING

Split-second decisions and risk-taking behavior are key elements of motor sports. Clearly, music of any sort and at any tempo is a potential distraction during these sports, and it is therefore not recommended. It can, however, play a central role in preparing drivers and riders for competition. The pit lane is often a hive of journalists and photographers, corporate sponsors, celebrities, engineers, and even autograph hunters. All of these people have little regard for a driver's or rider's mental preparation. It is easy to be overcome by all of the attention and lose focus. A pair of over-ear headphones to block the roar of nearby engines and a soundtrack that relaxes the body but stimulates the mind toward task-specific visualization is the requirement. The precise level of activation to elicit with music depends on the individual; there is considerable variety in motor sports. Some performers, such as two-time MotoGP world champion Marc Márquez (Spain), need to be in a state of relative calm. Others, such as the rally driver Brian Deegan (Australia), need to be highly aroused: "I feel aggressive—that's when I'm at my best."

Many Formula One drivers have talked about their use of music before training or competition.

In the pre-competition phase, Hamilton creates his own listening bubble and visualizes the race.

Photo4/LaPresse//Icon Sportswire

For example, Lewis Hamilton soothes his anxiety and chills out by making music, at times with his trademark pooches, Roscoe and Coco, howling along. He sings and accompanies himself on guitar—for the most part, in solitary confinement.

> *I play a bit of everything really, Bob Dylan, Lenny Kravitz, Jimmy Hendrix. Reggae is my favorite to relax to. I was brought up on reggae. Whenever we had a big family get-together they would always be listening to reggae. I have been listening to Bob Marley since I was born.* (Garside, 2008)

Just before competition, Hamilton aims to switch gears mentally and ramps things up with hip-hop artists such as Tupac and Naz. Despite Hamilton's abundant musical talents, there's no chance of him joining his ex-girlfriend Nicole Scherzinger in the Pussycat Dolls quite yet!

# AIMING AND SHOOTING SPORTS: ARCHERY, BILLIARDS, BOCCIA BOWLS, CLAY PIGEON SHOOTING, CROQUET, CURLING, DARTS, GOLF, PETANQUE, POOL, SNOOKER, TARGET SHOOTING, TENPIN BOWLING

The role of music in fairly sedate aiming sports such as bowls and darts is essentially to prepare competitors mentally. In such sports, which require considerable immersion and concentration, music use is generally not permitted once competition gets under way. Nonetheless, pre-competition music takes two forms. First, players use music to block out distractions in the competitive environment, form their own listening bubbles, and create an optimal mind-set. Second, players use walk-on music to reinforce their identities, raise their spirits, and get the crowd behind them. It is, of course, possible to use both applications back to back—with a personal music player in the locker room and then the arena PA system just before play gets under way.

Aiming and shooting sports require a relatively low level of physiological arousal coupled with a low level of cognitive, or thought-related, anxiety to ensure optimal performance. The reason is that the movements required are fine and controlled and must be extremely accurate. When the heart is beating hard and negative thoughts are flying through the mind, stringing together a century break in snooker is extremely difficult. Some snooker players are known to have had parallel careers as a means by which to take their minds completely away from the demands of the competitive circuit. Before his recent retirement from the game, six-time world champion Steve Davis (UK) enjoyed a parallel career as a techno DJ—he is now making a seamless transition from breaking records on a snooker table to spinning them on a turntable.

The required psychological state for a competitor in an aiming or shooting sport is quite a balancing act, because confidence is not ordinarily the friend of relaxation. As in all sports, there is considerable inter-individual variation in terms of physiological and mental arousal. Nevertheless, most players benefit from achieving a calm and focused state of mind. I advise athletes in such sports not to think but to allow their instincts to rule; research has shown this approach to be successful (Wulf, 2013). It has been said that worry is a misuse of imagination and so music provides a means by which to harness the power of imagination toward positive ends.

One way in which to reinforce a positive mind-set is by use of a well-chosen walk-on tune. Walk-on music was introduced to snooker by promoter Barry Hearn and sent ripples through the snooker world back in 2010. It represented a notable departure from its rather dreary, working men's club image. Hearn imported it from other sports that he had also revitalized (i.e., boxing and darts) to bring the audience and the players a little closer together.

Snooker players are encouraged to select tracks with special meaning. Once introduced by the tournament MC, players walk from the edge of the arena toward the table, accompanied by their favored soundtrack. Players have shown a tendency to change their walk-on tracks from season to season to reflect how they feel about themselves or their personal expectations at the time, or to appeal to certain constituencies in the crowd. For example, during the 2013 season, Ronnie O'Sullivan, aka the Rocket, used a rather obscure track, "Drops Of Jupiter" by Train, possibly to reflect a growing sense of disillusionment. The lyrics allude to getting into the Milky Way and seeing only dim lights rather than the bright ones that were anticipated. Contrastingly, in 2014 he made the more purposeful but equally obscure choice of "A Man Of Determination" by George Lam, perhaps emblematic of his growing maturity as a player; it may even have been a nod to the increasing Chinese presence in the game.

The walk-on music innovation adopted by the snooker authorities has certainly increased the level of media interest in the sport; many commentators muse over the players' selections during major tournaments. The music also endears the players to the audience. Snooker players rarely say much in public (they tend toward introversion), so the music can give fans a view into players' psyches, and even into their hopes and dreams. Table 7.6 lists the walk-on tracks of the top-10 seeded players who took part in the 2014 World Championships at the Crucible Theatre in Sheffield, UK. The final was contested by the top-seeded players, Ronnie O'Sullivan and Mark Selby. Selby, whom O'Sullivan nicknamed the Torturer, emerged victorious by a score of 18 frames to 14.

There are different traditions across sports and, although walk-on music is now a staple of championship snooker, it is generally shunned in the world of golf. Whether this is reflective of the working class versus upper-middle-class origins of these two sports is hard to say, but they are packaged and marketed to people in very different social strata. Also, in sports such as snooker, the player's walk-on music seems to change from season to season and sometimes within a season. By way of contrast, in darts, players opt for more enduring walk-on tracks that stay with

**Table 7.6** Walk-On Music for the Top-10 Seeds at the 2014 Snooker World Championships

| Player | 2014 World Champs seeding | Track | Artist(s) or composer | Tempo (bpm) | Brief analysis |
|---|---|---|---|---|---|
| Ronnie O'Sullivan | 1 | A Man Of Determination | George Lam | 60 | This drum-crashing anthem from Hong Kong–based songster George Lam seems an unusual choice for the Rocket. Nonetheless, its relative obscurity to a British audience mirrors O'Sullivan's enigmatic qualities, whereas its traditional Eastern emphasis reflects the leanings of the sport in the twenty-first century. |
| Neil Robertson | 2 | Heart Of Courage | Two Steps From Hell | 68 | With a world championship gong under his belt, Roberson chose this dark and mysterious movie theme that embodies the serious, battling, and mature qualities he espoused at this high point in his career. |
| Mark Selby | 3 | Fast Fuse | Kasabian | 88 | The song is in keeping with Selby's character; he is known on the circuit as the Torturer. A repetitive riff with a brooding energy signifies the 2014 world champion's singular determination to win ugly if need be. |

| Player | 2014 World Champs seeding | Track | Artist(s) or composer | Tempo (bpm) | Brief analysis |
|---|---|---|---|---|---|
| Ding Junhui | 4 | Stronger | Kelly Clarkson | 120 | A somewhat unexpected and quirky choice from China's greatest player, the lyrics of the refrain echo Nietzsche's famous aphorism "What doesn't kill you makes you stronger." It could be that this message touches on Ding's recovery from the scars of several high-profile defeats that have spurred him on to unprecedented heights. |
| Barry Hawkins | 5 | My Love | Kele Le Roc | 80 | Galvanized by coach Terry Griffiths, the Hawk has become snooker's renaissance man, yet this track reflects his gentle-manly and warm approach to the sport. He exudes a love for snooker and a deep respect for his opponents. |
| Stuart Bingham | 6 | Get Lucky | Daft Punk feat. Pharrell Williams | 116 | Like Hawkins, Basildon-born baize boy Bingham is a kindly and positive figure. This summery pop tune with a wonder-ful groove conveys some of that open and optimistic energy. |
| Judd Trump | 7 | Animals | Martin Garrix | 128 | Famed for his flamboyant style of play and quirky footwear, young Bristolian Trump's choice of musical backup is no surprise with its hectic, waspish energy. Like the player himself, this track is brim-ming with hubris and caged emotion. |
| Marco Fu | 8 | Shine | Take That | 90 | Prolific break builder Fu is a perennial on the World Snooker Tour. This jaunty choral piece with its smooth harmonies is the perfect foil for his charisma and showmanship. |
| Shaun Murphy | 9 | *Superman* | John Williams | Varies | Known as the Magician, Shaun Murphy has an aura of greatness about him and is lauded by his fellow professionals for his impeccable potting. He also has a sense of humor, and this music choice is as much tongue-in-cheek self-mockery as it is flaming chutzpah. Either way, Murphy is a gilt-edged entertainer. |
| Stephen Maguire | 10 | Here I Go Again | Whitesnake | 84 | Stephen On-Fire Maguire is a player who thrives on his own occasionally destructive emotions. This ragged rock track encapsulates his demeanor at the table: macho, willful, and tempestuous, along with a dash of frustration and self-sabotage. |

*Note:* All of these tracks can be located on YouTube.

them throughout their careers; for example, Phil the Power Taylor (England) with "The Power" by Snap! prefaced by a stirring horn phrase from Copland's *Fanfare for the Common Man* and Simon the Wizard Whitlock (Australia) with "Down Under" by Men at Work. Sometimes the crowd latches onto a particular piece of music and ends up inadvertently picking it for a player. The Dutch Destroyer, Vincent van der Voort, used to come to the oche with Kasabian's "Fast Fuse," a reflection of his fiery and fast-paced style of play. Now he uses KC and the Sunshine Band's "Give It Up," ever since the crowd began to chant his name during the chorus, "van der Voort, van der Voort, Vincent van der Voort." It is no exaggeration to say that this has made a difference in his career given the strong bond it has created with his fans.

# SUMMARY

Sports are classified into meaningful clusters according to their skill components. This enables us to emphasize different music applications across the clusters: pre-task activation, anxiety control, mood regulation, distraction during training, confidence boosting, and so on. This chapter should help you find ways to use music to meet your needs or those of your athletes. I strongly encourage going beyond conventional uses of music; as Frankie Valli sang in the hit movie *Grease*, "conventionality belongs to yesterday." New gains in sport often require ingenious approaches that might appear slightly outlandish at first.

The judicious use of music can increase both the quality and consistency of sport performance. Familiar music is a constant and thus a comforting stimulus in what might otherwise be perceived as a threatening environment. Sport is a theater in which frailties are often laid bare for all to see. Music can take an athlete's mind off the pressure of the occasion, create a sense of self-control, bolster the ego, and fire him or her with passion. The precise function of music varies according to the characteristics of the individual (e.g., personality), the nature of the event (e.g., cognitive vs. motoric sport), and the importance of the competition (e.g., local league vs. major international championship).

In terms of the required mental approach, individual sports that require fine motor skills, such as snooker and darts, are very different from sports that require gross skills, such as powerlifting and shot putting. Qualities of music (e.g., tempo, loudness, harmony, lyrics) are selected to bring about the desired mind-set, which can also be triggered by a piece of music through a process psychologists call classical conditioning. Music is one of the few stimuli that can have a direct and predictable influence on an athlete's psychological state.

Music selection is unique to each person, as reflected in the playlists of well-known sportspeople such as Andy Murray (tennis) and Michael Phelps (swimming). The starting point is determining how the athlete wants to feel in the moments leading up to competition and then identifying specific tracks that embody such qualities. When using music as a training stimulus, many of the principles outlined in detail in chapter 4 for individual exercise apply to individual sports. A useful avenue for coaches and athletes to explore is the differentiated use of music (see figure 7.1), which has only recently attracted scientific interest. The idea is to use music in training only when it is most needed (e.g., in the closing stages of a 10-km run) and not throughout a session. This is one way to banish conventionality and embrace innovation in music applications.

# 8

# Team Sport Training and Performance

*I can't listen to that much Wagner. I start getting the urge to conquer Poland.*
—Woody Allen, actor, director, screenwriter, comedian, musician, and playwright

Music has long played a starring role in the on-field drama of team sports. It is woven into the fabric of prominent sports such as soccer, American football, and ice hockey. Many years before the advent of personal listening devices and digital hi-fi systems, players used chants in the locker room to strengthen their unions, fans roared their club's anthem in stadiums, and teams sang raucously in club bars to cap a victory. The songs, chants, and anthems were passed on from one generation to the next, and so the sport–music tradition has continued in perpetuity.

The use of music in the team sport context has had much more to do with tradition and team culture than with systematic mood regulation or performance enhancement. Moreover, until relatively recently, it was seldom used to facilitate team training or to expedite recovery from training. In fact, music application is one domain in which sport science has lagged well behind its sister discipline, exercise science. Some forward-thinking coaches, such as Pete Carroll of the NFL's Seattle Seahawks, have embraced the use of music in training with apparent success and considerable approval from their players (see the sidebar Carroll Concert for Seattle Seahawks' Super Bowl XLVIII Victory). One reason for using loud music—as in the Seahawks example—is to force athletes to overcome the distraction it creates and promote nonverbal communication.

Using a similar approach to chapter 7, this chapter groups team sports that have common characteristics, based on the supposition that music interventions can be applied within the entire cluster of sports in that section. As in chapter 7, the clustering of sports is based primarily on skill classifications. However, most team sports entail a variety of skills (e.g., dribbling vs. free-throw shooting in basketball) and include specialist roles for players (e.g., the kicker vs. the quarterback in American football) that do not facilitate the tight classification presented in tables 7.1 and 7.2 in chapter 7. The music-related techniques presented in this chapter can, in many cases, also be applied across clusters. From the many examples presented, you should be able to discern which are most relevant to you or the athletes in your charge.

## SERVE-AND-RETURN SPORTS: BADMINTON, HANDBALL, SQUASH, TABLE TENNIS, TENNIS, VOLLEYBALL

With the exception of volleyball, which has court-based (six players) and sand-based (two players)

# CARROLL CONCERT FOR SEATTLE SEAHAWKS' SUPER BOWL XLVIII VICTORY

The 2014 Super Bowl champions Seattle Seahawks and their charismatic coach Pete Carroll are well known for the use of a theme song—The Verve's "Bittersweet Symphony"—when taking to the field of play or celebrating a game-clinching field goal. In preparing for Super Bowl XLVIII, an entirely different kind of verve surrounded the team. Carroll's Seahawks practiced to a loud and incessant hip-hop soundtrack.

Early in the week that preceded the Super Bowl, Carroll would sneak in the odd James Brown or Earth, Wind & Fire classic from his youth, but by Friday, news reporters covering the Seahawks' practice needed Shazam, an app that identifies pieces of music, to find out exactly what they were listening to. Some of the tracks the reporters managed to identify are listed in table 8.1 along with an analysis.

There was a party atmosphere at the practices by all accounts. Maybe the coaches had to shout a little louder to be heard over the strains of Ludacris and Snoop Dogg, but

The Seattle Seahawks' successful Super Bowl campaign of 2014 had a significant musical component that was instigated by coach Pete Carroll.

**Table 8.1** Tracks Accompanying Seattle Seahawks' Training in Preparation for Super Bowl XLVIII

| Track | Artist(s) | Tempo (bpm) | Brief analysis |
|---|---|---|---|
| Hold Me Back | Rick Ross | 63 | Certainly not one for the kids given the use of explicit lyrics from the outset. The underlying beat is rather heavy and lumbering, although at the same time rhythmically complex. This complexity leads the listener to perhaps feel the tempo at double the speed, or 126 bpm. The refrain is all about not being held back and striving to play hard and tough whatever the hand that life deals you. This is certainly not as |

| Track | Artist(s) | Tempo (bpm) | Brief analysis |
|---|---|---|---|
| | | | polished a rap performance as others in the Seahawks' playlist, but it carries a powerful message from the urban wastelands of southern American states. |
| We Ready | Archie Eversole feat. Bubba Sparxxx | 75 | Opens with the familiar melody of Steam's (1969) anthemic lyric from "Sha Na Na Hey Hey Kiss Him Goodbye," but it's slowed down and replaced with a lyric about being ready, which also serves as the track's main hook. Typical of the idiom, the rap sections ooze bravado and machismo. The artists hail from the state of Georgia, and therefore this track resonates with star players that the Seahawks drafted, such as Percy Harvin and Jesse Williams. |
| Last Of A Dying Breed | Ludacris feat. Lil Wayne | 82 | This one is also explicit and, as is characteristic of Ludacris, the lyrical content is brash to the extreme. Interleaving the dense rap are some uplifting brass figures—the sort you might expect during the titles of a boxing movie. The refrain holds particular appeal to players nearing the end of their careers, such as linebacker Heath Farwell (32) and backup quarterback Tarvaris Jackson (30). The lyrics allude to Ludacris being a prime example of a dying breed of lyricists. |
| We Own It | 2 Chainz feat. Wiz Khalifa | 86 | A catchy and well-produced track closely associated with the hit movie *Fast & Furious 6*. With a heavy-duty beat from the outset, it's easy to see why this is an excellent choice for bolstering esprit de corps and getting the players immersed in the moment. The lyrics mention those you ride with and how to own the moment. |
| Bad Meets Evil | Fast Lane feat. Eminem and Royce Da 5'9 | 87 | This is a high-octane rap performance and, like many of the Seahawks' preferred tracks, is laden with profanities. The refrain echoes the Seahawks' ride in the fast lane of professional athletics and the final push toward the ultimate goal to be victorious. |
| Ambitionz Az A Ridah | Tupac | 87 | The piece opens with a sample from a boxing MC: "Let's get ready to rrrrumble!" The lyrics are propulsive, highly anti-establishment, and self-aggrandizing—perhaps just what is needed to pep up the players a couple of days before the biggest game of their lives. It has a weighty Tupac beat coupled with a super-heavyweight performance. |
| More Bounce To The Ounce | Zapp & Roger | 105 | A distinct departure from the Seahawks' hard-core rap-centric playlist, this 1980 track has an infectious funk groove that immediately prompts the desire to "shake your thang." The few lyrics are predicated on the words in the title with permutations thereof. This selection might be described as a timid duck among a gaggle of angry geese, but the groove has been sampled for a number of recent hip-hop tracks, which is perhaps where the association lies. |

*Note:* All of these tracks can be located on YouTube.

*(continued)*

**Carroll Concert for Seattle Seahawks' Super Bowl XLVIII Victory** *(continued)*

the players were certainly having fun and fully engaged with each other both during and between plays. In fact, between snaps, the entire defensive line was dancing on the field! Even the veteran quarterback coach, Carl Smith, 65 with an ailing hip, was seen swaying. This brought a wry smile to the face of Coach Carroll.

Following a crushing 43-8 victory over the Denver Broncos (the third largest point differential in Super Bowl history), one of the Seahawks' most revered players, fullback Michael Robinson, had this to say about Carroll's approach:

> *Football is a game. A game. Pete has figured that out and makes football fun—all aspects of it: practices, travel, games. One of our goals is to play at a level other teams can't match. That's precisely what you saw tonight. What do you see when you see a team running around practicing to music all week? They're loose. They're full of energy. And that's what we are. I know it works for us. (Kelly, 2014)*

And what does the ever-youthful Coach Carroll have to say about the importance of music? It was during the period 2000 to 2009, when he was head coach of the USQ Trojans, that he first realized the potential of music as a coaching tool. Back then he told reporters: "Music is the fabric of so many things that connect us and elevate us. It's music that defines the human experience" (Pompei, 2014).

versions, the sports in this section were featured in their individual forms in chapter 7. These activities all entail a serve to initiate play, rallying, volleying, smashing, feigning, and so forth, and are characterized by discrete and serial skills that are open and closed, generally cognitive, with fine and gross elements—quite a complex mix! Add to this the requirement for sharp reactions, eye–hand coordination, and high fitness levels, and it is clear that the sports featured in this section place particularly high mental and physical demands on their players.

Music can play several roles in these sports, including bringing players together (i.e., enhancing team cohesion), prompting imagery, bolstering confidence, and relieving pre-competition anxiety. Given the very high physical demands of sports such as tennis and squash, music can also play a recuperative role, although this application has seldom been explored by coaches or sport therapists in any systematic way. While attending international beach volleyball tournaments, I have observed that loud dance or rock music is often played during match play. This is clearly part of the marketing ploy for that sport, which is in a relative state of infancy. The purpose of

such music is to enthuse and animate the crowd. An important consequence of beach volleyball authorities' music policy is that players need to develop superior nonverbal communication skills (e.g., through the use of hand gestures) to optimize their competitive endeavors.

One of the strongest doubles partnerships in the world of tennis has been that of Venus and Serena Williams, the formidable Williams sisters. Individually, they have secured 29 grand slam singles titles and, as a collective, a massive 14 grand slam doubles titles. Perhaps their sibling rivalry leads them to be so domineering whenever they join forces as a doubles team. The sisters have their own Venus and Serena pre-match soundtrack, which is taken from a documentary film that shines a light on their progression from their days in Compton (one of the most deprived areas on the California coast) to global superstardom (see www.songonlyrics.com/soundtracks/venus-and-serena-soundtrack-list.html for a trailer).

The soundtrack, produced by the much-acclaimed Wyclef Jean, is unique in the sporting world in that it is autobiographical, galvanizing, and inspirational to the sisters. It begins with a hard-core rap track by N.W.A. titled "Straight

Outta Compton," which foregrounds the gang culture, youths clashing with police, and wholesale social breakdown that surrounded the Williamses' formative years. The second track, "Venus (I'm Ready)" performed by Wyclef Jean, has an entirely different vibe. It is positive in its rhythmic energy, harmonic content, and central message, which serves to pay homage to Venus, the mythological Roman goddess of love and beauty. This is a clever juxtaposition on the part of Wyclef, who structured the song as a type of love letter to the older of the two sisters.

As an individual player, Venus has been in the shadow of Serena for most of her professional career. Accordingly, the affirmations in the second track, such as the likening of Venus's service to a bolt of lightning, may well hold special significance for her. The third track, by Nuno Bettencourt and Gary Cherone, is amusingly titled "Hole Hearted." The lyrics of this dynamic, guitar-led song reflect the daily struggles the sisters must endure to remain at the top of their game.

The key message to extract from this rather incredible meshing of two sisters' deep-seated ambition, the film, and the soundtrack, is that small groups, such as those that travel together for racket sports or volleyball, have many commonalities—perhaps in where they hail from, their ethnic backgrounds, their cultural experiences, or their aspirations. These can be used to create a soundtrack that holds special meaning for all members of the team. The soundtrack can instill a sense of common purpose and enable players to prepare mentally. Music has the power to pull together the various strands of our identities and represent who we truly are in the face of adversity.

# PADDLE SPORTS: CANOEING, DRAGON BOAT RACING, KAYAKING, ROWING

These water-borne sports are very much cut from the same cloth; they all entail team races in which an oar, paddle, or other implement is used to propel the craft. In some variants, such as the canoe slalom, competitive placings are decided through a time trial format. More commonly, though, teams compete directly in neighboring lanes just as track and field athletes do in the sprint distances. Each aquatic discipline employs a stroke characterized by an irregular rhythm between its drive and recovery phases. This emphasis on the rhythmic components of the movement is even more acute in canoeing and kayaking, because competitors must balance strokes on either side of the vessel. Moreover, all members of the team must stroke in unison to achieve maximal efficiency. For this reason, coxswains in rowing and dragon boat racing have often employed some form of metronome or drumbeat. Indeed, a traditional Chinese drum at the prow of the vessel is an intrinsic part of dragon boat racing.

The imperative to maintain a given tempo, described as a stroke rate, gives music a pronounced role in training sessions and mental rehearsals. Unfortunately, the stroke rates typically encountered in these sports are much lower than the tempo of the desired music (the opposite problem to that of runners). Using rowing as an example, a solution is to perform one stroke for every four musical beats. So, a typical 30-strokes-per-minute rowing cadence would tie in with a piece of dance music that has a 120 bpm tempo (e.g., "Music" by Madonna). This makes musical sense because four beats often form a bar, or measure, within the time signature of a piece (see chapter 1). It goes almost without saying that music with a regular, even, and pronounced rhythm is essential for this purpose. Syncopated and otherwise complex rhythms may be distracting and counterproductive. Paddle sports have a justified reputation for being arduous, not least because they make full use of the musculature of each limb and the core—the whole body, in effect. This places considerable demands on the cardiovascular system.

Given the monotonous and strenuous nature of the activity (particularly rowing), music is vitally important in these sports. Its role may be to promote positive feeling states during training sessions and to provide lyrical affirmations that boost confidence and inspire team spirit in the face of a grueling endeavor. Lyrics that reference the activity, such as those featured in Soundgarden's intense, moody rock track "Rowing" (58 bpm), are also of benefit. Some rowers favor a more abstract lyrical approach by using pieces that refer obliquely to their activity such as "Robot Rock" by Daft Punk (112 bpm).

# HIGH-CONTACT FIELD SPORTS: AMERICAN FOOTBALL, AUSTRALIAN RULES FOOTBALL, GAELIC FOOTBALL, RUGBY LEAGUE, RUGBY UNION

The field sports featured in this section, which are essentially territorial and possession based, have a long and proud music tradition. These sports are characterized by alternating periods of offense and defense; the main goal is to breach the opposing team's defenses while maintaining one's own. Passing, tackling, and running with the ball are common skills, and each team member needs to maintain a level of tactical awareness. The skills involved in each field sport can vary greatly, and individual players must often adopt specialist roles (e.g., linebacker or kicker in American football). The attentional demands on players in various positions, and thus their optimal arousal levels, can also vary. Consider the broad focus and cool head the rugby fly-half needs to scan the field and make the play, versus the fairly narrow focus and brute force of a prop forward holding up the scrum or driving in a maul.

Team cohesion has both social and task-related aspects (Carron, Hausenblas, & Eys, 2005). Social cohesion concerns the team's desire to spend time together outside of the playing and training environment (e.g., going to parties and eating in restaurants), whereas task cohesion relates to how well the team cleaves together in the pursuit of competitive goals. Given the strong collective cul-

The All Blacks' fearsome haka in full flow.

tures in such sports, social cohesion often mirrors task cohesion. Music applications can be directed toward both aspects of cohesion. Despite the fact that having a high level of social cohesion is not a prerequisite for sporting success, it certainly helps (Carron et al., 2005).

The main role of music in the high-contact field sports featured in this section is to bolster the sense of team unity and prepare players mentally so that they are optimally aroused and ready for the rigors of game play. Music or music combined with recent video highlights can be played on the team bus or in the locker room immediately before the game (see case study 2 in chapter 9). Groundbreaking research in the area of business management has demonstrated that music with pronounced bass frequencies has power-inducing qualities (Hsu et al., 2014); such perceptions of power are highly desirable in high-contact sports. Table 8.2 lists tracks that have been used in the pre-game phase by well-known teams and it is notable that only the tracks used by NFL teams have pronounced bass frequencies. Players can also heighten the sense of team unity by making

music themselves and engaging in ornate pre-game rituals.

Many rugby and Gaelic football teams engage in what's colloquially known as a team stomp in the locker room immediately before walking onto the pitch. This involves the players coming into a huddle and holding each other tightly. Often, the team captain details some of the key technical aspects to focus on, and then the players sing the team anthem or chant at a high volume while stomping their feet frenetically. The ritual is rounded off with back slapping, chest beating, and other gestures that might be more familiar to zoologists than psychologists. On many occasions I have even witnessed players head butting lockers (and heavily denting them) after a stomp to get suitably aroused. This approach does not suit all players (particularly those who function at their best with a relatively low level of arousal), so team managers should also allow some individual preparation time to ensure that all players feel at their best.

Many other pre-match rituals involving chanting are used in field sports. The New Zealand rugby union team known as the All Blacks

**Table 8.2**   Pre-Game Tracks to Enhance Team Cohesion

| Track | Artist(s) or composer | Tempo (bpm) | Used by |
|---|---|---|---|
| The Real New York Giants Theme Song | Audiobrain | 87 | NFL's New York Giants |
| Who's Got It Better | Bailey DaChamp | 101 | NFL's San Francisco 49ers |
| I'm Shipping Up To Boston | Dropkick Murphys | 129 | NFL's New England Patriots |
| Gold Coast Suns Theme Song | N/A | 130 | Gold Coast Suns Australian rules football team |
| Great Western Sydney Giants Theme Song | N/A | 141 | GWS Giants Australian rules football team |
| Fourteen Men | Wolfe Tones | 85 | Dublin GAA Gaelic football team |
| Jimmy's Winning Matches | Rory and the Island | 95 | Donegal GAA Gaelic football team |
| The Gambler | Kenny Rogers | 87 | England rugby union team |
| NSW Waratahs team song | N/A | 97 | NSW Waratahs rugby union team (Australia) |
| Mighty Quinn | Gotthard | 99 | Harlequins RFC rugby union team (UK) |
| Old Faithful | Eddy Arnold | 63 | Hull FC rugby league team (UK) |

*Note:* All of these tracks can be located on YouTube.

famously issues a Maori martial challenge known as the haka; this is conducted on the pitch while squaring up to the opposition players. The haka entails loud chanting, tribal dancing, intimidating facial expressions, and a finale in which the players give the opposition a long, harsh stare. Such acts of collective bravado not only ready the players, but also stir the passion of the fans.

Sport sociologists often point out that sport serves as a token for tribal warfare, and watching the Maori haka, it is hard to dispute this notion (Young, 2013). Australian rules football has a catalog of songs that fans sing to greet the players and help them prepare emotionally for the task at hand. Two of the best known are "Power To Win" (Port Adelaide) and "When The Saints Go Marching In" (St. Kilda). Fans are encouraged to use such powerful anthems through publication of lyrics in match programs and sing-alongs that are prompted by the stadium announcer. This can create a home advantage because opposing players are forced to narrow their focus to block out the wall of sound. A great example of this is the Seattle Seahawks' stadium, which reputedly is the loudest in the world. This was said to contribute to a strong home record en route to their Super Bowl victory of 2014.

> *To watch the All Blacks' haka opposed by the Tongan's Sipi Tau (war dance), search "The Haka—New Zealand vs. Tonga" on YouTube.*

As with all sports popularized in the land of the free, triumphant and stirring music is encoded within the DNA of American football from the marching bands that provide fanfare at high school football games to the pomp of the NFL Super Bowl half-time show. However, an emerging trend is revealing the extent to which music is now integral to many of the training camps organized by the NFL's leading teams. The majority of teams now use music during practices, and in a big way. It comes as no surprise in a sport dominated by vigor, rippling muscles, and testosterone that the musical choices lean toward the high octane: the Buffalo Bills favor rap classics; the Philadelphia Eagles opt for a blend of techno house music, rap, and pop tunes; and Florida's Jacksonville Jaguars blast an eclectic mix that includes Outkast, U2, and Journey.

Buffalo's general manager, Doug Whaley, believes that music is sweeping the training grounds of professional teams because it reflects a wider youth culture: "For so many of them [young people], their motto is, 'Life's better with a soundtrack'" (King, 2014). The role music plays between drills in training is akin to its pre-competitive function in power events (see chapter 7). Cameron Wake of the Miami Dolphins explained: "You get your morale and your mood up. You feel lively and ready for the drill" (King, 2014). Perhaps the most head-scratching fact about the new musical revolution in the National Football League is that two of the biggest abstainers are the New Orleans Saints and the New York Giants. Who could have written the script for that?

---

## SWING LOW, SWEET CHARIOT

Anthemic chanting reverberating around a stadium can be a source of inspiration to the players. It also allows the fans to express their appreciation, or indeed disdain, for whatever is happening on the field of play. Most of the great teams involved in contact sports have a distinctive chant that sounds out from the stands. For the England rugby union team, it's the rousing African-American spiritual "Swing Low, Sweet Chariot." Although perhaps an unlikely choice for the England faithful, given that the hymn can be traced back to the blight of slavery, it was spontaneously adopted in March 1988 during a game against Ireland, when Chris Oti, a black player, scored a sensational hat trick. The singing of "Swing Low," whether in the stands or the players' locker room, promotes feelings of patriotism, togetherness, and pride. It has taken on a new and entirely different meaning and significance through the medium of association.

---

# SUBJECTIVELY SCORED TEAM SPORTS: PAIR SKATING, RHYTHMIC GYMNASTICS, SYNCHRONIZED DIVING, SYNCHRONIZED SWIMMING

With the notable exception of synchronized diving, artistic team sports that are subjectively scored have an umbilical relationship with music in that the soundtrack is integral to the competitive experience. The sports in this section predominantly consist of skills that are serial, closed, gross, and motor in nature (see chapter 7). As a whole, they are characterized by expressiveness and routines that have been highly practiced over many months. Because subjectively scored sports can be extremely anxiety provoking, music can serve a vital role in calming athletes' nerves prior to performance.

In preparation for competition, teams in subjectively scored sports build routines around carefully chosen themes. For example, synchronized swimming routines are often built around broad themes such as the seasons or the ocean, which the team must express collectively. One of the most highly acclaimed ice dance performances of all time, Jayne Torvill and Christopher Dean's dramatic "Paso Doble (Capriccio Espagnol)," was predicated on the theme of the Spanish bullfight. Dean played the role of the majestic matador, while Torvill depicted the evanescent cape. Listening to a track related to the music used in

*To watch Torvill and Dean's spellbinding performance at the 1984 Figure Skating World Championships in Ottawa, Canada, search "Jayne Torvill & Christopher Dean OSP Paso Doble WC Ice Dance 1984" on YouTube.*

competition can reinforce these expressive themes in the period that leads up to competition (e.g., Spanish guitar music with a paso doble rhythm for Torvill and Dean's "Paso Doble"). Athletes in subjectively scored sports may also benefit from using music to help them recuperate from the stressful cauldron of competition.

In addition to its aesthetic contributions, music can support the training and preparation of athletes in subjectively scored team sports. Aesthetic disciplines often involve a sequence of movements and skills (e.g., arm strokes, throws, and egg-beating kicks in synchronized swimming), and rhythmic music can mark the structure of the routine by providing cues that aid rehearsal. Much as bobsled and road cycling teams might use music to facilitate memorizing a course, ice dancers and pair skaters can use music to mentally rehearse the timing elements of a routine while traveling together. In this way, the team shares an attentional focus and emotional state in keeping with the performance, in terms of both its technical and aesthetic characteristics. Music is the ideal conduit for this shared experience, particularly if an element of learning is involved through the use of the same music prior to training sessions in the weeks leading up to competition.

On the day of the event, team competitors do not have quite the vulnerability to anxiety and negative thought processes that individual competitors do. Nevertheless, pre-event music can take team members' minds off the judging for their event and onto the actions they need to complete to build a solid performance. Accordingly, a steady beat, warm harmonies, and strong lyrical affirmations are recommended. A slight word of caution: Although I have written much about music's capacity to integrate teams and facilitate bonding, it can have the opposite effect of dividing groups if individuals within the group listen to music in their own bubbles. This is especially so in sports that require explicitly coordinated performances such as pair skating, synchronized swimming or diving, and rhythmic gymnastics. A further advisory note concerns the overexposure to pieces that accompany competition. For example, pair skaters who listen to their performance piece on repeat may become desensitized to its emotional impact; some even come to detest the sound of these pieces. Olympic ice dance champions Jayne

Torvill and Christopher Dean (1984) might well be forgiven for being sick of the characteristically repetitive rhythm of Ravel's *Bólero*.

The teamwork element can place a larger premium on timing than we find in individual subjectively scored sports such as diving and artistic gymnastics. For example, in rhythmic gymnastics team events, an object such as a ball may be passed among the members as they coordinate individual movements in a formation. To complete this sequence, the gymnasts require a common temporal reference point. As a routine is developed, musical rhythm can provide a perfect template to aid skill learning and integration among team members.

Team members in subjectively scored sports must be truly in unison technically, emotionally, and expressively, and music can help. Because of the sweeping, graceful movements that characterize these sports, music of the ambient (aka new age) and classical genres is a particularly apt choice to create the right mind-set prior to competition. Pieces such as *Call of the Sea* by David Arkenstone or Chopin's Nocturne in E flat major, op. 9, no. 2 would serve this function well, as would compositions associated with dance, such as the overture to Tchaikovsky's ballet *Swan Lake*. Gymnasts and skaters typically exude an artistic sensibility, if not before they entered the sport,

then as a result of their experiences within it. This heightened sense of musicality and aesthetics may enable team members to bond using their common experiences, tastes, and cultural reference points. On the rink, in the pool, and in the gymnasium, music can bring teams together and help them create a shared language of expression.

# BAT-AND-BALL TEAM SPORTS: BASEBALL, CRICKET, ROUNDERS, SOFTBALL

The bat-and-ball sports in this section are hugely popular because we have all played at least one of them during our school days in the spring and summer months. In the Americas and East Asia, baseball is a multimillion-dollar industry, whereas in certain parts of the British Commonwealth, such as India, cricket is followed almost like a religion. Music applications in these sports tend to span the pre-match phase and then punctuate aspects of match play. National cricket teams such as England have dabbled with using music as part of a psych-up strategy (see the sidebar Freddie Flintoff's Ring of Fire), but not in any systematic way.

## FREDDIE FLINTOFF'S RING OF FIRE

Cricket, a seemingly placid sport that is popular in the British Commonwealth, has not traditionally been strongly associated with pre-match singing in the locker room. That all changed when England played India in the final test in Mumbai in 2006. Led by their charismatic and sometimes unpredictable captain, Andrew "Freddie" Flintoff, the England cricket team sang the country classic "Ring Of Fire" by Johnny Cash just before entering the fray. Subsequently, Flintoff was asked by an Indian reporter to explain the significance of the song to the England team. Flintoff could barely keep a straight face: "Eh . . . it's just a song that the boys like," he explained.

Flintoff knew the real connection, but it would have been distinctly impolite to explain that the song's title was an unintended reference to the after-effects of eating spicy food; indeed, most of the team had been dogged by stomach upsets during the test series. It was said that the atmosphere in the England locker room during the lunch interval on the final day was akin to a rugby match. With "Ring Of Fire" blaring out at full blast, the players whipped themselves up into a hand-clapping, feet-stomping frenzy.

# THE FOURTH BASS IN BASEBALL

A baseball player's walk-up song, whether heading to the mound or the batter's box, can reveal a great deal. In some instances, the music serves a psych-up or priming function; in others, it is a personal favorite that represents the player's attitude, personality, or even style of play. Baseball occupies a unique place in the world of sport in that it is a team sport and an individual sport all rolled into one. The use of music in baseball heightens the emotional intensity of the game and creates a closer link between players and the legions of spectators; it imprints an individual identity onto the collective endeavor. Table 8.3 lists some of the biggest names in Major League Baseball (MLB) along with their walk-up tunes and some brief analyses regarding what their selections might say about them.

**Table 8.3** Famous American Baseball Players and Their Walk-Up Songs

| Player (Team) | Track | Artist(s) | Tempo (bpm) | Style | Brief analysis |
|---|---|---|---|---|---|
| Mariano Rivera (New York Yankees) | Enter Sandman | Metallica | 123 | Heavy metal | Metallica performed this classic track at Yankee Stadium for the veteran pitcher's final game in the fall of 2013. It's a rousing piece, but not in a nice way; the unnerving guitar harmonies might cause palpitations! The lyrics make reference to a child's nightmares: "Sleep with one eye open, gripping your pillow tight." Rivero, known by the epithet the Sandman, perhaps saw himself as the batting team's worst nightmare. |
| Alex Rodriguez (New York Yankees) | Already Home | Jay-Z | 81 | Hip-hop | With one of the most formidable batting records in MLB history, Rodriguez had the self-assurance to tell the fans, and more important, the opposing team, that he was almost on the home plate even before swinging his bat. |
| Mike Trout (Los Angeles Angels) | Started From The Bottom | Drake | 86 | Hip-hop | This is a seriously brash track with explicit lyrics that signal Trout's ascendance through the ranks and the closeness he feels toward his Angels. The lyrics celebrate rising from the bottom of the pile to the top and how this demands a collective effort. |
| Salvador Perez (Kansas City Royals) | Balada Boa | Gusttavo Lima | 129 | Latin Pop | This effervescent Latin number is oozing with energy and whatever the Spanish equivalent for *joie de vivre* might be. The lyrics allude to getting ready to party hard, and party is precisely what Perez intends to do, having crushed one out of the park. |
| Alexei Ramírez (San Diego Padres) | Danza Kuduro | Don Omar feat. Lucenzo | 130 | Reggae-ton | The Puerto Rican favorite Omar sings and raps about seduction, backed by a propulsive beat laced with electric accordion runs. This tune clearly speaks to Ramírez' Latin roots and his Hispanic fan base. The lyrics use the metaphor of taming the ocean, which for Ramírez may pertain to humbling the opposition. |

*(continued)*

Table 8.3 *(continued)*

| Player (Team) | Track | Artist(s) | Tempo (bpm) | Style | Brief analysis |
|---|---|---|---|---|---|
| Matt Joyce (Pittsburgh Pirates) | I Can't Stop | Flux Pavilion | 70 | Dubstep | A bass-heavy dubstep tune with a looped lyric that is sampled from the Jay-Z and Kanye West track "Who Gon Stop Me." It tells the fans and opposing team that he's going to go all the way—he's in a state of perpetual motion! |
| Dustin Pedroia (Boston Red Sox) | Still D.R.E. | Dr. Dre feat. Snoop Dogg | 93 | Hip-hop | This classic hip-hop track has more 'tude than you could shake a bat at! The iconic 1999 video remains etched in many people's memory with Dr. Dre and Snoop Dogg cruising around the Compton area of Los Angeles in lowriders. Dre's central message that clearly resonates with Pedroia is "I'm still here baby, and I'm at the top of my game, so don't be messing with me, ya hear!" |
| Aaron Hicks (New York Yankees) | California Love | Tupac feat. Dr. Dre | 92 | Hip-hop | This is a classic West Coast rap track, and given that Hicks hails from Long Beach, California, it is perhaps an all-too-obvious choice for him. The groove is totally infectious, and the refrain celebrates the state's fun-loving nature, emphasizing that Californians know how to party. The talented switch-hitter is pre-empting the celebration of another home run. |

*Note:* All of these tracks can be located on YouTube.

"Enter Sandman"
Written by James Hetfield, Lars Ulrich, and Kirk Hammett
Published by Creeping Death Music (GMR)
All Rights Reserved. Used by Permission.

Baseball, rounders, and softball are closely related in terms of the skills required, among them eye–hand coordination, precise timing, and good acceleration off the mark. Unlike rounders and softball, baseball has been professionalized since the late 19th century, and so the spectacle for the crowd has always been a salient issue for organizers and promoters. Baseball players often have a walk-up song for when they are getting ready to bat or pitch (see the sidebar The Fourth Bass in Baseball). This appears to animate the crowd while also offering a powerful cue for the players as well as a means for self-expression. In rounders and softball, players can use music in the pre-event phase to fire them up for the game (e.g., "Ready To Go" by Republica), bolster their confidence (e.g., "Light It Up [Remix]" by Major Lazer feat. Nyla & Fuse ODG), or enhance their focus (e.g., "Smack That" by Akon feat. Eminem).

In bat-and-ball sports, as well as in others with high technical demands, music is inadvisable in certain instances. For example, in the early stages of learning, before a skill becomes automatic, a high degree of information-processing capacity is required to master the techniques (e.g., hitting a curveball in baseball). The parallel processing of music and kinesthetic, or bodily, cues can result in a performance decrement. Sometimes, players need to be acutely aware of the actions of other players. In cricket, for example, with the leather-encased ball flying at the batsman's head at up to 100 mph (161 km/h), a player needs to detect subtle auditory cues to ascertain the nature of the bowler's delivery (e.g., the bowler's foot placement on delivery or the sound the ball makes during its single bounce on the pitch). Along similar lines, while learning a new skill, such as how to catch a high ball in rounders or softball, verbal feedback from a coach is crucial; music can be an unnecessary distraction that inhibits the learning process.

# COURT-BASED BALL GAMES: BASKETBALL, DODGEBALL, KORFBALL, NETBALL

The team sports in this section are fast and highly interactive and so require good tactical awareness. In particular, given the task interdependence in sports such as basketball and korfball, the task-related cohesion of a team is crucial. In such sports, music is used for team preparation in the locker room, during pre-game warm-ups, and to facilitate post-game recuperation. It can also aid recuperation and promote recovery during training. Indeed, recent research from Israel has shown that upbeat music can enhance the cool-down by speeding up the rate of lactate clearance in the musculature (Eliakim et al., 2012, 2013).

Court-based ball games are both physically and mentally taxing. The post-training and post-game phases lend themselves particularly well to the use of music to speed up recovery and engender a sense of revitalization. Music is seldom used in this way by team sport athletes; this is a novel, evidence-based way sport professionals can aid the recovery process of their athletes (e.g., Jing & Xudong, 2008; Karageorghis et al., 2014; Savitha, Mallikarjuna, & Chythra, 2010). Table 8.4 contains a selection of post-task lyrical tracks for general consumption that check all the right boxes in terms of rhythmic, harmonic, and lyrical content. To optimize the recuperation process, players can suggest tracks, perhaps in the range of 60 to 90 bpm, from which a playlist can be created. The playlist should begin with the fastest tracks and progress toward the slowest to tap the power of entrainment (see chapter 2). The Group Music Selection Tool from chapter 3 can be used to facilitate the democratization of the music selection process. See the following sidebar for some application-specific rewording.

## USING THE GROUP MUSIC SELECTION TOOL TO CREATE A RECUPERATIVE MUSIC PLAYLIST

What are your three favorite slow-tempo, soothing music selections to listen to while recovering from a high-intensity training session or game? Also, which three slow-tempo tracks might be suitable for recovering from a high-intensity training session or game, but not necessarily soothing for you?

**Preferred tracks:**

1. Title: _____     Artist: _____

2. Title: _____     Artist: _____

3. Title: _____     Artist: _____

**Nonpreferred tracks that might also work for this purpose:**

1. Title: _____     Artist: _____

2. Title: _____     Artist: _____

3. Title: _____     Artist: _____

**Table 8.4** Lyrical Tracks for Post-Game Recuperation

| Track | Artist(s) | Tempo (bpm) | Brief analysis |
|---|---|---|---|
| Bloodstream | Ed Sheeran | 91 | This mellow, guitar-driven track from the Suffolk songster has a light, breezy energy; the scattered and psychedelic themes in the lyrics reflect the often hectic post-game mind-set. |
| Free Fallin' | John Mayer | 89 | Mayer's soft, reassuring voice reverberates throughout this quietly joyous song that espouses a theme of letting go and relinquishing control. |
| Stay With Me | Sam Smith | 85 | A slow, steady beat underpins warm piano chord sequences and the sparse declamations of a gospel choir. The centerpiece of the track is Smith's heartfelt, tender falsetto vocal, which takes you to another place. |
| Here With Me | Dido | 83 | Londoner Dido gives generous evidence of her Celtic roots in this lilting, anthemic ballad that is infused with messages of rest and acceptance. |
| You Make Me Feel Brand New | The Stylistics | 78 | The delivery in this soulful 1974 piece is smooth and jazzy with warm harmonies that blend well with the lyrical themes of regeneration and revitalization. |
| Teardrop | Massive Attack | 77 | This ambient trip-hop track juxtaposes subtle drum patterns and sparse bass tones with a spiraling lullaby laced with mystery to conjure comforting imagery. |
| Someone Like You | Adele | 68 | Adele is the *chanteuse de nos jours*, and in this signature song, she gives a rich and enchanting vocal performance that rides on waves of soft piano arpeggios. Simplicity and strong words, gently delivered, are incredibly therapeutic. |
| Can You Feel The Love Tonight | Elton John | 64 | Sirs Elton John and Tim Rice joined forces to create a spellbinding soundtrack serenade for Disney's iconic *Lion King*. The warm, noble brass theme of the intro gives way to an intimate vocal that tells a timeless story of acceptance and peace. |
| Breathe Me | Sia | 60 | As the mix progresses, listeners are directed toward a more serene mental state. The lyrical expression gently caresses and transports them to a tranquil place with its breathy, somnolent vocals. |
| Redemption Song | Bob Marley | 58 | A message of insurrection and protest is belied by Marley's tranquilizing vocal presence and plaintive guitar strums. This track marks the fitting end of a recuperative musical journey that has pacified an aching body while uplifting the mind. |

*Note:* These tracks are suitable for recuperation from any team sport, and their use should not necessarily be restricted to the sports in this section. All of the tracks in table 8.4 can be located on YouTube.

Among the sports presented in this section, basketball has a well-established music culture, particularly in the United States, but netball, dodgeball, and korfball do not. In the latter three sports, music plays more of an individualized role (i.e., players use personal listening devices to prepare mentally) rather than being part-and-parcel of a collective preparation. The comparison with basketball shows another stark difference. Basketball is strongly associated with an urban culture that permeates every aspect of it—the language players use, the clothes players and fans wear, the tattoos that adorn players' bodies, the muscle cars they drive, and of course, urban music. In comparison to other team sports, there seems to be considerable homogeneity in what individual players listen to and the music played during games (e.g., to entertain the crowd, introduce the players, punctuate breaks in the play, celebrate high-points). Wherever such cultural homogeneity exists, it is much easier for sport professionals to implement music-related interventions, because music is a cultural phenomenon.

## AIMING SPORTS: BOWLS, CURLING, PETANQUE, TENPIN BOWLING

With the exception of curling (a winter team sport performed on an icy court known as a curling sheet), all of the sports in this section are featured in their individual forms in chapter 7. Because bowls, petanque, and tenpin bowling can also be played in small teams, some additional music considerations come into play (bowls is played in teams of two, petanque is played in teams of two or three, and tenpin bowling is played in teams of two to five). These sports require fine motor skills given the premium on precision. Accordingly, music serves a pre-competition function to enable players to prepare mentally, with a calm and focused state often being the most desirable.

Aiming sports require a high level of cooperation and dialogue, and music can be used to promote team ideals, key foci, and a sense of togetherness. For example, Delta Goodrem's evocative ballad "Together We Are One" could be combined with photographs of the coach and team members from occasions when they achieved success together. The images can be viewed on cell phones or tablets to engender a sense of unity and collective effort. Music is not permitted during play, and the pre-competition use of personal music devices might force a wedge between teammates rather than bring them closer together. There is a need, therefore, to identify where and when to use pre-event music. An ideal location that will not interfere with players from other teams and officials is the car or van on the way to a tournament. This comes with the added advantage of players not having to carry audio equipment into competition venues.

A physically calming but mentally stimulating piece of music can gently get athletes' competitive juices flowing without causing them to expend too much nervous energy. Extramusical associations and lyrical affirmations can also be exploited for maximum effect. Despite the fact that these sports are not associated with a strong musical culture, several notable recordings are suitable as pre-event tracks because of their lyrical content and the messages they relay. A sample of these is presented in table 8.5.

## INTERACTIVE TEAM SPORTS: HOCKEY, ICE HOCKEY, LACROSSE, SOCCER, ULTIMATE

The sports in this section are highly interactive, fast-paced, and territorial. They all require a broad range of skills in terms of the classifications presented in tables 7.1 and 7.2, and two of them, ice hockey and soccer, have a strong musical heritage. In English soccer (called football), for example, records date back to the late 19th century of chants on terraces; Norwich City's "On The Ball" is the oldest football song still in use today. British scholar Dave Russell argued that, in comparison with the late 20th century, the relationship between music and team sport in those early days was largely natural, organic, and unforced: "Sport and music did not so much 'crossover' as draw from a common cultural pool" (Russell, 2014, p. 303). In the modern game, virtually all players have their own playlists, many of which are made public through online media such as Spotify, and every professional team has a range of tracks that are blasted over the stands or used to heighten the sense of team cohesion in the locker room (e.g., Liverpool FC's "You'll Never Walk Alone").

The sport of ice hockey is extremely interactive and includes a lot of bodily contact; thus, players are associated with relatively high levels of arousal (akin to American football and rugby). For example, Drew Stafford (Buffalo Sabres) and Jaromir Jagr (New Jersey Devils) use heavy metal music at an insane tempo in the pre-game phase to feel sufficiently psyched. During the game, many clubs employ an organist or even a special effects crew to mark the plays with musical excerpts and rev up the crowd. This also brings the fans and

**Table 8.5**   Pre-Event Tracks for Aiming Team Sports

| Track | Artist(s) or composer | Tempo (bpm) | Sports suitable for |
|---|---|---|---|
| Flower Of Scotland | Roy Williamson | 66 | Curling |
| Let's Go Bowling | Camera Obscura | 76 | Tenpin bowling |
| The Bowling Song | Asleep at the Wheel | 80 | Tenpin bowling |
| Alison (My Aim Is True) | Elvis Costello and the Attractions | 89 | Bowls, curling, petanque, tenpin bowling |
| I'm A Bowler | Hillbilly Beats | 90 | Tenpin bowling |
| Golden Touch | Razorlight | 95 | Bowls, curling, petanque, tenpin bowling |
| Scotland The Brave | Sir Harry Lauder | 102 | Curling |
| Petanque | Kalope | 120 | Petanque |
| One Vision | Queen | 121 | Bowls, curling, petanque, tenpin bowling |
| Push The Button | Sugababes | 126 | Curling |
| Crown Green Bowls | The BBC Concert Orchestra | 138 | Bowls |
| Soul Riff (BBC TV *Bowls* theme music) | Douglas Wood | 139 | Bowls |
| Rival Bowler | Shave | 142 | Tenpin bowling |
| Theme From Petanque | Petanque | 159 | Petanque |

*Note:* All of these tracks can be located on YouTube.

players closer together; music almost functions as a common denominator in the competitive sphere.

In any given team, players require different levels of arousal to perform at their best; therefore, coaches and team managers need to strike a balance between individual and team preparation. On several occasions, Rio Ferdinand, the former England and Manchester United captain, provided considerable insight regarding his prematch playlist (see the sidebar His Name Is Rio and He Dances in the Sand). As a general rule, the closer the team gets to start time, the more the preparations need to be oriented toward the team as a whole so that players commence with a united front rather than as ball hoggers or glory hunters. At a team level, music can conjure the right kind of imagery or visualization for the task at hand, motivate the players immediately before they step onto the pitch or the ice, and aid postmatch relaxation.

Coaches and team managers in interactive sports also need to consider how music or the noise generated by an away crowd might affect their players. At the 2010 FIFA World Cup in South Africa, several prominent players such as Steven Gerrard (England) and Cristiano Ronaldo (Portugal) complained about the deafening sound of the vuvuzelas—2-foot (60 cm) plastic horns that produce a loud monotone note. Television audiences also complained the world over and forced broadcasters to turn down the sound of the crowd during live transmissions. To prepare for the din of a hostile crowd, players can listen to recordings of crowds over the PA system during training in the buildup to the match (this is known as simulation training). Of course, no audio recording can replicate the huge sonic tapestry created by an 80,000-strong crowd, but some preparation is far better than none.

Players in interactive, territorial sports can make use of the full breadth of music applications (i.e., pre-task, in-task, post-task). Beyond using music to psych up or train to, many players also use it to relieve the boredom of biweekly travel to away venues. Canadian NHL ice hockey teams, for example, routinely need to make journeys in

# HIS NAME IS RIO AND HE DANCES IN THE SAND

Star defender Rio Ferdinand was one of the most recognizable faces in the English premiership. He played in defense at center-back and represented the England soccer team on more than 80 occasions, including appearances in two FIFA World Cups. Ferdinand is well known for his use of pre-match music and has commented on this to the world's media on numerous occasions. Like 91 percent of the British public, Ferdinand particularly enjoys listening to music while driving and has one of the swankiest car stereo systems money can buy. The mix of music he uses changes from game to game based on a range of factors—the importance of the upcoming match, his current mood, and the type of mind-set he wants to create.

Table 8.6 shows a selection of tracks Ferdinand likes to use in the pre-match phase along with some brief analyses of their potential psychological effects.

**Table 8.6**  Rio Ferdinand's Pre-Match Track Selections

| Track | Artist(s) | Tempo (bpm) | Style | Brief analysis |
| --- | --- | --- | --- | --- |
| Game Over | Tinchy Stryder feat. Giggs, Professor Green, Tinie Tempah, Devlin, Example, and Chipmunk | 65 | Grime | This edgy 2012 track pulls few punches with its hard-core lyrical content. A sizzling beat underpins a succession of swaggering deliveries from Stryder, Pro Green, and co. that focus on themes of conspicuous consumption and living to excess. The raw, confrontational, and alpha male energy may be the perfect prime for Rio as he prepares for each game. |
| Three Little Birds | Bob Marley | 74 | Reggae | Moving from "Game Over" to "Three Little Birds" feels like going from a war zone to a christening. Although there is an obvious clash of musical styles here, Rio's purpose in listening to Bob Marley's gentle lilt is clear: it's all about warmth and positivity, the perfect antidote to pre-match nerves. |
| Hammer Dem Down | Lutan Fyah | 84 | Reggae | This effervescent roots reggae number builds on the Caribbean flavor of Marley's iconic ballad. Themes of rising up against oppression and asserting rightful claims fit well with the approaching battle on the pitch and the need to unify in order to vanquish the opposition. |
| Started From The Bottom | Drake | 86 | Hip-hop | This rap track trumpets Drake's ascent to stardom and success from humble beginnings. A theme that pervades the song is that the artist remained true to himself and kept his original team of supporters around him. |

*(continued)*

Table 8.6    *(continued)*

| Track | Artist(s) | Tempo (bpm) | Style | Brief analysis |
|---|---|---|---|---|
| Work Out | J Cole | 93 | Hip-hop | Of all Rio's choices, this is the most enigmatic. A mid-tempo rap about an imagined sexual liaison, "Work Out" has a salacious edge and might carry a meaning that is very personal to Rio. The clue to its use may lie in the title and the imagery in the song, which is about energy and self-expression. |
| Wonderman | Tinie Tempah feat. Ellie Goulding | 93 | Hip-hop | With its motifs of hardships overcome, transcendence, and superlative performance, this piece is imbued with all the affirmations needed before entering the arena. The synth keyboard track quotes the early video game themes that would have populated the aspiring young Rio's soundscape. |
| Fools Gold | Stone Roses | 113 | Rock | This track, which was introduced to Rio by former Manchester United teammate Gary Neville, is doubtless here for both its musical and extramusical qualities. The iconic bass riff lends the song an irresistible rhythmic power, whereas its status as one of the great indie anthems from Mancunian poster boys, the Stone Roses, makes it synonymous with the city and its most famous export. |
| Harder, Better, Faster, Stronger | Daft Punk | 123 | House | The title of this piece seems to reference the Olympic motto of *Citius, Altius, Fortius*. The empowering suggestion is laid over an infectious groove and a fast beat, which ramps the heart rate up to a higher frequency. This track is perfect for amping a player up before heading into the fray. |

*Note:* All of these tracks can be located on YouTube.

excess of 3,000 miles (4,828 km). Brazilian soccer players use percussion instruments to relieve boredom and anxiety while also maintaining a sense of unity and fun. When the hands are busy, anxious thoughts are less prevalent.

At the 2014 FIFA World Cup in Brazil, the home nation arrived at every game with the team samba band in full swing. The musical director, or MD, was Daniel Alves, who both sings and plays the drums. Dante strummed a guitar, Jo shook a tambourine, and Willian often got involved in the action, as did Neymar. The players enjoy making music on the team plane, on the team bus, and in the locker room just before matches. No wonder they're known worldwide as the Samba Boys.

*Psychologists say it is very important in the dressing room and coming from the hotel to the stadium that you do something with your hands, with your mouth . . . if you just sit there worrying, clutching your hands, that does not help. If you play something, it helps them relax. That's why we give them the drums and things. . . . Since 1970 we have done this. We buy instruments for them, and they play on the bus instead of saying, "Oh my God, we are going to play Germany or England in a World Cup game." That does not help.*

Insight from former Brazil soccer coach Carlos Alberto Parreira ("Key to Brazilian success," 2006)

*To watch a video that illustrates how music constitutes a central part of the Samba Boys' pre-game preparation, search "Samba Brazil football team" on YouTube.*

The sports of field hockey, lacrosse, and ultimate (formerly known as ultimate Frisbee) have yet to establish a strong music culture. Table 8.7 lists some tracks along with brief analyses related to their use in pre-game visualization, pre-game psych-ups, and post-game recuperation. The purpose of table 8.7 is to get you thinking more deeply

**Table 8.7**   Tracks for Visualization, Psych-Up, and Post-Game Recuperation

| Track | Artist(s) | Tempo (bpm) | Brief analysis |
|---|---|---|---|
| **Pre-match visualization** | | | |
| *Nessun Dorma* | Luciano Pavarotti | 54 | Puccini's famous aria from *Turandot* has become a sporting anthem ever since it was used to accompany the BBC's coverage of the 1990 FIFA World Cup in Italy. It immediately conjures images of striving for glory, heartfelt passion, and sporting immortality. |
| I Believe I Can Fly | R. Kelly | 60 | What bolder statement of self-empowerment could there be? Whether it's soaring to catch a Frisbee or sprinting through the centerfield like GB hockey star Nick Caitlin, this track is sure to promote inspiring imagery. |
| Heroes | David Bowie | 113 | This powerful and evocative piece is driven by Brian Eno's wailing guitar licks and Bowie's call to arms. If the Berlin wall can be brought down, then so can the other team's back line! |
| **Pre-game psych-up** | | | |
| The Power | Snap! | 109 | This energetic anthem has all the ingredients to inspire players for action and bolster their self-belief. The song boasts a killer hook coupled with the ideal lyrics to accompany the pre-game psych-up. |
| All Together Now | The Farm | 112 | A powerful and evocative tribute to the impromptu England vs. Germany soccer matches of 1916 that took place in the neutral territory of WWI's no man's land; this classically inspired piece has become associated with several teams and instills a sense of unity and shared purpose. |
| Jai Ho (You Are My Destiny) | Nicole Scherzinger feat. the Pussycat Dolls and A.H. Rahman | 137 | The title of this powerful track means "victory be yours" in Hindi, and it instantly conjures images of the triumphant denouement of the 2008 movie *Slumdog Millionaire*. Mesmerizing Indian rhythms and soaring harmonies combine to make it both uplifting and energizing. A must for Indian hockey players! |
| **Post-game recuperation** | | | |
| Orinoco Flow | Enya | 115 | Enya's soothing vocal tones combine with a river of harmony to make this the perfect restorative piece after a hard-fought game. |
| Lovely Day | Bill Withers | 98 | A salute to the positive energy of a beautiful summer's day when everything is going well, this track maintains a soothing tone through Bill Withers' gravelly, sincere vocals. |
| Albatross | Fleetwood Mac | 68 | This shimmering instrumental piece calms the spirit and replaces any post-game tension with a floating serenity and assured calm. A perfect backdrop for reflecting on a performance. |

*Note:* All of these tracks can be located on YouTube.

about the key facets of music selection and, as with all of the playlists in this book, is indicative rather than definitive. You will, of course, make track selections and segue tracks based on your own needs or those of the athletes you work with.

# TEAM SAILING

Team sailing competitions that feature yachts, dinghies, and other craft vary considerably in terms of the duration of the event, the number of races in each regatta, and the size of the crew. Many yacht races cover thousands of nautical miles, whereas other sailing events such as the famous America's Cup consist of a series of regattas that may take place within an enclosed harbor. There is also great variability in the duration of events; some are completed inside a day, whereas others, such as the International Sailing Federation World Cup, are serialized over an entire season. The Olympic sailing program features a variety of classes crewed by two members, which is in stark contrast to longer series, such as the aforementioned America's Cup, which permits a maximum of 11 crew members, including a skipper and a tactician.

In global sailing competitions, team membership can consist of crew from various nations. For example, Oracle Team USA, the defending America's Cup champions in 2013, was composed of sailors from the United States, Australia, New Zealand, Great Britain (Sir Ben Ainslie, the most decorated Olympic sailor), the Netherlands, Italy, and Antigua and Barbuda. In such a climate of international collaboration, music may play a role in unifying team members from different cultures by giving them a common focus. In this way, music can serve as a type of abstract social gel.

Despite their genteel appearance, some sailing competitions are highly adversarial, which gives rise to the need for music to reinforce collective efficacy (i.e., the crew's shared belief in its capability to achieve its desired outcomes against rival crews) and team morale. Team sailing results are determined more by team cohesion and confidence than by the equipment and craft. Indeed, the specifications for the vessels used in sailing competitions are highly regulated to ensure that racing is always competitive. Because training

for team sailing entails a considerable amount of downtime, tedium, and repetition, music can provide stimulation, distraction, and enjoyment both before and after training sessions. Given that the pattern of movements in sailing is determined by the elements, music does not have a synchronous application in these sports. Also, safety and technical drawbacks make the use of music aboard the boat undesirable.

In terms of affirmations, sailing or traveling across water is a common theme in both classical and popular music. The tracks in table 8.8, which can be used before and after sailing to promote team unity, have been chosen from a vast array of sailing-related music. The world's oceans have provided the inspiration for hundreds, if not thousands, of popular songs and compositions through the ages.

# MISCELLANEOUS CATEGORY: BOBSLED, RELAY RACES, TUG OF WAR, WATER POLO

This section addresses four sports that seem totally unrelated in terms of their skill demands and the environments in which they are played. Because they didn't fit snugly into any of the other sections, they are grouped in this final miscellaneous category. Many of the music applications covered earlier in this chapter can be used in these sports. Although the skills and environments may differ, desired outcomes such as team unity, a shared sense of purpose, and an optimal pre-competition mind-set are the same.

In terms of its overall structure, water polo has close ties with interactive team sports such as soccer and hockey, although it is played in a swimming pool. During the match, music does not have a role to play, but it can be used by individual players en route to the competition venue and then by the team as a whole in the locker room to prepare mentally.

Tug of war is an unusual sport often seen at summer festivals, county fairs, or town sporting events. Again, music is seldom used during a contest, but many tracks could be used for a team's

**Table 8.8**  Sailing-Related Songs to Promote Team Unity

| Track | Artist(s) | Tempo (bpm) | Genre |
|---|---|---|---|
| Sail Away | David Gray | 68 | Pop |
| The Sea | Morcheeba | 75 | Pop |
| If I Had A Boat | Lyle Lovett | 92 | Pop/country |
| Rock The Boat | Aaliyah | 93 | Hip-hop |
| Silent Sea | KT Tunstall | 101 | Pop/folk |
| All Hands On Deck | Tinashe feat. Iggy Azalea | 101 | Pop |
| The Tide Is High (Get The Feeling) | Atomic Kitten | 104 | Pop |
| A Pirate Looks At Forty | Jack Johnson | 108 | Pop/folk |
| Sail Away | Enya | 115 | Ambient |
| Drop In The Ocean | OMI feat. AronChupa | 123 | Reggae fusion |

*Note:* All of these tracks can be located on YouTube.

pre-competition preparation. Three examples are "I'm Pulling Through" by Diana Krall, "Two Tribes" by Frankie Goes to Hollywood, and "Pull Me Back" by Leah Turner.

The skills germane to relay running differ from those of the other sports in this section; with the exception of the baton changeover, relay races involve little interaction or interdependence. My background in track and field has taught me that athletes tend to use music individually during the warm-up phase. They do not use it while drilling for the competition because the incoming runner has to shout "Hand" or the name of the outgoing runner. The outgoing runner is focused intently on picking out the shout among a chorus of similar shouts in adjacent lanes.

In the warm-up phase of a relay race, the competing shouts are often every bit as prevalent or distracting as they are during the race itself, because all the relay athletes warm up at the same time. One of the most productive uses of music is to create a highlight video portraying the squad executing smooth changeovers and set it to a unifying piece of music chosen by the squad members. Pieces that I have used in such high-

light videos include "Pass Out" by Tinie Tempah, "Reach Out, I'll Be There" by the Four Tops, and "Reach Out And Touch (Somebody's Hand)" by Diana Ross. Evocative pieces of music can be used en route to the track; see the sidebar One Moment in Time for the Great Britain Olympic Bobsled Team.

# SUMMARY

Carefully selected music can serve a rainbow of functions in team sport environments. Making music can be a great distraction that relieves pre-game nerves; players chant passionately before a game to enhance their esprit de corps; and music is blasted in locker rooms to psych players up. Sometimes music is integrated with highlight videos to enhance players' confidence in the lead-in to an event. Fans are encouraged to adopt anthems, live music performances keep fans revved up during half-time intervals, and players are introduced or rewarded (when they excel) with certain pieces of music. Still other uses of music are to celebrate or console and to aid recuperation following a game or training session.

## ONE MOMENT IN TIME FOR THE GREAT BRITAIN OLYMPIC BOBSLED TEAM

My long-time friend and colleague, Peter Terry, worked as team psychologist for the Great Britain bobsled team at the 1998 Olympic Winter Games in Nagano, Japan. Following decades in the doldrums of international bobsled, the four-man GB team had slowly eroded the advantage held by the world's top teams at the preceding two olympiads, finishing sixth in the 1992 Albertville Games and fifth in Lillehammer in 1994. Terry planned for the team to clinch the medal that had proven elusive to Britain since the Innsbruck Games of 1964.

In addition to being the squad's psychologist, Terry sometimes drove the team van, although it was in the former role that he excelled. As they approached the bobsled track each day for training and on the two competition days, he would pop on Whitney Houston's 1988 Olympic anthem "One Moment In Time." Terry would instruct the athletes to visualize themselves calmly and decisively seizing the moment with the strong extramusical associations of the song functioning as the perfect aural backdrop. On the final day of competition, they seized their moment in a storming final run that won them the bronze medal by the narrowest of margins.

What is perhaps most interesting about this story is that Terry managed to get a bunch of testosterone-charged, tough-as-nails servicemen to consent to the playing of such a feminine and cheesy piece of pop schmaltz. This probably speaks volumes about Terry's charisma and credibility—it's not just the songs you play, but the way you play 'em! It's also striking how the last song that you listen to can linger in your head . . . and sometimes to good effect.

The advent of new technologies has resulted in music being used in more sophisticated ways. For example, music and video can be edited relatively quickly and cheaply now, and with the addition of verbal primes, can make for a potentially powerful pre-match intervention. Nonetheless, the use of music is not always advisable in team sport environments; at times, even during match play, it can provide an unwanted distraction. The practice of novel skills and the provision of feedback from a coach can be disrupted by the presence of music, unless played at a very low intensity (<60 dBA). Teams that will be playing in unfamiliar locations (e.g., European or American teams playing in South Africa, Brazil, or the West Indies) should engage in some simulation practice before departure. This will accustom them to the unfamiliar sounds they will hear and the ways home fans will seek to throw them off their game (e.g., with vuvuzelas, samba drums, and steel drums).

A key principle is the democratization of music selection—that is, the athletes for whom the music is intended should be involved in its selection. Coaches and team managers are often from generations or cultural backgrounds different from those of the players; accordingly, they should be wary of imposing their own musical tastes, which can cause considerable angst. Having as many team members as possible involved in music selection gives them a sense of empowerment and autonomy, while also ensuring an optimal music program. The main message here is democratize or antagonize!

# 9

# Sport Case Studies and Playlists

*It would be possible to describe everything scientifically, but it would make no sense; it would be without meaning, as if you described a Beethoven symphony as a variation of wave pressure.*

—Albert Einstein

This section presents two case studies that complement those presented at the end of part II. The first is based on an individual sporting pursuit (running); the second illustrates the dynamics of a team sport (American football). The approaches detailed in these case studies can be applied by sport practitioners to a wide range of sporting scenarios; the key is to absorb the main principles and then apply them creatively. As before, the case studies are broadly based on real people and teams I have worked with and cover a range of music applications.

## CASE STUDY 1: FRIEDA'S RUN FOR FREEDOM

Frieda enjoyed running from a young age, although she never excelled competitively. She just liked the sense of freedom and well-being that running gave her. Being relatively uncoordinated, other activities such as dance and popular team sports such as netball never really appealed to Frieda. Living just a stone's throw from the banks of the Brisbane River meant that she had a truly magnificent urban riverscape as the backdrop for her early-morning runs and, for most of the year, great weather to boot.

Frieda left school at 18 and went to work as an administrator for a local firm that distributed electrical goods all over southeastern Australia. During her first few years with the firm, she found it hard to do any sport-related activity at all; her job was so engrossing and demanding that it left her feeling drained at the end of each workday. She would go for the occasional jog or swim on the weekends, but that was about the limit of her physical endeavors. As the years progressed, exercise and physical activity became less of a priority for Frieda, and she formed a habit of spending her evenings watching on-demand videos on her laptop and gossiping with girlfriends on Skype.

By her mid-20s Frieda realized that the job had taken its toll on her fitness and once super-healthy lifestyle. She wanted to exercise more often and perhaps join a club where she could meet some new people and put the fizz back into her existence. She managed to negotiate some flextime with her line manager whereby she could start and finish work an hour later on Mondays, Wednesdays, and Fridays. This gave her a window during the workweek to recommence early-morning runs and combine these with more intense sessions on the weekends. Frieda joined a running club based at a local university, where she encountered a gaggle of like-minded people. She had an array of running partners to choose from, and several group activities and competitions were organized on the weekends.

## Music and Motivation

Despite the new work pattern and abundance of running buddies, Frieda found it far harder to motivate herself for running than she had in her late teens. There were so many competing demands on her time now. She had become a supervisor at work, and the constant planning threw up an array of minor issues that consistently seemed to undermine her best intentions. Frieda needed a helping hand, a boost of some sort. She noticed that many of the athletes in her running club used ergonomically designed MP3 players during their runs and made great capital of the songs on their playlists: "When I'm flagging, I whack on some up-tempo Crowded House and I'm just cruising along again!" revealed one of her running buddies. Online, Frieda noticed that the athletes often exchanged playlists via Facebook or Twitter. Many discussed their song selections in relation to the runs they were planning, saving the most energizing beats for hill climbs, sprints, and the final 10 or 15 minutes of a run.

Frieda had always been a big music fan, but ever since her physical education teacher told her that "real athletes listen only to their bodies," she never thought seriously about combining running with music. Although deep down Frieda knew that there was an element of truth in what her teacher had said all those years ago, she wanted to participate in athletics just to be fit and healthy. She wasn't so concerned about joining the elite or competitive outcomes, as long as she was gradually improving her personal best times, or at least retaining the ability to run fluently rather than simply jogging or plodding. Frieda was also increasingly struggling to find something that would distract her from the everyday trials and tribulations of the office.

iStock.com/m-imagephotography

Brisbanian Frieda finds that she is able to enhance her running ability with the aid of musical accompaniment.

## Musical Running Method

Frieda asked Tom, a guy from the running club she'd started dating, for an MP3 player for her 25th birthday. When she had used a music player before during her high school days, it was bulky, the music tracks were difficult to upload to the device, and headphones were a distraction (besides which, they never stayed in her ears!). From her conversations with other members of the running club, she learned that the latest equipment was ergonomically designed and far easier to use. Although that request for an MP3 player was a simple action, it cemented her commitment to take running more seriously. It was like the point in a journey when the ticket is bought and it's too late to pull out.

Tom's gift was to prove pivotal to Frieda's running career. The music literally put a spring in her step and made each run an enormous pleasure that she actively looked forward to. She began to realize that her running renaissance had actually brought music back into her life. At school, Frieda

had been an avid and dedicated dance music fan, singing along to her favorite tunes in her bedroom, much to the annoyance of her father. Since work had taken over her life and she'd moved into a new apartment, she had gotten out of the habit of listening to music, partly out of fear of sparking confrontations with her elderly neighbors and partly because there was always something else to do. Now she was looking forward to her runs, because they were the time in the week that she could feel the wonderful flow of musical rhythm. Running allowed her to fully respond to and engage with the music; in fact, the two became synonymous in her mind.

At the suggestion of one of the senior coaches at the running club, Frieda began logging how she felt after each run on her smartphone using two simple snapshot measures known as the Feeling Scale and Felt Arousal Scale (see chapter 3). The fruit of this informal experiment was that she noticed a distinct difference between how she felt immediately after a run without music and how she felt after a run with music (see figure 9.1).

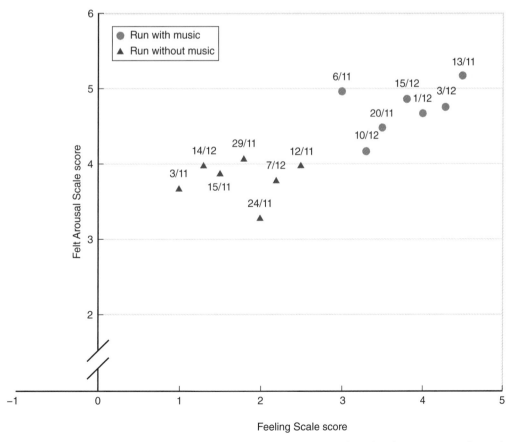

**Figure 9.1**   Feeling Scale scores and Felt Arousal Scale scores immediately after runs conducted with and without music.

The music made her feel slightly livelier and more in tune with her body, which made the running experience more pleasurable (on occasion, she felt as though she could continue almost indefinitely). And rather than thinking about what was happening at the office, Frieda often found herself singing along to the music and receiving a huge boon from the lyrics of her favorite tunes (e.g., "Baby we were born to run").

## Synchronous Approach Gives a Performance Boost

Frieda soon realized that, in addition to boosting her motivation and distracting her from work-related thoughts, music could help her run slightly faster. An added benefit was that she was able to distribute her effort more evenly, particularly during longer runs. She achieved this by synchronizing her stride rate to the musical beat in some of her sessions. To maintain an even cadence, she would take slightly longer strides when descending a hill, and shorter ones when ascending. Frieda achieved this synchronicity by taking a whole stride cycle, or two steps per beat. She enjoyed compiling her playlists the evening before a run. In fact, she became so proficient at this that she began to align her playlists with her target times for common time trial distances (see Frieda's 10-km playlist in table 9.1). Members of Frieda's running club began to ask whether she would be willing to share some playlists after seeing her reduce her 10-km road race time from

**Table 9.1** Frieda's Synchronous Running Playlist for a 10-km Run at a 45-Minute Pace

| Track | Artist(s) | Tempo (bpm) | Strides per minute (spm) |
|---|---|---|---|
| Lullaby | Nickleback | 68 | 136 |
| Paradise | Coldplay | 70 | 140 |
| Stitches | Shawn Mendes | 75 | 150 |
| Linger | Guy Sebastian feat. Lupe Fiasco | 76 | 152 |
| Here's To Never Growing Up | Avril Lavigne | 82 | 164 |
| Just Like Fire | P!nk | 82 | 164 |
| Tightrope | Janelle Monae feat. Big Boi | 83 | 166 |
| 1955 | Hilltop Hoods feat. Montaigne and Tom Thum | 84 | 168 |
| Royals | Lorde | 85 | 170 |
| All The Little Lights | Passenger | 86 | 172 |
| Stay With Me | Sam Smith | 86 | 172 |
| Heart Attack | Demi Lovato | 87 | 174 |
| Somebody To You | The Vamps feat. Demi Lovato | 88 | 176 |
| Behind The Scenes | Brittany Cairns | 90 | 180 |
| Cheap Thrills | Sia feat. Sean Paul | 90 | 180 |
| Boom Clap | Charli XCX | 92 | 184 |
| Work | Rihanna feat. Drake | 92 | 184 |
| Little Submarines | The Black Keys | 93 | 186 |
| Special | SIX60 | 95 | 190 |
| Don't | Ed Sheeran | 95 | 190 |

*Note:* All of these tracks can be located on YouTube.

51:29 minutes to a blistering 42:48 minutes in the space of just six months.

## Differentiated Music Use

Another ploy that Frieda used to enhance her running performance was the differentiated use of music—that is, playing music only when she most needed it and not throughout a run. At certain times, she would not need music at all— particularly during the early part of a run when the scenery or her running partner kept her mind sufficiently occupied. Frieda found that when she wanted to step up a gear or the going felt really tough, she would reach for the play button. Moreover, environmental challenges such as a strong headwind or a steep hill were also much easier with a blast of music.

When using the differentiated approach, Frieda initiated any brief playlist with what she thought of as a power song—a piece of asynchronous music that would send her motivation levels skyrocketing. Her favorite power song was a fast dancey number from the mid-1980s titled "Freedom" by the legendary British pop duo Wham! The fast beat, uplifting harmonies, and zany declamations made Frieda feel as though she was a fully charged power cell. The song had particularly special meaning for Frieda, because she remembered that, years ago, her mother enjoyed dancing to it whenever it was on the radio. Frieda developed a list of power songs in a systematic way by personally rating the motivational qualities of each song using the Brunel Music Rating Inventory-3 (see chapter 3). Frieda listened to and rated a number of tracks each month, but used only the highest-scoring ones as power songs in the differentiated application of music (see table 9.2).

## The Sound of Race Days

Use of the MP3 player was, of course, not permitted during most races, so Frieda chose to use it only for some of her runs. When she was with her running club on the weekends and completing more intense sessions such as interval or paarlauf training (a form of team relay in which each runner completes multiple efforts at a high intensity), she didn't use music so that she could manage comfortably without it during competition. Also, at those higher intensities, Frieda was less able to focus on the music and her stride rate was far more variable, because she often had to jostle for position in a pack of athletes. What she did notice, however, was that during races she could hear the music in her mind's ear; when her heart and lungs were screaming "Stop!" the imagined beat and inspiring lyrics encouraged her to persevere.

## Using Music to Soothe

At first, Frieda finished her runs leaving just enough time to shower and start her workday.

**Table 9.2**   Frieda's Running "Power Songs" Along With Her BMRI-3 Scores

| Track | Artist(s) | Tempo (bpm) | BMRI-3 score |
|---|---|---|---|
| Freedom | Wham! | 134 | 42 |
| Love Shack | B-52s | 133 | 41 |
| Wanna Be Startin' Somethin' | Michael Jackson | 122 | 40 |
| Good Feeling | Flo Rida | 128 | 40 |
| Bang Bang | Jessie J feat. Ariana Grande and Nicki Minaj | 150 | 40 |
| Pump It | The Black Eyed Peas | 154 | 40 |
| Girls Like | Tinie Tempah feat. Zara Larsson | 120 | 39 |
| Spinning Around | Kylie Minogue | 120 | 39 |
| When A Fire Starts To Burn | Disclosure | 124 | 39 |
| Do It Now | Mashd N Kutcher | 128 | 38 |

*Note:* All of these tracks can be located on YouTube.

This didn't work well for the simple reason that she was often too fired up to concentrate on the minutiae of her desk work. Her mind was full of the scenery she had enjoyed, and the dynamic music was still ringing in her ears. She also felt as though she was overheating and, on one occasion, had to sneak out of the office under false pretenses to grab another shower to cool down. To reverse this feeling of being stimulated and amped, Frieda began adding a few songs to the end of her play-lists to help her recuperate as she strolled along the riverbank (see examples in table 9.3).

These pieces induced a relaxed and contemplative state of mind. In time, Frieda began to look forward to these stolen chill-out moments and viewed them as a reward following her strenuous exertions. She particularly enjoyed the purity of voice and melodiousness of the British soprano singer Laura Wright. The stirring operatic arias, warm ballads, and mellow instrumental tracks

**Table 9.3**  Frieda's End-of-Run Recuperative Music Selections

| Track | Artist(s)/ composer | Tempo (bpm) | Brief analysis |
|---|---|---|---|
| Symphony No. 7 in A Major, op. 92: Allegretto | Laura Wright/ Beethoven | 107 | Laura's angelic voice creates a sense of ascendancy following a hard run. The warm harmonies allow Frieda to dissociate from the pain in her legs and ride a wave of positive energy. |
| Golden Lady | Stevie Wonder | 101 | The unique, soulful voice of Stevie soothes the body and spirit. The chorus speaks directly to Frieda as she visualizes herself as the enigmatic Golden Lady. |
| You Gotta Be | Des'ree | 95 | This uplifting and gently soaring ballad is full of positive messages about keeping cool, being calm, and staying together. |
| Come Away With Me | Norah Jones | 81 | Norah Jones' voice exudes relaxation and calmness in this characteristically soft and tranquil piece infused with subtle piano riffs. |
| Make You Feel My Love | Adele | 73 | The tempo drops down and gives Adele the time to express powerful and tender emotions in a restrained and brooding delivery that induces feelings of serenity and security. |
| Imagine | John Lennon | 72 | Lennon's *magnum opus* shares a sparse, rolling piano arrangement with the previous two tracks and perfectly expresses the concept of peace in a way that Frieda finds therapeutic, yet uplifting. |
| On The Wings Of Love | Jeffrey Osborne | 71 | The crystalline clarity of Osborne's voice and his unfettered spirit soothes Frieda as she celebrates the rewarding feeling of being in love with her running. |
| *Nessun Dorma* | Laura Wright/ Giacomo Puccini | 65 | A track with powerful extramusical associations given that Pavarotti's rendition became the theme tune for the Italia 1990 FIFA World Cup. This chilled-out version has a much more contemporary feel with the energy developing gradually toward a momentous "Vinceró" ("I will win") ending. |
| You Are So Beautiful | Joe Cocker | 62 | Frieda returns to the backbone of her playlist with a piano-led, heartfelt soul number from balladeer par excellence Joe Cocker, whose voice cracks with emotion as he delivers a message of acceptance in the chorus. |
| *O Euchari in Leta Via* | Laura Wright/ Hildegard von Bingen | 55 | With a slow heartbeat echoing in the background, this classical track performed by the artist known as the Sporting Soprano, is the perfect antidote to a tortuous run. The "O Euchari" lyric is as much re-energizing as it is ethereal. |

*Note:* All of these tracks can be located on YouTube.

that Frieda chose seemed to capitalize on the gushing feeling of euphoria at the end of her runs—a mixture of achievement, relief, and sheer joy.

## Lessons Learned

Frieda had succumbed to a state of relative inactivity, which is what happens to many young adults when they start their first office jobs. They are so eager to put the hours in and impress the boss that health-related activities such as exercising and maintaining a balanced diet often come a distant second to their need for achievement. Despite sometimes exuding gruff exteriors, bosses and line managers are not ogres. Frieda discovered that she was able to negotiate some flextime so that she could indulge her passion for running. The use of music during some runs put wind in her sails; she was able to forget about what was going on at the office and become immersed in the task at hand. Moreover, the fact that she was out running in an environment that she found inspiring had a restorative effect, which resulted in her being better able to cope mentally with the stresses of her professional life. She also became adept in creating playlists that facilitated running to the beat; this allowed her to apply the force of rhythm to a specialized purpose and achieve some highly respectable times in distance events. It appears that Frieda's physical education teacher had given her some poor advice.

# CASE STUDY 2: COACH ANDERSON SEEKS A NEW "SOUND SYSTEM"

Coach Ray "Butch" Anderson was a long-serving football coach at a high school on the West Coast of the United States. He ate, slept, and breathed football—a true gridiron devotee. Coach Anderson took pride in developing young players and was a much-admired and well-respected member of his community. Until a couple of seasons previously, the Eagles had enjoyed regular county- and even state-level success. Since then, their performances had inexplicably nosedived, to the point that they struggled even to win friendly games against teams from much smaller schools;

the Eagles were predators turned prey. Coach Anderson could see that the players' morale was ebbing away, but he couldn't put his finger on the source of their woes.

## Eagles' Sport Psychologist

The strong imperative to turn the fortunes of the team around led Coach Anderson to seek the services of a sport psychologist, Dr. Arnold Byford, who specialized in team and group dynamics. Dr. Byford was well known in the local community because, 14 years prior to earning a football scholarship to Penn State, he had been the Eagles' star quarterback. He had retained some involvement with the Eagles and was often a VIP on game nights. "Doc, I want you to take a no-stone-left-unturned approach in helping me get this here team back to its winning ways" was Coach Anderson's emphatic instruction. The psychologist spent some weeks carefully observing the Eagles in training and competition. He also took time to speak with key players, support staff, and even parents; it was important to get a sense of what had caused the team's malaise.

From his interactions, Dr. Byford gauged that the Eagles lacked team unity and a collective sense of purpose. In his day, the players interacted constantly and were only too eager to discuss an upcoming game or review a previous one. Now it seemed that the players were obsessed with checking their Facebook status or viewing Twitter and Pinterest feeds. Even during water breaks in training, players were often observed sneaking to the sidelines to switch on their cell phones to receive their social networking fix or read text messages. During away games, most team members played video games on their tablets or listened to their own music on the bus. Beyond the taunting and blustering that is part-and-parcel of high school football, little meaningful interaction was evident. The psychologist began to wonder whether the lack of a code of conduct regarding cell phone use might be having a negative influence on the team's performance.

Rather than imposing a blanket ban, Dr. Byford advised Coach Anderson to limit players' access to their cell phones to key points, such as during training sessions or half-time breaks in games. Cleverly, he encouraged the use of the phones to enhance team unity and cohesion. Dr. Byford asked one of the support staff to take regular video footage of each play in training and at games. He then worked with the school's media technician to create a highlights video each week that was set to an inspirational song selected by the players.

Track suggestions were collated by one of the team's captains using the quick-and-easy Group Music Selection Tool (see chapter 3). He would subsequently pass on the track suggestions to Dr. Byford. This video essentially shined a spotlight on effective teamwork as well as moments of individual brilliance such as crunching tackles or electrifying touchdowns. Plays that were very technical or audacious were presented in slow motion, and peak moments were coordinated with crescendos, breakbeats, or melodic high points in the music. In this way, the music heightened the emotional intensity of the action the players saw on screen.

## KA-POW!

Coach Anderson began to highlight the best play of the week, which became known by the acronym POW (play of the week). At first, the players were skeptical of the intervention, even gently mocking it. However, this undercurrent of derisory banter was creating unity in itself without anyone being consciously aware of it. Over the course of a few weeks, the POW nomination had won the players' attention and became a focal point. Something of a debate would spring up each week regarding who would merit the POW this time around and whether the music would be a good fit with the personality and style of the featured player. Seamlessly, the POW award went from being a dubious honor to a valued one. The innovation also took players' minds off their demotivating deluge of defeats. They had an alternative source of motivation that was under their own control, and so they engaged more with the team as a whole and with their sport.

## Motivational Videos With Music

Coach Anderson posted each week's motivational video on the team's official Facebook page the night before games and encouraged his players to download it to their phones. The players would, as a matter of course, then watch the video and discuss it with their teammates in the lead-up to each game. He knew that this exposure would create a high level of engagement because it played well to the boys' egos. The videos had different foci from week to week; some emphasized the defensive line, others highlighted explosive running plays, and a few spotlighted players who had excelled in their special roles. Significantly, all of the videos illustrated good teamwork and the collective celebration of successful plays. The videos got players thinking much more about all their true priorities, rather than being distracted with self-indulgent activities to relieve boredom.

Encouraged by the success of these motivational videos set to music, Dr. Byford advised Coach Anderson to take things a step further. Rather than listening to their own music on headphones, players suggested pre-game tracks at the midweek team meeting, again using the Group Music Selection Tool with which they were now well familiar. The suggestions were used to compile playlists that were played on the stereo system of the team bus or a boombox in the locker room at home games (see table 9.4). Three of the tracks (marked by asterisks in table 9.4) were so popular with the players that they became team anthems and were heartily adopted by supporters.

## Pre-Game Prep

The music became an integral part of the team's pre-game preparation, activating the players and rallying the fans behind the team when delivered over the PA system. Dr. Byford often conducted systematic observations of the players using the Music Listening Observation Tool (M-LOT; see chapter 3) to gauge how they would respond to certain tracks. The observations showed him and the coaching team the types of tracks that fully engaged and animated the players in the pre-game phase (see the example in figure 9.2 on page 208). The lyrics of the pre-game songs often reinforced the unity and implacability of the team. Hearing the songs also reminded the players that it was time to be mentally sharp and fully prepared physically; the music conditioned them to feel ready and alert.

## Gradual Turnaround of Form

The fortunes of the team didn't pick up overnight, because they had developed a losing habit that

**Table 9.4** Tracks Suggested by Eagles Players for the Pre-Game Phase

| Track | Artist(s) | Tempo (bpm) | Genre |
|---|---|---|---|
| Disa My Ting | T-Pain feat. Kardinal Offishall | 65 | Hip-hop |
| All Day | Kanye West feat. Allan Kingdom and Paul McCartney | 66 | Hip-hop |
| Who Gon' Stop Me | Jay-Z feat. Kanye West | 67 | Hip-hop |
| Put On | Young Jeezy feat. Kanye West | 70 | Hip-hop |
| Hard In Da Paint | Waka Flocka Flame | 72 | Hip-hop |
| All I Do Is Win | DJ Khaled feat. Ludacris, Rick Ross, T-Pain, & Snoop Dogg | 75 | Hip-hop |
| Pop Bottles | Birdman feat. Lil Wayne | 75 | Hip-hop |
| Can't Tell Me Nothing | Kanye West | 80 | Hip-hop |
| I'm Ready (Explicit) | The Diplomats | 83 | Hip-hop |
| Lose Yourself | Eminem | 86 | Hip-hop |
| Til I Collapse | Eminem feat. Nate Dogg | 86 | Hip-hop |
| You're Going Down | Sick Puppies | 91 | Rock |
| Hate Me Now | Nas feat. Puff Daddy | 91 | Hip-hop |
| Victory | Puff Daddy feat. the Notorious B.I.G. & Busta Rhymes | 92 | Hip-hop |
| If I Can't | 50 Cent | 94 | Hip-hop |
| Can't Stop, Won't Stop | Young Gunz | 100 | Hip-hop |
| Tubthumping* | Chumbawamba | 104 | Pop |
| Fester Skank | Lethal Bizzle feat. Diztortion | 107 | Grime |
| Jump Around | House of Pain | 107 | Hip-hop |
| Another One Bites The Dust* | Queen | 110 | Rock |
| Get Ugly | Jason Derulo | 111 | Hip-hop |
| Sirius/Eye In The Sky | Alan Parsons Project | 112 | Ambient dance |
| The Final Countdown* | Europe | 118 | Rock/pop |
| Start Me Up | Rolling Stones | 123 | Rock |
| Welcome To The Jungle | Guns N' Roses | 123 | Rock |
| Enter Sandman | Metallica | 123 | Rock |
| Seven Nation Army | The White Stripes | 125 | Rock |
| Hit Me With Your Best Shot | Pat Benatar | 128 | Pop/rock |
| Song 2 | Blur | 130 | Rock |
| Whoomp! (There It Is) | Tag Team | 130 | Hip-hop |
| Thunderstruck | AC/DC | 133 | Rock |
| Crazy Train | Ozzy Osbourne | 137 | Rock |
| Kernkraft 400 | Zombie Nation | 140 | Dance |

*Note:* All of these tracks can be located on YouTube.

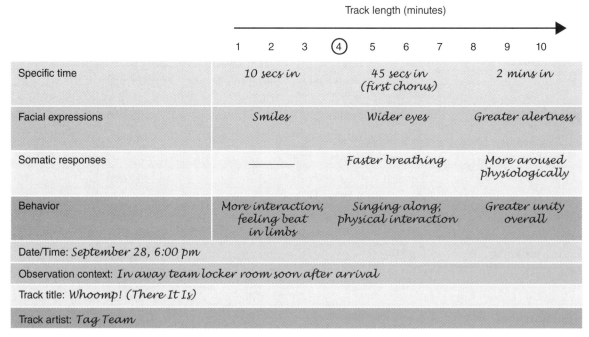

**Figure 9.2**   Music Listening Observation of the Eagles by Dr. Arnold Byford.

had to be broken. Often, when they had worked themselves into a winning position by the start of the fourth quarter, they would suffer a turnover and concede points on almost every possession. Taking his cue from the work that Dr. Byford had initiated, Coach Anderson knew that he needed to spring an extra-special intervention during half time. Football is all about rituals, so in the final minutes before the team strode out to take the field one Friday night, Coach Anderson invented a new tradition. The Eagles were 6 games in and stood 2 and 4, making tonight a must-win, a virtual playoff game before the playoffs had even begun. To make matters worse, they had been turned over twice and had only two field goals to show for their possession, trailing poorly at 25-6.

The team had fallen into a pattern of feigning relaxation in the locker room. There was plenty of banter and joshing going on, but cliques would form: the kickers hung out near the door, and the defensive linemen held down one corner of the room like anchors. Another problem was the lack of focus. Eavesdropping on the players would reveal conversations about a keg party or the attributes of certain cheerleaders.

It was clear that the reason for the behavior was that the players didn't want to talk about the elephant in the room: the game. Coach Ander-

son had gotten tired of speeches, too; he'd long since memorized some inspirational talks from YouTube, such as Al Pacino's classic rallying call in the film *Any Given Sunday*. Of course, he had changed the wording a little, just enough so that the players wouldn't recognize the source. But he had gone to the well too many times with the speeches and said too many things that sounded the same. In fact, his deliveries seemed to have the opposite effect, drawing attention to the lack of motivation among the players rather than heightening it. He knew it was time to tilt his sails in a different direction.

Coach Anderson reasoned that what the team needed was unity and focus. So on this day he shouted for the team to huddle together and shut up for a minute; then hold that silence. A surprised hush gave way to stillness, and in that stillness something was happening. They were all confronting the reality of the game, thinking about what it said about the team as a whole. Then Coach Anderson dealt his trump card. He hit the play button on the boombox. What the players heard next was Queen's stadium rock salvo "Another One Bites The Dust." Following suggestions from a couple of the players, the team had used this number on the bus before, and it had gone down extremely well.

There was something quite direct and aggressive about the bass line, and the brash sentiment of the track seemed right for that moment. As the second chorus fired up, Randy Ortega, the team's middle linebacker—who often led by example—simply stood up and hollered "C'mon guys!" He clapped in time with the bass-line just prior to the lyric "Another one bites the dust" (110 bpm). It wasn't long before he was joined by the entire defensive line and by the next bar, every player was at it, chanting as they went. Coach Anderson smiled and tipped his head back. "You bang that drum! Yeah," he yelled. He had recognized a turning point in the team's attitude. They had made a subtle shift from "we're trying all these tricks so why are we still on the losing team?" to "we're trying all these tricks and we'll keep trying them until we find the one that makes us a winning team again."

## Ascent of the Eagles

In three decades of coaching, that moment burned brightest in Coach Anderson's memory. It reminded him of a quote from his time at Michigan Tech: "A great teacher can hold the door open, but the pupils must enter by themselves." The striking thing about that game was that the Eagles regained the lead, scoring with all three possessions in the third quarter only to lose it again to trail by 10 with two minutes remaining. After calling a time-out, Coach Anderson knew exactly what the players needed to hear. He stepped into the huddle, paused for emphasis, and then started clapping those three beats. It was like a trigger that took them all back to the locker room; they sucked it up like the coals on a barbeque drawing in the oxygen and glowing red hot.

The Eagles got the touchdown they so desperately needed, and the field goal was slotted right through the center of the posts, but they lost the game in overtime. It almost didn't matter, though, because something took place that day that was bigger than a single season. They didn't make the playoffs that year but they did win the regional bowl the following season and the state game two years after that. To this the day, the fans at Eagle Field stomp their feet to the same three beats and enjoy what is known in the trade as a home-field advantage—one of the best in the West!

Coach Anderson gets his team fired up in the locker room.

# Summary Points for Part III

1. Because of the greater focus on performance outcomes in sport relative to exercise, music is most often used to enhance performance (e.g., as part of a pre-competition routine).

2. Some of the key functions of music in sport are to regulate arousal, reduce anxiety, instill a sense of self-control, provide key foci through lyrical cues, facilitate mental rehearsal, enhance team cohesion, and expedite the process of recuperation following events and training.

3. In training, music can be used to aid skill learning, enhance the memory of serial skills (e.g., navigating a bobsled track), and regulate repetitive activities such as running and swimming.

4. Music can lose its impact if used continuously and so a helpful alternative is the application of differentiated music—playing music only when it is most needed.

5. Both individual and team sports can be clustered on the basis of common skills, physical demands, playing environment, and so on. Similar music-related interventions can be applied within these clusters, and some can be used across sport clusters (e.g., the use of slow-tempo recuperative music to aid post-competition recovery).

6. Some sporting environments are not conducive to the use of music during competition (e.g., aerial and water-based sports), but it can serve an important role pre-competition (e.g., anxiety reduction).

7. Sportspeople are more likely than exercisers to take advantage of extramusical associations in their music selections given the potent imagery and positive mind-set that such associations can engender (e.g., see the sidebar One Moment in Time for the Great Britain Olympic Bobsled Team in chapter 8).

8. Music has an important role in ego strengthening, especially in combative, high-contact, subjectively scored, and injurious sports.

9. Rather than simply functioning as a pre-event prime or ergogenic aid in training, music can play a ceremonial role in the realm of sport that reinforces team identity, bonding, and hostility toward the opposition (e.g., the All Blacks' haka). This function can incorporate fans and players to create a holistic and culturally rewarding experience.

10. Whenever possible, practitioners should embrace technology when creating playlists for individual athletes and teams. This can considerably enhance the potency of their interventions and perceived competence (e.g., in the pre-competition phase, using an app such as Flipagram with images of peak performances that revolve to the accompaniment of an inspiring and meaningful music selection).

# What Do You Now Know About Music in Exercise and Sport?

At the beginning of this book, I encouraged you to tackle 25 questions to gauge how much you knew about the application of music in exercise and sport. Now that you've come to the end of the book, here are 25 more questions, in the same format and at the same level of difficulty as those you attempted earlier, to help you assess the degree to which your knowledge has improved.

You will find the answers in the Answers to Quizzes section. As before, add the points for your correct answers and multiply this number by 4 to turn it into a percentage (e.g., if you get 20 correct answers, 20 × 4 = 80, which makes your score 80 percent). If you score less than 75 percent, you might want to revisit the sections in the book that relate to the questions you got wrong to fill in any gaps in your knowledge.

I hope this test helps you develop the confidence to apply what you have learned to your professional and personal endeavors.

## MULTIPLE-CHOICE QUESTIONS

1. Which of the following types of effect is *not* associated with music listening in sport and exercise settings?

   a. psychological

   b. psychophysical

   c. physiological

   d. psychotic

2. When we say that music serves as an ergogenic aid, what exactly do we mean?

   a. Music gives its users a competitive advantage.

   b. Music allows athletes to perform at a higher intensity (e.g., lift a heavier weight than they can without music).

   c. Music allows athletes to endure an activity for longer.

   d. all of the above

3. Which of the following modes of aerobic exercise is quite difficult to select musical accompaniment for?

   a. running

   b. stepping

   c. rowing

   d. cycling

4. Which of these statements best describes asynchronous music?

   a. music that is neither motivating nor demotivating

   b. music that exercisers and athletes do not consciously move in time with

   c. music that has irregular rhythms and is characterized by the speeding up and slowing down of the tempo

   d. music that has a beat to which exercisers and athletes do not synchronize their movements

5. Which of the following statements best describes the effects of music at higher exercise or training intensities?

   a. Music distracts performers from sensations of effort and fatigue while also enhancing feeling states.

   b. Music does not influence performers working at high intensities.

   c. Music helps performers focus more intently on the activity.

   d. The intensity of the activity dominates performers' awareness, but music can still influence how they feel.

6. How is music thought to influence perceptions of exertion and fatigue?

a. By virtue of the limited channel capacity of the nervous system

b. By occupying working memory with thoughts pertaining to lyrics and musical structure

c. By acting directly on pain receptors to reduce their activation

d. By stimulating the release of neurotransmitters associated with euphoria and well-being

7. Motivational music is characterized by which musical features?

a. fast tempo, bright harmonies, and a syncopated rhythm

b. fast tempo, strong rhythm, and lyrics with affirmations of movement

c. memorable melody, major key, and pronounced rhythm

d. moderate tempo, regular rhythm, and lyrics with affirmations of movement

8. In the asynchronous application of music, which of these statements best describes the relationship between exercise or training intensity and music tempo preference?

a. Fast music is always the best choice for exercise, regardless of how hard the person is working.

b. Fast music is suitable for explosive events, whereas long bouts of endurance work require slower music with a regular pulse.

c. The tempo of the music should closely match the heart rate of the exerciser or athlete through the range of work intensity.

d. Preferences for music tempo range from 120 to 140 bpm depending on the intensity level of the exercise or training activity.

9. How might music be used by a professional basketball team in relation to their games?

a. post-task to facilitate and structure recovery

b. pre-task to increase arousal (i.e., psych up) and team cohesion

c. in-task to facilitate concentration between plays and generate crowd support

d. all of the above

10. For which type of physical activity would it be generally inadvisable to use a personal music device?

a. road cycling

b. performing heavy Olympic lifts shortly after learning a new technical element

c. running in a big city marathon

d. all of the above

11. Which of the following is a key principle in devising an exercise-to-music program?

a. Select up-to-date music.

b. Select music with an ear-catching melody.

c. Involve the prospective participants in the selection process.

d. Play the music really loudly so that it dulls participants' pain and causes them to come back for the next class.

12. Which of these musical qualities is *not* associated with post-task recuperative music?

a. regular pulse

b. simplistic rhythmic structure

c. intricate melodies

d. tempo in the range of 60 to 70 bpm

13. Which of these music intensity (volume) ranges would be appropriate to accompany high-intensity exercise?

a. 85 to 95 dBA

b. 55 to 65 dBA

c. 65 to 75 dBA

d. 95 to 105 dBA

14. Which application of music would be ideal for a powerlifter performing a bench press in training?

a. in-task stimulative music to help time the movement and increase arousal during the lift

b. pre-task stimulative music to help the lifter psych up

c. pre-task instrumental music to aid focus and attention to key technical points

d. in-task sedative music to combat unnecessary muscle tension and limit fatigue

15. The main consideration when selecting music that a baseball team will use en route to a competition is

a. choosing music that reinforces the group's identity and ethos

b. selecting music with affirmations of movement

c. picking a music program that will increase players' arousal levels

d. using selections that are currently in the billboard top 10

# SHORT-ANSWER QUESTIONS

16. Why do exercisers and athletes listen to music after they have finished working out?

_____

_____

_____

17. The terms *tempo* and *rhythm* are often confused by people. How would you explain the main difference between them to a child?

_____

_____

_____

18. Describe the mechanisms that underlie the effects of music on attention during a steady treadmill run that is slightly below the ventilatory threshold.

_____

_____

_____

19. Outline briefly the ways walk-up music might influence a baseball batter and team fans.

_____

_____

_____

20. What should be considered when selecting musical accompaniment for Lucy Harkos, a 46-year-old mother of two who is embarking on a weight loss program?

_____

_____

_____

21. Which characteristics of the task should be considered when selecting musical accompaniment for a sport training session?

_____

_____

_____

22. What musical features contribute most to the motivational qualities of music in a gymnasium setting?

_____

_____

_____

23. What considerations should be borne in mind when selecting music for a sport team?

_____

_____

_____

24. Why is selecting music for rowing considerably more difficult than selecting music for either running or cycling?

_____

_____

_____

25. What are the main safety considerations associated with using music while cycling?

_____

_____

_____

Answers on page 216.

# ANSWERS TO QUIZZES

## ANSWERS TO WHAT DO YOU KNOW ABOUT MUSIC IN EXERCISE AND SPORT?

1. c. the lyrical content, tempo, and rhythmic qualities

2. d. Assists participants in the pre-task phase by priming them for the task at hand; provides an in-task stimulus that lifts mood, distracts attention from fatigue-related sensations, and facilitates moving to the beat; and enhances post-task recovery.

3. b. the blood flows away from the inner ear (the cochlea) toward the working muscles, making the inner ear far more susceptible to damage from the sound vibrations

4. d. these women are likely to have grown up listening to Madonna's music, and thus, it holds a particularly special meaning for them

5. a. of a relatively high tempo, of loud intensity, and rather evocative

6. d. the male voice is generally an octave lower than the female voice, and this difference may account for gender differences in how sound frequencies are processed by the brain

7. a. complete immersion in an activity to the point at which nothing else seems to matter

8. d. It should conjure the type of imagery desired by the team for the task at hand, instill a sense of unity and cohesion, and include strong lyrical affirmations.

9. b. Music reduces inefficiencies in the movement chain when applied synchronously.

10. c. 8 to 12 percent

11. a. the relatively slow tempo is almost perfect for taking a stride cycle to each beat

12. d. using auditory and visual stimuli in combination facilitates greater distraction than using either auditory or visual stimuli alone

13. a. attention is focused on things unrelated to the task, such as problem solving, daydreaming, or music

14. d. canvassing class members and highlighting when a track suggested by a particular person is used

15. b. the music conjures images that have become associated with the music through prior life experiences, TV, film, radio, or the Internet (e.g., striving for Olympic glory and Vangelis' *Chariots of Fire* theme from the movie of the same name)

16. beats per minute (bpm)

17. How fast a piece of music feels, regardless of its tempo (there is a subjective element to this)

18. Any of the following are acceptable: improve mood, regulate arousal, increase level of dissociation, enhance enjoyment, relieve boredom, conjure task-relevant imagery, prompt a flow experience, promote positive self-talk

19. The task at hand (particularly the movement rate and pattern), the work intensity, their personal characteristics (e.g., age, gender, personality), and their cultural backgrounds

20. The choice of music tempo during exercise or training is related to working heart rate, but the relationship is not a straightforward linear one. Participants report tempo preferences within a narrow range of ~120 to ~140 bpm. Toward the top end of this range, there is a plateau in terms of preference for faster tempi when exercise intensity exceeds a moderate level (over 60 percent of maximum). Music tempi above 140 bpm do not appear to lead to correspondingly high preference scores when participants work at high intensities (over 80 percent of maximum).

21. 65 to 75 dBA (this is the intensity of the sound at ear level)

22. Any of the following are acceptable: wide accessibility of music online, free choice, ability to manage playlists, sense of self-determination or autonomy, ability to alter the playlist in accordance with how they feel, more hygienic than using earphones that have been used by others

23. Music is part of a broader youth culture, and young people use music and music artists to form their identities.

24. The conscious use of music as a type of auditory metronome to regulate the rate of movement patterns

25. When it distracts from safety-relevant information, when exercisers or athletes need to direct their full attention toward skill learning (i.e., in the early stages of learning), when a stream of instructions from a trainer or coach needs to be heard, and when exercisers or athletes are working at very high intensities and need to focus on internal body sensations

# ANSWERS TO WHAT DO YOU NOW KNOW ABOUT MUSIC IN EXERCISE AND SPORT?

1. d. psychotic
2. d. all of the above (a competitive advantage, perform at a higher intensity, and endure for longer)
3. c. rowing
4. b. music that exercisers and athletes do not consciously move in time with
5. d. The intensity of the activity dominates performers' awareness, but music can still affect how they feel.
6. a. By virtue of the limited channel capacity of the nervous system
7. b. fast tempo, strong rhythm, and lyrics with affirmations of movement
8. d. Preferences for music tempo range from ~120 to ~140 bpm depending on the intensity level of the exercise or training activity.

9. d. all of the above (in-task, pre-task, and post-task)
10. d. all of the above (road cycling, heavy lifting after learning a new technical element, running in a big city marathon)
11. c. Involve the prospective participants in the selection process.
12. c. intricate melodies
13. c. 65 to 75 dBA
14. b. pre-task stimulative music to help the lifter psych up
15. a. choosing music that reinforces the group's identity and ethos
16. To aid relaxation and post-task recovery
17. Tempo is the speed of the music—whether it is fast, slow, or in between. Rhythm is the pattern of the beats over time. [You can take a simple rhythm—such as *shave and a haircut, two bits*—and clap it at different speeds, or *tempi*. The best way to demonstrate musical terms to a child may be to play a musical example rather than use a verbal description.]
18. The afferent nervous system, which deals with incoming signals, has a limited channel capacity, and so sensory stimuli such as music can block the internal fatigue-related signals associated with physical exertion.
19. Walk-up music can animate the crowd and psych up, or prime, the player. It can also reinforce the player's identity, unnerve the opposition, or give the player a verbal cue of his main focus (e.g., "Smack That" by Akon feat. Eminem).
20. The music should include pieces that reflect Lucy's musical preferences with some emphasis on the type of music she listened to during her formative years. The music should feature pronounced rhythms, tempi conducive to exercise performance (~120 to ~140 bpm), pleasing melodies, and lyrics with affirmations of physical activity (e.g., "So you need to, make the body move"). Further, the music should hold some personal meaning for Lucy, perhaps through extramusical associations and identification with particular artists.

21. The intensity and mode of the activity, the need to synchronize movement with the music's rhythm, and whether the task is self-led or directed by a coach or instructor

22. Tempo (speed), rhythm (the distribution of notes over time and their accentuation), meter (the feel of the music's speed), modality (major or minor harmony), melody (tune), harmony (the combination of notes), lyrics, extramusical associations, and instrumentation

23. Music should reinforce the sport team's identity through lyrical and other associations. The genre of the music (e.g., hip-hop, dance, rock) should be in line with the group members' preferences and cultural backgrounds. Ideally, it should also be stimulating and evocative.

24. Rowing is a relatively complex motor skill in which the time distribution of the performance elements (drive and recovery phases) is unequal. This raises the issue of where the strong beat should fall in the music: should it be during the catch (beginning of the stroke) or at the finish? The answer really depends on personal preference.

25. Music should not be used when cycling on roads or sidewalks because cyclists cannot hear the noises (including warning sounds) made by pedestrians and drivers. They may also be distracted from important safety-relevant information (a car about to pull out). Cyclists must always think ahead and be ever mindful of numerous potential hazards. Music should be used only for stationary cycling (e.g., in spinning classes).

# GLOSSARY

**activation**—One's level of energy, alertness, and bodily arousal.

**aerobic activities**—Lower-intensity activities such as jogging that rely predominantly on oxygen to release energy from food.

**aerobic capacity**—The capacity of humans to take in oxygen, transport it around the body, and use it in working muscle cells.

**affective valence**—The intrinsic attractiveness (positive valence) or aversiveness (negative valence) of an event, object, or situation.

**anaerobic activities**—Activities of a higher intensity that rely predominantly on the chemical energy stored within muscles (e.g., weightlifting, sprinting) and induce breathlessness.

**arousal**—The intensity of psychological experience, ranging from deep relaxation to the greatest excitement. Arousal has both psychological and physiological dimensions and can be interpreted with either a positive or negative valence (e.g., excitement vs. panic).

**association (as opposed to dissociation)**—Focusing inside the body or on task-relevant information (e.g., respiration rate, stride rate, technique), or both.

**asynchronous music**—An application of music in which there is no conscious synchronization between either musical tempo or meter and a person's movement patterns. Synchronous movement may occur without conscious awareness.

**blood pressure**—The force exerted by blood against the walls of the arteries. Systolic pressure is the highest pressure that results from the contraction of the heart; diastolic pressure is the lowest pressure that occurs during the resting phase of the heart cycle.

**breakbeat**—A point in a piece when the music rests (stops) to feature a brief percussion solo that is often syncopated and more complex than the main beat.

**breakdown training**—In weight training, involves reaching muscle fatigue by reducing the weight that is lifted once the exerciser has fatigued with the initial weight.

**cadence**—The pedaling or movement rate; this term is most often applied to running and cycling.

**circuit training**—A form of high-intensity conditioning or resistance training that uses a circuit of sequential exercises. When one circuit is completed, the exerciser begins at the first exercise again to complete the next circuit. The time between exercises in circuit training is short (10 to 30 seconds), and the recovery period between circuits is generally two to six minutes long.

**classical conditioning (also referred to as Pavlovian or respondent conditioning)**—A form of learning in which a response to a stimulus is trained by using an existing response to a different stimulus.

**cognitive anxiety**—Thought-related anxiety that drives physical responses such as muscular tension.

**consonance**—A combination of notes that, when played at the same time, sounds pleasant to most people (as opposed to dissonance).

**crescendo**—A musical term that means "getting louder."

**cycle ergometry**—Exercise involving cycling on a static exercise bike.

**diminuendo**—A musical term that means "getting quieter."

**dissociation**—Focusing outside the body on task-irrelevant information (e.g., the landscape, environmental sounds) or daydreaming.

**dynamics**—From the Greek *dynamis,* which means "power," dynamics refers to the notations on a musical score that tell the performer how forcefully (and also in what style) to play the notes.

**dynamometer**—A device for measuring force, torque, or power.

**entrainment**—The tendency of biological rhythms such as heart rate and breathing rate to alter their frequency toward that of a musical pulse.

**ergogenic**—Improving physical performance by either delaying fatigue or increasing work output.

**ergometer**—A stationary exercise machine that records cardiorespiratory performance (e.g., a cycle ergometer).

**extramusical associations**—Associations people have with pieces of music that connect them with experiences, ideas, places, people, memories, and cultural phenomena.

**genre**—A type of music that is based on convention and stylistic criteria (synonymous with *idiom*).

**harmony**—A sound created when notes or melodies combine (e.g., the sound made when members of a barbershop quartet sing in unison). The meshing of notes acts, in part, to shape the mood of the music to make people feel happy, sad, surprised, anxious, or calm.

**heart rate**—The number of times the heart contracts in a minute. Heart rate is measured in beats per minute (bpm) and is often used to establish work intensity during exercise or training.

**homeostasis**—The process by which an organism maintains the constant internal conditions necessary for life.

**idiom**—See *genre*.

**in-task music**—Music heard during physical activity or sport.

**kettlebell**—A cast-iron or steel weight (resembling a cannonball with a handle) that is used to perform ballistic exercises that combine cardiorespiratory, strength, and flexibility training.

**kinesthetic**—The sense of bodily position, movement, and stress, particularly in relation to neighboring parts of the body.

**lactate**—An acid produced in the muscles during high-intensity exercise as a result of fatigue. It limits exercise performance when it accumulates in large quantities.

**lactate clearance**—The clearance of lactate from the muscles into the bloodstream; also known as buffering.

**maximal heart rate**—The highest heart rate a person can achieve during exercise (often estimated using the simple formula 220 minus age).

**melody**—The recognizable tune of a piece of music; a series of notes that constitutes the most prominent and often the highest (in terms of pitch) part of the score. People often catch themselves singing, humming, or whistling the melody of pieces of music.

**meter**—As distinct from tempo, meter concerns how tones are grouped over time. It depends on the listener's perception of the pulse and when it is expected to occur. Meter relates to whether a person taps her foot hard or lightly in response to a piece of music, and how the taps in this series join to create larger units.

**negative training**—Loading a body movement in only the down, or muscle-lengthening (eccentric), phase.

**neurotransmitters**—Bodily chemicals that transmit signals from neurons (electrically excitable cells) to target cells.

**no-music control**—A condition in an experiment involving no music that is used to gauge the effect of an experimental condition that includes music. The no-music control provides a point of comparison that enables the researcher to gauge the magnitude of the experimental effect.

**norepinephrine**—A chemical that is both a stress hormone that facilitates the fight-or-flight response and a neurotransmitter.

**oudeterous**—A term used by the author and his colleagues to describe music that is neutral in its motivational qualities; that is, neither motivating nor demotivating (see Karageorghis, Terry, & Lane, 1999).

**oxygen uptake**—The amount of oxygen used by an individual in a minute; also written as $\dot{V}O_2$.

**post-task music**—Music that is heard after physical activity or sport.

**powerlifting**—A strength-based sport or training activity that consists of three attempts at lifting maximal weight on three lifts: squat, bench press, and deadlift. This requires the application of strength at high speed (hence, the word *power*).

**pre-task music**—Music used to arouse, relax, or regulate the mood of an individual or a team or exercise group prior to a competition or activity.

**priming**—Priming techniques create temporary states of activation or internal readiness. The interaction of an environmental prime, such as a piece of music, with internal readiness, influences a person's perceptions and evaluations, as well as his motivations and subsequent behaviors.

**pyramid training**—A method of strength training in which the exerciser starts with a light weight for a high number of repetitions. In each set, the weight is increased and the repetitions are decreased. After performing a small number of repetitions at the top of the pyramid (one to three), the weights are gradually reduced and the repetitions increased until the first set of the pyramid is reached.

**respiration rate (RR)**—The number of breaths taken in a minute.

**slow training**—The combination of very slow speeds of lifting and lowering weights.

**sound intensity**—The sound power per unit area.

**sound pressure**—The local pressure deviation from the ambient (average, or level, equilibrium) atmospheric pressure caused by a sound wave. In air, sound pressure can be measured using a microphone; in water, with a hydrophone. In simple terms, it is the physical disruption caused by a sound wave.

**stage training**—A workout regimen in which the required number of repetitions and sets is performed for each exercise before moving to the next exercise.

**superset**—The combination of two or more exercises to maximize the amount of work completed by a muscle or group of muscles.

**synchronous music**—Music that is used to facilitate a conscious synchronization between movement patterns and the tempo or meter of the musical piece (also referred to as auditory–motor synchronization).

**syncopation**—An unexpected rhythmic feel that occurs when the rhythmic emphasis is placed off the main beat. Syncopation can also result from the way the main beat is accented. In the case of common time (four quarter notes to the bar), the strongest beat is the first in the bar, and the second strongest is the third in the bar. Popular styles of music such as swing and reggae place strong emphasis on beats 2 and 4 and are thus characterized by syncopated rhythms.

**tempo**—The speed or rate at which music is played; most commonly expressed in beats per minute (bpm).

**volume**—The sound intensity level (as heard) of a piece of music (see also *dynamics, sound intensity,* and *sound pressure*).

**$\dot{V}O_2max$**—A common measure of cardiorespiratory fitness that represents the maximal amount of oxygen a person can extract from the air during exercise. It is measured in milliliters per kilogram of body weight per minute.

# REFERENCES

Alessio, H.M., & Hutchinson, K.M. (1991). Effects of submaximal exercise and noise exposure on hearing loss. *Research Quarterly for Exercise and Sport, 62*, 413-419.

Amato, P.R. (2000). The consequences of divorce for adults and children. *Journal of Marriage and Family, 62*, 1269-1287.

American College of Sports Medicine. (2011). Quantity and quality of exercise for developing and maintaining cardiorespiratory, musculoskeletal, and neuromotor fitness in apparently healthy adults: Guidance for prescribing exercise. *Medicine & Science in Sports & Exercise, 43*, 1334-1359.

Anshel, M.H., & Marisi, D.Q. (1978). Effects of music and rhythm on physical performance. *Research Quarterly, 49*, 109-113.

Atan, T. (2013). Effect of music on anaerobic exercise performance. *Biology of Sport, 30*, 35-39.

Atkinson, G., Wilson, D., & Eubank, M. (2004). Effects of music on work-rate distribution during a cycling time trial. *International Journal of Sports Medicine, 25*, 611-615.

Bacon, C.J., Myers, T.R., & Karageorghis, C.I. (2012). Effect of music-movement synchrony on exercise oxygen consumption. *Journal of Sports Medicine and Physical Fitness, 52*, 359-365.

Barwood, M.J., Weston, J.V., Thelwell, R., & Page, J. (2009). A motivational music and video intervention improves high-intensity exercise performance. *Journal of Sports Science and Medicine, 8*, 435-442.

Bateman, A., & Bales, J. (Eds.). (2008). *Sporting sounds: Relationships between sport and music*. London: Routledge.

Beedie, C.J., Terry, P.C., & Lane, A.M. (2005). Distinctions between emotion and mood. *Cognition and Emotion, 19*, 847-878.

Berkowitz, R.L., Coplan, J.D., Reddy, D.P., & Gorman, J.M. (2007). The human dimension: How the prefrontal cortex modulates the subcortical fear response. *Reviews in the Neurosciences, 18*, 191-207.

Berlyne, D.E. (1971). *Aesthetics and psychobiology*. New York: Appleton-Century-Crofts.

Bharani, A., Sahu, A., & Mathew, V. (2004). Effect of passive distraction on treadmill exercise test performance in healthy males using music. *International Journal of Cardiology, 97*, 305-306.

Biddle, S.J.H., Mutrie, N., & Gorely, T. (2015). *Psychology of physical activity: Determinants, well-being and interventions* (3rd ed.). London: Routledge.

Bigliassi, M., Barreto-Silva, V., Kanthack, T.F.D., & Altimari, L.R. (2014). Music and cortical blood flow: A functional near-infrared spectroscopy (fNIRS) study. *Psychology & Neuroscience, 7*, 545-550.

Bishop, D.T., Karageorghis, C.I., & Kinrade, N.P. (2009). Effects of musically-induced emotions on choice reaction time performance. *The Sport Psychologist, 23*, 59-76.

Bishop, D.T., Karageorghis, C.I., & Loizou, G. (2007). A grounded theory of young tennis players' use of music to manipulate emotional state. *Journal of Sport & Exercise Psychology, 29*, 584-607.

Bishop, D.T., Wright, M.J., & Karageorghis, C.I. (2014). Tempo and intensity of pre-task music modulate neural activity during reactive task performance. *Psychology of Music, 42*, 714-727.

Bood, R.J., Nijssen, M., van der Kamp, J., & Roerdink, M. (2013). The power of auditory-motor synchronization in sports: Enhancing running performance by coupling cadence with the right beats. *PLoS ONE, 8*, e70758.

Borg, G.A.V. (1982). Psychophysical bases of perceived exertion. *Medicine & Science in Sports & Exercise, 14*, 377-381.

Borg, G.A.V. (1998). *Borg's perceived exertion and pain scales*. Champaign, IL: Human Kinetics.

Borg, G.A.V. (2004). Scaling experiences during work: Perceived exertion and difficulty. In N. Stanton, A. Hedge, K. Brookhuis, E. Salas, & H.W. Hendrick (Eds.), *Handbook of human factors methods* (pp. 95-103). New York: CRC Press.

Carron, A.V., Hausenblas, H.A., & Eys, M.A. (2005). *Group dynamics in sport* (3rd ed.). Morgantown, WV: Fitness Information Technology.

Chamorro-Premuzic, T., & Furnham, A. (2007). Personality and music: Can traits explain how people use music in everyday life? *British Journal of Psychology, 98*, 175-185.

Chan, A.S., Ho, Y.-C., & Cheung, M.-C. (1998). Music training improves verbal memory. *Nature, 396*, 128.

Charnas, D. (2007, August 28). Does music belong in your yoga class? *Yoga Journal*. Retrieved from www.yogajournal.com/article/teach/does-music-belong-in-your-class

Chtourou, H., Jarraya, M., Aloui, A., Hammouda, O., & Souissi, N. (2012). The effects of music during warm-up on anaerobic performances of young sprinters. *Science & Sports, 27*, e85-e88.

Clark, I.N., Baker, F.A., & Taylor, N.F. (2016). The modulating effects of music listening on health-related exercise and physical activity in adults: A systematic review and narrative synthesis. *Nordic Journal of Music Therapy, 25*, 76-104.

Clark, I.N., Taylor, N.F., & Baker, F.A. (2012). Music interventions and physical activity in older adults: A systematic literature review and meta-analysis. *Journal of Rehabilitation Medicine, 44*, 710-719.

Clynes, M., & Walker, J. (1982). Neurobiologic functions of rhythm time and pulse in music. In M. Clynes (Ed.), *Music, mind, and brain: The neuropsychology of music* (pp. 171-216). New York: Plenum Press.

Crust, L. (2008). Perceived importance of components of asynchronous music during circuit training. *Journal of Sports Sciences, 26*, 1547-1555.

Crust, L., & Clough, P.J. (2006). The influence of rhythm and personality in the endurance response to motivational asynchronous music. *Journal of Sports Sciences, 24*, 187-195.

Daily Mirror. (2007). Interrogation: Andy Murray. Retrieved from www.mirror.co.uk/3am/celebrity-news/interrogation-andy-murray-486032

Deutsch, J., & Hetland, K. (2012). The impact of music on pacer test performance, enjoyment and workload. *Asian Journal of Physical Education & Recreation, 18*, 6-14.

Edworthy, J., & Waring, H. (2006). The effects of music tempo and loudness level on treadmill exercise. *Ergonomics, 49*, 1597-1610.

Ekkekakis, P. (2003). Pleasure and displeasure from the body: Perspectives from exercise. *Cognition and Emotion, 17*, 213-239.

Ekkekakis, P. (2013). *The measurement of affect, mood, and emotion: A guide for health-behavioral research.* New York: Cambridge University Press.

Eliakim, M., Bodner, E., Eliakim, A., Nemet, D., & Meckel, Y. (2012). Effect of motivational music on lactate levels during recovery from intense exercise. *Journal of Strength and Conditioning Research, 26*, 80-86.

Eliakim, M., Bodner, E., Meckel, Y., Nemet, D., & Eliakim, A. (2013). Effect of rhythm on the recovery from intense exercise. *Journal of Strength and Conditioning Research, 27*, 1019-1024.

Eliakim, M., Meckel, Y., Nemet, D., & Eliakim, A. (2007). The effect of music during warm-up on consecutive anaerobic performance in elite adolescent volleyball players. *International Journal of Sports Medicine, 28*, 321-325.

Elliott, D., Carr, S., & Savage, D. (2004). Effects of motivational music on work output and affective responses during sub-maximal cycling of a standardized perceived intensity. *Journal of Sport Behavior, 27*, 134-147.

Eysenck, H.J. (1967). *The biological basis of personality.* Springfield, IL: Charles C. Thomas.

Eysenck, M.W., Derakshan, N., Santos, R., & Calvo, M.G. (2007). Anxiety and cognitive performance: Attentional control theory. *Emotion, 7*, 336-353.

Farah, M. (2013, October 7). Mo Farah: This is my moment, my race—I will not be beaten at the London Olympic Games. *Daily Telegraph.* Retrieved from www.telegraph.co.uk/sport/othersports/athletics/10361764/Mo-Farah-This-is-my-moment-my-race-I-will-not-be-beaten-at-the-London-Olympic-Games.html

Flatischler, R. (1992). The influence of musical rhythmicity in internal rhythmical events. In R. Spintge, & R. Droh (Eds.), *Music medicine* (pp. 241-248). St Louis, MO: MMB Music.

Folley, M. (2014, February 18). All smiles for Vanessa Mae despite violinist finishing LAST on Olympic skiing debut. *Mail Online.* Retrieved from www.dailymail.co.uk/sport/winterolympics/article-2561900/WINTER-OLYMPICS-2014-All-smiles-British-violinist-Vanessa-Mae-despite-finishing-dead-Giant-Slalom.html

Franěk, M., van Noorden, L., & Režný, L. (2014). Tempo and walking speed with music in the urban context. *Frontiers in Psychology, 5*, 1361.

Fritz, T.H., Hardikar, S., Demoucron, M., Niessen, M., Demey, M., Giot, O., Li, Y., Haynes, J.-D., Villringer, A., & Leman, M. (2013). Musical agency reduces perceived exertion during strenuous physical performance. *Proceedings of the National Academy of Sciences of the United States of America, 110*, 17784-17789.

Gardner, J. (1991). *The art of fiction: Notes on craft for young writers.* New York: Vintage Books.

Garside, K. (2008, March 21). Lewis Hamilton uses music to keep away blues. *Telegraph.* Retrieved from www.telegraph.co.uk/sport/columnists/kevingarside/2295048/Lewis-Hamilton-uses-music-to-keep-away-blues.html

Ghaderi, M., Rahimi, R., & Ali Azarbayjani, M. (2009). The effect of motivational and relaxation music on aerobic performance, rating perceived exertion and salivary cortisol in athlete meals. *South African Journal for Research in Sport, Physical Education & Recreation, 31,* 29-38.

Goerlich, K.S., Witteman, J., Schiller, N.O., Van Heuven, V.J., Aleman, A., & Martens, S. (2012). The nature of affective priming in music and speech. *Journal of Cognitive Neuroscience, 24,* 1725-1741.

Hagen, J., Foster, C., Rodríguez-Marroyo, J., De Koning, J.J., Mikat, R.P., Hendrix, C.R., & Porcari, J.P. (2013). The effect of music on 10-km cycle time-trial performance. *International Journal of Sports Physiology and Performance, 8,* 104-106.

Hagins, M., Moore, W., & Rundle, A. (2007). Does practicing hatha yoga satisfy recommendations for intensity of physical activity which improves and maintains health and cardiovascular fitness? *BMC Complementary and Alternative Medicine, 7,* 40.

Hardy, C.J., & Rejeski, W.J. (1989). Not what, but how one feels: The measurement of affect during exercise. *Journal of Sport & Exercise Psychology, 11,* 304-317.

Hayakawa, Y., Miki, H., Takada, K., & Tanaka, K. (2000). Effects of music on mood during bench stepping performance. *Perceptual & Motor Skills, 90,* 307-314.

Henderson, J. (1998, February 18). Red-hot rhythm and blues. *Athletics Weekly,* 4-7.

Herholz, S.C., & Zatorre, R.J. (2012). Musical training as a framework for brain plasticity: Behavior, function, and structure. *Neuron, 76,* 486-502.

Hernández-Peón, R., Brust-Carmona, H., Peñaloza-Rojas, J., & Bach-y-Rita, G. (1961). The efferent control of afferent signals entering the central nervous system. *Annals of the New York Academy of Science, 89,* 866-882.

Hewston, R.M., Lane, A.M., & Karageorghis, C.I. (2008). Development and initial validation of the Music Mood-Regulation Scale (MMRS). *E-Journal of Applied Psychology, 4,* 15-22.

Hsu, D.Y., Huang, L., Nordgren, L.F., Rucker, D.D., & Galinsky, A.D. (2014). The music of power: Perceptual and behavioral consequences of powerful music. *Social Psychological and Personality Science, 6,* 75-83.

Hutchinson, J.C., & Karageorghis, C.I. (2013). Moderating influence of dominant attentional style and exercise intensity on responses to asynchronous music. *Journal of Sport & Exercise Psychology, 35,* 625-643.

Hutchinson, J.C., Karageorghis, C.I., & Jones, L. (2015). See hear: Psychological effects of music and music-video during treadmill running. *Annals of Behavioral Medicine, 49,* 199-211.

Hutchinson, J.C., Sherman, T., Davis, L., Cawthon, D., Reeder, N.B., & Tenenbaum, G. (2011). The influence of asynchronous motivational music on a supramaximal exercise bout. *International Journal of Sport Psychology, 42,* 135-148.

Hyde, K.L., Lerch, J., Norton, A., Forgeard, M., Winner, E., Evans, A.C., & Schlaug, G. (2009). The effects of musical training on structural brain development: A longitudinal study. *Annals of the New York Academy of Sciences, 1169,* 182-186.

International Association of Athletics Federations. (2015). Competition rules 2016-2017. Monaco: IAAF. Retrieved from http://www.iaaf.org/about-iaaf/documents/rules-regulations

Iwanaga, I. (1995). Harmonic relationship between preferred tempi and heart rate. *Perceptual & Motor Skills, 81,* 67-71.

Jackson, S.A., & Csikszentmihalyi, M. (1999). *Flow in sports: The keys to optimal experiences and performances.* Champaign, IL: Human Kinetics.

Jackson, S.A., Eklund, R.C., & Martin, A. (2010). *The flow scales manual.* Mind garden. Retrieved from www.mindgarden.com/flow-scales/467-flow-manual.html#horizontalTab1

Jing, L., & Xudong, W. (2008). Evaluation on the effects of relaxing music on the recovery from aerobic exercise-induced fatigue. *Journal of Sports Medicine and Physical Fitness, 48,* 102-106.

Jones, L., Karageorghis, C.I., & Ekkekakis, P. (2014). Can high-intensity exercise be more pleasant? Attentional dissociation using music and video. *Journal of Sport & Exercise Psychology, 36,* 528-541.

Juslin, P.N. (2009). Emotion in music performance. In S. Hallam, I. Cross, & M. Thaut (Eds.), *The Oxford handbook of music psychology* (pp. 377-389). Oxford, UK: Oxford University Press.

Juslin, P.N., & Laukka, P. (2004). Expression, perception, and induction of musical emotions: A review and a questionnaire study of everyday listening. *Journal of New Music Research, 33,* 217-238.

Juslin, P.N., & Västfjäll, D. (2008). Emotional responses to music: The need to consider underlying mechanisms. *Behavioral and Brain Sciences, 31,* 559-575.

Karageorghis, C.I. (1991). *An analysis of the effects of music on performance*. Unpublished bachelor's dissertation, Brunel University London, Uxbridge, UK.

Karageorghis, C.I. (2014). Run to the Beat: Sport and music for the masses. *Sport in Society, 17*, 433-447.

Karageorghis, C.I. (2016). The scientific application of music in exercise and sport: Towards a new theoretical model. In A.M. Lane (Ed.), *Sport and exercise psychology* (2nd ed., pp. 276-322). London: Routledge.

Karageorghis, C.I., Hutchinson, J.C., Jones, L., Farmer, H.L., Ayhan, M.S., Wilson, R.C., Rance, J., Hepworth, C.J., & Bailey, S.G. (2013). Psychological, psychophysical, and ergogenic effects of music in swimming. *Psychology of Sport and Exercise, 14*, 560-568.

Karageorghis, C.I., & Jones, L. (2014). On the stability and relevance of the exercise heart rate–music-tempo preference relationship. *Psychology of Sport and Exercise, 15*, 299-310.

Karageorghis, C.I., Jones, L., & Low, D.C. (2006). Relationship between exercise heart rate and music tempo preference. *Research Quarterly for Exercise and Sport, 26*, 240-250.

Karageorghis, C.I., Jones, L., Priest, D.L., Akers, R.I., Clarke, A., Perry, J.M., Reddick, B.T., Bishop, D.T., & Lim, H.B.T. (2011). Revisiting the relationship between exercise heart rate and music tempo preference. *Research Quarterly for Exercise and Sport, 82*, 274-284.

Karageorghis, C.I., Jones, L., & Stuart, D.P. (2008). Psychological effects of music tempi during exercise. *International Journal of Sports Medicine, 29*, 613-619.

Karageorghis, C.I., Mouzourides, D.A., Priest, D.L., Sasso, T.A., Morrish, D.J., & Walley, C. (2009). Psychophysical and ergogenic effects of synchronous music during treadmill walking. *Journal of Sport & Exercise Psychology, 31*, 18-36.

Karageorghis, C.I., & Priest, D.L. (2012a). Music in the exercise domain: a review and synthesis (Part I). *International Review of Sport and Exercise Psychology, 5*, 44-66.

Karageorghis, C.I., & Priest, D.L. (2012b). Music in the exercise domain: a review and synthesis (Part II). *International Review of Sport and Exercise Psychology, 5*, 67-84.

Karageorghis, C.I., Priest, D.L., Terry, P.C., Chatzisarantis, N.L.D., & Lane, A.M. (2006). Redesign and initial validation of an instrument to assess the motivational qualities of music in exercise: The Brunel Music Rating Inventory-2. *Journal of Sports Sciences, 24*, 899-909.

Karageorghis, C.I., Priest, D.L., Williams, L.S., Hirani, R.M., Lannon, K.M., Bates, B.J., & Williams, C. (2010). Ergogenic and psychological effects of synchronous music during circuit training. *Psychology of Sport and Exercise, 11*, 54-68.

Karageorghis, C.I., Stevens, R.C., Hamer, M., Bruce, A.C., & Pottratz, S.T. (2014). Psychological and psychophysiological effects of recuperative music following exhaustive exercise. *Proceedings of the 2014 British Association of Sport and Exercise Sciences Conference*. Burton on Trent, UK: British Association of Sport and Exercise Sciences.

Karageorghis, C.I., & Terry, P.C. (1997). The psychophysical effects of music in sport and exercise: A review. *Journal of Sport Behavior, 20*, 54-68.

Karageorghis, C.I., & Terry, P.C. (2009). The psychological, psychophysical, and ergogenic effects of music in sport: A review and synthesis. In A. Bateman & J. Bale (Eds.), *Sporting sounds: Relationships between sport and music* (pp. 13-36). London: Routledge.

Karageorghis, C.I., Terry, P.C., & Lane, A.M. (1999). Development and initial validation of an instrument to assess the motivational qualities of music in exercise and sport: The Brunel Music Rating Inventory. *Journal of Sports Sciences, 17*, 713-724.

Karageorghis, C.I., Terry, P.C., Lane, A.M., Bishop, D.T., & Priest, D.L. (2012). The BASES expert statement on use of music in exercise. *Journal of Sports Sciences, 30*, 953-956.

Kelly, D. (2014, February 3). Super Bowl 48's Super Seahawks: Pete Carroll's cultural & schematic philosophies apparent in Seattle's playoffs run. *Field Gulls*. Retrieved from www.fieldgulls.com/football-breakdowns/2014/2/3/5374724/super-bowl-48-seahawks-pete-carrolls-richard-sherman-marshawn-lynch

Key to Brazilian success: plenty of sex. (2006, March 30). Retrieved from http://www.smh.com.au/news/world-cup-2006/key-to-brazilian-success-plenty-of-sex/2006/03/30/1143441275656.html

King, P. (2014, August 4). The maturation of Cam. *MMQB*. Retrieved from http://mmqb.si.com/2014/08/04/cam-newton-carolina-panthers-maturation

Kodzhaspirov, Y.G., Zaitsev, Y.M., & Kosarev, S.M. (1988). The application of functional music in the training sessions of weightlifters. *Soviet Sports Review, 23*, 39-42.

Koelsch, S., & Skouras, S. (2014). Functional centrality of amygdala, striatum and hypothalamus in a "small-world" network underlying joy: An fMRI study with music. *Human Brain Mapping, 35,* 3485-3498.

Kornysheva, K., von Cramon, D.Y., Jacobsen, T, Schubotz, R.I. (2010). Tuning-in to the beat: Aesthetic appreciation of musical rhythms correlates with a premotor activity boost. *Human Brain Mapping, 31,* 48-64.

Lane, A.M., Davis, P.A., & Devonport, T.J. (2011). Effects of music interventions on emotional states and running performance. *Journal of Sports Science and Medicine, 10,* 400-407.

Laukka, P., & Quick, L. (2013). Emotional and motivational uses of music in sports and exercise: A questionnaire study among athletes. *Psychology of Music, 41,* 198-215.

Leeds, J. (2010). *The power of sound: How to be healthy and productive using music and sound* (2nd ed.). Rochester, VT: Healing Arts Press.

Leman, M., Moelants, D., Varewyck, M., Styns, F., van Noorden, L., & Martens, J. (2013). Activating and relaxing music entrains the speed of beat synchronized walking. *PLoS ONE, 8,* e67932.

Levesque, C., & Pelletier, L.G. (2003). On the investigation of primed and chronic autonomous and heteronomous motivational orientations. *Personality and Social Psychology Bulletin, 29,* 1570-1584.

Levitin, D. J. (2007). *This is your brain on music: Understanding a human obsession.* London: Atlantic Books.

Levitin, D.J., & Tirovolas, A.K. (2009). Current advances in the cognitive neuroscience of music. *Annals of the New York Academy of Sciences, 1156,* 211-231.

Lim, H.B.T. (2012). *Effects of varied music applications in cycle ergometry.* Unpublished doctoral dissertation, Brunel University London, Uxbridge, UK.

Lim, H.B.T., Atkinson, G., Karageorghis, C.I., & Eubank, M. (2009). Effects of differentiated music exposure during a 10-km cycling time trial. *International Journal of Sports Medicine, 30,* 435-442.

Lim, H.B.T., Karageorghis, C.I., Romer, L.M., & Bishop, D.T. (2014). Psychophysiological effects of synchronous versus asynchronous music during cycling. *Medicine & Science in Sports & Exercise, 46,* 407-413.

Lind, E., Welch, A.S., & Ekkekakis, P. (2009). Do 'mind over muscle' strategies work? Examining the effects of attentional association and dissociation on exertional, affective and physiological responses to exercise. *Sports Medicine, 39,* 743-764.

Lindgren, F., & Axelsson, A. (1988). The influence of physical exercise on susceptibility to noise-induced temporary threshold shift. *Scandinavian Audiology, 17,* 11-17.

Loizou, G., & Karageorghis, C.I. (2015). Effects of psychological priming, video, and music on anaerobic exercise performance. *Scandinavian Journal of Medicine & Science in Sports, 25,* 909-920.

Loizou, G., Karageorghis, C.I., & Bishop, D.T. (2014). Interactive effects of video, priming, and music on emotions and the needs underlying intrinsic motivation. *Psychology of Sport and Exercise, 15,* 611-619.

Lyttle, T., & Montagne, M. (1992). Drugs, music, and ideology: A social pharmacological interpretation of the acid house movement. *The International Journal of the Addictions, 27,* 1159-1177.

Mann, M.R. (2004). Erging to music. *Ultra-Fit Magazine, 14*(7), 76-78.

McCown, W., Keiser, R., Mulhearn, S., & Williamson, D. (1997). The role of personality and gender preference for exaggerated bass in music. *Personality and Individual Differences, 23,* 543-547.

McMorris, T. (2004). *Acquisition and performance of sports skills.* Chichester, UK: Wiley.

Mesagno, C., Marchant, D., & Morris, T. (2009). Alleviating choking: The sounds of distraction. *Journal of Applied Sport Psychology, 21,* 131-147.

Michel, W., & Wanner, H.U. (1973). Effect of music on sports performance. *Schweizerische Zeitschrift fur Sportmedizine, 2,* 141-169.

Molnar-Szakacs, I., & Overy, K. (2006). Music and mirror neurons: From motion to 'e'motion. *Social Cognitive and Affective Neuroscience, 1,* 235-241.

Nakamura, P.M., Pereira, G., Papini, C.B., Nakamura, F.Y., & Kokubun, E. (2010). Effects of preferred and nonpreferred music on continuous cycling exercise performance. *Perceptual & Motor Skills, 110,* 257-264.

Nakashima, T., Naganawa, S., Sone, M., Tominaga, M., Hayashi, H., Yamamoto, H., Liu, X., & Nuttall, A. L. (2003). Disorders of cochlear blood flow. *Brain Research Reviews, 43,* 17-28.

Neher, A. (1962). A physiological explanation of unusual behavior in ceremonies involving drums. *Human Biology, 34,* 151-160.

Nethery, V.M. (2002). Competition between internal and external sources of information during exercise: Influence on RPE and the impact of the exercise load. *Journal of Sports Medicine and Physical Fitness, 42,* 172-178.

North, A.C. & Hargreaves, D.J. (2008). Music and taste. In A.C. North, & D.J. Hargreaves (Eds.), *The social and applied psychology of music* (pp. 75-142). Oxford, UK: Oxford University Press.

Pain, M.A., Harwood, C., & Anderson, R. (2011). Pre-competition imagery and music: The impact on flow and performance in competitive soccer. *The Sport Psychologist, 25,* 212-232.

Park, M., Hennig-Fast, K., Bao, Y., Carl, P., Pöppel, E., Welker, L., Reiser, M., Meindl, T., & Gutyrchik, E. (2013). Personality traits modulate neural responses to emotions expressed in music. *Brain Research, 1523,* 68-76.

Patton, N.W. (1991). *The influence of musical preference on the affective state, heart rate, and perceived exertion rations of participants in aerobic dance/exercise classes.* Doctoral dissertation, Texas Women's University. Microform Publications, University of Oregon, Eugene, OR (University Microfiche No. UNIV ORE: U092 344-345).

Phillips-Silver, J., & Keller, P.E. (2012). Searching for roots of entrainment and joint action in early musical interactions. *Frontiers in Human Neuroscience, 6,* 26.

Pompei, D. (2014, April 4). Age is just a number. *Sports on Earth.* Retrieved from www.sportsonearth.com/article/70926684/how-seattle-seahawks-head-coach-pete-carroll-stays-young

Priest, D.L., & Karageorghis, C.I. (2008). A qualitative investigation into the characteristics and effects of motivational music in exercise and sport. *European Physical Education Review, 14,* 351-371.

Priest, D.L., Karageorghis, C.I., & Sharp, N.C.C. (2004). The characteristics and effects of motivational music in exercise settings: The possible influence of gender, age, frequency of attendance, and time of attendance. *Journal of Sports Medicine and Physical Fitness, 44,* 77-86.

Radford, G.P. (2007). Under the threshold: Is there more than meets the eye? *Fairleigh Dickinson University Magazine.* Retrieved from www.fdu.edu/newspubs/magazine/07ws/subliminal1.html

Rejeski, W.J. (1985). Perceived exertion: An active or passive process? *Journal of Sport Psychology, 75,* 371-378.

Rendi, M., Szabo, A., & Szabó, T. (2008). Performance enhancement with music in rowing sprint. *The Sport Psychologist, 22,* 175-182.

Russell, D. (2014). 'See, the conquering hero comes! Sound the trumpets, beat the drums': Music and sport in England, 1880–1939. *Sport in Society, 17,* 303-319.

Russell, J.A. (1980). A circumplex model of affect. *Journal of Personality and Social Psychology, 39,* 1161-1178.

Sanchez, X., Moss, S.L., Twist, C., & Karageorghis, C.I. (2014). On the role of lyrics in the music–exercise performance relationship. *Psychology of Sport and Exercise, 15,* 132-138.

Savitha, D., Mallikarjuna, R.N., & Chythra, R. (2010). Effect of different musical tempo on post-exercise recovery in young adults. *Indian Journal of Physiology and Pharmacology, 54,* 32-36.

Scherer, K.R., & Zentner, M.R. (2001). Emotional effects of music: Production rules. In P.N. Juslin & J.A. Sloboda (Eds.), *Music and emotion: Theory and research* (pp. 361-392). Oxford, UK: Oxford University Press.

Schneider, S., Askew, C.D., Abel, T., & Strüder, H.K. (2010). Exercise, music, and the brain: Is there a central pattern generator? *Journal of Sports Sciences, 28,* 1337-1343.

Scott, L.M., Scott, D., Bedic, S.P., & Dowd, J. (1999). The effect of associative and dissociative strategies on rowing ergometer performance. *The Sport Psychologist, 13,* 57-68.

Sebanz, N., Bekkering, H., & Knoblich, G. (2006). Joint action: Bodies and minds moving together. *Trends in Cognitive Sciences, 10,* 70-76.

Simpson, S.D., & Karageorghis, C.I. (2006). The effects of synchronous music on 400-m sprint performance. *Journal of Sports Sciences, 24,* 1095-1102.

Smoll, F.L., & Schultz, R.W. (1978). Relationships among measures of preferred tempo and motor rhythm. *Perceptual & Motor Skills, 46,* 883-894.

Stevinson, C.D., & Biddle, S.J.H. (1999). Cognitive strategies in running: A response to Masters and Ogles (1998). *The Sport Psychologist, 13,* 235-236.

Stubbs, D. (2012, August 6). What are the songs that inspire Usain Bolt? *NME.* Retrieved from www.nme.com/blogs/nme-blogs/what-are-the-songs-that-inspire-usain-bolt

Tammen, V.V. (1996). Elite middle and long distance runners [sic] associative/dissociative coping. *Journal of Applied Sport Psychology, 8,* 1-8.

Tarrant, M., North, A.C., & Hargreaves, D.J. (2001). Social categorization, self-esteem, and the estimated musical preferences of male adolescents. *Journal of Social Psychology, 141,* 565-581.

Tate, A.R., Gennings, C., Hoffman, R.A., Strittmatter, A.P., & Retchin, S.M. (2012). Effects of bone-conducted music on swimming performance. *Journal of Strength and Conditioning Research, 26,* 982-988.

Tenenbaum, G. (2001). A social-cognitive perspective of perceived exertion and exertion tolerance. In R.N. Singer, H.A. Hausenblas, & C. Janelle (Eds.), *Handbook of sport psychology* (2nd ed., pp. 810-822). New York: Wiley.

Tenenbaum, G., Lidor, R., Lavyan, N., Morrow, K., Tonnel, S., Gershgoren, A., Meis, J., & Johnson, M. (2004). The effect of music type on running perseverance and coping with effort sensations. *Psychology of Sport and Exercise, 5,* 89-109.

Terry, P.C. (1995). The efficacy of mood state profiling with elite performers: A review and synthesis. *The Sport Psychologist, 9,* 309-324.

Terry, P.C., & Karageorghis, C.I. (2011). Music in sport and exercise. In T. Morris & P.C. Terry (Eds.), *The new sport and exercise psychology companion* (pp. 359-380). Morgantown, WV: Fitness Information Technology.

Terry, P.C., Karageorghis, C.I., Mecozzi Saha, A., & D'Auria, S. (2012). Effects of synchronous music on treadmill running among elite triathletes. *Journal of Science and Medicine in Sport, 15,* 52-57.

Terry, P.C., Lane, A.M., Lane. H.J., & Keohane, L. (1999). Development and validation of a mood measure for adolescents. *Journal of Sports Sciences, 17,* 861-872.

Thayer, R.E., Newman, J.R., & McClain, T.M. (1994). Self-regulation of mood: Strategies for changing a bad mood, raising energy, and reducing tension. *Journal of Personality and Social Psychology, 67,* 910-925.

The Hits. (2013). Ed Sheeran & Robin Thicke make Andy Murray's Wimbledon playlist. Retrieved from www.thehitsradio.com/music/news/ed-sheer-an-robin-thicke-andy-murrays-wimbledon-playlist

Ünal, A., de Waard, D., Epstude, K., & Steg, L. (2013). Driving with music: Effects on arousal and performance. *Transportation Research Part F: Psychology and Behaviour, 21,* 52-65.

Uppal, A.K., & Datta, U. (1990). Cardiorespiratory response of junior high school girls to exercise performed with and without music. *Journal of Physical Education and Sport Science, 2,* 52-56.

van der Zwaag, M.D., Westerink, J.H.M.D., & van den Broek, E.L. (2011). Emotional and psychophysiological responses to tempo, mode, and percussiveness. *Musicae Scientiae, 15,* 250-269.

Waterhouse, J., Hudson, P., & Edwards, B. (2010). Effects of music tempo upon submaximal cycling performance. *Scandinavian Journal of Medicine and Science in Sports, 20,* 662-669.

Waterlow, L. (2013, June 7). Raving about fitness: Exercise is now the way to get high as fun new dance class takes inspiration from the 90s. *Mail Online.* Retrieved from www.dailymail.co.uk/femail/article-2337607/Raving-fitness-Exercise-way-high-fun-new-dance-class-takes-inspiration-90s.html

Wilson, E.M., & Davey, N.J. (2002). Musical beat influences corticospinal drive to ankle flexor and extensor muscles in man. *International Journal of Psychophysiology, 44,* 177-184.

Woodman, T., & Hardy, L. (2003). The relative impact of cognitive anxiety and self-confidence upon sport performance: A meta-analysis. *Journal of Sports Sciences, 21,* 443-457.

Wulf, G. (2013). Attentional focus and motor learning: A review of 15 years. *International Review of Sport and Exercise Psychology, 6,* 77-104.

Yamamoto, T., Ohkuwa, T., Itoh, H., Kitoh, M., Terasawa, J., Tsuda, T., Kitagawa, S., & Sato, Y. (2003). Effects of pre-exercise listening to slow and fast rhythm music on supramaximal cycle performance and selected metabolic variables. *Archives of Physiology and Biochemistry, 111,* 211-214.

Yamashita, S., Iwai, K., Akimoto, T., Sugawara, J., & Kono, I. (2006). Effects of music during exercise on RPE, heart rate and the autonomic nervous system. *Journal of Sports Medicine and Physical Fitness, 46,* 425-430.

Young, K. (2013). *Sport, violence and society.* New York: Routledge.

Zatorre, R.J., Halpern, A.R., Perry, D.W., Meyer, E., & Evans, A.C. (1996). Hearing in the mind's ear: A PET investigation of musical imagery and perception. *Journal of Cognitive Neuroscience, 8,* 29-46.

Zell, E., & Krizan, Z. (2014). Do people have insight into their abilities? A metasynthesis. *Perspectives on Psychological Science, 9,* 111-125.

# FURTHER READING

## BOOKS AND BOOK CHAPTERS

Ball, P. (2011). *The music instinct: How music works and why we can't do without it.* New York: Vintage.

Bateman, A. (Ed.). (2015). *Sport, music, identities.* New York: Routledge.

Berger, J., & Turow, G. (Eds.) (2013). *Music, science, and the rhythmic brain: Cultural and clinical implications.* London: Routledge.

Bicknell, J. (2010). *Why music moves us.* Basingstoke, UK: Palgrave Macmillan.

Bishop, D.T., & Karageorghis, C.I. (2009). Managing pre-competitive emotions with music. In A. Bateman & J. Bale (Eds.), *Sporting sounds: Relationships between sport and music* (pp. 59-84). London: Routledge.

Blumenstein, B., Bar-Eli, M., & Tenenbaum, G. (Eds.). (2002). *Brain and body in sport and exercise.* Chichester, UK: John Wiley & Sons.

Campbell, P. (2010). *Songs in their heads: Music and its meaning in children's lives.* Oxford, UK: Oxford University Press.

Cochrane, T., Fantini, B., & Scherer, K.R. (2013). *The emotional power of music: Multidisciplinary perspectives on musical arousal, expression, and social control.* Oxford, UK: Oxford University Press.

Coker, W. (1972). *Music and meaning.* New York: Free Press.

Csikszentmihalyi, M. (1990). *Flow: The psychology of optimal experience.* New York: Harper & Row.

DeLiege, I., & Davidson, J.W. (Eds.). (2011). *Music and the mind: Essays in honour of John Sloboda.* Oxford, UK: Oxford University Press.

DeNora, T. (2000). *Music in everyday life.* Cambridge, UK: Cambridge University Press.

DeNora, T., & Bergh, A. (2009). From wind-up to iPod: techno-cultures of listening. In N. Cook, D. Wilson-Leech, & E. Clarke (Eds.), *Cambridge companion to recorded music* (pp. 102-114). Cambridge, UK: Cambridge University Press.

Deutsch, D. (Ed.) (1998). *The psychology of music* (2nd ed.). London: Academic Press.

Gabrielsson, A. (2001). Emotions in strong experiences with music. In P. Juslin & J.A. Sloboda (Eds.), *Music and emotion: Theory and research* (pp. 431-449). Oxford, UK: Oxford University Press.

Gabrielsson, A. (2011). *Strong experiences with music: Music is much more than just music.* Oxford, UK: Oxford University Press.

Gabrielsson, A., & Juslin, P.N. (2003). Emotional expression in music. In R.J. Davidson, K.R. Scherer, & H.H. Goldsmith (Eds.), *Handbook of affective sciences* (pp. 503-534). New York: Oxford University Press.

Hallam, S., Cross, I., & Thaut, M. (Eds.). (2016). *The Oxford handbook of music psychology.* Oxford, UK: Oxford University Press.

Hargreaves, D.J., & North, A.C. (2008). *The social and applied psychology of music.* Oxford, UK: Oxford University Press.

Hellmuth Margulis, H. (2013). *On repeat: How music plays the mind.* Oxford, UK: Oxford University Press.

Hesmondhalgh, D. (2013). *Why music matters.* Hoboken, NJ: Wiley-Blackwell.

Hodges, D.A., & Sebald, D.C. (2011). *Music in the human experience: An introduction to music psychology.* London: Routledge.

Honing, H. (2013). *Musical cognition: A science of listening.* Piscataway, NJ: Transaction.

Juslin, P., & Sloboda, J.A. (2001). *Music and emotion: Theory and research.* London: Oxford University Press.

Karageorghis, C.I. (2008). The scientific application of music in sport and exercise. In A.M. Lane (Ed.), *Sport and exercise psychology* (pp. 109-137). London: Hodder Education.

Karageorghis, C.I. (2014). Music-based interventions. In R.C. Eklund & G. Tenenbaum (Eds.), *Sage encyclopedia of sport and exercise psychology* (pp. 494-496). New York: Sage.

Karageorghis, C.I. (2014). Run to the Beat: Sport and music for the masses. In A. Bateman (Ed.), *Sport, music, identities (Sport in the global society—contemporary perspectives)* (pp. 141-155). London: Routledge.

Karageorghis, C.I., & Bird, J.M. (2016). *Under Pressure*: Music-related interventions in high-performance domains. In A. Mornell (Ed.), *Art in motion III* (pp. 149-173). Frankfurt, Germany: Peter Lang.

Karageorghis, C.I., Ekkekakis, P., Bird, J.M., & Bigliassi, M. (in press). Music in the exercise and sport domain: Conceptual approaches and underlying mechanisms. In M. Leman, M. Lesaffre, & P.-J. Maes (Eds.), *Routledge companion to embodied music interaction*. London: Routledge.

Karageorghis, C.I., & Terry, P.C. (2009). The psychological, psychophysical and ergogenic effects of music in sport: A review and synthesis. In A. Bateman & J. Bale (Eds.), *Sporting sounds: Relationships between sport and music*. London: Routledge.

Karageorghis, C.I., & Terry, P.C. (2011). *Inside sport psychology*. Champaign, IL: Human Kinetics.

Lane, A.M. (Ed.). (2016). *Sport and exercise psychology* (2nd ed.). London: Routledge.

Lawrence, D. (2009). *The complete guide to exercise to music* (3rd ed.). London: A & C Black.

LeDoux, J. (1996). *The emotional brain: The mysterious underpinnings of emotional life*. London: Simon & Schuster.

Levitin, D.J. (2008). *The world in six songs: How the musical brain created human nature*. New York: Dutton.

Liggett, D. (2000). *Sport hypnosis*. Champaign, IL: Human Kinetics.

Loizou, G., & Karageorghis, C.I. (2009). Video, priming and music: Effects on emotions and motivation. In A. Bateman & J. Bale (Eds.), *Sporting sounds: Relationships between sport and music* (pp. 37-58). London: Routledge.

Lucaccini, L.F., & Kreit, L.H. (1972). Music. In W.P. Morgan (Ed.), *Ergogenic aids and muscular performance* (pp. 240-245). New York: Academic Press.

MacDonald, R.A.R., Kreutz, G., & Mitchell, L. (2012). *Music, health, and wellbeing*. New York: Oxford University Press.

Mannes, E. (2011). *The power of music: Pioneering discoveries in the new science of song*. New York: Walker & Company.

Mellalieu, S., & Hanton, S. (2008). *Advances in sport psychology*. New York: Routledge.

Mithen, S. (2005). *The singing Neanderthals: The origins of music, language, mind and body*. London: Weidenfeld & Nicholson.

Morris, T., Terry, P.C., & Gordon, S. (Eds.). (2007). *Sport and exercise psychology: International perspectives*. Morgantown, WV: Fitness Information Technology.

North, A.C., & Hargreaves, D.J. (2008). *Music and social psychology*. Oxford, UK: Oxford University Press.

Patel, A.D. (2008). *Music, language, and the brain*. New York: Oxford University Press.

Peretz, I. & Zatorre, R.J. (Eds.). (2003). *The cognitive neuroscience of music*. London: Oxford University Press.

Plutchik, R. (1994). *The psychology and biology of emotion*. New York: HarperCollins.

Powell, J. (2010). *How music works: The science and psychology of beautiful sounds, from Beethoven to the Beatles and beyond*. New York: Little, Brown, and Company.

Richardson, J., Gorbman, C., & Vernallis, C. (2013). *The Oxford handbook of new audiovisual aesthetics*. New York: Oxford University Press.

Roerdink, M. (2008). *Anchoring: Moving from theory to therapy*. Netherlands: IFKB.

Sacks, O. (2007). *Musicophilia*. London: Picador.

Simon, P., & Szabo, T. (2013). *Music: Social impacts, health benefits and perspectives*. Hauppauge, NY: Nova Science.

Sloboda, J.A., & Juslin, P.N. (2001). Psychological perspectives on music and emotion. In P.N. Juslin & J.A. Sloboda (Eds.), *Music and emotion: Theory and research* (pp. 71-104). New York: Oxford University Press.

Starr, G.G. (2013). *Feeling beauty: The neuroscience of aesthetic experience*. Cambridge, MA: MIT Press.

Storr, A. (1997). *Music and the mind*. London: HarperCollins.

Tan, S., Cohen, A.J., Lipscomb, S.D., & Kendall, R.A. (2013). *The psychology of music in multimedia*. Oxford, UK: Oxford University Press.

Tan, S., Pfordresher, P., & Harré, R. (2010). *Psychology of music*. London: Psychology Press.

Temperley, D. (2010). *Music and probability*. Cumberland, RI: MIT Press.

Terry, P.C. (2004). Mood and emotions in sport. In T. Morris & J. Summers (Eds.), *Sport psychology: Theory, applications and issues* (2nd ed., pp. 31-57). Brisbane, Australia: Wiley.

Thaut, M.H. (2008). *Rhythm, music and the brain: Scientific foundations and clinical applications*. New York: Routledge.

Theorell, T. (2014). *Psychological health effects of musical experiences: Theories, studies and reflections in music health science*. Dordrecht, Netherlands: Springer.

Weinberg, R.S., & Gould, D. (2015). *Foundations of sport and exercise psychology* (6th ed.). Champaign, IL: Human Kinetics.

Williams, J.M. (Ed.). (2009). *Applied sport psychology: Personal growth to peak performance* (6th ed.). New York: McGraw Hill.

Wilson, F.R. (1986). *Tone deaf and all thumbs?* New York: Viking.

# JOURNAL ARTICLES

Alter, D.A., O'Sullivan, M., Oh, P.I., Redelmeier, D.A., Marzolini, S., Liu, R., Forhan, M., Silver, M., Goodman, J.M., & Bartel, L.R. (2015). Synchronized personalized music audio-playlists to improve adherence to physical activity among patients participating in a structured exercise program: A proof-of-principle feasibility study. *Sports Medicine—Open, 1,* 23. doi:10.1186/s40798-015-0017-9

Annesi, J.J. (2001). Effects of music, television, and a combination entertainment system on distraction, exercise adherence, and physical output in adults. *Canadian Journal of Behavioral Science, 33,* 193-202.

Ayers, L.P. (1911). The influence of music on speed in the six day bicycle race. *American Physical Education Review, 16,* 321-324.

Bassett, J., West, S., & Shores, K. (2011). The effects of asynchronous music on the physical activities of youth in supervised recreation activities. *Journal of Park and Recreation Administration, 29,* 80-97.

Baumgartner, T., Lutz, K., Schmidt, C.F., & Jancke, L. (2006). The emotional power of music: How music enhances the feeling of affective pictures. *Brain Research, 1075,* 151-164.

Becker, N., Brett, S., Chambliss, C., Growers, K., Haring, P., Marsh, C., & Montemayor, R. (1994). Mellow and frenetic antecedent music during athletic performance of children, adults, and seniors. *Perceptual & Motor Skills, 79,* 1043-1046.

Becker, N., Chambliss, C., Marsh, C., & Montemayor, R. (1995). Effects of mellow and frenetic music and stimulating and relaxing scents on walking by seniors. *Perceptual & Motor Skills, 80,* 411-415.

Beckett, A. (1990). The effects of music on exercise as determined by physiological recovery heart rates and distance. *Journal of Music Therapy, 27,* 126-136.

Beisman, G.L. (1967). Effect of rhythmic accompaniment upon learning of fundamental motor skills. *Research Quarterly, 38,* 172-176.

Bernardi, L., Porta, C., Casucci, G., Balsamo, R., Bernardi, N.F., Fogari, R., & Sleight, P. (2009). Dynamic interactions between musical, cardiovascular, and cerebral rhythms in humans. *Circulation, 119,* 3171-3180.

Biagini, M.S., Brown, L.E., Coburn, J.W., Judelson, D.A., Statler, T.A., Bottaro, M., Tran, Tai, T., & Longo, N.A. (2012). Effects of self-selected music on strength, explosiveness, and mood. *Journal of Strength & Conditioning Research, 26,* 1934-1938.

Bigliassi, M. (2015). Use the brain: Complementary methods to analyse the effects of motivational music. *Frontiers in Human Neuroscience, 9,* 508.

Bigliassi, M., Silva, V.B., Altimari, L.R., Vandoni, M., Codrons, E., & Buzzachera, C.F. (2015). How motivational and calm music may affect the prefrontal cortex area and emotional responses: A functional near-infrared spectroscopy (fNIRS) study. *Perceptual & Motor Skills, 120,* 202-218.

Bigliassi, M., Silva, V.B., Karageorghis, C.I., Bird, J.M., Santos, P.C., & Altimari, L.R. (2016). Brain mechanisms that underlie the effects of motivational audiovisual stimuli on psychophysiological responses during exercise. *Physiology & Behavior, 158,* 128-136.

Bird, J.M., Hall, J., Arnold, R., Karageorghis, C.I., & Hussein, A. (2016). Effects of music and music-video on core affect during exercise at the lactate threshold. *Psychology of Music.* Advance online publication. doi:10.1177/0305735616637909

Birnbaum, L., Boone, T., & Huschle, B. (2009). Cardiovascular responses to music tempo during steady-state exercise. *Journal of Exercise Physiology online, 12,* 50-57.

Bishop, D.T. (2010). 'Boom Boom How' Optimising performance with music. *Sport and Exercise Psychology Review, 6,* 35-47.

Bishop, D.T., Wright, M.J., & Karageorghis, C.I. (2014). Tempo and intensity of pre-task music modulate neural activity during reactive task performance. *Psychology of Music, 42,* 714-727.

Blumenstein, B., Bar-Eli, M., & Tenenbaum, G. (1995). The augmenting role of biofeedback: Effects of autogenic, imagery and music training on physiological indices and athletic performance. *Journal of Sports Sciences, 13,* 343-354.

Boutcher, S.H., & Trenske, M. (1990). The effects of sensory deprivation and music on perceived exertion and affect during exercise. *Journal of Sport & Exercise Psychology, 12,* 167-176.

Brownley, K.A., McMurray, R.G., & Hackney, A.C. (1995). Effects of music on physiological and affective response to graded treadmill exercise in trained and untrained runners. *International Journal of Psychophysiology, 19,* 193-201.

Burger, B., Thompson, M.R., Luck, G., Saarikallio, S., & Toiviainen, P. (2013). Influences of rhythm- and timbre-related musical features on characteristics of music-induced movement. *Frontiers in Psychology, 4,* 184.

Caty, G. Pieters, T., Liistro, G., & Reychler, G. (2013). Influence of music with a fast tempo on the 6-minute walk test in COPD patients. *Annals of Physical and Rehabilitation Medicine, 56,* e327.

Chanda, M.L., & Levitin, D.J. (2013). The neurochemistry of music. *Trends in Cognitive Sciences, 17,* 179-193.

Chapados, C., & Levitin, D.J. (2008). Cross-modal interactions in the experience of musical performances: Physiological correlates. *Cognition, 108,* 639-651.

Chen, J.L., Penhune, V.B., & Zatorre, R.J. (2008). Listening to musical rhythms recruits motor regions of the brain. *Cerebral Cortex, 18,* 2844-2854.

Chin, T., & Rickard, N.S. (2012). The Music Use (MUSE) questionnaire: An instrument to measure engagement in music. *Music Perception, 29,* 429-446.

Chow, E.C., & Etnier, J.L. (2016). Effects of music and video on perceived exertion during high-intensity exercise. *Journal of Sport and Health Science.* Advance online publication. doi:10.1016/j.jshs.2015.12.007

Clark, I.N., Baker, F.A., Peiris, C.L., Shoebridge, G., & Taylor, N.F. (2016). The Brunel Music Rating Inventory-2 is a reliable and valid instrument for older cardiac rehabilitation patients selecting music for exercise. *Psychology of Music, 44,* 249-262.

Clark, I.N., Baker, F.A., & Taylor, N.F. (2012). The effects of live patterned sensory enhancement on group exercise participation and mood in older adults in rehabilitation. *Journal of Music Therapy, 49,* 180-204.

Clark, I.N., Baker, F.A., & Taylor, N.F. (2016). The modulating effects of music listening on health-related exercise and physical activity in adults: a systematic review and narrative synthesis. *Nordic Journal of Music Therapy, 25,* 76-104.

Copeland, B.L., & Franks, B.D. (1991). Effects of types and intensities of background music on treadmill endurance. *Journal of Sports Medicine and Physical Fitness, 31,* 100-103.

Coutts, C.A. (1961). Effects of music on pulse rates and work output of short duration. *Research Quarterly, 1,* 17-21.

Crust, L. (2004). Carry-over effects of music in an isometric muscular endurance task. *Perceptual & Motor Skills, 98,* 985-991.

Crust, L. (2004). Effects of familiar and unfamiliar asynchronous music on treadmill walking endurance. *Perceptual & Motor Skills, 99,* 361-368.

De Bourdeaudhuij, I., Crombez, G., Deforche, B., Vinaimont, F., Debode, P., & Bouckaert, J. (2002). Effect of distraction on treadmill running time in severely obese children and adolescents. *International Journal of Obesity, 26,* 1023-1029.

Debarnot, U., & Guillot, A. (2014). When music tempo affects the temporal congruence between physical practice and motor imagery. *Acta Psychologica, 149,* 40-44.

Digelides, N., Karageorghis, C.I., Papapavlou, A.J., & Papaioannou, A. (2014). Effects of asynchronous music on students' lesson satisfaction and motivation at the situational level. *Journal of Teaching in Physical Education, 33,* 326-341.

Dillon, E.K. (1952). A study of the use of music as an aid in teaching swimming. *Research Quarterly, 23,* 1-8.

Dorney, L., Goh, E.K.M., & Lee, C. (1992). The impact of music and imagery on physical performance and arousal: Studies of coordination and endurance. *Journal of Sport Behavior, 15,* 21-33.

Dwyer, J.J.M. (1995). Effect of perceived choice of music on exercise intrinsic motivation. *Health Values: The Journal of Health Behavior, Education & Promotion, 19*(2), 18-26.

Dyer, B.J., & McKune, A.J. (2013). Effects of music tempo on performance, psychological, and physiological variables during 20 km cycling in well-trained cyclists. *Perceptual & Motor Skills, 117,* 484-497.

Dyrlund, A.K., & Wininger, S.R. (2008). The effects of music preference and exercise intensity on psychological variables. *Journal of Music Therapy, 45,* 114-134.

Eliakim, M., Meckel, Y., Gotlieb, R., Nemet, D., & Eliakim, A. (2012). Motivational music and repeated sprint ability in junior basketball players. *Acta Kinesiologiae Universitatis Tartuenis, 18,* 29-38.

Elliott, D., Carr, S., & Orme, D. (2005). The effect of motivational music on sub-maximal exercise. *European Journal of Sport Science, 5,* 97-106.

Ferguson, A.R., Carbonneau, M.R., & Chambliss, C. (1994). Effects of positive and negative music on performance of a karate drill. *Perceptual & Motor Skills, 78,* 1217-1218.

Gabana, N.T., Van Raalte, J., Hutchinson, J.C., Brewer, B.W., & Petitpas, A.J. (2014). The effects of music and a coxswain on attentional focus, perceived exertion, motivation, and performance during a 1000 m ergometer rowing sprint. *Journal of Applied Sport Psychology, 27*, 288-300.

Geisler, G., & Leith, L.M. (2001). Different types of asynchronous music and effects on performance of basketball foul shot. *Perceptual & Motor Skills, 93*, 734.

Gfeller, K. (1988). Musical components and styles preferred by young adults for aerobic fitness activities. *Journal of Music Therapy, 25*, 28-43.

Ghaderi, M., Azarbaijani, M.A., Alinejad, H.A., Atashak, S., Shamsi, M.M., & Ghaderi, D. (2012). Influence of music type listening on anaerobic performance and salivary cortisol in male athletes. *Pedagogika, 12*, 162-167.

Ghaderi, M., Rahimi, R., & Azarbayjani, M.A. (2009). The effect of motivational and relaxation music on aerobic performance, rating perceived exertion and salivary cortisol in athlete males. *South African Journal for Research in Sport, Physical Education and Recreation, 31*, 29-38.

Gluch, P. (1993). The use of music in preparing for sport performance. *Contemporary Thought on Performance Enhancement, 2*, 33-53.

Goosey-Tolfrey, V.L., West, M., Lenton, J.P., & Tolfrey, K. (2011). Influence of varied tempo music on wheelchair mechanical efficiency following 3-week practice. *International Journal of Sports Medicine, 32*, 126-131.

Grahn, J. (2012). See what I hear? Beat perception in auditory and visual rhythms. *Experimental Brain Research, 220*, 51-61.

Grahn, J. (2012). Neural mechanisms of rhythm perception: Current findings and future perspectives. *Topics in Cognitive Science, 4*, 585-606.

Grahn, J.A., & Brett, M. (2007). Rhythm and beat perception in motor areas of the brain. *Journal of Cognitive Neuroscience, 19*, 893-906.

Grahn, J., & Rowe, J.B. (2013). Finding and feeling the musical beat: Striatal dissociations between detection and prediction of regularity. *Cerebral Cortex, 23*, 913-921.

Hall, K.G., & Erickson, B. (1995). The effects of preparatory arousal on sixty meter dash performance. *Applied Research in Coaching and Athletics Annual, 10*, 70-79.

Hallett, R., & Lamont, A. (2014). How do gym members engage with music during exercise? *Qualitative Research in Sport, Exercise and Health, 7*, 411-427

Hohler, V. (1989). Sport and music. *Sport Science Review, 12*, 41-44.

Hume, K.H., & Crossman, J. (1992). Musical reinforcement of practice behaviors among competitive swimmers. *Journal of Applied Behavior Analysis, 25*, 665-670.

Iwanaga, I. (1995). Relationship between heart rate and preference for tempo of music. *Perceptual & Motor Skills, 81*, 435-440.

Jarraya, M., Chtourou, H., Aloui, A., Hammouda, O., Chamari, K., Chaouachi, A., & Souissi, N. (2012). The effects of music on high-intensity short-term exercise in well-trained athletes. *Asian Journal of Sports Medicine, 3*, 233-238.

Jia, T., Ogawa, Y., Miura, M., Ito, O., & Kohzuki, M. (2016). Music attenuated a decrease in parasympathetic nervous system activity after exercise. *PLoS ONE, 11*, e0148648.

Johnson, G., Otto, D., & Clair, A.A. (2001). The effect of instrumental and vocal music on adherence to a physical rehabilitation exercise program with persons who are elderly. *Journal of Music Therapy, 38*, 82-96.

Johnson, J., & Siegel, D. (1987). Active vs passive attentional manipulation and multidimensional perceptions of exercise intensity. *Canadian Journal of Sport Sciences, 12*, 41-44.

Juslin, P.N. (2013). From everyday emotions to aesthetic emotions: Towards a unifying theory of musical emotions. *Physics of Life Reviews, 10*, 235-266.

Kämpfe, J., Sedlmeier, P., & Renkewitz, F. (2011). The impact of background music on adult listeners: A meta-analysis. *Psychology of Music, 39*, 424-448.

Karageorghis, C.I., Drew, K.M., & Terry, P.C. (1996). Effects of pretest stimulative and sedative music on grip strength. *Perceptual & Motor Skills, 83*, 1347-1352.

Karageorghis, C.I., & Priest, D.L. (2008). Music in sport and exercise: An update on research and application. *The Sport Journal, 11*. Retrieved from www.thesportjournal.org/article/music-sport-and-exercise-update-research-and-application

Karageorghis, C.I., Vlachopoulos, S.P., & Terry, P.C. (2000). Latent variable modelling of the relationship between flow and exercise-induced feelings: An intuitive appraisal perspective. *European Physical Education Review, 6*, 230-248.

Kerrigan, F., Larsen, G., Hanratty, S., & Korta, K. (2014). 'Gimme shelter': Experiencing pleasurable escape through the musicalisation of running. *Marketing Theory, 14*, 147-166.

Koç, H., & Curtseit, T. (2009). The effects of music on athletic performance. *Ovidius University Annals, Series Physical Education and Sport/Science, Movement and Health, 1,* 43-47.

Koelsch, S., Fritz, T., von Cramon, D.Y., Müller, K., & Friederici, A.D. (2006). Investigating emotion with music: An fMRI study. *Human Brain Mapping, 27,* 239-250.

Lanzillo, J.J., Burke, K.L., Joyner, A.B., & Hardy, C.J. (2001). The effects of music on the intensity and direction of pre-competitive cognitive and somatic state anxiety and state self-confidence in collegiate athletes. *International Sports Journal, 5,* 101-110.

Large, E.W. (2000). On synchronizing movements to music. *Human Movement Science, 19,* 527-566.

Leow, L.-A., Rinchon, C., & Grahn, J. (2015). Familiarity with music increases walking speed in rhythmic auditory cuing. *Annals of the New York Academy of Sciences, 1337,* 53-61.

Levitin, D.J., & Cook, P.R. (1996). Memory for musical tempo: Additional evidence that auditory memory is absolute. *Perception & Psychophysics, 58,* 927-935.

Lima-Silva, A.E., Silva-Cavalcante, M.D., Pires, F.O., Bertuzzi, R., Oliveira, R.S.F., & Bishop, D. (2012). Listening to music in the first, but not the last 1.5 km of a 5-km running trial alters pacing strategy and improves performance. *International Journal of Sports Medicine, 33,* 813-818.

Lin, J.-H., & Lu, F.J.-H. (2013). Interactive effects of visual and auditory intervention on physical performance and perceived effort. *Journal of Sports Science and Medicine, 12,* 388-393.

Lopes-Silva, J.P., Lima-Silva, A.E., Bertuzzi, R., & Silva-Cavalcante, M.D. (2015). Influence of music on performance and psychophysiological responses during moderate-intensity exercise preceded by fatigue. *Physiology & Behavior, 139,* 274-280.

MacDougall, H.G., & Moore, S.T. (2005). Marching to the beat of the same drummer: The spontaneous tempo of human locomotion. *Journal of Applied Physiology, 99,* 1164-1173.

Macnay, S.K. (1995). The influence of preferred music on the perceived exertion, mood, and time estimation scores of patients participating in a cardiac rehabilitation exercise program. *Music Therapy Perspective, 13,* 91-96.

Macone, D., Baldari, C., Zelli, A., & Guidetti, L. (2006). Music and physical activity in psychological well-being. *Perceptual & Motor Skills, 103,* 285-295.

Madison, G., Paulin, J., & Aasa, U. (2013). Physical and psychological effects from supervised aerobic music exercise. *American Journal of Health Behavior, 37,* 780-793.

Matesic, B.C., & Cromartie, F. (2002). Effects music has on lap pace, heart rate, and perceived exertion rate during a 20-minute self-paced run. *The Sports Journal, 5*(1). Retrieved from www.thesportjournal.org/article/tag/music/page/4/

Menon, V., & Levitin, D.J. (2005). The rewards of music listening: Response and physiological connectivity of the mesolimbic system. *NeuroImage, 28,* 175-184.

Moens, B., & Leman, M. (2015). Alignment strategies for the entrainment of music and movement rhythms. *Annals of the New York Academy of Sciences, 1337,* 86-93.

Moens, B., Muller, C., van Noorden, L., Franêk, M., Celie, B., Boone, J., Bourgois, J., & Leman, M. (2014). Encouraging spontaneous synchronisation with D-Jogger, an adaptive music player that aligns movement and music. *PLoS ONE, 9,* e114234.

Nethery, V.M., Harmer, P.A., & Taaffe, D.R. (1991). Sensory mediation of perceived exertion during submaximal exercise. *Journal of Human Movement Studies, 20,* 201-211.

Overy, K. (2012). Making music in a group: Synchronization and shared experience. *Annals of the New York Academy of Sciences, 1252,* 65-68.

Pates, J., Karageorghis, C.I., Fryer, R., & Maynard, I. (2003). Effects of asynchronous music on flow states and shooting performance among netball players. *Psychology of Sport and Exercise, 4,* 413-427.

Pearce, K.A. (1981). Effects of different types of music on physical strength. *Perceptual & Motor Skills, 53,* 351-352.

Perham, N., & Sykora, M. (2012). Disliked music can be better for performance than liked music. *Applied Cognitive Psychology, 26,* 550-555.

Pfister, T., Berrol, C., & Caplan, C. (1998). Effects of music on exercise and perceived symptoms in patients with chronic obstructive pulmonary disease. *Journal of Cardiopulmonary Rehabilitation, 18,* 228-232.

Plante, T.G., Gustafson, C., Brecht, C., Imberi, J., & Sanchez, J. (2011). Exercising with an iPod, friend, or neither: Which is better for psychological benefits? *American Journal of Health Behavior, 35,* 199-208.

Potteiger, J.A., Schroeder, J.M., & Goff, K.L. (2000). Influence of music on RPE during 20 minutes of moderate intensity exercise. *Perceptual & Motor Skills, 91,* 848-854.

Powell, W., Stevens, B., Hand, S., & Simmonds, M. (2010). Sounding better: Fast audio cues increase walk speed in treadmill-mediated virtual rehabilitation environments. *Annual Review of CyberTherapy and Telemedicine, 8*, 161-164.

Pujol, T.J., & Langenfeld, M.E. (1999). Influence of music on Wingate anaerobic test performance. *Perceptual & Motor Skills, 88*, 292-296.

Ramji, R., Aasa, U., Paulin, J., & Madison, G. (2015). Musical information increases physical performance for synchronous but not asynchronous running. *Psychology of Music.* Advance online publication. doi:10.1177/0305735615603239

Razon, S., Basevitch, I., Land, W., Thompson, B., & Tenenbaum, G. (2009). Perception of exertion and attention allocation as a function of visual and auditory conditions. *Psychology of Sport and Exercise, 10*, 636-643.

Reychler, G., Mottart, F., Boland, M., Wasterlain, E., Pieters, T., Caty, G., & Liistro, G. (2015). Influence of ambient music on perceived exertion during a pulmonary rehabilitation session: A randomized crossover study. *Respiratory Care, 60*, 711-717.

Romero, A.J. (2012). A pilot test of the Latin active hip hop intervention to increase physical activity among low-income Mexican-American adolescents. *American Journal of Health Promotion, 26*, 208-211.

Ruscello, B., D'Ottavio, S., Padua, E., Tonnelli, C., & Pantanella, L. (2014). The influence of music on exercise in a group of sedentary elderly women: An important tool to help the elderly to stay active. *Journal of Sports Medicine and Physical Fitness, 54*, 536-544.

Sandstrom, G.M., & Russo, F.A. (2013). Absorption in music: Development of a scale to identify individuals with strong emotional responses to music. *Psychology of Music, 41*, 216-228.

Savitha, D., Sejil, T.V., Rao, S., Roshan, C.J., & Avadhany, S.T. (2013). The effect of vocal and instrumental music on cardiorespiratory variables, energy expenditure and exertion levels during submaximal treadmill exercise. *Indian Journal of Physiology and Pharmacology, 57*, 159-168.

Schaefer, R.S. (2014). Auditory rhythmic cueing in movement rehabilitation: Findings and possible mechanisms. *Philosophical Transactions of The Royal Society B: Biological Sciences, 369*, 20130142. Retrieved from http://rstb.royalsocietypublishing.org

Scherer, K.R (2004). Which emotions can be induced by music? What are the underlying mechanisms? And how can we measure them? *Journal of New Music Research, 33*, 239-251.

Schie, N.A., Stewart, A., Becker, P., & Rogers, G.G. (2008). Effect of music on submaximal cycling. *South African Journal of Sport Medicine, 20*, 28-31.

Schwartz, S.E., Fernhall, B., & Plowman, S.A. (1990). Effects of music on exercise performance. *Journal of Cardiopulmonary Rehabilitation, 10*, 312-316.

Seath, L., & Thow, M. (1995). The effect of music on the perception of effort and mood during aerobic type exercise. *Physiotherapy, 81*, 592-596.

Sejdić, E., Jeffery, R., VandenKroonenberg, A., & Chau, T. (2012). An investigation of stride interval stationarity while listening to music or viewing television. *Human Movement Science, 31*, 695-706.

Shaulov, N., & Lufi, D. (2009). Music and light during indoor cycling. *Perceptual & Motor Skills, 108*, 597-607.

Sherman, J., & Richmond, S. (2013). Listening to music prior to anaerobic exercise improves performance. *Journal of Athletic Medicine, 1*, 66-69.

Sievers, B., Polansky, L., Casey, M., & Wheatley, T. (2013). Music and movement share a dynamic structure that supports universal expressions of emotion. *PNAS Proceedings of the National Academy of Sciences of the United States of America, 110*, 70-75.

Sloboda, J. (2008). The ear of the beholder. *Nature, 454*, 32-33.

Smirmaul, B.P.C., dos Santos, R.V., & da Silva Neto, L.V. (2015). Pre-task music improves swimming performance. *The Journal of Sports Medicine and Physical Fitness, 55*, 1445-1451.

Smoll, F.L., & Schultz, R.W. (1982). Accuracy of motor behavior in response to preferred and nonpreferred tempos. *Journal of Human Movement Studies, 8*, 123-138.

Spilthoorn, D. (1986). The effect of music on motor learning. *Bulletin de la Federation Internationale de l'Education Physique, 56*, 21-29.

Stork, M.J., Kwan, M., Gibala, M.J., & Martin Ginis, K.A. (2014). Music enhances performance and perceived enjoyment of sprint level interval exercise. *Medicine & Science in Sports & Exercise, 47*, 1052-1060.

Styns, F., van Noorden, L., Moelants, D., & Leman, M. (2007). Walking on music. *Human Movement Science, 26*, 769-785.

Szabo, A., Small, A., & Leigh, M. (1999). The effects of slow- and fast-rhythm classical music on progressive cycling to voluntary physical exhaustion. *Journal of Sports Medicine and Physical Fitness, 39*, 220-225.

Szmedra, L., & Bacharach, D.W. (1998). Effect of music on perceived exertion, plasma lactate, norepinephrine and cardiovascular hemodynamics during treadmill running. *International Journal of Sports Medicine, 19,* 32-37.

Tan, F., Tengah, A., Nee, L.Y., & Fredericks, S. (2014). A study of the effect of relaxing music on heart rate recovery after exercise among healthy students. *Complementary Therapies in Clinical Practice, 20,* 114-117.

Templin, D.P., & Vernacchia, R.A. (1995). The effect of highlight music videotapes upon the game performance of intercollegiate basketball players. *The Sport Psychologist, 9,* 41-50.

Tenenbaum, G., Lidor, R., Lavyan, N., Morrow, K., Tonnel, S., Gershgoren, A., Meis, J., & Johnson, M. (2004). The effect of music type on running perseverance and coping with effort sensations. *Psychology of Sport and Exercise, 5,* 89-109.

van der Vlist, B., Bartneck, C., & Mäueler, S. (2011). moBeat: Using interactive music to guide and motivate users during aerobic exercising. *Applied Psychophysiology and Biofeedback, 36,* 135-145.

Van Dyck, E., Moens, B., Buhmann, J., Demey, M., Coorevits, E., Dalla Bella, S., & Leman, M. (2015). Spontaneous entrainment of running cadence to music tempo. *Sports Medicine—Open, 2,* 15.

Vlachopoulos, S.P., Karageorghis, C.I., & Terry, P.C. (2000). Hierarchical confirmatory factor analysis of the flow state scale in an exercise setting. *Journal of Sports Sciences, 18,* 815-831.

White, V.B., & Potteiger, J.A. (1996). Comparison of passive sensory stimulations on RPE during moderate intensity exercise. *Perceptual & Motor Skills, 82,* 819-825.

Young, S.C., Sands, C.D., & Jung, A.P. (2009). Effect of music in female college soccer players during maximal treadmill test. *International Journal of Fitness, 5,* 31-36.

Ziv, G., & Lidor, R. (2011). Music, exercise performance, and adherence in clinical populations and the elderly: A review. *Journal of Clinical Sport Psychology, 5,* 1-23.

# INDEX

*Note:* The italicized *f* and *t* following page numbers refer to figures and tables, respectively.

# ABOUT THE AUTHOR

@ESPNMag

**Costas Karageorghis, PhD, CPsychol, CSci, FBASES, AFBPsS,** is a reader in sport psychology in the department of life sciences at Brunel University London, UK. He is internationally renowned for his research on the effects of music in the realm of exercise and sport. Karageorghis is a chartered member of the British Psychological Society, a chartered member of the Science Council, and a double-accredited member of the British Association of Sport and Exercise Sciences, which elected him a fellow in 2010.

Karageorghis is coauthor of the popular text *Inside Sport Psychology* (2011), which has been translated into three languages. He has also published 10 book chapters, 75 peer-reviewed journal articles, and 100 professional papers in sport and exercise psychology. His music-related research has been featured in media outlets such as the *Times, New York Times, Wall Street Journal, Washington Post, Sydney Morning Herald, ESPN The Magazine,* and *National Geographic.* He has presented his research at conferences throughout the world, serving eight times as a keynote speaker. Karageorghis has worked with numerous international athletes and sport organizations as well as international corporations such as Nike, Spotify, International Management Group, Red Bull, Speedo, and Sony.

From 2007 to 2011, Karageorghis served as head coach of the Great Britain Students track and field team. He has also managed and coached the Brunel University London track and field team since the early 1990s, leading it to seven British Universities championships.